MW00535318

The Beatles and Humour

The Beatles and Humour

Mockers, Funny Papers, and Other Play

Edited by Katie Kapurch, Richard Mills,
and Matthias Heyman

BLOOMSBURY ACADEMIC
NEW YORK • LONDON • OXFORD • NEW DELHI • SYDNEY

BLOOMSBURY ACADEMIC
Bloomsbury Publishing Inc
1385 Broadway, New York, NY 10018, USA
50 Bedford Square, London, WC1B 3DP, UK
29 Earlsfort Terrace, Dublin 2, Ireland

BLOOMSBURY, BLOOMSBURY ACADEMIC and the Diana logo
are trademarks of Bloomsbury Publishing Plc

First published in the United States of America 2023

Copyright © Katie Kapurch, Richard Mills, and Matthias Heyman, 2023

Each chapter copyright by the contributor, 2023

For legal purposes the Acknowledgments on p. 39 constitute
an extension of this copyright page.

Cover design: Louise Dugdale
Cover photo by John Pratt/Stringer/Getty Images

All rights reserved. No part of this publication may be reproduced or
transmitted in any form or by any means, electronic or mechanical,
including photocopying, recording, or any information storage or
retrieval system, without prior permission in writing from the publishers.

Bloomsbury Publishing Inc does not have any control over, or responsibility for,
any third-party websites referred to or in this book. All internet addresses given in this
book were correct at the time of going to press. The author and publisher regret any
inconvenience caused if addresses have changed or sites have ceased to exist, but can
accept no responsibility for any such changes.

Whilst every effort has been made to locate copyright holders the publishers
would be grateful to hear from any person(s) not here acknowledged.

A catalog record for this book is available from the Library of Congress.

ISBN:	HB:	978-1-5013-7934-5
	ePDF:	978-1-5013-7937-6
	eBook:	978-1-5013-7938-3

Typeset by Integra Software Services Pvt. Ltd.

To find out more about our authors and books visit www.bloomsbury.com
and sign up for our newsletters.

Dedicated to Beatle people, friends near and far

"And when I go to town I wanna see all three." Ringo Starr, "Early 1970"

Contents

List of Illustrations   ix

Introduction: Mockers, Funny Papers, and Parading with Ringo:
Why the Beatles Are Still in Play
Katie Kapurch, Matthias Heyman, and Richard Mills   1

Part 1   Playing Together   19

1   The Beatles and the Bard, the Walrus and the Eggman: Playing
with William Shakespeare and Lewis Carroll and/as Perspective
by Incongruity *Katie Kapurch*   21

2   I Laugh and Act Like a Clown: The Beatles as Paradoxical Clowns
Matthias Heyman   41

3   Defuse, Dilute, Deflate: The Beatles Turn It On and Laugh It Off
Aviv Kammay   59

4   Billy Preston and the Beatles *Get Back*: Black Music and
the Wisdom of Wordplay and Wit
Mike Alleyne, Walter Everett, and Katie Kapurch   75

Part 2   Playing Solo   113

5   Madcap Laughs: The Evolution of John Lennon's Humor
Jeffrey Roessner   115

6   "Shall We Dance? This Is Fun!": Paul McCartney's Popular
Song Pastiches *David Thurmaier*   133

7   "I Was So Young When I Was Born": George Harrison and
the Mansion of Mirth *John Covach*   151

8   George Martin, Parlophone Records, and Great Britain's
Funnymen *Kenneth Womack and Ed Zareh*   169

9   Yoko Ono's Avant-Garde Humor
Stephanie Hernandez   187

Part 3 Playing in Context   199

10 Bug Music: Beatle Memes in 1960s American Sitcoms
     Matthew Schneider   201
11 The Beatles and the Birth of British Comedy in the 1960s with
     Beyond the Fringe and *Monty Python's Flying Circus*
     Richard Mills   217
12 Pastiche, Parody, or Post-Irony? The Beatles' Influence on Tears
     for Fears *Mark Spicer*   235

Editor and Contributor Bios   251
Index   255

List of Illustrations

Figures

7.1 Humor in George Harrison songs through 1973   159
7.2 Humor in select George Harrison videos after 1973   165
12.1 Strategic intertextual musical references in "Sowing the Seeds
     of Love": a) Verse vamp ("I Am the Walrus"), b) Chorus ("Hello,
     Goodbye"), c) Baroque trumpet in the third chorus ("Penny Lane,"
     "All You Need Is Love"), d) Curt Smith's countermelody in Verse 3
     (self-reference to Tears for Fears' own "Shout")   242

Tables

4.1 January, 1969, performances involving Billy Preston   105
11.1 Comedy and Music in the Long 1960s   223
12.1 Chronology of Tears for Fears studio albums   238

List of Illustrations

Maps

Introduction: Mockers, Funny Papers, and Parading with Ringo: Why the Beatles Are Still in Play

Katie Kapurch, Matthias Heyman, and Richard Mills

Meet the Mockers

"Are you a mod or a rocker?" inquires a journalist, her sophisticated remove indicating this is both a serious question and one she doesn't really care about. "Uh, no, I'm a mocker," responds Ringo Starr, his delivery droll before he breaks into a smile. The journalist giggles, her aloofness momentarily broken by the joke.

In the press conference scene of *A Hard Day's Night* (1964), this dialogue is buttressed with many other clever one-liners, such as John Lennon's reply to a question about how the Beatles found America: "Turn left at Greenland," he answers with a straight face—and then an exaggerated snarky smile. Lennon shocks another journalist when he seems to write "TITS" on her notepad after she asks him about his hobbies. To a question about what the Beatles call their haircut, George Harrison dryly offers the name "Arthur." Meanwhile, McCartney repeatedly answers, "No, actually, we're just good friends," to questions that don't warrant that response, indicating the frequency he is asked about his love life. These responses playfully engage with the press while showing the absurdity of their questions, reminding the viewer that the Beatles don't take themselves too seriously—even if audiences do. Moreover, the Richard Lester film claims, Beatles won't be co-opted by the establishment.

The press conference scene and other scenarios in *A Hard Day's Night*, while scripted and edited to intensify the battery of their punchlines, took inspiration from the Beatles' actual quips. Screenwriter Alun Owen lifted the first example from an April 1964 Q-and-A during which Paul McCartney offered "mockers" as an answer to a question about whether he preferred Mods or Rockers. The query was designed to gauge his allegiance in a subcultural war that exploded the very next month when violence between those groups erupted in Brighton, forever immortalized in the Who's film, *Quadrophenia* (1979). Owen, who travelled with the Beatles to learn about them, recognized what made them so attractive: "The thing about the boys is this great joy of being alive that they put across" (qtd. in Stark 2005, 110). Owen's screenplay captures the sense of fun that the Beatles projected, something Harrison (who is usually inclined to sarcasm and irony) admitted was real: "We had fun, you know, we really had fun" (qtd. in Stark 2005, 110).

The Beatles often used humor to diffuse tension during actual press conferences, especially the one after they landed at JFK Airport in New York City, where journalists showed up to poke holes in the bubble of excitement surrounding the band's arrival. When asked if they were "four Elvis Presleys," Starr immediately responded, "It's not true, it's not true" in an Elvis imitation, taking the air out of the question and its implications; this and other banter appeared spontaneous—even to the Beatles themselves who laughed at each other. Steven L. Hamelman also points to the Beatles' own laughter, situating it in a longer tradition and explaining its consequences:

> Steeped in British music hall routine, the Beatles are quick to laugh in the films *A Hard Day's Night* (1964) and *Help!* (1965), and the two *Live at the BBC* boxsets (1994/2013) are filled with the sound of pop stars voicing their joie de vivre. The Beatles' giggles, guffaws, and chuckles bring joy to listeners who seek the personal touch—for laughter shows openness and vulnerability. … [L]aughter is a powerful emotional and thematic force in the studio and on stage.
>
> (2019, 177)

The Beatles' fresh, united front made them worth listening to at the time and is one fans have wanted to join ever since. Who doesn't want a group of friends with whom to reach the "toppermost of the poppermost" (Lennon's joke) while laughing along the way?

The examples we cite above are some of the most iconic, rehearsed in clips and memes in social media ad nauseum but still getting a laugh after all these years. The chapters in this book consider such examples, interrogating their historical significance. This volume also reaches well beyond the obvious to explore dimensions of the band's humor that warrant theoretically guided investigations. The Beatles may not have always taken themselves seriously, but their comedic techniques and other playful devices are not the stuff of simplicity. Rather, these are subjects that have commanded the arts since antiquity. As Aristophanes' chorus of birds advises in a comedy first staged in 414 BCE, "Man is a truly cunning creature."

Humor has been theorized ever since the ancient Greeks, so from Aristophanes we could go in countless different directions. In this volume, our contributors have isolated particular techniques and generic conventions to make new cases and to provide fresh insights about the band. *The Beatles and Humour* thus explores many different aspects of the Beatles' humor in relation to the band's music, as well as non-musical discourse. "Humor," as we broadly approach it in this collection, includes the demonstration of and adherence to formal conventions and techniques of comedy and its attendant genres, along with other forms of play.

Mikhail Bakhtin's concept of status-inverting carnivalesque helps foreground playful creation, surrealism, and parody, all features of the Beatles' humor (1965/1984). Bakhtin observed the "comic rituals of the feast of fools, the feast of the ass, and the various comic processions and ceremonies of other feasts," which sanctioned nonnormative play: "The feast was a temporary suspension of the entire official system with all its prohibitions and hierarchic barriers. For a short time life came out of its usual, legalized and consecrated furrows and entered the sphere of utopian freedom. The very brevity of this freedom increased its fantastic nature and utopian radicalism, born in the festive atmosphere of images" (1965/1984, 89). In various ways, the Beatles provide similar excursions within the bounds of mass media, skirting and flirting with accepted norms (such as those related to gender), especially within their decade of the 1960s; chapters that consider clowns and the role of the fool take up these concerns in this book. As a global mass-mediated phenomenon, the Beatles are also now a corporatized entity with a master narrative—rules others can playfully flout, too.

The irreverent fun that the Beatles offered listeners and fans was similar to what *The Goon Show* had given them. As Lennon announced, "We were sons of *The Goon Show* … We were of an age. We were the extension of that rebellion in a way" (qtd. in Stark 2005, 109). Recognizing this radio program as one of the Beatles' formative influences, Steven D. Stark explains, "in postwar Great Britain, comedy helped form the mass consciousness of the Beatles' generation in much the same way rock did in America. Nothing did more to shape that new comic sensibility than *The Goon Show*" (2005, 107). Running from 1951 until 1960, the BBC radio program starred Spike Milligan and Peter Sellers and provided "listeners, many of them young, a weekly does of anarchic, surrealistic insolence with three or four skits per half hour" (2005, 107). Stark goes on to explain some typical Goon scenarios: "Listeners to the show were treated to the exploits of Professor Osric Pureheart, who was designing a lead violin for deaf people, or British hero Neddie Seagoon and Major Denis Bloodnok with his curry addiction. Sound effects might come from heavily edited donkey farts" (2005, 107). While still recognized as expert practitioners of free association, some Goon jokes now sound outdated, especially in their offhanded ableism, casual racism, and other offenses. Contributors probe such issues in the humor of the Beatles, who aspired to be like the Goons, "a collaborative group that wrote and performed its own material" (Stark 2005, 109).

Following the examples of their predecessors, including the Goons and many others mentioned throughout this book, and laughing all the while, the Beatles perfected the art of play—whether they were playing with words in song or clowning around together in an abandoned field or cracking each other up during a concert. They played with instruments, other sound-making objects, and technology in the studio and with each other in a variety of geographical locations (both cinematic and real), including Buckingham Palace and an Indian retreat. Subsequent artists have picked up on the play motif, paying tribute to the Beatles through affectionate parody and otherwise playful pastiche, as well as satire.[1] Late twentieth- and early twenty-first-century rappers and hip-hop artists, for example, Signify on the band to debunk and celebrate the Beatles' authority at the very same time; that rhetorical strategy is also available in music and discourse of the Black artists that the Beatles idolized.[2] Here and throughout this book, we show how humor is intrinsic to the music itself, as well as to the band's persona and legacy.

---

[1] Recognizing the importance of parody and satire to British humor, Russ Bestley explains the difference between the two:
    Parody requires a degree of prior knowledge or familiarity with context, as Jerry Palmer suggests: "Parody always consists of the imitation (allusion, if not direct quotation or misquotation) of some other text or texts, even if only by using stylistic devices which are typical of the text(s) in question. … The role of imitation means that, from the first, intertextuality is integral to parody" (84). Satire, meanwhile, is a mode of social criticism that adopts a scornful, mocking, or sarcastic tone in order to improve, destroy, or increase awareness of the object of its ridicule (2019, 77).
[2] For more on this, see Kapurch and Smith (2023), as well as Chapter 4 in this collection.

Mockers in/and Music

This book argues the Beatles' humor should not be considered separate from the music and other artistry.[3] Without a doubt, the Beatles' longevity is connected to their collective sense of humor, as well as other comic, comedic, and playful elements present in their musical, cinematic, and other visual texts. Four parts made a whole, with each member of the band versed in the comedic tools of irony, sarcasm, wordplay, and even nonsense. John, Paul, George, and Ringo complemented each other, but they played different instruments (literally and figuratively), an observation Oliver Lovesey makes as he summarizes the Beatles' comedy:

> Having all members of the band showcase their talents was a feature of the variety revue medium in which the group emerged. They perfected the press conference and photo shoot as comedy fests, and their first two comic films hugely boosted their profile, just as earlier they had performed a spoof of *A Midsummer Night's Dream*, available on YouTube. George Martin, their producer, had recorded Peter Sellers, and his work with the comic genius greatly elevated [Martin] in their estimation and no doubt facilitated their willingness to experiment with often comic sound effects, and the band created remarkable comedy set pieces such as "You Know My Name (Look Up the Number)."
>
> (2019, 173)

Together, the Beatles demonstrate what seems like an innate gift for timing and deadpan wit, especially in *A Hard Day's Night*, *Help!* and *Magical Mystery Tour*, the former of which drew immediate comparisons to the Marx Brothers. In the 1964 film, as Cecil Wilson wrote in the *Daily Mail*, the Beatles "emerge as a comedy act who also happen to play and sing" (qtd. in Stark 2005, 106). In a non-scripted context, as Lovesey suggests, the band's press conferences and interviews reveal an aptitude for self-awareness, improvisation, and one-liners. Songs such as "Piggies," "I Am the Walrus," and "Maxwell's Silver Hammer" show how the music itself is informed by comedic genres, including parody, satire, surrealism, and observational humor.

The former Beatles did not lose their comedic sensibilities when they were apart, but they often seemed to be missing the others to complete the set up or

---

[3] *The Beatles and Humour* is also a timely follow-up *The Routledge Companion to Popular Music and Humor*, evidence of growing interest in humor in relation to music. Editors Thomas M. Kitts and Nick Baxter-Moore's volume is premised on the idea that "the element of humor interacts with the artistic and social aspects of the musical experience" (2019, i), which supports our argument about the Beatles' humor informing all aspects of their artistry and an appreciation of their reception, then and now.

punchline, making their reunion in the *Anthology* project all the more appealing to fans. As postmodern subjects, the Beatles were always self-reflexive about their artistry, including their jokesomeness. In 1969, Lennon offered a case in point, explaining the role that humor was playing in his peace campaign with Yoko Ono, his new partner in comedy: "That's part of our policy, is not to be taken seriously, because I think our opposition, whoever they may be, in all their manifest forms, don't know how to handle humour! We are humorous, we are, what are they, Laurel and Hardy" (Lennon 1969). In effect moving on from the Marx Brothers-Beatles, Lennon announced his new comedic team—a duo.

Even with all of the funny business going on from the beginning to the end, the role that humor plays in the Beatles' oeuvre and their reception has not received sustained scholarly scrutiny, which *The Beatles and Humour* aims to provide.[4] The reasons for critical gaps to date may have to do with the fact that the Beatles' comedic timing and other skills are so bound up in their musicianship and marketing that their talent as comedians has been taken as a given or taken for granted. Comedy is a major dramatic and literary genre with a long history, but for musicians, artistic legitimacy[5] isn't always earned by making 'em laugh, to borrow the imperative from an iconic number from *Singin' in the Rain* (1952). Such musical comedies were, in fact, some of the US media instrumental in shaping the Beatles' comedic sensibilities, a point reflected in Lennon's Laurel and Hardy reference to the American-British duo. Just as the Beatles' musical influences cannot be traced to a single source, neither can their sense of humor— although the city of Liverpool is surely the beginning of that story.

From Liverpool to the Funny Papers

The Beatles' dry delivery and cheeky wit can and have been connected to British humor writ large, with comedy as a discursive strategy stemming from a rigid class structure. As the journalist Ray Connolly noted, "Traditionally, the only

---

[4] We are definitely not the first ones to find the Beatles funny. When we say "sustained," we refer to the absence of scholarly books singularly devoted to the Beatles and humor. By "scholarly," we refer to monographs and edited collections rooted in specific disciplinary approaches with relevant critical theory and documentation of sources. As references to scholars and historians throughout this Introduction indicate, numerous studies of the Beatles and/or comedy in music have already approached and theorized the band's humor as part of a larger project. John Covach's 1990 article about the Beatles and the Rutles is an early and significant contribution to this trajectory of thought in the academic setting. To our knowledge, Covach, who is also a contributor to this collection, is the first academic to theorize the Beatles' humor.

[5] As Kitts and Baxter observe, "popular musicians who consistently resort to humor may not be 'taken seriously' as artists" (2019, 2).

way you could answer back to the upper-classes without being insolent was by being funny" (qtd. in Stark 2005, 106). The Beatles, according to Stark, "deftly combined two types of humor endemic to the English: They were both verbally deft and masters of more basic standup humor like the comedy of George Formby" (Stark 2005, 109). As a member of the George Formby Appreciation society, Harrison in particular seemed to have been a fan of this comedian and more so his trademark ukulele (for more on this, see the chapter devoted to Harrison in this collection). At the end of "Free as a Bird," the 1995 song that reunited the three living Beatles with the voice of their deceased bandmate, the Beatles even included Formby's own catchphrase, "Turned out nice again." In doing so, they nodded both to his influence and the British music hall tradition to which he belonged—all of that visualized at the end of the music video for "Free as a Bird."

But humor in *Liverpool*, "where everyone considers him- or herself an amateur comedian," is distinctive (Stark 2005, 105). Liverpool-based Beatles historian David Bedford speaks from his own experiences when he claims, "The Beatles could not have come from any other city" (2020, 19). Bedford goes on, citing historian John Belchem, who explains, "Liverpool is in the North of England, but not really of it. We are living in the people's republic of Merseyside" (2020, 19). Stark offers more geographical context, making the case for how Liverpudlian humor found distinctive expression in the Beatles:

> In the fifties, comedians from northern England such as Arthur Askey and Ken Dodd blanketed the radio waves and those vaudeville-like music halls still in operation. Liverpool comedians were known for playing the underdog, which, as self-defined outsiders, came naturally to them and appealed to the English fondness for humor that upset the class system. Yet twist that a little and you end up with the Beatles' kind of anti-establishment humor that the young found very appealing later in the sixties, as earlier comedians such as the Marx Brothers also enjoyed a renaissance.
>
> (2005, 109)

Bedford also identifies the band's comedic influences, situating them in a Liverpool context: "If you go back and watch interviews the Beatles did, especially in America, then the humor they brought can be traced back to the natural wit of the Scousers, and the influence of the Goons" (2020a, 24). Punctuating this point, Bedford cites an apropos joke: "When asked what he thought of Beethoven, Ringo replied, I love him. Especially his poems" (2020a, 24).

Lennon cited Liverpool as comedic training ground in December 1970, pointing to the often-profound stakes of comedic relief:

> Liverpool is a very poor city, and tough. But people have a sense of humor because they are in so much pain. So they are always cracking jokes, and they are very witty. It's an Irish place, too; it is where the Irish came when they ran out of potatoes, and it's where black people were left or worked as slaves or whatever. It is cosmopolitan, and it's where sailors would come home with blues records from America. Liverpool has the biggest country & western following in England besides London—always besides London because there is more of it there. I heard country & western music in Liverpool before I heard rock & roll.
>
> (qtd. in Wenner 2000, 146)

Lennon might have been listing disparate factors, but it's no coincidence that people in Liverpool, many of them descended from Irish immigrants, had a penchant for country music, a genre formatively shaped by Anglo-Irish-Scots people living in the Appalachian region of the United States, as well as other demographics, specifically Black Americans (who, for example, innovated the banjo).

Lennon's mention of country in relation to Liverpool's comic ethos warrants consideration.[6] Country music frequently includes humorous exaggeration and comparison in its lyrics—even sadness to the point of excess can be a point of comic relief. Exploring the under-examined role of humor in a musical genre known for sad songs, Don Cusic considers country's outright comedians (Rod Brasfield, the Duke of Paducah, and Minnie Pearl, the latter whose trademark gag was a hat with a pricetag hanging from it). Cusic also points to the genre's mainstays:

> Perhaps the most 'serious' artist in the history of country music was Hank Williams. At least he is most well known for his songs of hurt and heartache while his tragic life story is considered the quintessential saga of a country star. Yet Hank Williams had a healthy dose of humor in a number of his songs; in fact, his first recording to reach the Billboard charts was 'Move It On Over,' a song detailing the woes of a husband who comes in late and must sleep in the dog house. "This doghouse here is mighty small / But it's better than no house at all".
>
> (1993, 47)

Such ironic comparisons (especially when they are sexual in nature) appealed to the Beatles, whose take on Buck Owens's "Act Naturally" illustrates this point, too. This song has self-deprecating humor that works on multiple levels, especially in relation to acting. The speaker sings about becoming a famous actor, but by

---

[6] For more about the Beatles, Liverpool, and country music, see Bedford (2020b).

1965 the Beatles had attained fame not only as Beatles, but also as actors in their films. Starr's droll voice sings about acting naturally,[7] which is what their films tried to represent them doing, but, according to director Richard Lester, it was Starr who was the most natural onscreen; this is why he was featured more than the others in their first two films. (McCartney, who tried too hard and thus acted unnaturally, had his solo scene cut from *A Hard Day's Night*.) So, even though Starr sings a humble song, he is in fact the Beatle with the most acting talent—as evidenced by his solo career, too.

Ringo continued to sing about being the fool in other songs with the Beatles, as well as in his first solo record full of covers, *Sentimental Journey* (1970). This album was intended as a tribute to the songs, like "I'm a Fool to Care," that his parents' loved. Starr's musical return to Liverpool brings us back to a point Lennon raised in his commentary on the city: he mentions but is rather offhanded about the city's connection with slavery and its thriving Caribbean community, whose immigrants had, in fact, settled in the Liverpool 8 (L8) district in which Ringo grew up. This community is pertinent to a forthcoming chapter that addresses calypso and the Beatles' indebtedness to humor in Black music. As that chapter shows, the Beatles' Liverpudlian-rooted senses of humor remained planted even when the band changed musical styles and when its members eventually grew apart as the 1960s went along.

By the end of the decade, the Beatles still alluded to songs familiar to their families and Liverpool "sing-songs," calling on pop standards such as "Bye Bye Blackbird" like one would use an inside joke with a friend; Starr also includes this song on *Sentimental Journey*.[8] The idea that the Beatles' did not lose their Liverpudlian humor-heritage is one of the points made by Peter Jackson's re-edit of footage that was first the dreary, unhumorous *Let It Be* (1970). With *The Beatles: Get Back* (2021), as multiple chapters in this collection point out, Jackson restores some of the humor formerly lost to the archives. At the time of their break-up, however, the Beatles did release music evidencing their ability to mock serious situations and to undercut their own importance.

"You Never Give Me Your Money" is part of the *Abbey Road* medley, widely considered a last gasp of band togetherness. In this song, McCartney quibbles, "you only give me your funny papers," a reference to the Apple-related business

---

[7] "Embracing the comic paradox of fabricated authenticity or acting naturally was a feature of four representative British bands of the mid-1960s, all of whom incorporated aspects of comedy in their stage personae from DIY pantomime to verbal slapstick, circuses, and performances of transvestism" (Lovesey 2019, 169).

[8] For more on how the song "Bye Bye Blackbird" functions as an inside joke in the Beatles' recorded music, see Kapurch and Smith (2023).

woes giving the Beatles internal trouble (Everett 1999, 226; 260). In the midst of loss, this meta-textual humor—a joke about a jokesome-text—is a coping mechanism. The "paper-chasing" in another 1969 song, "Two of Us," includes another comparable reference to Apple, but here again is an occasion to see humor as the Beatles' own coping mechanism: in one run-through of the song, Paul announces, "Take it, Phil!," which Everett calls "a vivid reminder that Paul and John began their vocal harmonizing in emulation of Phil and Don Everly" (1999, 226). As they appeared to do for each other, in times of trouble the Beatles remain a cultural salve for many, their humor a major ingredient to this function.

Roll Up: Invitations to Play through Pastiche

To date, explorations of the Beatles' humorous dynamics and invitations to play have often focused on how audiences and other performers interact with the band. Twenty-first century Beatles fans can, for example, participate in their own Beatle play on the famous zebra crossing in London or the rebuilt Cavern Club in Liverpool, which has become a kind of Beatles playground. The impetus to interact, in fact, goes back to the Beatles' heyday. One of the main paradigms of 1960s art, according to Arthur Marwick, was spectator involvement: "the participation of reader, viewer, listener, or audience could be pronounced as to become a major element in a work, as in certain types of theatre calling for audience participation, or an in an assemblage composed of mirrors" (1998, 317). Yoko Ono, as one of the forthcoming chapters explains, was on the cutting edge of this movement.

Participatory culture is now commonplace, extensively theorized by scholars building on the foundational work of Henry Jenkins, and a feature of popular culture writ large. Today, musicians and other celebrities are basically required to cultivate participation among their fanbases in a social media-driven landscape. In the twenty-first century, then, the Beatles' humor has, in effect, been kept alive by the recirculation of their images and texts via memes and gifs. "The Teatles," for example, enjoys a very wide following, including members of the Beatles' inner circle. Teatles creator, Huw Spink, is devoted to collecting and sharing images of the Beatles in various postures of tea drinking and is active on multiple social media platforms, periodically publishing an ongoing series of booklets with images and essays. Teatling is a perfect—and persistently amusing—example of how fans "play" with the Beatles.[9]

---

[9] For more about Huw Spink's Teatlemania, see White (2021).

Richard Mills's *The Beatles and Fandom: Sex, Death and Progressive Nostalgia* (2019) includes many instances of fan activity that qualify as Beatle play, including tourism, fanfiction, and slash pairings. Mills's work demonstrates the extent to which Beatles fan activity is based on playful transgression, arguing that Beatles heritage tourism digitizes physical space into online play with fan videos; fanfiction appropriates the Beatles' image into carnivalesque comedy, and slash fiction places the Beatles in humorous and heavily eroticized scenarios. Mills argues that "the majority of fandom is humorous," including, for example, "colloquial letters to *Beatles Monthly* concerning 'kissing Ringo's conk'" (2019, 158). He also points to "[c]onventions where the Beatles phenomenon is celebrated with good-natured bonhomie and ironic obsession," including the "self-deprecating" humor of established Beatles' historians, such as Hunter Davies, Ian MacDonald, and Philip Norman, the latter who offered a "complete volte-face on his McCartney thesis" (2019, 92–3).

Like Mills, Katie Kapurch has also addressed fan play and imitation, particularly through gender-related lenses. In her study of the Beatles and girl-culture melodrama, she considers slash videos on YouTube, including one that uses the Britney Spears's song "Womanizer" as a soundtrack to images of Paul McCartney winking and being generally flirty: "The pairing … suggests that McCartney is the subject and addressee of the song, the 'Superstar' whose womanizing ways are 'charming' but need to be avoided by the speaker" (2016, 215). This, for Kapurch, is evidence of twenty-first-century girls playing with the Beatles like dolls, creating new stories out of old images, while also imitating the kind of wit the Beatles projected. As more evidence of the comedic in Beatles' fan experiences, Mills likewise cites "the transgressive fan vids on *YouTube* [that] range from the sentimental to the outrageously comic" (2019, 158). Mills also addresses tourism: "The Beatles walk in Liverpool and London run the full gamut from serious oration to stand-up comedy, depending on the tour guide that is!" (2019, 159). Appealing strongly to tourists seeking time travel (or the sensation of it) are tribute bands, whose "stage craft lends itself to spontaneous improvised humor which changes each night depending on audience reaction" (2019, 159).

But not all tribute bands are created equal. To find a unique position among the hundreds of tribute bands, Matthias Heyman argues, many so-called bender bands "approach the Beatles' music in a more satirical, parodic, or pastiche-like manner, in the process blurring ideological boundaries surrounding genre, gender, race, and place" (2021, 84). While some fans appreciate the originality that results from a playful approach, he claims, others value tribute bands that prioritize visual and aural mimicry (2021, 91). Still, even look-alikes and other clone bands invoke the comedic, albeit not always intentionally (Heyman 2020, 3). Imitating recognizable Beatle body postures and gestures or using fake Scouse accents may be part of the game, and one cannot help to chuckle at the occasional clumsiness that results from such artificial hyperreality.

As Heyman also notes, the very first Beatles tribute act was indeed a parodic band, the Rutles, the Beatles-pastiche-turned-actual-band created by Pythons Eric Idle and Neil Innes (2021, 79). The Rutles' parody, ironically, shines a light on how funny the Beatles could be. These comedians could be outrageous and irreverent, in part, because the Beatles were apt to laugh at themselves.

Even though the Beatles were fun and funny, to date, existing scholarly treatments of the Beatles' humor are largely concerned with the Rutles.[10] John Covach's "The Rutles and the Use of Specific Models in Musical Satire" offered a musicological analysis of two Rutles tracks included in their first film *All You Need Is Cash* (1978), using Leonard Meyer's theory of style to unravel the intertextual dimensions in both songs vis-à-vis their models (1990, 123–4). Covach argues that, in order for the musical satire to work, the listener is required "to identify various intertexts" and "complex set of associations," resulting in a "more complicated and richer" understanding of these songs (1990, 142–3; 144).

While Covach focused on two works from the film's soundtrack, more recently, Kenneth Womack revisited the Rutles' mockumentary from a cultural-historical perspective. In "*All You Need Is Cash*: Skewering a Legend with the Prefab Four" (2019), he lays bare the creation, production, and reception of the film and its protagonists, tracing its history from Innis' Bonzo Dog Doo-Dah Band, featured in *Magical Mystery Tour* (1967), and Idle's *Rutland Weekend Television* (1975–6) to their copyright sue in 1978 by ATV, the then-holder of the Beatles song catalogue. Womack contends that *All You Need Is Cash* is not merely a parody but also a way to "exploit Beatles fans' nostalgic memories of life during their 1960s-heyday" (2019, 274). He comes to an insightful conclusion about what the Rutles expose about ongoing interest in the subject of their parody:

> However ephemeral such pop-music phenomena as the Beatles may be, they perversely toy with our nostalgic desires to become whole yet again and to regain the lost connections of our irretrievable pasts. The Rutles, through their

---

[10] Since the Rutles have been the subject of previous study (e.g., Covach 1990; Womack 2019), they receive less attention in this volume.

comic pretensions and their silly love songs, remind us that the effort, while tempting and, at times, emotionally satisfying, is invariably rooted in the absurd.

(2019, 279)

Fan communities, as well as tribute bands ranging from amateurs to professional Pythons, provide concrete illustrations of the play that accounts for the Beatles' endurance, but the Beatles' popularity is also not limited to die-hard devotees.

Through a sustained focus on humor, we provide answers to questions asked by academics and by commentators every time the Beatles reappear prominently in a news cycle: Why do the Beatles matter? Why do they still appeal? What makes them unique? While others have addressed these questions with attention to the Beatles' musical innovation and other artistry, we make a specific case for humor. The short answer to the questions above: the Beatles laughed and make us laugh. But laughing with the Beatles is also an invitation to think critically about society and, as Lennon prompted listeners, to imagine better alternatives for living.

This Book

This collection examines some of the formative influences on the band's humor, their output as a group and as individuals, and the texts produced in response to the Beatles; it is not, however, comprehensive to each of these categories. The music theorists and musicologists contributing to this collection reveal how listeners aurally experience the band's humor and experimentation, isolating specific techniques and other musical features. Contributors with expertise in literature, film, and other media also consider techniques, especially those available in lyrics, media-specific forms and conventions, and symbolic constructs. Pastiche, parody, and wordplay emerge consistently throughout these chapters, each one offering its own theoretical orientation for approaching these and other concepts.

Contributors explore the formative influences on and evolution of ideological concepts in music, lyrics, and other discourse. Historical readings also provide a rich framework for understanding biographical and other contextual concerns. Many of the contributors to this collection are presenting critical stances about the Beatles' humor, attuned to issues of class, gender, sexuality, race, and ability. Contributors are also often thinking across time periods. They probe the changing nature of humor for the band and its individual artists, making connections between the Beatles and their past and the Beatles and their ongoing legacy.

The chapters in Part One: Playing Together focus on the Beatles as a group while also isolating techniques that characterize their output during the 1960s. Some of these chapters ask how the Beatles intersect with other comedians, humorists, and artists skilled in the art of wordplay that came before or alongside them. In "The Beatles and the Bard, the Walrus and the Eggman: Playing with William Shakespeare and Lewis Carroll and/as Perspective by Incongruity," Katie Kapurch introduces the Beatles' use of perspective by incongruity, a technique used by William Shakespeare and Lewis Carroll; in doing so, she introduces a literary precedent for the Beatles' humor and techniques addressed throughout the collection.

In "I Laugh and Act Like a Clown: The Beatles as Paradoxical Clowns," Matthias Heyman uses theater scholar Richard Weihe's theory of the paradox of the clown to explore various acts of clowning, joking, and fooling around present in the Beatles' work and representation. Organized around seven forms of paradoxical play, such as border play, gender play, and language play, his chapter sheds new light on a selection of the band's songs, lyrics, films, videos, press conferences, and stage performances, revealing that, while the Beatles are not literal clowns, they certainly share the humorous "unity of opposites" characteristic of clowns. Continuing a focus on techniques that span the band's tenure, in "Defuse, Dilute, Deflate: The Beatles Turn It On and Laugh It Off," Aviv Kammay examines the Beatles' self-directed humor. These self-reflexive strategies account for the band's appeal and helped them maintain their identity as lads with working-class roots in Liverpool.

Also considering how the Beatles call back to their roots, Mike Alleyne, Walter Everett, and Katie Kapurch explore influences not typically associated with the Beatles' humor, their Black musical predecessors and contemporaries. Using scenes from *The Beatles: Get Back* (2021) as a touchstone, "Billy Preston and the Beatles *Get Back*: Black Music and the Wisdom of Wordplay and Wit" expands our understanding of the Beatles' debts to multi-genre Black artists while revealing many of Preston's heretofore unexplored musical contributions, putting them in dialogue with the band's Black sources.

The chapters in Part Two: Playing Solo provide deeper dives into the Beatles and members of their inner circle as individual artists, offering insight into their contributions to the Beatles and solo careers. In "Madcap Laughs: The Evolution of John Lennon's Humor," Jeffrey Roessner reveals how Lennon used humor as a tool for social critique—as well as self-directed mockery and reform. With a particular focus on the duality of laughing and crying, Roessner investigates what he recognizes as Lennon's "emotional duplicity," offering an important analysis of the nature of Lennon's ridicule, actions now considered in the realm of cancel culture. David Thurmaier also shines a new light on a former Beatle in "Shall We Dance? This Is Fun!: Paul McCartney's Popular Song Pastiches." Focusing on McCartney's pastiche of American and British popular song traditions, Thurmaier gives us new ways to think about the Cute One's humor and a better appreciation of what Lennon derided as "granny songs." Continuing to consider an individual Beatle in a new light, John Covach explores the relationship between humor and detachment in Harrison's music. In "I Was So Young When I Was Born": George Harrison and the Mansion of Mirth," Covach reveals the Indian philosophical underpinnings of Harrison's approach to play in his lyrics, music, and music videos.

Maintaining a focus on how individuals shaped the Beatles, Kenneth Womack and Ed Zareh argue for appreciating Beatles producer in "George Martin, Parlophone Records, and Great Britain's Funnymen." Their historical analysis encourages us to see Martin as a kind of auteur, whose visions shaped the Beatles and other zany British acts of the 1950s and 1960s. Following an investigation of this respected member of the Beatles' collective is a chapter that considers a member of the Beatles' inner circle long subject to unfair sexist and racist ridicule. Stephanie Hernandez's "Yoko Ono's Avant-Garde Humor" considers pieces from *Grapefruit*, as well as texts produced in response to Ono, to advance both an appreciation for the humorous and critical aspects of her playful art, as well as her status as an avant-garde artist worthy of appreciation.

The chapters in Part Three: Playing in Context consider media that intersect and engage with the Beatles, both during the 1960s and afterwards. In "Bug Music: Beatle Memes in Sixties American Sitcoms," Matthew Schneider productively uses the meme as a theoretical guide, analyzing a host of American television programs that spoofed the Beatles. Through their parody of "bug music," these shows' jokes used the Beatles to navigate the decade's rapid change. Focusing on the other side of the pond, Richard Mills considers a British context, putting the Beatles in conversation with their contemporaries and immediate successors in "The Beatles and the Birth of British Comedy in the 1960s with *Beyond the Fringe* and *Monty Python's Flying Circus*." Mills shows how these three troupes relate to each other, invoking the surreal and the carnivalesque to engage in political critique. Continuing to consider the Beatles' relevance to a British political context, Mark Spicer's analysis moves us into the 1980s. In "Pastiche, Parody, or Post-Irony? The Beatles' Influence on Tears for Fears," Spicer reveals the Beatles' relevance to the band's critique of Thatcher-era British society, opening the door for future work on pastiche beyond (or in conversation with) the Rutles.

This book is not comprehensive to the corpus of possibilities related to the comic and comedic aspects of the Beatles phenomenon; we see the chapters in this collection as opening the door for more work on the Beatles and humor. A reader might also observe that we do not include a chapter devoted to everyman Ringo Starr, whose musicianship is frequently characterized by collaboration and whose vast comedy-oriented solo output warrants separate investigation. In this collection, Starr appears so often as a point of humor—or the humorous glue—that we found a chapter devoted to him in the context of the Beatles was re-treading material already covered throughout the other chapters, in addition to this introductory chapter. Indeed, this introduction begins with and returns to Ringo, too, offering one last case in point: Starr's parade and the events leading up to it in *A Hard Day's Night*.

In *A Hard Day's Night*, one of the running jokes is that Paul's grandfather is "very clean"—even though he's actually the opposite (similar to how the actor is also not McCartney's actual relation despite other appeals to verisimilitude). The gag is an allusion to Wilfrid Brambell's role as the pronounced "dirty old man" in the British sitcom, *Steptoe and Son*, which aired on the BBC starting in 1962. Functioning as a kind of trickster-fool in the Beatles film, Brambell's character constantly sows discontent, and Ringo is eventually tasked with keeping an eye on the old man. Bored, grandfather grows increasingly annoyed as he observes Ringo reading a book, admonishing the drummer for his choice. Ringo retorts, "you can learn from books," but grandfather keeps provoking Ringo, encouraging him to make the most of his life by "parading the streets!" The Beatle's subsequent outing amounts to a series of mishaps and a missed final run-through while the band waits for Ringo to reappear. Grandfather promised glory, but Ringo aimlessly wanders the streets, looking forlorn (in reality, Starr was hungover when he filmed these scenes). After a brief encounter with a "fellow deserter," a kid named Johnny, Ringo seems to realize that he misses his bandmates, who soon rescue him from the briefest of stints in jail. As the four Beatles run—and laugh—through the streets soundtracked by "Can't Buy Me Love," the audience learns, as does Ringo, that parading is way more fun with the Beatles.

Still, maybe Ringo was also onto something when he defended his book. Taking cues from Starr and Paul's grandfather, this book offers its own parade of sorts: humor-related historical contexts, intertexts, and theoretical concepts are offered in the service of fools, clowns, and friends, including the Beatle people who show that playing with the Beatles keeps the band in play.

References

Bakhtin, Mikhail M. 1965/1984. "*From Rabelais and His World*." Translated by Helene lswolsky. In *The Bakhtin Reader*, edited by Pam Morris, 195–244. New York: Oxford University Press.

Bedford, David. 2020a. "The Beatles in Liverpool." In *The Beatles in Context*, edited by Kenneth Womack, 19–27. Cambridge: Cambridge University Press.

Bedford, David. 2020b. *The Country of Liverpool: The Nashville of the North*. Liverpool: David Bedford, Liddypool.

Bestley, Russ. 2019. "'Anarchy in Woolworths': Punk Comedy and Humor." In *The Routledge Companion to Popular Music and Humor*, edited by Thomas M. Kitts and Nick Baxter-Moore, 76–84. New York: Routledge.

Covach, John. 1990. "The Rutles and the Use of Specific Models in Musical Satire." *Indiana Theory Review* 11: 119–44.

Cusic, Don. 1993. "Comedy and Humor in Country Music." *Journal of American Culture* 16, no. 2 (Summer): 45–50.

Everett, Walter. 1999. *The Beatles as Musicians:* Revolver *through the* Anthology. New York: Oxford University Press.

Hamelman, Steven L. 2019. "*I Never Said I Was Tasteful*: Lou Reed and the Classic Philosophy of Humor." In *The Routledge Companion to Popular Music and Humor*, edited by Thomas M. Kitts and Nick Baxter-Moore, 177–85. New York: Routledge.

A Hard Day's Night. 1964. Dir. Richard Lester. United Artists.

Heyman, Matthias. 2020. "Ladies and Gentlemen, It's (Not) the Beatles: Recreating The White Album." *Rock Music Studies* 7, no. 3: 254–68. https://doi.org/10.1080/1940115 9.2020.1792186.

Heyman, Matthias. 2021. "Recreating the Beatles: The Analogues and Historically Informed Performance." *Journal of Popular Music Studies* 33, no. 2: 77–98. https://doi.org/10.1525/jpms.2021.33.2.77.

Kapurch, Katie. 2016. "Crying, Waiting, Hoping: The Beatles, Girl Culture, and the Melodramatic Mode." In *New Critical Perspectives on the Beatles: Things We Said Today*, edited by Kenneth Womack and Katie Kapurch, 199–220. New York: Palgrave Macmillan.

Kapurch, Katie, and Jon Marc Smith. 2023. *Blackbird: How Black Musicians Sang the Beatles into Being—and Sang Back to Them Ever After*. University Park: Penn State University Press.

Kitts, Thomas M. and Nick Baxter-Moore. 2019. "An Introduction." In *The Routledge Companion to Popular Music and Humor*, edited by Thomas M. Kitts and Nick Baxter-Moore, 1–9. New York: Routledge.

Lennon, John. 1969. Interview by David Wigg. May 8, 1969. Transcription by Jay Spangler. *Beatles Interviews Database*. https://www.beatlesinterviews.org/db1969.0508.beatles.html.

Lewisohn, Mark. 2013. *The Beatles: All These Years—Volume 1: Tune In, Extended Special Edition*. New York: Little, Brown.

Lovesey, Oliver. 2019. "The British Invasion of the Wild West: Country Parody in the Rolling Stones and Other British Bands." In *The Routledge Companion to Popular Music and Humor*, edited by Thomas M. Kitts and Nick Baxter-Moore, 169–76. New York: Routledge.

Marwick, Arthur. 1998. *The Sixties: Cultural Revolution in Britain, France, Italy and the United States c. 1958–74*. Oxford: Oxford University Press.

Mills, Richard. 2019. *The Beatles and Fandom: Sex, Death and Progressive Nostalgia*. London: Bloomsbury Academic.

Stark, Steven D. 2005. *Meet the Beatles: A Cultural History of the Band That Shook Youth, Gender, and the World*. New York: HarperCollins.

Wenner, Jann S. 2000. *Lennon Remembers*. London and New York: Verso.

White, Stephen. "A Beatles Fan Spent Years Collecting over 400 Photos of the Fab Four Drinking Tea." *The Guardian*. October 7, 2021. https://www.mirror.co.uk/3am/celebrity-news/beatles-fan-spent-years-collecting-25163804.

Womack, Kenneth. 2019. "*All You Need Is Cash*: Skewering a Legend with the Prefab Four." In *The Routledge Companion to Popular Music and Humor*, edited by Thomas M. Kitts and Nick Baxter-Moore, 273–80. New York: Routledge.

Part One

Playing Together

1

The Beatles and the Bard, the Walrus and the Eggman: Playing with William Shakespeare and Lewis Carroll and/as Perspective by Incongruity

Katie Kapurch

In 1964, the Beatles stepped onstage wearing their signature black Beatle boots, mop-top haircuts, … and the fanciful gear of Elizabethan actors. The occasion for the mismatch was a one-hour televised special, *Around the Beatles*, taped in London on April 28. Trading guitars for trumpets, John, Paul, and George heralded the beginning of the performance while Ringo waved a flag. What followed was a rollicking take on one of the Bard's iconic play-within-a-play from *A Midsummer Night's Dream*, first performed in 1605. This is the comedy in which Shakespeare spoofs tragic representations of lovers, including his own, with an Act V performance of Ovid's account of Pyramus and Thisbe. The Beatles' take on this spoof was not the only time the band delivered the Bard. In another example of meta-textual layering, the Beatles included lines from the tragedy *King Lear* in "I Am the Walrus," implicitly nodding back to their debut. These examples—the Beatles in *Midsummer* and *Lear* in the Beatles—are two frequently referenced intersections between the Beatles and Shakespeare.[1]

---

[1] Matthew Schneider (2019) argued for a reading of "The End" in relation to a Shakespearean couplet: "In Barry Miles' *Many Years from Now*, Paul McCartney said 'I wanted [the *Abbey Road* medley] to end with a little meaningful couplet, so I followed the Bard and wrote a couplet'. That lyric— 'And in the end, the love you take/Is equal to the love you make'—aptly captures the Beatles' core message in what John Lennon praised as a 'cosmic, philosophical line'. It also raises the question of Shakespeare's influence on the Beatles." Schneider noted some of the Beatles' Shakespearean intersections that I discuss throughout this chapter. Elsewhere, Schneider also discusses the Beatles' debt to Carroll, "the English traditions foremost portrayer of childish delight" and "a powerful transmitter to later artists [such as the Beatles] of the psychically complex Blakean and Wordsworthian child" which finds particular expression "in the songs and personae of John Lennon and Ringo Starr" (2008, 145).

The Beatles get a lot of credit for self-referentiality, but the Bard was doing that more than three centuries prior. The *Midsummer* performance and "I Am the Walrus" also show how the Beatles were replanting (or transplanting) signs from one category into another, something they didn't just do with Shakespeare. They played with musical categories, drawing on existing genres and mixing their techniques.[2] The Beatles' seemingly long, girlish hair is another well-known example of what seemed like gendered mismatching at the time.[3] In doing so, the Beatles frequently offered contradictory pairings akin to what twentieth-century rhetorical theorist Kenneth Burke termed "perspective by incongruity."[4] This is a technique used prodigiously by Shakespeare, as Burke recognized, and therefore one I define in more detail with examples from the sixteenth-century English playwright.

This chapter positions Shakespeare as a guide to the Beatles' humor, particularly irony via metaphor and other puns, along with self-referential and intertextual allusions. I open with a play not typically referenced in conjunction with the Beatles, *All's Well That Ends Well*, whose scoundrel Paroles offers relevant illustrations of Burke's notion of perspective by incongruity.[5] This play's gender reversals raise that subject in relation to the Beatles, leading to the incongruity of the Beatles in the Bard. Their *Midsummer* performance, in effect, serves to parody the band's own love story, especially the Lennon-McCartney partnership. More literary intersections continue to provide occasions for seeing perspective by incongruity, witnessed in the joining of Shakespeare and Lewis Carroll within the setting of the Beatles' "I Am the Walrus." The imagery in this song, much of which the Beatles claimed was nonsense, is enriched with attention to Carroll's use of perspective by incongruity, revealing unacknowledged metaphorical possibilities. In particular, Lennon's eggman and walrus become meaningful in conversation with Shakespearean precedent. Reading the Beatles through the Bard, as well as Carroll, opens new ways of thinking about the band's humor and ongoing relevance.

---

[2] See Walter Everett's two-volume *The Beatles as Musicians* (1999; 2001) for a song-by-song analysis that illustrates the Beatles' numerous lifts and borrowings from many musical genres.

[3] See Ehrenreich, Jacobs, and Hess (1986), the landmark reception study of the Beatles' appeals to girls and the effects of their long hair and other visual markers of style; see Kapurch (2021), which accounts for Ehrenreich et al. and the scholarship that follows them while positioning the Beatles as gender fluid.

[4] Addressing "Eleanor Rigby," Graham and Luttrell (2019) apply Burke's concept of perspective by incongruity to disparate musical forms in the Beatles' music, focusing on the string arrangement in the 1966 song and noting the generic conventions of pop-rock music at the time.

[5] Burke famously did not offer a systematized theory of this and other concepts; scholars have since tried to systematize his thinking, developing methods for its application; see, for example, the scholarship of Barry Brummett. For the purposes of this chapter, I am using "perspective by incongruity" in its basic sense: "a deliberate misfit" (Burke 1935/1984, 90). I do this to probe the consequences of seemingly mismatched intertextual pairings and other contradictions and reversals.

Introducing Perspective by Incongruity with Paroles in *All's Well That Ends Well*

"Humor," as Thomas Brothers' study of the Beatles (and Duke Ellington's orchestra) posits, "is often about shifting meaning, a sudden glimpse of an unfixed point of view" (2021, 265). To illustrate, Brothers points to the surreal quality of Beatles' *Pepper* uniforms, a visual corollary to the humor that pervades the album's songs: "a way of puncturing all limiting concepts and opening into a bigger view of life that is 'fluid and chanting all the time and evolving,' as McCartney put it" (2021, 265). What Brothers describes here is akin to perspective by incongruity and its altering effects.

A "metaphorical extension" that applies a commonly held notion to a new setting, perspective by incongruity often provokes laughter *and* critical thoughtfulness: "A word belongs by custom to a certain category—and by rational planning you wrench it loose and metaphorically apply it to a different category" (Burke 1935/1984, 308). Mark C. Long provides a useful summation of Burke's definition and its origins:

> Burke develops the term "perspective by incongruity" in reference to the stylistic principle of Nietzsche that invokes metaphor to stress "a kind of vision got by seeing one order in terms of another" (*CS* 216). Burke adds that although Nietzsche exemplified the procedure, it was Bergson who came nearest to making incongruity a system by proposing to deliberately cultivate contradictory concepts (*PC* 94). In brief, a perspective by incongruity is a "deliberate misfit"; it "appeals by exemplifying relationships between objects which our customary rational vocabulary has ignored."
>
> (1997, 90)

Nobody did this better than Shakespeare, who, according to Burke, "could make new 'metaphorical extensions' at random. He could leap across the categories as readily as walking. The mortmain of dead metaphors ('abstractions') that has gripped us since his time has rigidified this original liquidity" (1937/1984, 230).

There are many examples of perspective by incongruity in Shakespeare's work, so many that you could probably just open a play at random and find one. For admirable but saucy wordplay, scholars often look to *All's Well That Ends Well*'s Paroles,[6] the rascal whose name literally means "words" in French (Maus 2016, 2640). Peter Ackroyd describes the "military braggart," as "a creature of prolific

---

[6] For the spelling of Paroles's name, I follow the 2016 edition of *The Norton Shakespeare*; elsewhere, the character's name has been spelled Parolles.

and meaningless words who can now be firmly identified as a Shakespearian 'type,'" adding that "Shakespeare loved those who dwelled in a wilderness of words" (2005, 437). Here, Ackroyd's descriptions deal in opposites to expose the contradictions, paralleling Paroles's rhetorical accomplishments via metaphor, irony, and other puns.[7]

Here's an apt example from the beginning of *All's Well*, where Shakespeare via Paroles discursively "leaps" with metaphor, pulling us along, laughing:

> Virginity breeds mites, much like a cheese; consumes itself to the very paring, and so dies with feeding his own stomach. Besides, virginity is peevish, proud, idle, made of self-love, which is the most inhibited sin in the canon. Keep it not; you cannot choose but loose by't: out with 't! within ten year it will make itself ten, which is a goodly increase; and the principal itself not much the worse: away with 't!
>
> (I.1.133–40)[8]

Virginity, mites, and cheese prompt immediate laughter in the audience, especially given the repulsiveness of overly aged cheese.[9]

Mite-ridden cheese is a metaphorical corollary to the unattractiveness of dated virginity. Paroles genders virginity, comparing "her" age to such things as a courtier's once-stylish-now-out-of-style cap, joining a male head with a symbolically female cap to accentuate heterosexual relations; that cap is compared to similarly out-of-fashion objects, "the brooch and the toothpick," as well as a "withered pear" (I.1.145–50). Paroles is making the case that, unlike pies and porridge, virginity does not age well, repeating "withered pear" twice more to punctuate his point: "it looks ill, it eats drily" (I.1.150–2). Virginity leads to vaginal depletion, according to Paroles, who insists that anatomy itself is affected and afflicted by lack of use. This is no doubt sexist and ageist (he's not making the same case for an unused phallus), but at the same time Paroles does counter other sexist views of a young woman's virginity as a prize.

---

[7] Pun is defined in relation to a "'bistable illusion,' one of those pictures which looked at one way is a rabbit and another a duck. The eye, more consistent than the mind, cannot see both at the same time but instead puts our mind into a high-frequently oscillation between the two worlds" (Lanham 1991, 128).

[8] Paroles's dialogue is quoted in its prose presentation following Greenblatt et al. (2016).

[9] Burke uses a cheese metaphor to characterize interpretation itself, as Long points out: "In *Permanence and Change* Burke observes that the universe 'would appear to be something like a cheese; it can be sliced in an infinite number of ways—and when one has found his pattern of slicing, he finds that other men's slices fall in the wrong places' (103). I take Burke's first point to be that the possibility of infinite slicing patterns is a felicitous condition for the human tendency to hit upon serviceable patterns of slicing" (1997).

Paroles's discourse involves what Burke terms casuistic stretching, which is "designed to 'remoralize' by accurately naming a situation already demoralized by inaccuracy" (Burke 1937/1984, 309). The weird and unexpected pairings warrant reflection about whether virginity is indeed something to value and maintain, especially, as Paroles points out to Helen (the play's heroic heroine), given biblical restrictions against masturbation. It is, after all, Helen's proclamation about maintaining her virginity that prompts Paroles, who elsewhere in this scene notes that mothers cannot be virgins. So when virgins are lauded, according to him, mothers are implicitly criticized, and this can't be right because it would throw the sanctity of motherhood itself into question. Upending the idea that having sex for the first time is a loss, Paroles likewise argues that sex can yield ten more virgins, a financial metaphor that renders loss a gain and reverses the idea that virginity is cultural capital.

Sex is almost always present in pop songs, of course, but you can find it everywhere in Shakespeare, too—especially the comedies, since they are concerned with romantic pairings and all their attendant messiness. Sex is the obvious subject of Paroles's exposition on virginity, which is compared with cheese subject to expiration. Paroles is Shakespeare's fool (the character who is often a crafty wordsmith) and *All's Well* is a comedy, so the play does not punish its fool as a scapegoat. Paroles is allowed, albeit "in a reduced capacity," to reintegrate into society as he owns and accepts his rascally nature: "Simply the thing I am, shall make me live" (Maus 2016, 2641; IV.3.316–17). As Harold Bloom memorably explains, "Many critics have disliked Parolles, but I cannot imagine why; he is a splendid scoundrel, perfectly transparent to anyone of good sense, which of course does not include Bertram," elsewhere described as "a spoiled brat" (1998, 346; 345). Bloom continues in this vein: "Parolles is a mere braggart soldier, an imposter, a liar, a leech, considerably more interesting than the warring and whoring Bertram" (1998, 348).

Illustrating the play's obvious gender reversals, the character Bertram is the object of the aforementioned heroic-heroine Helen's quest to win him (for a second time, actually, since he refuses to acknowledge their marriage the first go around). As Katharine Eisaman Maus explains of *All's Well*, "The gender reversals in the plot ... make the difference in conventional expectations for men and women vividly clear ... these deviations implicitly challenge conventional gender roles, making them artificial and restrictive" (2016, 2635). Maus's insight about gender in *All's Well* is relevant to the Beatles, especially the young men they were in the early 1960s. The Beatles' well-known gendered incongruities have some precedent in *All's Well* and, more broadly, the British theatrical tradition, which consistently allowed for cross-dressing and other camped-up performances with men routinely playing the parts of women until the late seventeenth century.

The four lads from Liverpool, who were ascending to pop stardom in 1964, experienced economic and social boons as they became Beatles. These were not unlike the mobility and gains of fairy-tale heroes of European folklore, a source for *All's Well That Ends Well*, which "retells [the] popular tale of fantastic upward mobility, but with the genders reversed: the resourceful young quester is female, the marital prize male" (Maus 2016, 2635). Much has been said about the Beatles' gender play—whether their long hair or appeals to girls or girlishness in the songs themselves.[10] But Maus's insight is relevant to another way the Beatles intersect with the Bard vis-à-vis gender and romantic storylines: their performance of the play-within-a-play that parodies lovers, in retrospect, parodies their own band romance.

Who Are the Lovers?: The Beatles in *A Midsummer Night's Dream*

With Shakespeare in mind, images of the four Beatles physically running around in their films parallel the four lovers running across the stage in *A Midsummer Night's Dream*. In the play, the characters' mishaps and misunderstandings are largely owed to another fool, the trickster Puck. This rascal is a "keen mixer," to borrow the phrase Paul uses for Grandfather, who plays the fool of *A Hard Day's Night*. Elsewhere in this film, McCartney parodically issues one line from *Hamlet*, "O, that this too, too solid flesh would melt," holding a fake nose and wearing a self-important makeshift toga before turning to camera, interjecting "zap!" with a hairdryer as substitute gun (Lester 1964).

The title of *A Hard Day's Night* has a literary vibe applicable to the often-chaotic content of *A Midsummer Night's Dream*, which takes place over the course of one night. Likewise, the action of the Beatles' film is confined to a two-day time span—also pushing toward a performance. "A Hard Day's Night," also a song title, derives from one of Starr's malapropisms, long recognized for

---

[10] For more on these gender dynamics, see Ehrenreich et al. (1986); Kapurch (2016, 2021).

mismatched phrasings that seem to make sense, such as "Tomorrow Never Knows." This might be why the Beatles manager Brian Epstein, who had a theatrical background and knew Shakespeare well, once said, "I don't know whether it was William Shakespeare or Ringo Starr who said: 'When this business stops being fun, I'm giving it up'" (1967/1998, 180). The incongruous pairing points to an essential irony about work as fun, which is exactly how the Beatles made their business—music—seem.

A Hard Day's Night culminates in the televised concert, a performance-in-a-performance scenario that recalls the last act of *Midsummer*. Act V begins as the rag-tag itinerant troupe of craftsman stage their show, which is the aforementioned play-within-a-play that the Beatles performed the same spring they filmed *A Hard Day's Night*. In the televised performance of *Around the Beatles*, the members of the band take on the parts of the play's craftsman, who attempt to depict the tragedy of Pyramus (Paul) and Thisbe (John), accompanied by Moonshine (George) and antagonized by Lion (Ringo). In playing the craftsman playing these Ovidian parts, however, the Beatles are also playing the Beatles—another layer of textuality that confirms their skill not just as musicians but as actors.[11] They *expertly* perform the parts of *inept* craftsmen in accordance with the very Beatle identities they were using this program to establish. The performance is often cited as testament to the band's comic ability and evidence of their Britishness given the Bard's inextricable link to British culture and its comedic traditions.[12]

All of the Beatles are aware of the camera, but none more so than McCartney, who often makes facial gestures to wink and otherwise flirt with the viewer at home. (Harrison does a little bit of this with his eyebrows in the opening, too.) Paul-as-Pyramus, ever the Cute One, is also attuned to the rowdy, interjecting crowd members present in the performance space; he keeps getting distracted by the interjections, frequently pointing with his finger, a favorite gesture of McCartney's, as if to redirect attention onto the scene. In another meta-textual moment occurring in tandem with the play's meta-textual lines, Paul-as-Pyramus

[11] "The scenes and sounds of the Beatles' *Dream* sequence ... signal the band's working knowledge and familiarity with the medium of television, and also a breezy anarchy and iconoclasm, impelled by the same cultural confidence that empowered a generation of new, working-class, a generation of new, working-class, class, provincial and demob-happy entertainers in the post-Second-World-War World-War period" (Hansen 2010, Loc. 1127–9).

[12] "Through this performance of Shakespeare, the Beatles signal their awareness of the time's *Dream/* dream-making, playing up their status as players. Their parody draws attention to the significance of impersonation to popular music: the Beatles acted as much on record or in their films as they do in this Shakespearean burlesque, and as such are conscious of their power and status as marketable performers, and their audience's role in sustaining them" (Hansen 2010, Loc. 1105–8).

gives the script's stage directions: "this is Thisbe's cue, and she comes in and we look through the"—but he interrupts the scripted line, gesticulating for the audience be quiet. Sporting an ugly wig and with a blacked-out tooth, Lennon, ever the Smart One, mostly performs Thisbe with an overly dry straight face, sometimes breaking into a higher-pitched vocal register. John-as-Thisbe begins speaking with a gruffer voice than anyone has ever heard from Lennon (making Ringo-as-Lion, who is waiting for his turn onstage, laugh). Lennon doubles down on brutish masculinity as a counterpoint to both his own costume (a sleeveless dress) and McCartney's feminine cuteness.

John-as-Thisbe mostly ignores the crowd, well aware of how his dry delivery, in addition to the humor of his cross-dressing, is playing with the "audience" playing the play's unruly Athenians.[13] Lennon, accompanied by George-as-Moonshine, perfectly times the mimed action needed for knocking and door-opening sound effects, the kind of gags he grew up hearing on *The Goon Show*. As the Quiet One, George-as-Moonshine dutifully serves as set piece, shining on the other Beatles, but he does a kind of sarcastic "Don't Bother Me" routine with the audience, mostly ignoring them after his introduction in order to perform the light-shining duties. Meanwhile the Funny One, Ringo, is loveable and cuddly as the should-be scary lion, who is actually harmless—an interesting persona for a drummer, who plays the most physically demanding instrument. Ringo-as-Lion's roar, an adorable effort and hardly intimidating, corresponds to that very mismatch.

Lion, if you remember, is thought to have attacked Thisbe by Pyramus, who kills himself when he mistakes her bloodied veil as proof of her death. The lovers' protracted deaths include multiple gags in *Midsummer*'s script and are played for laughs. In the Beatles' case, John-as-Thisbe cracks Paul-as-Pyramus up and takes a turn shouting at the audience. This is funny because Lennon hasn't really broken yet, controlling the timing of the outburst to signal the mock-seriousness of the death. The camera is overhead as the songwriting partners are lying on the floor, getting married in pretend death and holding hands as they say "Adeiu," which sounds like "I do." They turn Shakespeare's line into "Adieu, Adew, I do

---

[13] Hansen pays particular note to the dynamic of the audience playing the audience, noting that girls and young women function as groundlings, while the young men in the boxes call attention to another host of issues: "The elevated male malcontents also deride the pretensions of the performers, betraying regional tensions latent in this emerging aesthetic: 'Go back to Liverpool'. These interjections police a range of divisions that the Beatles transgressed in their performative formative experiments … : divisions between province and metropolitan centre, between popular and high culture, and between 'authenticity' and 'performance'" (2010, Loc. 1142–6).

like to be beside the seaside" (qtd. in Hansen 2010, Loc. 1166). With a nod to a British music hall song from 1907, the kind of inside joke frequently shared among the two, Lennon and Paul are both laughing by the end, looking at each other as the scene ends.

Part of the humor of Shakespeare's play-within-the-play as often performed in *Midsummer* proper involves the craftsmen playing Pyramus and Thisbe and their required intimacies, including the kiss through the Wall, played by another craftsman. The irony is, of course, that in Shakespeare's day (and before that) men were always playing the women's roles. Long considered Shakespeare's parody of both Ovid and the death scene in his own *Romeo and Juliet*, the Pyramus-and-Thisbe scene is also a send up of the kept-apart lovers and their own rather trifling concerns in *Midsummer*. Although the Beatles mostly speed through the wall scene, Lennon and McCartney aren't resistant to touching each other; John-as-Thisbe knows Paul-as-Pyramus is adorable, coaxing more cuteness out of McCartney—all captured by the camera given McCartney's ability to play for its close-up.

The Beatles' performance of the Pyramus-and-Thisbe scene becomes, especially after we know how the band ended and could never reunite after Lennon's death, a parody of the band's love story, particularly the Lennon-McCartney partnership. In January 1969, Lennon and McCartney implicitly revisited the sketch when acknowledging the romantic dimensions of "Two of Us." The following exchange during that month's recording sessions is another example of meta-textual awareness since McCartney even realizes their songs are working together like a narrative:

Paul. It's like, after "Get Back"—'We're on our way home'.
John. Yeah.
Paul. So there's a story. And there's another one—"Don't Let Me Down."
       [sings] "Oh! Darlin' I'll never let you down ..."
John. Yeah. It's like you and me are lovers.
Paul. Yeah. (Jackson 2021; Beatles 2021, 139)

Peter Jackson's *The Beatles: Get Back* stops here, playing the scene for sentimentality and foreshadowing, with Paul's "yeah" a sad acknowledgement of the impending breakup. But the companion book includes what followed:

John. We shall have to camp it up for those two [songs].
Paul. Yeah, well, I'll be wearing my skirt on the show anyway.
       (Beatles 2021, 139)

McCartney and Lennon reprise the Pyramus and Thisbe gag—with McCartney offering to play the Cute One in a performance again. This was way before anyone started using the word "bromance" or referring to fan-fiction's pairings of McCartney and Lennon as the ship "McLennon."[14]

In the Beatles' 1964 *Midsummer* performance, multiple puns and visual gags appear as the bandmembers play with Shakespeare's already pun-ridden lines; Paul-as-Pyramus, for example, pulls out a comically under-sized sword. Lennon then deflates the whole enterprise with a transition into the next segment: "Enough of this [?] rubbish, we'd like to bring on something good now, some girls, hee hee [he leers], we'd like to bring on the Vernon Girls, and two of the girls from the film *The West Side Story* [*sic*], the Jets ..." (qtd. in Hansen 2010, 1166–70). The transition, which overtly claims heterosexual desire, might seem to "correct" the homoerotic charge that the Pyramus and Thisbe scene has given the room. But, as the *Get Back* example shows, the Beatles would go on to more gender play, especially that which served romantic readings of the bandmembers' interpersonal dynamics.

Lennon is no Paroles, the scoundrel that scholars laud for verbal deft, but Lennon's rascally nature and his own penchant for wordplay leads us to more perspective by incongruity via naughty boys—and curious girls.

Leering with *Lear* and Alice: The BBC Bard, the Eggman, and the Walrus

The Beatles, and especially Lennon, liked to play the naughty boys with their use of puns, such as the repeated "tit" added to "Girl." That disguised vocable takes a little revenge upon the title character for rendering the speaker a fool. The Beatles issued many other (better) verbal witticisms in lyrics, scripted dialogue, and interviews (although, as I mention before, these were usually not examples of Shakespearean-level casuistic stretching as defined by Burke). Lennon even accuses Starr of being a "naughty boy" in *Help!* with a pun about buzzing and

---

[14] See Kapurch for more on fan creations that re-imagine the Lennon-McCartney relationship: "The Beatles' capacity to unite [twenty-first century] girls through the representation of same-sex intimacy is especially prevalent in the texts that some girls create and post online ... In girls' YouTube videos, John, Paul, George and Ringo's images are used to imagine narratives both related and unrelated to Beatle biographies ... In general, girls imagine and reinterpret Lennon and McCartney's partnership as one of lost love, the melodramatic tenet that the Beatles' early crying songs address again and again" (2016, 214–15).

later plays with that phrase in "I Am the Walrus," when it's not clear if the boy has been naughty because he's been a girl or if "boy" is an expression of wonder at how naughty the girl has been. In this psychedelic romp, the Bard's own verbal wit appears as the Beatles play with Shakespearean verse, adding lines from *King Lear* to the end of the song.

Lennon explained how this pairing came to be, adding to his list of the song's random bits:

> There was even some live BBC radio. They were reciting Shakespeare or something and I just fed whatever lines were on the radio right into the song. We did about half a dozen mixes and I just used whatever was coming through at that time. I never knew it was *King Lear* until, years later, somebody told me—because I could hardly make out what he was saying.
>
> (Beatles 2000, 273)

In the song, the most audible lines include Oswald's pronouncement, "O! untimely death," to which Edgar responds, calling Oswald "a serviceable villain" (IV.6.243; 244). These phrases—both reliant on incongruous pairings—follow bizarre verses and a chorus in which Lennon's speaker announces himself the walrus. Right away, we see a mismatch in the pairing of lines from a tragedy with the surreal music and lyrics of "I Am the Walrus," a song full of strange imagery and ideas that don't seem to go together, such as "sitting on a cornflake" and getting a suntan when it's raining. These activities are performed by a speaker who also portends to be an eggman accompanied by other eggmen.

Who is an eggman? How does one become an eggman? The metaphorical character is a little like Paroles's courtier wearing a vaginal cap—a female-symbolic object positioned in relation to a man. The nickname is thought to be in reference to the Animals' Eric Burdon, who, as his own egg timer, cracked eggs on women when he orgasmed, a kind of "untimely death" if you consider *le petit mort*. Of course, the Beatles' insertion of *Lear* (whose tragic plot centers on a king driven mad by the events his choices set in motion) is not an *intentional* comment on orgasm-as-little-death. Likewise, the Beatles may not have made the connection between Oswald pronouncing his death and the death-like brokenness of another eggman, Humpty Dumpty. His genre is invoked by the song's nursery-rhyme phrase, "see how they run," lifted from "Hot Cross Buns" (and revisited in "Lady Madonna").

Lennon insisted "I Am the Walrus" was "just saying a dream—the words don't mean a lot" (Beatles 2000, 273). The song is one of Lennon's nonsense-for-nonsense's sake songs, intended to flummox critics who annoyed both Lennon and McCartney with tiresome readings and interpretations, which *Sgt. Pepper's Lonely Hearts Club Band* had encouraged in 1967. As Roessner points out, Lennon saw musicians as having two choices: "they can either play rock 'n' roll or 'go bullshitting off into intellectualism'" (2006, 152). Not long after *Pepper*, Lennon also explained his position to biographer Hunter Davies:

> It's nice when people like it [our music], but when they start "appreciating" it, getting great deep things out of it, making a thing of it, then it's a lot of shit. It proves what we've always thought about most sorts of so-called art. It's a lot of shit. We hated all that shit they wrote and talked about Beethoven and ballet, all kidding themselves it was important. Not it's happening to us ... Let's stick that in there, we say, that'll start them puzzling. I'm sure all artists do, when they realize it's a con. I bet Picasso sticks things in. I bet he's been laughing his balls off for the last 80 years.
>
> (qtd. in Roessner 2006, 153)

Even so, the metaphors—however they got into "I Am the Walrus"—have meaning in their transplanted setting, especially when we continue contemplating the inclusion of Shakespeare.

The incongruous pairing of Shakespeare's dialogue with the Beatles' music and lyrics is a thought-provoking mismatch, initiating questions about the nature of and relationship between high art and popular culture. Does the inclusion of Shakespeare make the Beatles' song high art? This, again, was not the goal in 1967:

> [*Pepper*] is highly experimental, but it is also funny. Apparently, most critics took the music too seriously for Lennon and McCartney. During the last years of the Beatles and on into their solo careers, both Lennon and McCartney satirized those who insisted on finding hidden meaning in their work or intellectually analyzing their music.
>
> (Roessner 2006, 152)

The absorption of Shakespeare into mass culture like the Beatles connects to another question that arises from the seemingly random insertion of *King Lear* into "I Am the Walrus": does the appearance of the Bard in the Beatles put Shakespearean drama back into a rightful category, theater for the masses? The appearance of Shakespeare in this pop song is a reminder that the majority of Shakespeare's original audiences were groundlings and that his plays were attenuated to their concerns—especially what would make them laugh. As

Hansen argues, "The Beatles performed or registered complex rhetorical and cultural shifts, as Shakespeare did" (2010, Loc. 1075).[15]

A reader might still be wondering: wasn't the inclusion of *King Lear* the result of chance and coincidence, dependent on whatever the BBC was playing on the radio?[16] That bit of randomness would seem to serve the others in "I Am the Walrus," a song full of supposedly incongruous, unrelated images. But this Shakespearean tragedy is all about dishonest and withheld communication—which leads to inaccurate interpretations. The scene inserted into "I Am the Walrus," in fact, deals with those very themes: when he dies, Edgar discovers a letter Oswald was carrying; the letter exposed the murderous schemes of Goneril, one of Lear's daughters. Not only do the lines themselves contain oxymoronic word pairings; the lines also address what can be known or understood, motifs that relate to Lennon's motivation and his Carroll intertext.

When Lennon argued against interpretation of his work as high art, he echoed Carroll, who eschewed overinterpretations of his surreal imagery, insisting on his work as amusement for children and issuing his critique in the texts themselves. When the Beatles saw the high-art designation as a category that reduced creativity and limited meaning, their concerns bespoke a generational struggle consistent with what motivated Carroll's project. Robert M. Polhemus identifies in Carroll what must have appealed strongly to Lennon about the Alice books:

> Children are subject to authority, but Carroll puts authority in doubt and questions it. The Alice fiction deals with the crisis of authority in modern life, and readers are drawn to solve it. People project their wishes and beliefs and concerns onto these fictions as they lay them upon children. Like the parables of the Bible, like dreams, like depicted fantasies, Carroll stipulates a hermeneutics of subject ingenuity and a multiplicity of views. These malleable texts resist closure of meaning; they remain open-ended and dialogical.
>
> (1994/2013, 343)

The "malleable" Carroll-intertext brings these issues about perspective and interpretation to bear on "I Am the Walrus."

[15] "Beatles' songs implicated auditors in a 'quasi-Shakespearean fusion of first and second person, me and you' (122). The band's inclusive words 'unsettle gender in lyrics', just as Shakespeare 'delimits early modern culture in part by cross-dressing and unsexing the sexual difference upon which it is grounded' (132). So both the Beatles and Shakespeare evoke 'Bottomesque dissent' against early modern and modern Elizabethan establishments, even as they speak to and for changing nations (129)." (Hansen 2010, Loc. 1075–9).

[16] For more on the significance of this random event as it relates to 1960s' art, see Hansen (2010, Loc. 1176–90).

Carroll's Alice books, beginning with *Alice's Adventures in Wonderland* (1865), followed by *Through the Looking-Glass* less than a decade later, are another case study in perspective by incongruity. As Schneider puts it, "In mocking sense ... by holding it up to a mirror and creating nonsense, Carroll paradoxically underscores the need for nonsense" (2008, 144). Carroll imagined a slew of characters incongruous in and of themselves as they traverse surreal situations: a worrying rabbit running around with a timepiece, a caterpillar with a pipe, a cat whose head floats about its body. Alice's movement through the looking glass and her size predicaments are both illustrations of and commentary on disparity, which is meta-textual perspective by incongruity. Rather than looking into a mirror, Alice falls *through* a mirror and tries to see things clearly but becomes more confused by the curious things she encounters. As she expands and shrinks within fantastic settings whose trifles mirror the "real world," the reader sees the foolishness of the latter. Carroll was a keen observer of middle-class rituals (especially the consumption of tea and soup), which Alice encounters in various forms on the other side, too. Alice's excursions are constant encounters with perspective, insight Harrison seems to lift when he reminds the listener of their place in the broader scheme of things: "you're really only very small / and life goes on within you and without you."

The influence of Carroll on Lennon is well-known because Lennon frequently credited him, even announcing he wanted to "be" Carroll, especially after the publication of his nonsense writings and sketches *In His Own Write* (1964) (Beatles 2000, 176). Claiming that Alice was one of the texts he used to "live", Lennon revealed, "I was passionate about 'Alice in Wonderland' and drew all the characters. I did poems in the style of the Jabberwocky. I used to live Alice" (qtd. in Gopnik 2015). Lewisohn notes that Lennon documented this love when he was asked to provide influences "up to the age of eleven," explaining, "John was given the Alice books as birthday presents and reread them once a year— though he never bothered to find out if Carroll wrote anything else" (2013, 49). Schneider explains the debt: "Lennon, ever the risk-taker and transgressor, represented the fear side of the beauty/fear duality, taking as his impetus the hallucinogenic dimension of Carroll's Blake-influenced Alice books," whose "bizarre dreamscapes ... also gave them a long afterlife" (2008, 146–47).

Lennon sometimes spoke of Alice next to other literary texts, such as *Just William*, but elsewhere he noted, "My main influences for writing were always Lewis Carroll and *The Goon Show*, a combination of that," linking two formative comedic texts for his generation, including the other Beatles (qtd. in Lewisohn 2013, 59). Along with the Goons, Alice was a point of connection with

McCartney, who, while not necessarily an Alice obsessive, was familiar with the texts: "The more hours John and Paul spent together the more they found these things out, uncovering humor and harmony right down the line. They'd both read *Alice in Wonderland* and *Just William*, though Paul had read *Alice* once or twice whereas John still feasted on it every few months and had folded Lewis Carroll's vocabulary into his own" (Lewisohn 2013, 8).

Realizing the depth of Lennon's habituation to Carroll's Alice texts leads us to one of the central images in "I Am the Walrus." Alice encounters the original eggman, Humpty Dumpty, in *Through the Looking-Glass*, first published in December 1871. He's argumentative from the start of their encounter, taking issue with her assessment of him as an egg; she clarifies, "I said you *looked* like an egg, Sir ... And some eggs are very pretty, you know" (Carroll 1897/2013, 157). They proceed to argue about Alice's name (this eggman thinks it's "stupid" because it doesn't mean anything) while she attempts to urge him off of the too-narrow wall, thinking about his breakability but wanting to shield his ego (Carroll 1897/2013, 158). Humpty proudly informs her that the king has promised to rescue him with horses and men if such a thing were to happen, which, of course, Alice knows will take place. Carroll's extraction of the character of Humpty Dumpty from the nursery rhyme allows the reader to question the logic of that well-known text and the authority for which it stands. In *Through the Looking-Glass*, Humpty proclaims to be all knowing about poems, but he does not know his own poem and that the king, another authority, won't be able to put him back together. Applicable to this episode is Schneider's apt characterization of the Alice books: "Nonsense mocks sense; but in mocking it, it evokes it; nonsense pays unwitting homage to sense" (2008, 144).

In a similar way, Lennon extracts Humpty Dumpty (though not admitting to it), essentially renaming him with the label Humpty resisted. Lennon's "eggman" provokes overinterpreting critics, the very people Humpty's representation critiqued in Carroll's text. As Alice's and Humpty's conversation unfolds, constantly derailed by his contrariness, puns on concepts related to looking and hearing appear in a meta-discourse on language. Humpty arrogantly philosophizes on the nature of words, things he can employ and otherwise put to work for him: "When *I* use a word ... it means just what I choose it to mean—neither more nor less" (Carroll 1897/2013, 162). In doing so, "he picks up the other theory Dodgson plays with in this book, that words are wholly arbitrary signs" (Gray 2013, 158). Since Humpty proclaims himself to be an expert, Alice asks this egg-man to help her understand the nonsense "Jabberwocky" poem. Humpty agrees, proudly discoursing on the act of interpretation: "I can explain all the poems that ever were invented—and a good many that haven't been invented yet" (Carroll 1897/2013, 162). But his "analysis" involves assigning each word his own made-up meanings based on the words' sound-alike possibilities.

Lennon said that his eggman "could have been the pudding basin, for all I care" (Beatles 2000, 273). But he did own another Carroll allusion in "I Am the Walrus," citing "The Walrus and the Carpenter," calling it "beautiful" (Beatles 2000, 273). This is the narrative poem that Tweedledee and Tweedledum recite to Alice prior to her Humpty encounter. In the ballad, the Walrus offers a grand claim: "'The time has come,' [...] / 'To talk of many things.'" What follows is a random list of the ordinary: "shoes—and ships—and sealing wax—/ Of cabbages and kings" (Carroll 1897/2013, 139). Kings are thus rendered small by the association—more perspective by incongruity. This is a similar one at work in the tragedy of *King Lear*, whose king makes himself small when he relinquishes power. He has done this, however, because he was tricked: he could not see how two of his daughters were manipulating him with their false declarations of love; he incorrectly judges another honest daughter as a result. An incorrect judgement is also the outcome of "The Walrus and the Carpenter."

By the end of "The Walrus and the Carpenter," sight and perspective—what Alice is able to understand based on what the Tweedles tell and withhold—are at stake. Taking place on a beach (the kind of shore which Lennon would invoke in "Lucy in the Sky With Diamonds"), the poem's hungry title characters summon a parade of oysters, who line up "in a row" (like the policemen in "Walrus") and who somehow walk without feet. The oysters are a little like Lear, tricked into offering themselves up. "The walrus," Schneider explains, "looks in John Tenniel's illustrations for *Looking-Glass* like a portly Victorian gentleman, a gruff but lovable city banker" (2008, 144). The Walrus expresses remorse, but the Carpenter requests more bread, butter, and pepper, constantly dissatisfied and thus unsatisfied with his portion.

After the twins' recitation, Alice attempts to interpret the poem, wondering to whom she should give her sympathies. She immediately judges the Carpenter, leaning toward the Walrus because of his remorse, but the twins interrupt her, explaining that the Walrus was actually hoarding oysters, inhaling them behind his napkin. Alice is confused and out of her element: her attempts to judge the morality of the characters belie the kind of response she, as a Victorian young lady, has been trained to provide. Carroll's "demonic parodies" critique "Victorian sentiments in which well brought-up girls like Alice would have been schooled—those morality tales in sing-song verse that were intended to preserve in children their ignorance of what John Lennon called, in his own comment on his own ventures into Carrollian nonsense, the 'hidden cruelties' of life" (Schneider 2008, 143). It's little wonder that Alice has trouble determining the villain of the Tweedles' incomplete nonsense poem; she concludes, "Well! They were both very unpleasant characters—" and then she is conveniently interrupted by the sound of a steam engine (Carroll 1897/2013, 141).

Predicaments of sight and perspective are also at stake in the lyrics of "I Am the Walrus," with its repetitive hot-cross-buns calls to "see how they run" or fly, as well as numerous other invitations to witness surreal images. These include the Beatles' own title character from "Lucy in the Sky With Diamonds," the kicking of Edgar Allan Poe, smiling pigs, and other everyday images engaged in weird doings. Lennon's speaker questions whether chanting Hare Krishna will lead to a new point of view, too. Perspective is thus at stake in the composition and reception of the song; anyone attempting an interpretation (as I am doing!) has to account for Lennon's comments on his planned nonsense. The song is indeed rich—and its richness comes in large part from the transplanted poetry of Shakespeare and Carroll, the latter whose image was even transplanted into the Beatles' *Pepper* cover.

Though Carroll represents the disruption of Alice's interpretation within the pages of *Through the Looking-Glass*, the Tweedles' poem has still been read as an allegory of politics, nations, and religion, with the Walrus often positioned as a capitalist. Ironically, Lennon rejected overwrought interpretations of his own work, but he seemed to forget about Alice's correction because he eventually bought into the latter reading of Carroll. He regretted that he had aligned himself with the greedy Walrus character:

> It never dawned on me that Lewis Carroll was commenting on the capitalist system. I never went into that bit about what he really meant, like people are doing with The Beatles' work. Later I went back and looked at it and realized that the walrus was the bad guy in the story, and the Carpenter was the good guy. I thought, "Oh, shit, I've picked the wrong guy. But that wouldn't have been the same, would it? "I am the carpenter ...".
>
> (Beatles 2000, 273)

Lennon essentially creates his own serviceable villain with his walrus, assigning him to Paul in the following year's "Glass Onion," another song obsessed with looking and one that plays with the text-within-a-text concept.

Literary Intersections and Perspective
by Incongruity ... with Pie!

As we have seen, food is great fodder for puns and other jokes. Years before he was the walrus, Lennon conjured the story of a man on a flaming pie as a way of explaining the band's name: "Many people ask what are Beatles? Why Beatles? Ugh, Beatles, how did the name arrive? So we will tell you. It came in a vision—a man appeared on a flaming pie and said unto them, 'From this day on you are Beatles with an A.' Thank you, Mister Man, they said, thanking him" (qtd. in Lewisohn 2013, 423). Resembling Carroll-type nonsense, this joke parodies origin stories, spoofing self-important, near-biblical explanations with an unlikely pairing, a magical deity-like sage on a pie. Pies appear all over the Beatles' oeuvre and are even one of the places they will hide a joke: the fish-and-finger pie of "Penny Lane." A "pie," such a commonplace staple in British cuisine, is also one of Shakespeare's aforementioned metaphors: a pie, like porridge, is a thing that dates well, Paroles says, in contrast to virginity. This kind of imagery appears in the works of Carroll, as well another nonsense influence, Edward Lear, who both parodied their fellow Brits' fixation with certain food and drink.[17]

The Beatles frequently punned on everyday objects, like pies, along with social scenarios. These, of course, included sex; think of the oral sex implied by the wordplay in "Please Please Me." Such silliness might be dismissed as a trifle, as the subjects of the Beatles' early works—and thus the songs themselves—often are. But much great art, from the low to the high and everything in between, has been built out of trifles—as Paroles's discourse on cheese and virginity proves. Shakespeare, Carroll, and other British predecessors provide a depth to the humor at work in the Beatles' texts, especially songs that audiences today are encountering outside of and distended from their original 1960s' contexts (and even the albums themselves). Along with the literary precedents, perspective by incongruity is a useful technique for appreciating the Beatles' ongoing appeal and why humor is so vital to the longevity of their music and other output.

---

[17] While Lear is another nonsense influence, Schneider makes an important distinction: "In Lear, nonsense and sense do not, as they do in Carroll, *confront* each other" (2008, 144).

Acknowledgments

Special thanks to Jon Marc Smith for editorial contributions (along with happy hours spent laughing about fools and cheese). A debt of gratitude also goes to my former dissertation advisor and Kenneth Burke scholar, Barry Brummett.

References

Ackroyd, Peter. 2005. *Shakespeare: The Biography*. New York: Double Day.
Around the Beatles. 1964. Produced by Jack Good. Filmed on April 28, 1964. Aired on May 6. London: ITV.
Beatles, The. 2000. *The Beatles Anthology*. San Francisco: Chronicle.
Beatles, The. 2021. *The Beatles: Get Back*. London: Apple and Callaway.
Bloom, Harold. 1998. *Shakespeare: The Invention of the Human*. New York: Riverhead.
Brothers, Thomas. 2018. *Help! The Beatles, Duke Ellington, and the Magic of Collaboration*. New York: Norton.
Burke, Kenneth. 1935/1984. *Permanence and Change: An Anatomy of Purpose*. Third Edition. Berkeley: University of California Press.
Burke, Kenneth. 1937/1984. *Attitudes Toward History*. Third Edition. Berkeley: University of California Press.
Carroll, Lewis (Charles Lutwidge Dodgson). 1897/2013. *Through the Looking-Glass*, 1897 Edition, in *Alice in Wonderland*, edited by Donald J. Gray. Third Edition. New York: Norton.
Ehrenreich, Barbara, Elizabeth Hess, and Gloria Jacobs. 1986. *Remaking Love: The Feminization of Sex*. New York: Anchor Books.
Epstein, Brian. 1967/1998. *A Cellarful of Noise: The Autobiography of the Man Who Made the Beatles*. New York: Pocket Books.
Gopnik, Adam. 2015. "Who Can Be Finished with Alice?" Rev. of *The Annotated Alice*, by Martin Gardner. *The New Yorker*. October 11. https://www.newyorker.com/books/page-turner/who-can-be-finished-with-alice.
Graham, Phil, and Briony Luttrell. 2019. "A Rhetoric of Style: Eleanor Rigby and the Recording of Popular Music." *Social Semiotics* 29 (2): 222–39. doi:10.1080/10350330.2018.1434971.
Gray, Donald, ed. 2013. *Alice in Wonderland*. Third Edition. New York: Norton.
Hansen, Adam. 2010. *Shakespeare and Popular Music*. Kindle Edition. New York: Continuum.
Kapurch, Katie. 2016. "Crying, Waiting, Hoping: The Beatles, Girl Culture, and the Melodramatic Mode." In *New Critical Perspectives on the Beatles: Things We Said*

Today, edited by Kenneth Womack and Katie Kapurch, 199–220. New York: Palgrave Macmillan.

Kapurch, Katie. 2021. "The Beatles, Gender, and Sexuality: I am He as You Are He as You Are Me." In *Fandom and the Beatles*, edited by Kenneth Womack and Kit O' Toole, 139–61. Oxford: Oxford University Press.

Lester, Richard. 1964. *A Hard Day's Night*. United Artists.

Lewisohn, Mark. 2013. *Tune in: The Beatles: All These Years*. Volume 1. New York: Little, Brown.

Long, Mark C. 1997. "Tending to the Imagination: Perspective and Incongruity in William Carlos Williams and Kenneth Burke." Presented at the Modern Language Association Conference, Toronto, December. https://kbjournal.org/long_tending#:~:text=The%20analytical%20technique%20%22perspective%20by,into%20a%20way%20of%20seeing.

Maus, Katharine Eisaman. 2016. Introduction to *All's Well That Ends Well*. In *The Norton Shakespeare*, edited by Stephen Greenblatt et al., 2635–41. Third Edition. New York: Norton.

Polhemus, Robert M. 1994/2013. "Lewis Carroll and the Child in Victorian Fiction." In *Alice in Wonderland*, edited by Donald J. Gray, 341–345. New York: Norton.

Roessner, Jeffrey. 2006. "We All Want to Change the World: Postmodern Politics and the Beatles' White Album." In *Reading the Beatles: Cultural Studies, Literary Studies, and the Fab Four*, edited by Kenneth Womack and Todd F. Davis, 147–155. Albany: State University of New York Press.

Schneider, Matthew. 2008. *The Long and Winding Road from Blake to the Beatles*. New York: Palgrave.

Schneider, Matthew. 2019. Abstract for "Come Together: Fifty Years of Abbey Road." University of Rochester. September 27–29. Rochester, New York.

Shakespeare, William. 2016a. *All's Well That Ends Well, in The Norton Shakespeare*, edited by Stephen Greenblatt et al., 2642–707. Third Edition. New York: Norton.

Shakespeare, William. 2016b. *King Lear, in The Norton Shakespeare*, edited by Stephen Greenblatt et al., 2494–570. Third Edition. New York: Norton.

2

I Laugh and Act Like a Clown: The Beatles as Paradoxical Clowns

Matthias Heyman

Introduction: Everybody Loves a Clown[1]

During the infamous Bed-in for Peace in Amsterdam's Hilton Hotel in March 1969, John Lennon announced, "Yoko and I are quite willing to be the world's clowns [...] if by so doing it will do some good" (Fawcett 1980, 51). Just a few years earlier, however, he was reluctant about being associated with clowns: "I objected to the word 'clown' [in the lyrics of 'I'm a Loser'] because that was always artsy-fartsy, but Dylan had used it so I thought it was all right, and it rhymed with whatever I was doing" (Beatles 2000, 160). These comments reveal Lennon's ambiguous feelings and evolving understanding of what he thought being a clown implied. He even changes his definition, which parallels the variety of uses for the term "clown" across different historical, cultural, and social contexts. Clowns and their associated archetypes, such as fools, buffoons, jokers, and jesters, have a long and diverse history, from sacred Pueblo clowns over Commedia dell'Arte's Zanni characters to the more recent evil clowns (Pennywise, anyone?).[2] This makes devising an encompassing definition notoriously difficult.

In Western popular culture, clowns are commonly depicted as circus characters with colorful clothing and extravagant make-up who aim to evoke laughter. The connection between the Beatles and this particular clown stereotype is flimsy: Destructive Countdown Clowns are among the antagonists in *Yellow Submarine* (1968); at the official opening of the Apple Boutique in 1967, Pierre the Clown

---

[1] With some exceptions: according to Gary Lewis & the Playboys, their song's protagonist does not love clowns (1965, *Everybody Loves a Clown*).

[2] For more on the clown as a historical, cultural, and social figure, see, for example, Janik (1998), Davison (2013), Bouissac (2015), and Weihe (2016). Following Weihe (2016, 163), I use "clown" as a generic term in this chapter, encompassing Western comic figures' many variants and subtypes.

(real name: Pierre Picton) handed apples to the esteemed guests; and a red nose, today the clown's most symbolic facial feature, appears on rare occasions such as in the Magicians' scene in *Magical Mystery Tour* (1967).[3] But upon deeper scrutiny, clown characteristics can be connected to the Beatles in multiple ways, be it in their lyrics, their commentaries (written or otherwise), and their personae as presented on stage, in film, and in public appearances. Using theater scholar Richard Weihe's seven-pronged theory of the "paradox of the clown" (2016, 163), this chapter aims to demonstrate how the paradoxical clown is an integral part of the Beatles narrative, not through funny hats (although they would wear those sometimes) or extravagant make-up but through subtle and not-so-subtle comments, gestures, and lines.[4] Indeed, sometimes they *did* play the fool, to paraphrase Lennon (Beatles 1963/1994).

While it is challenging to identify the clown archetype's "irreducible, generalisable traits," as Anna-Sophie Jürgens et al. explain, "their contradictory nature—maintaining inconsistent, normally-opposing perspectives simultaneously—is a primary candidate as the one form common to all [its] variations" (2020, 3). According to Weihe (2016, 268–73), this form manifests itself in seven paradoxical ways of playing (*Spielformen* in German): (1) border play, (2) generation play, (3) body play, (4) gender play, (5) emotional play, (6) language play, and (7) morality play. In all seven, a Marxist dialectic, or "unity of opposites" (ibid., 268), occurs, for example, clowns exhibiting both child-like and senile characteristics.

The seven paradoxes are explored in the context of the Beatles in more depth below, the more relevant ones in more detail than the others.[5] Still, even the above list conveys how the four Beatles, individually and as a group, incorporated to some degree each of these forms of play: they were transgressive figures that crossed borders of class, age, gender, race, politics, and genre, and their music and lyrics were full of poetic subtleties that often carried emotional or moral meaning. This chapter aims to go beyond such generic observations and make explicit the various acts of clowning, joking, and fooling around present in the Beatles, their work, and their representation through these interrelated manifestations of paradoxical play.

---

[3] This is not an exhaustive list. The reader may be familiar with other clown references in Beatles or post-Beatles lore, such as Ringo Starr's clown cameo in the 1972 Apple film *Born to Boogie* (during the Marc Bolan—Elton John duet that opens "Children of the Revolution") or Paul and Linda McCartney dressing up as whiteface clowns during the 1975 Mardi Gras in New Orleans.

[4] All translations (from German) by the author.

[5] For this chapter, I kept the order of the seven paradoxes as Weihe (2016) presents them, although he does not specify his reasoning behind this seemingly random order.

Imagine There's No Countries: Border Play

The clown is a liminal figure, a character that freely moves between the borders of its world and those around him. In most literature on clowns, this is interpreted as crossing the boundary between the audience and the stage, often physically, when a clown ventures into the audience, but also in a metaphysical sense, for example, by breaking the fourth wall.[6] Both senses apply to the Beatles. For many of their live performances, they were strictly confined to the stage, even to the point of being literally encaged (at San Francisco's Candlestick Park, August 29, 1966). But during the Beatles' early years, when they still enjoyed a certain degree of anonymity, the band took great pleasure in engaging with their audience, entertaining—and occasionally offending—them with ad-libbed wisecracks, jokey impersonations (from Gene Vincent to *Coronation Street* character Leonard Swindley) and other kinds of antics (Lewisohn 2013, 701 and 934). This is often traced back to their Hamburg days, when Indra manager Bruno Koschmider, or rather his aide Willi Limpinsel, prodded the *Piedels* to "MACH SCHAU!" (ibid., 701, 711–12). Such border-crossing continued in their Cavern engagements. For the group's mushrooming fan base, this was an added attraction. "Cavernite" David John Smith remembered how "in between numbers they were a *comedy act*, looning about, and Lennon was doing his crips" (ibid., 1361; *italics in original*).[7] Indeed, their musical and visual charisma was crucial to their appeal with the early fans, but so was their "comedy sense," something which "the other Scouse bands didn't have," according to Smith, who compared the Beatles to a "*Rock 'n' Roll Goon Show*" (ibid., 1363; *italics in original*).

Moving from the clubs into national theaters and cinema's first and international concert halls and stadiums next, the Beatles necessarily had to upgrade their act, from "bar band or lunchtime diversion to a proper concert act" (Roessner 2015, 15). As their fame rose, the band "lost its basis in local culture [and] more boundaries were erected," as Roessner attests (ibid.). As a result, playing with the fourth-wall border became increasingly hard, especially since Brian Epstein, who began managing the band officially in January 1962, had the foursome tone down their wild behavior for the sake of professionalism (Lewisohn 2013, 1078). While Lennon never truly stopped his on-stage antics

---

[6] Julia Lane even argues that clowns are so liminal there are no walls at all; they operate in "a world that is not necessarily bound by the walls [...] of the performance space" (2016, 62).

[7] Lennon's "crips," the term used by this eyewitness, is crude slang for an offensive mockery of (mostly) physical disability.

that mocked disability, the Beatles became the relatively static stage act we can still witness in surviving concert footage. Only occasionally would they cross borders in a more physical sense, notably at the now legendary Shea Stadium concert on August 15, 1965. Seemingly triggered by the infinite pandemonium, the hysteric crowd of 55,600 bringing Beatlemania to a new level, the Beatles, and Lennon in particular, responded by gradually acting more and more manic, from mock-miming McCartney's gestures in the introduction to "Ticket to Ride" to speaking gibberish in his announcement of "A Hard Day's Night" (which is a form of language play, see below). The mayhem culminates in "I'm Down," the show's frantic finale. Having positively "lost his marbles," Lennon erupts in incontrollable laughter and plays—or rather, assaults—the Vox Continental organ with his elbows, leaving him nearly unable to sing the backing vocals.[8] Mach Schau, indeed!

Border play can also happen in a more figural sense, as in testing ideological boundaries. Indeed, clowns can break—and consequently question—political or social norms and limits (Weihe 2016, 269). Similarly, the Beatles were transgressive in many ways, including some discussed further below. Scholars have explored these aspects of the band's personae, often focusing on the impact they had on youth and counterculture.[9] A few examples, however, warrant further attention as they highlight how the Fab Four used comedy to challenge such figurative borders. During the Royal Command Performance on November 4, 1963, Lennon served as the band's literal "class clown" as he asked an audience that included the Queen Mother and Princess Margaret for their help: "For the people in the cheaper seats, clap your hands. And the rest of you, if you'd just rattle your jewelry" (Beatles 1963/1995). Seemingly an innocuous repartee, the well-prepared line (though perhaps changed last-minute to omit the F-bomb) shows how the Beatles were able to shrewdly comment on the class society their country still was, using lighthearted humor to "make the medicine go down," as Mary Poppins would have it several months later. In later instances, it was George Harrison who critiqued similar societal aspects of class, now through satirical lyrics such as those of "Taxman" (1966, *Revolver*) and "Piggies" (1968, *The Beatles*). The upbeat arrangement of "Piggies," with its faux-classical harpsichord and double string quartet accompanied by the occasional pig grunts, exudes a playfulness that contrasts the wry message and Harrison's deadpan delivery of the lyrics. Border play at its best.

---

[8] See Beatles (2000, 187), for the band's testimony of their Shae Stadium experience.
[9] See, for example, Inglis (2000), Gleed (2006), Collins (2020), Glynn (2021), and Campbell (2021).

Who's That Little Old Man?: Generation Play

"In the generation play, the clown unites the child and the adult," asserts Weihe (2016, 269). He clarifies that this doesn't mean that the clown *is* a child, but that the clown can exhibit child-like and childish behavior (2016). The paradox lies therein that this "adult child" lives and experiences two generations simultaneously (2016). Generation play may seem less relevant to the Beatles. Certainly, they at times behaved childishly ("ey Mister, can we 'ave our ball back!"), and some of their songs exude a child-like innocence, as exemplified by "Julia" (*The Beatles*, 1968), Lennon's ode to his two "mothers," one real but dead (Julia Stanley), the other adopted and alive (Yoko Ono).

But it is *A Hard Day's Night* (1964) that offers true instances of generation play in memorable scenes. The opening sequence of the Beatles' first film effectively propels us into the world of Beatlemania as Lennon, Harrison, and Starr attempt to escape a mob of teenage fans. Oddly, McCartney is nowhere to be seen. He appears only about one minute and a half into the movie, and our first glimpse of him shows him in disguise, donning an anchor-styled beard. Here is Paul, arguably the band's baby face, masquerading as an old man, seated next to an even older man, whom we later learn is his grandfather (Wilfrid Brambell), a "dirty old man" (see *Steptoe and Son*) soon to be pronounced "very clean" (Lester 1964).[10]

This sets up the first of several generation plays throughout the film, often featuring not only McCartney's granddad, a "king mixer" by all means, but also the Beatles separately (Lester 1964).[11] Indeed, the foursome regularly finds themselves in a situation where they combine childish clowning with a sense of mature wisdom. A notable scene has Lennon in a bathtub "larking about" as a little child, while Harrison, clearly the younger character, teaches Shake (John Junkin), the band's assistant, to shave using a safety razor (Lester 1964).[12]

[10] Also, note how the incognito McCartney reads a "distinguished" newspaper (even though it is the tabloid *Daily Express*), true to his temporary role as a "distinguished" fifty-something, while his grandfather reads the April 1964 issue of *For Men Only*, a risqué magazine, as evidenced by the scantily clad woman on the cover. While this can be seen as a pun on Brambell's "dirty old man" association, it can also be interpreted as another instantiation of generation play, with both men simultaneously exhibiting mature and immature traits.

[11] Remarkably, their following two films also feature the group as senior citizens. The airport scene in *Help!* (1965) reveals the disguised Beatles in various stages of late adulthood, with Lennon even confined to a wheelchair, while in *Yellow Submarine* (1968), the cartoon foursome experiences how the Sea of Time magically turns them into "half the lad[s they] used to be" first, and "senile delinquents" next (Dunning 1968). These movies, however, don't feature generation play to the same extent as *A Hard Day's Night*.

[12] Incidentally, the "Little Child" of the eponymous song, included on *With the Beatles* (1963), is more in line with the seventeen-year-old girl in "I Saw Her Standing There" (*Please Please Me*, 1963) and the many other "babies" mentioned in lyrics, the object of romantic love (and possibly more) rather than an actual kid.

Upon manager Norm's prodding (Norman Rossington), they leave for the car, but Lennon has surreally vanished from the bath, only to suddenly re-emerge as a responsible adult, scolding Norm for "messing around with that boat" (Lester 1964). Later in the movie, Harrison is mistaken for a teenage model tasked with opining on some shirts. He declares them "dead grotty" and is eventually dismissed for sharing his honest judgment (Lester 1964). One moment he's the teacher-adult, the next, he's a kid with an "utterly valueless opinion" who's supposed to be "right-wing" (Lester 1964). Two generations united in one clown.

Genuinely odd is one of the film's promotional trailers, filmed on April 3, 1964, outside Twickenham Film Studios. It shows the four lads in two baby prams behind microphones, a typewriter, a telephone, and a sign saying "You may telephone from here" at hand. It is unclear what these strollers have to do with the Beatles and their upcoming film, but with the benefit of hindsight, it offers an interesting counterplay to the generation play in *A Hard Day's Night*, now focused on the foursome in child mode rather than in the teenage and adult phases presented in the movie.[13]

With the exception of Starr's scene with "the kid" (David Janson) in *A Hard Day's Night*, the Beatles' generation play doesn't often feature kids. Babies are referenced in plenty of their lyrics—albeit mainly in a romantic sense, see footnote 12—but few songs have been written with actual kids in mind. Notable exceptions are "Yellow Submarine," "All Together Now," and even, by way of an Elizabethan lullaby by Thomas Dekker, "Golden Slumbers," all mainly McCartney compositions, unsurprising from a songwriter who said to "like children's minds and imagination" (Beatles 2000, 208). Similarly, while not a film explicitly marketed for children, *Yellow Submarine* (1968) has a certain appeal to the youngest generations. According to Harrison, "every baby, three or four years old, goes through *Yellow Submarine*" (Beatles 2000, 292). These and other instances, such as the near-opposite, geriatric-centric "When I'm Sixty-Four" (*Sgt. Pepper's Lonely Hearts Club Band*, 1968), reveal McCartney's empathy toward listeners of all ages.[14] Still, they are not the type of generational play described by Weihe (2016, 269).

---

[13] In another rare instance of a baby carriage appearing in (post-)Beatles lore, the music video to Harrison's "Crackerbox Palace" (*Thirty Three & 1/3*, 1976), directed by Monty Python's Eric Idle, prominently features the ex-Beatle as a baby (in said pram) and a uniformed school boy. Incidentally, it also comprises several clowns and other carnivalesque figures.

[14] McCartney has used other media to reach out to children, albeit mostly outside of his Beatles tenure. Notable examples are the animated short films he produced and (co-)voiced (*Rupert and the Frog Song*, 1994, *Tropical Island Hum*, 1997, and *Tuesday*, 2002) or the children picture books he authored (*Hey Grandude!*, 2019, and *Grandude's Green Submarine*, 2021).

Fallin', Yes, I Am Fallin': Body Play

When McCartney sings "Fallin', yes, I am fallin'" (in "I've Just Seen A Face," *Help!*, 1965), he's singing in a figurative sense. Falling in a literal sense, however, is an essential aspect of clowning. As Weihe explains, the clown's most characteristic movement is "stumbling and falling on the nose" (ibid., 270). Famously (and unscripted), Harrison is seen stumbling and falling in the opening sequence of *A Hard Day's Night* (and nearly repeats this gaffe in his 1974 promo clip for "Ding Dong, Ding Dong") while in the movie's escape sequence (with "Can't Buy Me Love" as non-diegetic music), the boys, or rather, the Threetles and Lennon's body-double, engage in all kinds of corporeal capers, inspired by director Richard Lester's and Peter Sellers' *The Running Jumping & Standing Still Film* (1959). Their other films feature slapstick-like shenanigans also, such as the Beatles being partly stripped of their clothes by a zealous hand dryer in *Help!* or the *Magical Mystery Tour* marathon.

Nonetheless, the paradox of body play lies in the ability to control and *lose* control of the body simultaneously (Jürgens et al. 2020, 3). The Beatles were not physical comedians in the line of such masters as Buster Keaton, Charlie Chaplin, or, closer to home, Benny Hill or Sellers (e.g., as Inspector Clouseau in the *Pink Panther* movies). Still, they displayed great control of their bodies in their shows, at least from 1962 on, after Epstein had tempered their Hamburg/Cavern cavorting (see above, under border play). In what was primarily a stagnant stage show, Harrison's "Liverpool leg" (Lewisohn 2013, 1427), their heads suddenly going from gentle bobbing to violent shaking, and Lennon's aforementioned and offensive "cripping" were distinctive gestures, indeed. Perhaps these are not the foursome's most hilarious moments, but it shows how they, in an amusing yet controlled manner, could briefly lose control to retain control, their subtle acts of body play being used to enhance musical unity, whip their fans into a frenzy, or defuse the tensions present in the audience or themselves.

You Should See Her in Drag: Gender Play

As I've noted elsewhere, "[m]ore than three decades of scholarship explores the Beatles' non-normative gender presentation," revealing an evolving understanding, from androgynous and homosocial to gender fluid (Heyman 2021, 95). Most recently, Katie Kapurch argues that the Beatles can be understood best in terms of gender fluidity, "a concept that better captures the appeal of the band's gendered spectrum in the early 1960s (and beyond) than androgyny does" (2021, 143). She explains that "[g]ender fluidity is the slide between masculine and feminine that does not have to occupy either one in the dominant position—but could or could not at any given time" (ibid.). Similarly, clowns have been interpreted as "gender ambivalent," using such means of expression as "androgyny, crossdressing, diva or macho behavior, sexism [i.e., *sexual innuendos*], asexuality, and others" (Weihe 2016, 270). Of interest here is the connection between the Beatles' gender fluidity and humor, which seems rather insubstantial. There are some instances of the Beatles in drag, such as Harrison during the 1963–64 *The Beatles Christmas Show* and Lennon playing Thisbe in a reworked episode of Shakespeare's *A Midsummer Night's Dream* (for the television special *Around the Beatles* on April 28, 1964). Furthermore, high-pitched, girlish voices appear a number of times, for example, on some of their Christmas records (which built on the British Christmas pantomime tradition, in which crossdressing is a performance convention), or to convey the girl's perspective in *A Hard Day's Night*'s "Tell Me Why" (in the line "Is there anything I can do?"). Lastly, some cursory references to characters in drag are made in the lyrics to, for example, "Ob-La-Di, Ob-La-Da" (1968, *The Beatles*) and "Polythene Pam" (1969, *Abbey Road*). While these are only superficial indications of comedic gender play, a general parallel can be drawn between the Beatles and clowns: in their unique way, both "unite masculinity and femininity"—and are therefore gender fluid, to use Kapurch's term—thereby embodying yet another aspect of the paradoxical clown (Weihe 2016, 271).

Some Kind of Solitude Is Measured Out in You: Emotional Play

The clown operates between a smile and a tear. Indeed, as Weihe observes, the very symbols of theater are, side by side, the smiling and crying masks, one denoting comedy, the other tragedy (2016, 271). Both emotional states, smiling and crying, are united in the clown, and smooth, sudden shifts between them are typical. For a clown, these are simply tools to interact with the audience: "The clown laughs and makes us laugh or he cries, either to elicit sympathy or to amplify [*and contrast, I would argue*] our laughter," Weihe explains (ibid.). For the Beatles, too, such emotional play offers a way to engage with their listeners.

These emotional contrasts are united in several Beatles songs, especially in the lyrics. This is exemplified by two compositions that reference clowns directly: "I'm A Loser" (1964, *Beatles for Sale*) and "You've Got to Hide Your Love Away" (1965, *Help!*). In the former, the duality of emotional play is brought up explicitly, as Lennon "laugh[s] and act[s] like a clown" only to reveal that "beneath this mask, [he is] wearing a frown." This conjures the trope of the sad clown. A similar sentiment of lost love is expressed in "You've Got to Hide Your Love Away." Here, Lennon is not the clown; rather, the clowns are those he has—defiantly or perhaps with resignation—invited to "gather 'round" in order to remind him to hide his love away, even after being ridiculed by these clowns. In one instance, Lennon portrays himself as a sad clown, in the other, his sadness is amplified and contrasted by the clowns around him.

Lennon admitted both songs to have been influenced by Bob Dylan, who similarly invokes the notion of clowns crying (in "A Hard Rain's A-Gonna Fall," 1963, *The Freewheelin' Bob*) or frowning (in "Like A Rolling Stone," 1965, single) (Beatles 2000, 160).[15] Dylan, however, uses this sad clown trope in a markedly different way. In "A Hard Rain's A-Gonna Fall," it is just one of the many characters that figure in this stream-of-consciousness protest song, whereas the clowns in "Like A Rolling Stone", too, are merely mentioned in the passing. Dylan's clowns are not engaged with; they are passive bystanders, not active participants in the song's storyline. Conceptually, the sad clown in "I'm A Loser" and "You've Got to Hide Your Love Away" is closer to the Everly Brothers' "Cathy's Clown" (1960, *A Date with the Everly Brothers*), a composition the Beatles frequently featured in their early days, and that was, indeed, sung by Lennon (Lewisohn 2013, 609 and 651–2). In all three instances, a dejected lover's introspective musings on betrayal, rejection, and public humiliation are accompanied by a happy beat and largely major-keyed melodies, an instantiation of emotional play expressed through the paradoxical relationship between a song's message (the lyrics) and its medium (the music). More importantly, the lyrics in all three songs employ clowns to draw out the contrast between the laughter and joy associated with clowns and the protagonist's despair and loneliness.

Lennon's use of sad clowns runs deeper than these obvious forms of emotional play suggest. The archetype of the sad clown is the so-called Pierrot, a whiteface clown with roots in the seventeenth-century *Comédie-Italienne*. Pierrot,

---

[15] There are other 1960s examples of Dylan referencing clowns, such as "Mr. Tambourine Man" (1965) and "Queen Jane Approximately" (1965). However, the clowns in these songs don't belong to the paradox of emotional play as Dylan doesn't frame them as sad clowns.

originally a naïve and somewhat melancholic character, is sometimes depicted with a tear dangling from one eye, a testimony to his tragic story of unrequited love, with Columbine, his object of desire, breaking his heart by preferring the happy-go-lucky Harlequin. In the aforementioned Lennon songs, the gloomy protagonist pines for unanswered love, too, making the reference to sad clowns more than a Dylanesque gimmick but an actual theatrical-literary device that connects these 1960s' works to continental Baroque theater traditions. Throughout the centuries, Pierrot took on a variety of guises and meanings, but in essence, he always remained a sad clown.[16]

In recent decades, the notion of the sad clown is often coupled with mental illness, even leading to the term "sad clown paradox," an established concept in modern-day psychology (Smith 2022).[17] As "I'm A Loser" is an early example of songs that expressed Lennon's emotional outcry for help as he went through a psychologically challenging period (other examples being "Help!" and "Nowhere Man"), his—perhaps intuitive—use of the sad clown trope in this song's lyrics is quite fitting (Beatles 2000, 158). While Lennon initially objected to using the word clown, he deep down may have identified with this metaphysical sad clown, making it more tolerable for him to include it in his lyrics (ibid., 160).

You May Feel the Words Are Not Quite Right: Language Play

For Weihe, the paradox of language play lies in how clowns exhibit a truly virtuoso control of language while possessing only a rudimentary ability to verbally express themselves or even be literally lost for words altogether (2016, 272). That the Beatles were linguistic virtuosos is clear. Their lyrics abound with cute rhyming, clever wordplay, and compelling storytelling. So too were they never want for words when speaking in public, for example, during press conferences. Thus, this paradox doesn't seem to apply to the Beatles.

Still, there are many instances during which the Fab Four were literally speechless. As they were often asked to mime the words to pre-recorded songs during televised or video-recorded performances, the (lead and backing) singers of the relevant song are seen singing but not heard in reality. True, the lyrics

---

[16] Arguably, the most iconic—and iconographic—Pierrot association by a musical artist is by David Bowie, who dressed up as a Pierrot for the artwork for "Ashes to Ashes" (*Scary Monsters (and Super Creeps)*, 1980) and its accompanying music video.

[17] See, for example, Janus (1975) and Fisher and Fisher (1981).

are heard, but the on-screen character(s) and music originate from a different source and time, making this a peculiar form of non-diegetic music. In a way, such miming renders the singer(s) speechless. While this stretches Weihe's understanding of speechlessness, it presented the otherwise so eloquent Beatles with an opportunity for silent comic relief (ibid.). For example, the 1965 "I Feel Fine" music video has Harrison singing to a punching ball. At first, he delivers his backing vocals properly, but when he notices the camera honing in on him, he starts singing out-of-sync gibberish, much to the amusement of himself and the others. It is unclear if Harrison really sang or merely mimed nonsense, but the effect is the same for the viewer. Miming to actual gibberish poses another problem altogether. In the 1966 studio clip of "Rain," Lennon has no issues miming his lyrics until he arrives at the final section. Realizing he has to mime live what on record is a vocal reversed in post-production, he cannot help grinning to himself, even shaking his head in disbelief at the surreal ordeal he is put to. To Richard Havers, it is a "highlight" of the video (2015).

The gibberish in "Rain" exemplifies how Weihe's proposition of silence and faulty speech (e.g., stuttering) as the opposite of virtuosic speech can be further expanded (2016, 272). Jürgens et al. explain that clowns at times tend "to speak in lunatic or in 'alternative' (unexpected, incomprehensible) ways" (2019, 3). Such "alternative" ways of speech are present in many Beatles songs, most of which were penned by Lennon (ibid.). Only a few contain actual incomprehensible nonsense, for example, in the final variation of "You Know My Name (Look Up The Number)" (1970, single) or in the third verse of the first take of "Don't Let Me Down" as performed live in the 1969 rooftop concert. In the former, the gobbledygook is intentional, whereas in the latter, it's a consequence of Lennon forgetting the lyrics.[18] Without missing a beat, he proffers an impromptu guide vocal. Utter nonsense, but it does the job, clearly to the hilarity of the other Beatles.

Post-1966 compositions such as "I Am The Walrus," "What's The New, Mary Jane," "Hey Bulldog," "Sun King," "Come Together," "Dig A Pony," and even "Revolution 9" best demonstrate the paradoxical unity present in the clown's language play: although the words in themselves are understandable to all, the

---

[18] Peter Jackson's *The Beatles: Get Back* (2021) reveals several other instances of the singer(s) using nonsense lyrics. However, in most cases this is the result of the songwriting process whereby the use of meaningless, placeholder lyrics allowed them to experiment with the words until the desired effect was achieved. One of the (obvious) exceptions is the gibberish lyrics sung to the traditional "The House of the Rising Sun" (Jackson 2021, part 1).

lyrics as a whole seem to signify nothing. And yet, these songs *work*. The lyrics make the music happen, trigger the listener, and, perhaps paradoxically, carry meaning and emotion. This fragile exercise, a balancing act between ridicule and honesty, can only be undertaken by a masterful songwriter with full command of language who is not afraid to unleash a surreal stream-of-consciousness-like speech. Such paradoxical language play was Lennon's forte. Already as a teenager, he showed a talent for absurdist yet clever writing, for example, in his self-made mock newspaper, *The Daily Howl* (Lewisohn 2013, 234–5). His prose, mainly influenced by The Goon Show and Lewis Carroll, culminated in *In His Own Write* (1964) and *A Spaniard in the Works* (1965), and many of his lyrics (ibid., 3 & 157).[19] Lennon, and by extension the Beatles, exemplifies the paradoxical aspects of the clown's language play.

Lastly, Weihe observes how the court jester (*Hofnarr*) is a "master of speech" and as such has an "exceptional linguistic tool at [his] disposal": *Narrenfreiheit* or the fool's liberty, which allows the clown to speak the truth freely and without risk of punishment (2016, 272). As such, clowns can comment on social and political circumstances and even act as moral compasses. This is briefly referred to above under border play, but it is also relevant to the following type of play: morality play.

Me Used to Be Angry Young Man: Morality Play

While those with coulrophobia may disagree, Weihe explains that "we intuitively think of the laughing clown as a positive figure" (2016, 273). He does clarify that since the 1980s, we have seen the rise of a more disturbing type of clown, namely the evil type (ibid.). In popular culture, one of the earliest evil clowns was Batman's nemesis the Joker (first appeared in the comic book series in 1940), but the type was popularized by the 1986 publication of Stephen King's *It* and its 1990 television adaption (Radford 2016, 64 & 67). However, the clown and its variants, such as the pre-renaissance harlequin or the Shakespearean fool, have always shown ambivalent characteristics. While such archetypes could be kind, friendly, and understanding, they sporadically behaved mischievously. As such, the clown appears to be simultaneously good and bad, a paradox described by Weihe as morality play (2016, 273).

---

[19] For more on the connection between the Beatles and (British) literature, see Schneider (2008, especially 130–4), for an analysis of Carroll's and the Goons' influence on Lennon.

While some fans tend to gloss over the more negative aspects of the Beatles' biographies (e.g., serial infidelities, occasional cruelty toward romantic partners and each other, and substance abuse), these "bad" sides were expressed in some of their music. These may even account for its appeal, much like the effect of Byronic heroes, who are dangerous bad-boy types in literature and other media.[20] This is exemplified by "Run for Your Life" (1965, *Rubber Soul*), with its death-threat beginning (though borrowed from the 1955 Elvis Presley single "Baby Let's Play House," written by Arthur Gunter), or "Getting Better" (1967, *Sgt. Pepper's Lonely Hearts Club Band*), which, despite the protagonist's claim toward self-betterment, opens with an admission of domestic abuse. It is perhaps unsurprising that Lennon, arguably the band's "bad boy," had a hand in the creation of both songs, either as the main author ("Run for Your Life") or collaborator (he provided the line about being cruel toward his woman in "Getting Better"). He later admitted that "Getting Better" was "a diary form of writing" whereby the cruelty referenced in the lyrics had a basis in reality (Sheff 1981, 154).

Furthermore, Lennon was no stranger to mocking others, especially those thought to be on the margins of (British 1960s) society. Elsewhere in this volume, Roessner considers Lennon's infamous on-stage antics and his off-the-record insulting of Jews and gay people (which often targeted Epstein), concluding that Lennon's own insecurity motivated his scorn (2023, 115–31). This wicked streak seems at odds with Lennon's later, carefully curated image as an advocate for social justice and equality, expressed notably in "Give Peace a Chance" (1969, single by the Plastic Ono Band), "All You Need Is Love" (1967, single), and even earlier songs such as "The Word" (1965, *Rubber Soul*) (ibid). Combined with the Beatles' messages of love and peace, such physical and verbal offenses send a mixed message, a clown-like one whereby good and bad are united.

Sometimes, the Beatles' artistic play (and other choices) got them into trouble, and 1966 was a disaster year in that respect. The band was criticized for the *Yesterday and Today* "butcher cover," but they also committed several intercultural offenses: they performed at Nippon Budōkan hall, a sacred site for many Japanese people, they accidentally snubbed the Philippines' First Lady, and Lennon's comments about the Beatles' being more popular than Jesus offended many white evangelical Christians in the southern United States.[21]

---

[20] I wish to thank Katie Kapurch for pointing out the connection with Byronic heroes.
[21] Steve Turner's *Beatles '66: The Revolutionary Year* (2016) is dedicated entirely to detailing this year's trials and tribulations.

Although the fallout from these situations was hardly amusing, the Beatles still managed to sneak in some quips when questioned about these and other sensitive matters, using humor to ease tensions. At the press conference held on August 24, 1966 in Los Angeles' Capitol Records Tower, the band seems ill at ease, weary, no doubt, but perhaps also wary of potentially provocative questions by polemic press members. Being increasingly knotted up in political and social debates, something Epstein always tried to prevent, they seem cautious about the press trying to frame them in a negative manner, particularly after the "more popular than Jesus" controversy. Still, the Beatles find witty ways to react to confrontational questions. For example, a reporter paraphrases from the July 1, 1966 edition of *Time* [from the anonymous write-up "Rock 'n' Roll: Going to Pot"] in which it is claimed that "Day Tripper" is about a prostitute and "Drive My Car" about a lesbian. McCartney smiles half-heartedly and seemingly nods in agreement: "Oh yeah" (Sterling, "Beatles Los Angeles Press Conference 1966"). To the question of what his true intent was when writing these songs, he matter-of-factly retorts: "We were just trying to write songs about prostitutes and lesbians, that's all" (ibid.). McCartney's quick witticism, greeted with laughter by those present, was not just about being funny; it was also a clever way to circumvent this potential minefield. If McCartney had tried to lecture the reporter on the actual subjects of changing gender roles and women's sexuality, the result would no doubt have been more media fallout. Instead, McCartney's retort made the reporter's question the set up for a joke all could share. The whole debacle is further deflated a few minutes later when Lennon quips about "Eleanor Rigby." Again making gay people the butt of the joke, he claims the song (a McCartney number) is about "two queers," causing the room to erupt with laughter (ibid.). This "bad" joke is another example of how Lennon's humor does not stand the test of time, while highlighting the role humor played as the Beatles navigated the consequences, good and bad, of their own musical play.

Conclusion: Gather 'Round All You Clowns

The Beatles were no clowns. They didn't wear oversized clothes, funny hats, whiteface make-up, and red noses, at least not regularly and as a part of their group identity and image. Furthermore, in the band's entire song catalog, there are only a handful of songs that feature clowns or jokers, and none of these are laugh-out-loud funny.

Yet, individually and as a group, they exhibited certain clown characteristics, mainly as seen through the lens of Weihe's seven paradoxical manifestations: (1) border play, (2) generation play, (3) body play, (4) gender play, (5) emotional play, (6) language play, and (7) morality play. Overall, these seven paradoxes allow us to better understand the Beatles and their work using different media, from their films to stage performances. The generational play central to the film *A Hard Day's Night*, their subtle use of comical body play in their live shows, Lennon's lyrical connections to the sad clown Pierrot; these are just a few examples of how the perspective of the paradoxical clown reveals a slightly different side to these otherwise well-known aspects of the Beatles' life and music.

The samples surveyed in this chapter provide only a glimpse of the possibilities Weihe's framework of clown paradoxes can offer in deepening and broadening our understanding of the Beatles. Other instances of paradoxical play are indeed found when further examining their output as a band or as solo artists. For example, by way of conclusion, let us take the one title in the Beatles catalog that references the fool, one of the most important subtypes of the clown. Where does "The Fool on The Hill" (*Magical Mystery Tour*, 1967) belong in Weihe's model? Does it figure under language play, as no sound this "man of a thousand voices" utters is ever heard? Does the song reveal yet another form of virtuoso speechlessness? Or does this fool fit better under emotional play, as an example of a sad clown? He grins rather foolishly, so we are told, yet he appears to be a tragic character, unknown, unheard, unloved. Perhaps not, as our protagonist refrains from sharing his feelings, incidentally—or not?—mirroring the gathered clowns' message in "You've Got to Hide Your Love Away." Maybe the clue to understanding this fool lies in body play? He "is keeping perfectly still," exactly as shown in the accompanying music video but so, too, can we see McCartney, the song's main author and presented as its protagonist in the video, jumping and running around like a little child. Following this observation, perhaps the fool *is* indeed a little child, wise in its innocence. Simultaneously, he seems somewhat of an old sage, knowing beyond his years. Could generation play be at stake? Whichever the interpretation(s), this final example aptly shows the richness of Weihe's paradoxical clown model as it allows us to reflect on the Beatles' music, lyrics, images, and words, spoken and written, from the vantage point of comedy and humor.

With clowns to the left and jokers to the right, this chapter hopefully offered an occasional good laugh in between. More importantly, attention to clowning reveals how the Beatles humorously played with borders, age, body, gender, emotion, and morality, challenging or re-enforcing our (pre)conceptions about their music, personae, and lives. To do so, they had to play the fool at times. But then again, it takes great wisdom to play the fool.

References

Beatles, The. 1963/1994. "Beatles Greetings." *Live at the BBC* (Disc 1, track 1). Apple Corps Ltd.

Beatles, The. 1963/1995. "Till There Was You." *The Beatles Anthology 1* (Disc 2, track 2). Apple Corps Ltd.

Beatles, The. 2000. *The Beatles Anthology*. San Francisco: Chronicle Books.

Bouissac, Paul. 2015. *The Semiotics of Clowns and Clowning: Rituals of Transgression and the Theory of Laughter*. London: Bloomsbury Publishing.

Campbell, Kenneth L. 2021. *The Beatles and the 1960s: Reception, Revolution, and Social Change*. New York: Bloomsbury Publishing.

Collins, Marcus. 2020. "'I Say High, You Say Low': The Beatles and Cultural Hierarchies in 1960s and 1970s Britain." *Popular Music* 39, no. 3–4: 401–19. https://doi.org/10.1017/S0261143020000458.

Davison, Jon. 2013. *Clown*. New York: Palgrave Macmillan.

Dunning, George, dir. 1968. *Yellow Submarine*. Digital restoration, 2012. Apple Records. DVD.

Fawcett, Anthony. 1980. *John Lennon 1940–80: One Day at a Time*. New York: Grove Press.

Fisher, Seymour and Rhoda L. Fisher. 1981. *Pretend the World Is Funny and Forever: A Psychological Analysis of Comedians, Clowns, and Actors*. Mahwah: Lawrence Erlbaum Associates, Inc.

Gleed, Paul. 2006. "The Rest of You, If You'll Just Rattle Your Jewelry: The Beatles and Questions of Mass and High Culture." In *Reading the Beatles: Cultural Studies, Literary Criticism, and the Fab Four*, edited by Kenneth Womack and Todd F. Davis, 161–8. Albany: State University of New York Press.

Glynn, Stephen. 2021. *The Beatles and Film: From Youth Culture to Counterculture*. London and New York: Routledge.

Havers, Richard. 2015. "+10, +11 Rain." *The Beatles 1+*. Liner notes to the 2DVD/CD box set. Apple Corps. Ltd.

Heyman, Matthias. 2021. "Recreating the Beatles: The Analogues and Historically Informed Performance." *Journal of Popular Music Studies* 33, no. 2: 77–98. https://doi.org/10.1525/jpms.2021.33.2.77.

Inglis, Ian. 2000. "Men of Ideas? Popular Music, Anti-intellectualism and the Beatles." In *The Beatles, Popular Music and Society: A Thousand Voices*, edited by Ian Inglis, 1–22. London: Palgrave Macmillan.

Jackson, Peter, dir. 2021. *The Beatles: Get Back*. Part 1. Apple Corps. Ltd. / Disney+.

Janik, Vicki K (ed.). 1998. *Fools and Jesters in Literature, Art, and History*. Westport: Greenwood Press.

Janus, Samuel. 1975. "The Great Comedians: Personality and Other Factors." *The American Journal of Psychoanalysis* 35: 169–74. https://doi.org/10.1007/BF01358189.

Jürgens, Anna-Sophie, Jarno Hietelahti, Lena Straßburger, and Susanne Ylönen. 2020. "Schlock Horror and Pillow Punches." *Comedy Studies* 11, no. 1: 1–11. https://doi.or g/10.1080/2040610X.2019.1692537.

Kapurch, Katie. 2021. "The Beatles, Gender, and Sexuality: I am He as You Are He as You Are Me." In *Fandom and the Beatles: The Act You've Known for All These Years*, edited by Kenneth Womack and Kit O'Toole, 139–66. New York: Oxford University Press.

Lane, Julia. 2016. "Impossibility Aside: Clowning and the Scholarly Context." PhD diss., Simon Fraser University.

Lester, Richard, dir. 1964. *A Hard Day's Night*. The 50th Anniversary Restoration, 2014. Second Sight Films. DVD.

Lewisohn, Mark. 2013. *The Beatles: All These Years—Volume One: Tune In*. Extended Special Edition. London: Little, Brown.

Radford, Benjamin. 2016. *Bad Clowns*. Albuquerque: University of New Mexico Press.

Roessner, Jeffrey. 2015. "From 'Mach Schau' to Mock Show: The Beatles, Shea Stadium and Rock Spectacle." In *The Arena Concert: Music, Media and Mass Entertainment*, edited by Robert Edgar, Kirsty Fairclough-Isaacs, Benjamin Halligan, and Nicola Spelman, 13–28. New York: Bloomsbury Publishing.

Roessner, Jeffrey. 2023 "Madcap Laughs: The Evolution of John Lennon's Humor." In *The Beatles and Humour: Mockers, Funny Papers, and Other Play*, edited by Katie Kapurch, Richard Mills, and Matthias Heyman, 115–31. New York: Bloomsbury Publishing.

Schneider, Matthew. 2008. *The Long and Winding Road from Blake to the Beatles*. New York: Palgrave Macmillan.

Sheff, David. 1981. *The Playboy Interviews with John Lennon and Yoko Ono*. Edited by G. Barry Golson. New York: Playboy Press.

Smith, Daniel. 2022. "The Sad Clown Paradox: A Theory of Comic Transcendence." *International Journal of Cultural Studies*. https://doi. org/10.1177/13678779221117176.

Sterling, Randal. "Beatles Los Angeles Press Conference 1966." YouTube Video, 16:41, July 31, 2011, https://youtu.be/O8MgItRRaTo.

Turner, Steve. 2016. *Beatles '66: The Revolutionary Year*. New York: Ecco.

Weihe, Richard. 2016. *Über den Clown: Künstlerische und Theoretische Perspektiven*. Bielefeld: transcript Verlag.

3

Defuse, Dilute, Deflate: The Beatles Turn It On and Laugh It Off

Aviv Kammay

The Duke Was Having Problems with the Message

During the Beatles' February 11, 1964 train ride from New York to Washington, Paul McCartney was asked to anticipate the Beatles' impact:

> Interviewer. "What place do you think that this story of the Beatles is gonna have in the history of Western culture?"
>
> Paul McCartney. "You must be kidding with that question. Culture? It's not culture."
>
> I. "What is it?"
>
> PM. "It's a good laugh!"[1]

McCartney's response is revealing. For the 21-year-old Liverpudlian, the very thought of publicly associating himself, his generation, the Beatles, rock and roll, or his hometown with the concept of "culture" necessitated an immediate and unambiguous rejection. To Paul's working-class mind, "culture" may have represented the ailments of unchecked snobbery, aloof artiness, and bourgeois self-importance. If so, the various antidotes—honesty, solidarity, rebellion—were summarized by the Beatle into a singular mechanism of resistance: "a good laugh."

In John A. Fisher's discussion of the semantic distinction between "high" and "low" art, laughter is linked to endeavors of "lower artistic status [as an] immediate physical reaction [...] that seems to bypass conscious reasoning" (2013, 478). And indeed, the reference to laughter in the dialogue above neutralized the potential elitist accolades the interviewer's question bestowed upon McCartney and the Beatles.

---

[1] A clip of this exchange, likely sourced from Albert and David Maysles's footage, appears in Howard (2016, 0:22:42 to 0:22:52).

But flirting with "high art" and ultimately cross-pollinating with intellectual elites were the unstoppable trajectory of the Beatles' path.[2] So impactful was their cultural presence in the 1960s that their contemporary critical reception "reconfigured debates over the relationship between high and low culture" (Collins 2020, 415). Prior to 1964, they had already been initiated into "high art" territory when critic William Mann (2006) devoted his observations of the band almost exclusively to the artistic quality of their 1963 musical output, highlighting their harmonic idiosyncrasies. The Fab Four would shortly become a fixture of the London milieu, where their rock and roll counterculture was "absorbed in the latest intellectual and artistic currents" (Stark 2005, 200). Musically, as Marianne Tatom Letts (2008) notes, the Beatles' introduction of orchestral sonorities into the pop aesthetic "[softened] the boundaries between musical genres" (2). Beatles songs would soon feature "high art" hallmarks such as experimentalism, philosophy, social critique, vulnerable introspection, and the study of styles from distant eras and places.

After the group disbanded in 1970, the pioneering work of Wilfrid Mellers (1973) and the landmark volumes by Walter Everett (1999; 2001) demonstrated that the Beatles music is art worthy of academic acceptance. In the twenty-first century, scholars continue to approach the band from an ever-growing array of socio-cultural, literary, and musical angles, this volume included. These works are complemented by symposia, enhanced by fan-generated knowledge (Mills 2020; Roessner 2016), and fuel local, institutional, or departmental teaching initiatives (Jenkins and Jenkins 2018). Add the first volume of Mark Lewisohn's (2013) colossal historical undertaking (with volumes II and III still to come) and reducing the Beatles to "a good laugh" seems ill-suited. Approaching the Beatles as "high art" has become a progressively established norm.

Academic acknowledgment of the Beatles can be attributed to their late-career "intellectual curiosity" (Feldman-Barrett 2021, 160), which coincided with cultural institutions beginning to allow popular music entry into previously exclusive domains (Collins 2020). Ian Inglis (2000) has noted that political, societal, and economical shifts in the 1960s led to an understanding that "popular music could and should be taken seriously—as industry, as entertainment, and as art" (6). He further asserts that the Beatles' societal position became akin to that of traditional intellectuals—"men of ideas"—despite the commercial nature

---

[2] "High art" is a category that should be challenged due to its race, gender, and class exclusions. In this chapter, it is designated for cultural contributions that have traditionally passed muster with Western academic institutional gatekeeping.

of popular music (9) and concludes that the "disjunction between the expected role of the 'pop star' and the increasingly diverse and innovative roles assumed by the Beatles—musical, social, political, professional—became one of the most striking components of their career" (14). While he maintains that they were surely proud to be considered influential, Inglis acknowledges the "professional cynicism" about the merits of their own work that exists in the Beatles' comments on their songs (15). Inglis characterizes this "cynicism" as the Beatles' version of modesty, yet they resisted intellectual categorization through their irreverence and wit, not lip-service clichés of humility.

As the Beatles matured in front of captivated followers and skeptics, they had little desire to publicly associate themselves with highbrow presumptuousness. Manifestations of this are found in Lennon and McCartney's dismissive responses to analyses of Beatles songs (e.g., Beatles 2000, 96; 2007; Everett 1999, 133, 180; Roessner 2006, 152–3). The Beatles' tendency to ridicule self-importance and social hierarchies is rooted in what Sheila Whiteley (2009) identifies as "their stubborn northern-ness, their Liverpool humor, and their disregard and contempt for the pomposity of class-based social relations" (216). McCartney's "good laugh" reaction to "culture" on the train to Washington represents a relatively tame signal of aversion toward a "high art" label and its associated vanity.

Unconfined by bourgeois norms of cordial flattery, the Beatles thrived inside the professional music world while lampooning it as outside observers. This casual irreverence in showbiz interactions was solidified in Alun Owen's scripted dialogue in *A Hard Day's Night* (1964), directed by Richard Lester (Neaverson 1997, 22). In the off-script reality of their career, the Beatles' blunt honesty was on full display whenever they teased journalists (MacDonald 2007, 22–3; Stark 2005, 108–9), or taunted music industry professionals (e.g., Graves 2022; Hertsgaard 1995, 38–9; Lewisohn 2013, 1228–9; Womack 2018, 200). But as their own music increasingly featured expressions of vulnerability, philosophy, and experimentalism, how did the Beatles direct this irreverence at themselves? How did they assure listeners that rock and roll's fun ethos was still behind this "high art"? Where is the "good laugh" within "serious" Beatles songs?

This chapter introduces *defusal*, *dilution*, and *deflation* as principal devices the Beatles deployed for self-directed humor in their music. These techniques served to counter their excursions into the realms of "high art," intellectualism, and style connoisseurship. Pierre Bourdieu's (1999) findings on parent-child class discrepancies provide a useful backdrop to this discussion because they include both the struggles and counteractions of individuals from working-class backgrounds who transitioned to the middle-class, as the Beatles did. Instances of defusal, dilution, and deflation correspond with acts of Benign Self-Directed Humor (Tsukawaki and Imura 2020), matching features of Asbjørn Øfsthus Eriksen's (2016) theory of humor in instrumental music, and Ron Aharoni's (2018) examination of carriers of meaning in humor. Drawing on these studies, my analysis highlights appearances of defusal, dilution, and deflation in career-spanning material, demonstrating a dedication to playful self-directed humor by the Beatles in their art, which consistently brings them back home.

Background and Theory: Daddy, Our Baby's Gone

The Beatles' wit exposed pretentiousness in traditionally dignified or hierarchical settings and kept in check their own role in those rituals. Similarly, humorous touches in their "heavier" music softened the Fabs' own artistic or philosophical signals (see Riley 2002). By defusing, diluting, or deflating content, the Beatles essentially functioned as both kings and jesters in their musical court. Aimed inwardly as much as outwardly, humor allowed them to alleviate anxiety, embarrassment, or guilt they may have felt over their position as lucky Scousers who made it big and outgrew their hometown.

The predicament of the upwardly mobile working-class child is identified by Bourdieu as a "most unexpected [...] feeling of *being torn* that comes from experiencing success as failure [or] transgression" (1999, 510, emphasis in original). As the children "fulfill the paternal will for [them] to succeed," they inescapably "become other" (510). The parent's message to the child is to "succeed, change, and move to the middle class," but also to "stay simple, [...] stick close to the little guys (to me)" (510). The Beatles' rise from Northern provinciality to "high art" may have been, as Oded Heilbronner (2008) suggests, "an expression of the successful [cross-class] social integration typical of the cultural life of England in the 1960s" (111). But even decades after their storied ascent, reverberations of discomfort were present. In a 2007 interview with *Liverpool Echo* Ringo Starr recalled that the Beatles were considered "traitors" for abandoning their hometown, and assured readers—forty-four years after moving away—that "even though we left we never let Liverpool down and we're always still proud of that heritage" ("Beatles" 2013). Even Ringo, the Beatle least associated with pretentiousness, hinted at guilt that had been lingering since the 1960s.

As for the remedy, the Beatles used self-directed humor in the music that most risked removing them from rock and roll, Liverpool, and their working-class roots. The deployment of this strategy fits Bourdieu's observations of behaviors meant to "neutralize the effects of the change [that separates] the individual from his father and from his peers" (1999, 510). Self-directed humor can "deal with anxieties as a defense mechanism" (Ziv 1984, 3). Ryota Tsukawaki and Tomoya Imura define the category Benign Self-Directed Humor as the "positive dimension of" self-directed humor (2020, 2) in which "anxiety and threats are diminished or removed by reinterpreting the stressful situation from a humorous perspective" (6). Self-directed humor in the Beatles' music playfully lightens the weight of profound statements. The effect dulls potential embarrassment about class position, reaffirming a bond between the Fabs and their roots.

The Beatles applied self-directed humor through the specific techniques of defusal, dilution, or deflation throughout their time as a band. All three terms refer to humorous gestures in relation to content, but they differ in their timing: A defusal is preemptive; a dilution occurs during a song; and a deflation occurs after the fact, rendering a fresh, lucid interpretation.[3] There are numerous examples, but this examination will focus on songs and albums the Beatles released, as well as some relevant live performances. Appearances of defusal, dilution, and deflation will be introduced in mostly chronological order, accentuating certain thematic connections that arise in music from different periods.

Analysis: Get Me Home for Tea

Precedents at the Star Club

During the band's final stint at the Star Club in Hamburg in late 1962 (Beatles 2008c; 2015), the hard rockin' Beatles don't seem invested in the ballads and other sentimental songs they have included in the setlist for their nightclub audience. The Beatles' on-stage humor at the Star Club prioritizes loyalty to a rock and roll aesthetic and attitude, as Lewisohn writes: "this is the old big-beat Beatles with bum-notes and personalities flying" (2013, 1517). Among the predominantly high-octane covers, the Beatles serve the occasional gentle, vulnerable tunes

---

[3] I briefly mentioned the terms with a few examples in Kammay (2021, 170–1).

with a grain of salt. Through verbal or musical mockery and wit, they defuse, dilute, and deflate the more tender selections.

The sentimentality of "A Taste of Honey" is defused when Paul introduces the number as "that [song] which George's gonna hate," and John ridicules the dramatic opening minor chord by running an exaggerated vocal warmup ("ba-ba-ba") along the bottom pentachord of the scale.[4] At a later Star Club set, another preemptively-defused love song is "To Know Her Is to Love Her." Paul reimagines the ballad's title as the sexually suggestive "To Know *It* Is to Love Her." Both this song and "A Taste of Honey" are eventually treated to deflation in addition to defusal, which will be discussed later.

After the next song, the rocker "Everybody's Trying to Be My Baby," Lennon whistles mock bird sounds as Paul introduces yet another ballad, "Till There Was You." Following Lennon's cue, McCartney begins to set the scene ("As we walk through the garden now, with the beautiful whistle of spotted—"), and Lennon jumps in to complete the defusal ("pelican in the garden of love!"). John's faux bird calls, moments before a quiet song that references birds, are reminiscent of the humor Eriksen finds in Richard Strauss's *Don Quixote*, where "imitation of bleating sheep [may be] offensive to the notion of symphonic orchestral music as a high art" (2016, 242). With whistles, garden walks, and pelicans, Lennon and McCartney signal to their Hamburg audience their awareness of the corny and the absurd.

Following their bird antics, "Till There Was You" begins, and the next mechanism of self-directed humor is applied. Throughout the song, Lennon relentlessly dilutes the "purity" of the ballad by mockingly repeating virtually every line sung by McCartney, a tease Lewisohn calls "a persistent piss-taking echo" (2013, 1520). Lewisohn likens this Paul-John dynamic to a "double act: the audience try to watch the singer but can't tear their eyes off his mate" (2013, 1520). It is defusal, dilution, and soon deflation that enable the Beatles to create this "double act" and exist both within and outside of "high art" and grandiosity. As "Till There Was You" reaches its end, Lennon presents a deflation, demanding, "I'd like a great round of applause," having completed his echo duty.[5]

Deflation continues to undercut the romantic content of "To Know Her Is to Love Her" and "A Taste of Honey," but the gestures are musical rather than

---

[4] Lennon similarly mocks elitism with this "warmup" routine earlier, when the Beatles pretend to receive a request for "Bach Fugue in B minor," proceeding to play Little Richard's "Kansas City."

[5] For an earlier, more aggressive example of Lennon's on-stage teasing of a crooning McCartney, see Lewisohn (2013, 834).

verbal. The closing major tonic chords in both songs are altered in Lennon and Harrison's fingers into blues-rock seventh chords.[6] These endings are incongruent with the musical idiom of the sentimental tunes. Incongruity in humor "is about the cognitive shift that we must make to recognize that a particular utterance [...] or something in the physical environment, causes us to change our stereotypical interpretation of what is described" (Nijholt 2020, 408). In music, this can involve "departures from stylistic norms and collisions between conflicting style systems" (Eriksen 2016, 245). Style-incongruity has implications related to class, since "[musical] styles are not 'neutral'; they represent values, because they may serve as markers for social class and cultural capital" (Eriksen 2016, 245). Deflating "To Know Her Is to Love Her" and "A Taste of Honey" in blues-rock fashion is consistent with the Beatles' class-consciousness.

The stylistic collision this deflation generates is uniquely enhanced in the performance of "A Taste of Honey." The cliché context of the major-chord ending in this minor/dorian ballad, the "Picardy third" touch, is especially far from the rock and roll idiom of Lennon and Harrison's closing chords. The deflation they apply reframes the raised third of the chord, playing a joke on its originally intended, arguably pompous purpose. This mechanism of humor fits Aharoni's notion of "a pointer [that] turns out to point at itself. [...] The pointer, ordinarily a transparent entity serving the meaning, suddenly becomes the protagonist" (2018, 14). In "A Taste of Honey" at the Star Club, upon hearing the surprising blues-rock closure of the song, the listener's attention is shifted to the raised third, a "transparent entity" which exists only to deliver the "Picardy" meaning, a "high art" European formula for an uplifting, hopeful ending. As it is presented in its new, blues-rock outfit, this European third inescapably becomes the butt of an incongruity joke.

Self-directed humor adds charm and self-awareness to the Beatles' witty gestures. But they sometimes attempted defusal to take cheap (and, in this case racist) shots at others. In his introduction to the Arthur Alexander love song "Where Have You Been (All My Life)," Lennon mocks African American Vernacular English by delivering a few lines in a stereotyped dialect. He fails, however, to draw reactions from the other Beatles or the audience. This preamble precedes what sounds like a sincere performance of the song.

---

[6] Heard in two Star Club performances of "A Taste of Honey." The recording of an earlier run abruptly cuts prematurely. A distant nod to this deflation gesture is heard in 1968 in the final chord of the gentle "Mother Nature's Son" on *The Beatles* (*The White Album*) (Beatles 2009), when a trumpet sneaks a bluesy 7th into the harmony.

Of the material available in the Star Club stage recordings, there are only two cases of gentle songs the Beatles do not defuse, dilute, or deflate. The first is the Lennon-McCartney original "Ask Me Why," soon to come out on the B-side of the Beatles' next single. The second is "Falling in Love Again," made famous by Marlene Dietrich in 1930, and performed by the Beatles with English-language lyrics written by McCartney (Lewisohn 2013, 1275, 1517). While these two songs contain original material, sparing them does not mean the Beatles avoided self-directed humor when dealing with their original creations. The Fabs would soon gladly mock elements in their own compositions. Their Star Club antics are prototypes for what would become common practice as their musical and career paths take them to new artistic domains.

Refusing to Fall: "Misery" and "If I fell"

A pronounced example of self-directed humor appears in an original Beatles song, "Misery," released on their debut album *Please Please Me* in 1963 (Beatles 2009). As the song fades out, Lennon's silly falsetto ("la-la-la") ridicules the tormenting romantic angst in the lyrics. Everett notes that John's vocal performances "often [sink] into low comedy" when "not expressive of love or anguish" (2001, 74–5). In that sense, a few deflating seconds in "Misery" anticipate Lennon's comical vocals in "Yellow Submarine" and "You Know My Name (Look Up the Number)," composed and recorded years later.[7]

Lennon is certainly expressive in his love song "If I Fell," but, self-conscious about his sincere vulnerability, he defuses it on both film and stage. In the sequence available in *A Hard Day's Night* (Lester 1964), Lennon performs the tune's preamble mockingly, directing his plea for faithful love at Starr. In a Philadelphia concert he introduces the number as "If I Fell *Over*" (Beatles 2008a). This type of device is what Aharoni describes as "the flattening of symbolic meaning. Metaphorical expressions are taken at face value" (2018, 14). Lennon's joke on the metaphorical "fall" is a self-directed jab at his own artistic tendencies. In Blackpool he introduces: "If I Fell … *just as if, right?*" (Beatles 2008b). Paul cracks up with John, and they require two attempts to properly start the number. Through this defusal, Lennon makes sure the audience distinguishes between the song's sensitive protagonist and himself.

---

[7] Available on *Revolver* and *Past Masters*, respectively (Beatles 2009).

Going Home with Ringo: "Yesterday"

McCartney's 1965 ballad "Yesterday" is described by scholars as a "small miracle" (Mellers 1973, 54) and "a masterwork of musical unity" (Womack 2007, 113). With its departure from typical rock and roll sonority, Paul expressed embarrassment about the song's highbrow potential and entrusted the Beatles' producer George Martin with avoiding a syrupy, vibrato-rich string arrangement (Everett 2001, 300–1). The astonishing result was far from schmaltz. Still, the added string-quartet necessitated both defusal and deflation from the class-conscious Beatles. "Yesterday" debuted on *Blackpool Night Out*, a live televised performance seen in Beatles (2003). As Harrison invites his bandmate to take the stage, he comically reminds the audience of the Beatles' working-class roots: "And so for Paul McCartney of Liverpool, opportunity knocks!" After McCartney finishes, Lennon gives him a fake bouquet, whose stems detach from the flowers. But John's verbal, less staged deflation is an even more impactful gag: "Thank you Ringo, that was wonderful!" The invocation of the beloved drummer is key here, and would become a consistently useful grounding mechanism for the Beatles.

Starr, some have claimed, has come to represent childhood and home in the Beatles' image, counterbalancing the artistic and intellectual explorations of his bandmates (Schneider 2008, 147). In the animated film *Yellow Submarine* (Dunning 1968), Ringo is introduced as an everyday lad from Merseyside, whereas the other Beatles enter the scene through "high art" stereotypes: experimentalism (John), philosophy (George), and exclusivity (Paul). Beyond the film, Starr often functions as a compass, pointing back home to Liverpool, youth, and carefree joy whenever his mates explore artsy or intellectual avenues.

"Yesterday," and later the introspective "Nowhere Man" and poignant "Eleanor Rigby," warrant counterweights, which Starr provides. All three singles are coupled with unassuming Ringo-led songs on the records' flipsides, diluting their heavy impact.[8] The first two were not even issued as singles in the UK, "Yesterday" explicitly due to Paul's embarrassment (Beatles 2000, 175). Even in its still tender but electric arrangement for the Beatles' 1966 tours, "Yesterday" is consistently followed on stage by Starr, singing the exciting rocker "I Wanna Be Your Man" (Lewisohn 1992, 226). In one Tokyo concert, McCartney completes "Yesterday" and proceeds to introduce the next number as "quite simply, Ringo!" (Beatles 2002). Doing away with the full title of "I Wanna Be Your Man" allows

---

[8] "Act Naturally," "What Goes On," and "Yellow Submarine." These singles are available as album tracks on *Help!*, *Rubber Soul*, and *Revolver*, respectively (Beatles 2009).

McCartney to keep the audience focused on the central deflating factor: Starr, the drummer who represents home.

Revolver and More Ringo-isms

Lennon needed Starr's wit to defuse the work that closes the Beatles' 1966 album *Revolver* (Beatles 2009). The track features tape loops and effects, and Lennon's lyrics are inspired by Timothy Leary's *The Psychedelic Experience*. He replaces his initial, experimentation-oriented song title ("Mark I") with "Tomorrow Never Knows," a witty, nonsensical "Ringo-ism." Lennon explained: "I gave it a throwaway title because I was a bit self-conscious [...]. So I took one of Ringo's malapropisms, which was like 'a hard day's night,' to take the edge off the heavy philosophical lyrics" (Beatles 2000, 209). Insecure about class and self-importance, Lennon turned to his trusted compass.

The Beatles' hesitancy about experimentation in *Revolver* is expressed from the album's start. The raspy count-in before "Taxman" presents a paradox. As a sound outside of the song, it allows the listener to peek behind the curtain and see the Beatles as people in the studio. Cultivating the feeling of shared humanity could perhaps counter the album's experimental aesthetic. Yet the count-in's robotic delivery and mechanical sonority shift the balance from "people" to "studio," absurdly exaggerating the artistic concept of *Revolver*. The secondary, more natural-sounding count, which abruptly arrives at a doubled tempo, is like a final, faint glimpse of Beatlemania, before the mechanisms of *Revolver*—studio effects, loops, sophisticated lyrics—take over. Eriksen finds that "exaggerating certain traits of a musical style" may result in humorous effects (2016, 247). Due to an "air of banality [...] the listener is distracted by unfortunate details that destroy the 'soulful' musical whole" (247). Through exaggeration in the opening seconds of *Revolver*, the Beatles, to some degree, mock their own experimentalism.[9]

A touch of incongruity also appears on *Revolver* in the final moments of "Tomorrow Never Knows," which closes the album with a deflation. Surrounded by the tape loops, the surprising honky-tonk piano provides the listeners with a sign of life in the automated world of the song. After a couple of trial runs, the pianist gets the hang of the Indian-influenced mixolydian idiom of the song.

---

[9]   Two years later, exaggeration can make a desire to die in "Yer Blues" sound funny. This *White Album* (Beatles 2009) track exaggerates its blues style with over-the-top words of agony and a heavily pronounced 12/8 meter, which increases in tempo when rock and roll is mentioned. Like "Helter Skelter" from the same album, this song is self-diluting due to exaggeration, allowing indulgence in style connoisseurship without risking embarrassing overcommitment.

This piano is the Beatles poking a hole in their experimental "high art" fantasy. Decades later, in the bittersweet reunion single "Free as a Bird" (Beatles 1995), a similarly unexpected banjolele afterthought transports the listener to postwar Liverpool. This deflation unambiguously guides the Beatles homeward, to the music of their childhood.

Growing Up, Still Mocking: *Sgt. Pepper* and Nostalgia

Sgt. Pepper's Lonely Hearts Club Band in 1967 (Beatles 2009) is an album that culturally establishes the Beatles' post-touring maturation. *Pepper* embodies what Jacqueline Edmondson (2017) calls the "change [in the Beatles'] form or nature [from] boy band [...] to artists" (90). But becoming London elites is betrayal, since, for the working-class, "success really means murdering the father" (Bourdieu 1999, 510). And murder they do, posing for *Pepper's* cover photo with images of "intellectual" musicians Stockhausen and Dylan among their chosen companions, abandoning the rock and roll icons of their youth like Elvis or Berry. They must then deflate *Pepper*, so they record a nonsensical snippet for side 2's runout groove, a gag that startles the listener after the fading final chord of the intense album-closer "A Day in the Life."

Following the release of *Pepper*, the Beatles mock their "high art" status in the anthemic single "All You Need Is Love."[10] While they place their own "She Loves You" chorus shoulder to shoulder with Bach in the coda, in the song's backing track they ridicule their pretension to be among the classics. McCartney and Harrison dilute the recording, playing rough, amateurish licks on orchestral instruments, double-bass and violin, respectively.[11] This semi-concealed gesture joins other diluting elements in the song, such as the vague, non-committal lyrics and the mantra-like repetitions. Jerzy Jarniewicz (2010) attributes these and similar subversive qualities in Beatles music to the group's cautious suspicion of unchallenged charismatic messaging, however revolutionary, which stems in part from their Liverpool upbringing. Their Summer of Love single thus doubles as a Northern, ironically performed universal anthem, a faux classic.

The nostalgic "Penny Lane," destined for *Pepper* but released earlier in 1967 as a single, features a "Eurovision" modulation, lifting the final chorus's key by a whole step. This pop-cliché device manufactures sensations of elation and

---

[10] The 1967 Beatles singles are all available on *Magical Mystery Tour* (Beatles 2009).
[11] This is best heard in Beatles (2010).

triumph, which the Beatles then deflate. Having removed a closing trumpet phrase from the mix, they end McCartney's song with a puzzlingly prolonged bare sound of high harmonium and cymbal, contrasting the posh aesthetic of the track. Coupled with "Penny Lane," Lennon's haunting Liverpool-fantasy song "Strawberry Fields Forever" is further deflated by the goofy "cranberry sauce" recitation during the coda.

Harrison's *Pepper* song, "Within You Without You," which showcases his increasing immersion in Indian music and philosophy, is deflated by pre-recorded laughter that ends the track. In this joke/no-joke attitude, Mellers has found "the quality that makes [the Beatles'] work so sensitively attuned to their generation" (1973, 188). The Beatles carried on using self-directed humor to keep power hierarchies and each other in check, maintaining a link to their youth and roots, even as they explore new, sophisticated musical terrains.

Laughing to the End: From the *White Album* to "Her Majesty"

Continuing the joke/no-joke path in 1968, George treats his gentle *White Album* (Beatles 2009) tune "Long Long Long" to a deflation. The sudden, uncalled-for ending on a Bb major guitar chord and the casual drum strikes break the spell of the mesmerizing song.[12] The result is an abrupt shift from a sincere air of spirituality to just another day at the office for the musicians. Elsewhere on the *White Album*, the strings' chromatically moving parallel tritones at the end of "Glass Onion" generate an artificial "sneer" effect (Everett 1999, 181). This enhances the already deflative nature of the song, poking fun at intellectual approaches to Beatles lyrics by spreading false clues about hidden meanings. Yet, when Starr wishes everyone "Good Night" at the closing of the *White Album*, even the affable Ringo cannot really deflate the impact of the avant-garde Lennon-Yoko Ono studio creation that precedes it, "Revolution 9." The lush arrangement of "Good Night" provides comfort, not a punchline.

Undoubtedly, releasing the *Yellow Submarine* film soundtrack (Beatles 2009) less than two months after the *White Album* provided some necessary incongruity. But a greater contrast to the aura of "Revolution 9" was to be the project that followed, a filmed-concert/live-album of "back-to-basics" Beatles music. The resulting 1970 album, *Let It Be* (Beatles 2009), released in the midst of the Beatles' disbandment, includes live arrangements as originally imagined, alongside

---

[12] The song is in F major, its coda tonicizing C minor/dorian. The Bb major chord resolves neither.

orchestral enhancements and overdubs. The song order in *Let It Be* sandwiches the vulnerable, hymn-like title track between falsetto mockery by John ("and now we'd like to do: Hark, the Angels Come"), and "Maggie Mae," a Liverpudlian folk tune about a sex worker who robs sailors. The falsetto defusal ridicules the religious undertones of "Let It Be," and the deflation completes the task, pulling us down from the ethereal "Mother Mary" to the distinctly earthly "Maggie Mae."

Abbey Road (Beatles 2009), the album released before *Let It Be* but recorded after most of the latter's content, ends with a powerful, majestic medley of "Golden Slumbers," "Carry That Weight," and "The End." Whirlwinds of intense emotions swirl, and then triumphant climax and resolution complete with strings and brass bring the exquisitely recorded album to a grand closure—until we are startled. In a maneuver akin to the ending of *Pepper*, the interruption short-circuits the listener's contemplation: an abrupt audio punch and a sudden comical miniature, "Her Majesty." This deflation, accidentally conceived in the studio and wholeheartedly welcomed, epitomizes how the Beatles first carry listeners away with sublime art, and then bring them back home giggling.

Outro: Knowing They're Happy and They're Safe

On January 24, 1969, *Let It Be* director, Michael Lindsay-Hogg, teased McCartney about the film's progress: "We've got a movie about smokers, nose pickers, and nail biters." McCartney responds: "We are rather uncouth, we're not an elite you know!" (Jackson 2022, 2:08:16 to 2:08:26). This exchange occurs five years after the train ride from NYC to Washington, and McCartney's instincts haven't seemed to change. For the Beatles, imaginative experimentation and delicate beauty were regularly complemented by a healthy dose of self-irreverence.

This chapter's analysis shows how the Beatles routinely defused, diluted, and deflated their own "high art" material.[13] From Liverpool to global stardom, the Beatles were conscious players in their artistic and social journey. Wary of straying too far from their roots, humor was their anchor. When their last released album, *Let It Be*, concludes with John's joke about passing "the audition," it is therefore fitting that the final sound we hear is of people having, to use Paul's words, "a good laugh."

---

[13] Additional instances of self-directed humor in some of the Beatles' recorded output and live performances exist beyond the ones mentioned here; the band's BBC sessions are also worthy of future examination.

References

Aharoni, Ron. 2018. "Shifting from Meaning to Its Carrier: A Common Denominator for Three Strains of Humour." *European Journal of Humour Research* 6, no. 3: 13–29.

Beatles, The. 1995. *Anthology 1*. Recorded 1958–1994. Apple, 2 CDs.

Beatles, The. 2000. *The Beatles Anthology*. San Francisco: Chronicle Books.

Beatles, The. 2002. "I Wanna Be Your Man." Recorded June 1966. Track 9 on *Live in Budokan*. Азия Records, compact disc.

Beatles, The. 2003. "Yesterday." Episode 4 in *The Beatles Anthology*. Television Documentary. ABC, 1995; Apple, DVD set.

Beatles, The. 2007. "Paul Interviewed by Tony Macarthur." Recorded November 1968. Track 3 on *1968 Disc 3*. Lazy Tortoise, CD set.

Beatles, The. 2008a. *Convention Hall Wisdom*. Recorded 1964–1965. Purple Chick, 2 CDs.

Beatles, The. 2008b. *Seattle Down*. Recorded July-August 1964. Purple Chick, 2 CDs.

Beatles, The. 2008c. *Star Club*. Recorded December 1962. Purple Chick, 2 CDs.

Beatles, The. 2009. *The Original Studio Recordings: Stereo Box*. Recorded 1962–1970. Apple, CD set.

Beatles, The. 2010. *Psychedelic Years Multi Tracks Separated II*. Recorded 1966–1968. WWII, 2 CDs.

Beatles, The. 2015. *Zu Laut!* Mobilephone. 2 hr., 10 min. DVD.

"Beatles world exclusive: 'Don't call us traitors'—Ringo." 2013. *Liverpool Echo*, Dec. 17, 2007, updated May 9, 2013. https://www.liverpoolecho.co.uk/news/liverpool-news/beatles-world-exclusive-dont-call-3497275.

Bourdieu, Pierre. 1999. "The Contradictions of Inheritance." In *The Weight of the World: Social Suffering in Contemporary Society*, edited by Pierre Bourdieu et al., translated by Priscilla Parkhurst Ferguson et al., 507–13. Stanford: Stanford University Press.

Collins, Marcus. 2020. "I Say High, You Say Low: The Beatles and Cultural Hierarchies in 1960s and 1970s Britain." *Popular Music* 39, no. 3–4: 401–19.

Dunning, George, dir. 1968. *Yellow Submarine*. Apple, 2012. 1 hr., 30 min. Blu-ray Disc.

Edmondson, Jacqueline. 2017. "The Act You've Known for All These Years: Discord and Harmony in the Third Space." In *The Beatles, Sgt. Pepper, and the Summer of Love*, edited by Kenneth Womack and Kathryn B. Cox, 89–97. Lanham: Lexington.

Eriksen, Asbjørn Øfsthus. 2016. "A Taxonomy of Humor in Instrumental Music." *Journal of Musicological Research* 35, no. 3: 233–63.

Everett, Walter. 1999. *The Beatles as Musicians: Revolver through the Anthology*. New York: Oxford University Press.

Everett, Walter. 2001. *The Beatles as Musicians: The Quarry Men through Rubber Soul*. New York: Oxford University Press.

Feldman-Barrett, Christine. 2021. *A Women's History of the Beatles*. New York: Bloomsbury.

Fisher, John A. 2013. "High Art Versus Low Art." In *The Routledge Companion to Aesthetics*, edited by Berys Gaut and Dominic McIver Lopes, 473–84. Abingdon: Routledge.

Graves, Mark. 2022. "The Beatles—Live at EMI House, Manchester Square, London (April 5, 1963) Stereo." January 10, 2022. Audio recording, 5:06. https://www.youtube.com/watch?v=qCrLtz4Yrik.

Heilbronner, Oded. 2008. "The Peculiarities of the Beatles: A Cultural-Historical Interpretation." *Cultural and Social History* 5, no. 1: 99–116.

Hertsgaard, Mark. 1995. *A Day in the Life: The Music and Artistry of the Beatles*. New York: Delacorte Press.

Howard, Ron, dir. 2016. *The Beatles Eight Days A Week: The Touring Years*. Universal Music Enterprises, 2016. 1 hr., 46 min. Blu-ray Disc.

Inglis, Ian. 2000. "Men of Ideas? Popular Music, Anti-intellectualism and the Beatles." In *The Beatles, Popular Music and Society: A Thousand Voices*, edited by Ian Inglis, 1–22. London: Palgrave Macmillan.

Jackson, Peter, dir. 2022. *The Beatles Get Back*. Episode 2, Disney+. 2 hr., 53 min. https://www.disneyplus.com/video/e16655bf-054c-4ff3-b4f6-a3e25fc1a2f1.

Jarniewicz, Jerzy. 2010. "The Beatles: Prophets or Fools of the Counterculture?" In *Fifty Years with the Beatles: The Impact of the Beatles on Contemporary Culture*, edited by Jerzy Jarniewicz and Alina Kwiatkowska, 71–8. Łódź: Łódź University Press.

Jenkins, Paul O., and Jenkins, Hugh, Editors. 2018. *Teaching the Beatles*. New York: Routledge.

Kammay, Aviv. 2021. "How Does It Feel to Be: Beatles Tribute Bands and the Fans Who Dream Them." In *Fandom and the Beatles: The Act You've Known for All These Years*, edited by Kenneth Womack and Kit O'Toole, 167–87. New York: Oxford University Press.

Lester, Richard, dir. 1964. *A Hard Day's Night*. The Criterion Collection, 2014. 1 hr., 27 min. Blu-ray Disc.

Letts, Marianne Tatom. 2008. "Sky of Blue, Sea of Green: A Semiotic Reading of the Film 'Yellow Submarine.'" *Popular Music* 27, no. 1: 1–14.

Lewisohn, Mark. 1992. *The Complete Beatles Chronicle*. London: Octopus.

Lewisohn, Mark. 2013. *The Beatles: All These Years—Volume One: Tune In*. Extended Special Edition. London: Little, Brown.

MacDonald, Ian. 2007. *Revolution in the Head: The Beatles' Records and the Sixties*. Chicago: Chicago Review Press.

Mann, William. 2006. "'What Songs the Beatles Sang …': The Times (London): December 23, 1963." In *Read the Beatles: Classic and New Writings on the Beatles, Their Legacy, and Why They Still Matter*, edited by June Skinner Sawyers, 45–7. London: Penguin.

Mellers, Wilfrid. 1973. *Twilight of the Gods: The Music of the Beatles*. New York: Viking.

Mills, Richard. 2020. *The Beatles and Fandom: Sex, Death and Progressive Nostalgia*. New York: Bloomsbury.

Neaverson, Bob. 1997. *The Beatles Movies*. London: Cassel.

Nijholt, Anton. 2020. "'All the World's A Stage': Incongruity Humour Revisited." *Annals of Mathematics and Artificial Intelligence* 88, no. 5–6: 405–38.

Riley, Tim. 2002. *Tell Me Why: The Beatles: Album by Album, Song by Song, the Sixties and After*. Cambridge: Da Capo.

Roessner, Jeffery. 2006. "We All Want to Change the World: Postmodern Politics and the Beatles' White Album." In *Reading the Beatles: Cultural Studies, Literary Criticism, and the Fab Four*, edited by Kenneth Womack and Todd F. Davis, 147–58. Albany: State University of New York.

Roessner, Jeffery. 2016. "Revolution 2.0: Beatles Fan Scholarship in the Digital Age." In *New Critical Perspectives on the Beatles: Things We Said Today*, edited by Kenneth Womack and Katie Kapurch, 221–40. London: Palgrave Macmillan.

Schneider, Matthew. 2008. *The Long and Winding Road from Blake to the Beatles*. New York: Palgrave Macmillan.

Stark, Steven D. 2005. *Meet the Beatles: A Cultural History of the Band That Shook Youth, Gender, and the World*. New York: HarperCollins.

Tsukawaki, Ryota and Imura, Tomoya. 2020. "The Light and Dark Side of Self-Directed Humor: The Development and Initial Validation of the Dual Self-Directed Humor Scale (DSDHS)." *Personality and Individual Differences* 157: 10.1016/j.paid.2020.109835.

Whiteley, Sheila. 2009. "The Beatles as Zeitgeist." In *The Cambridge Companion to the Beatles*, edited by Kenneth Womack, 203–16. New York: Cambridge University Press.

Womack, Kenneth. 2007. *Long and Winding Roads: The Evolving Artistry of the Beatles*. New York: Continuum.

Womack, Kenneth. 2018. *Sound Pictures: The Life of Beatles Producer George Martin—The Later Years, 1966–2016*. Chicago: Chicago Review Press.

Ziv, Avner. 1984. *Personality and Sense of Humor*. New York: Springer Publishing Company.

4

Billy Preston and the Beatles *Get Back*: Black Music and the Wisdom of Wordplay and Wit

Mike Alleyne, Walter Everett, and Katie Kapurch

A Lift

"You're giving us a lift, Bill," says John Lennon, characterizing the sun that Billy Preston shined on the Beatles' cloudy days of January 1969 (Jackson 2021[1]). Celebrating his arrival, George Harrison plays a bit of "A Taste of Honey," a number that Preston had often requested of the Beatles in Hamburg in 1962. This bit of studio interaction was captured during the *Get Back*-turned-*Let It Be* sessions and was included in Peter Jackson's *The Beatles: Get Back* (2021). Premiering on the streaming platform Disney+ in 2021, the eight-hour, three-part film is a massive re-edit of original *Let It Be* footage directed by Michael Lindsay-Hogg. As soon as the second installment of Jackson's film aired, memes of Preston's cool entrance into the studio,[2] where he takes off his coat and grooves along to what's playing, circulated widely on social media.

Fab fun seems to begin immediately upon Preston's appearance on January 22, 1969, and much retelling of old stories ensues. Paul McCartney tells Preston about the tour-opening concert in Copenhagen, June 4, 1964, when substitute drummer Jimmie Nicol couldn't get the floor-tom intro to "She Loves You";

---

[1] Available in Episode 2 (1:30:00); see also Beatles 2021, 131; Nagra roll 421A [Beatles 2001b, disc 2]. Here and elsewhere, explanatory notes provide additional information when relevant, such as the episode number and time stamp (hours:minutes:seconds) from *The Beatles: Get Back*, which is indicated in the parenthetical citation as "Jackson 2021." Explanatory notes may also include other sources for quoted material, such as the numbered Nagra rolls, as collected in the *Day By Day* and *Camera B Rolls* series (Beatles 2000–2003).
References to the "Nagra rolls" are to the numbered audiotapes ganged to either of the two cameras (A or B) shooting throughout both Twickenham and Apple Studios action. Much detail about individual Nagra-reel contents (and the various bootleg CDs on which the audio has been distributed) is found in Sulpy and Schweighardt (1997) and Sulpy (2001).

[2] Available in Episode Two (1:26:30).

they'd count "one, two" and he provided only silence, not the necessary cue for the band to enter. This and other tales bring laughter from all (Jackson 2021[3]). The change in attitude is not lost on a pleased George Martin, who tells Harrison and McCartney at the end of the day on the 24th, "you're all working so well together" (Jackson 2021[4]).

Along with the inclusion of Lennon's line about this "lift," other editorial choices in the newer film generally reinforce the standard characterization of Preston's cheerful contributions via keyboard. But he carried more than a good attitude. To the music, Preston brought a long-perfected understanding of exactly what touch of soul was required in a particular setting. The virtuosic keys player had begun playing, according to his own song "Music Is My Life," at "the age of three" (1972). He honed his skill throughout childhood and adolescence at Victory Baptist Church in Los Angeles, a launchpad for his entrée into the pop scene. Before the age of twelve, he was playing on stage and in church with gospel matriarch Mahalia Jackson and on television with Nat King Cole. In addition to playing with Sam Cooke, Ray Charles, and others throughout the 1960s, Preston accompanied Little Richard, whose 1962 tour was the occasion for Preston's initial meeting of the pre-fame Beatles in Hamburg. And it was as a member of Ray Charles's band from 1967 on that Preston's singular playing was again noticed by Harrison.

More than half a century after the *Let It Be* sessions, Disney+ subscribers responded enthusiastically to Preston—even though the depth of his involvement remains underrepresented in that eight-hour film.[5] Not only underrepresented, but misrepresented as well: perhaps Preston-centric film stock was in short

---

[3] Available in Episode Two (1:51:39+).
[4] Available in Episode Two (2:14:12).
[5] The Beatles' work in January, 1969, fills approximately ninety-two roughly discrete hours of film and accompanying audio tape. With other obligations, Preston would often show up well after the Beatles began their work for the day; still, he is audible in about thirty-one of the forty-nine hours shot following his initial appearance. (A tabulation of his presence in minutes per day: 160 of 288 on the 22nd, 226 of 289 on the 23rd, 65 of 288 on the 24th, 0 of 404 on the 25th, 294 of 375 on the 26th, 390 of 406 on the 26th, 390 of 406 on the 27th, all 376 on the 28th, 114 of 257 on the 29th, all 54 on the 30th ["rooftop" day], and 161 of 186 on the 31st.) Preston's screen time is not only much shorter than that of any Beatle, it is far less than his presence might have allowed. Despite the five cameras on the Apple roof for the 30 January concert (and another on a rooftop across the street), Preston's camera time is limited to his appearance when incidentally framed by one source trained on the frontline Paul and John together. When the bobbies appear directly behind him, a handheld camera picks him up, again not part of the intended view. However, there is some attention to his Rhodes solo during the second rooftop performance of "Don't Let Me Down." All this suggests that Billy's short shrift in *Get Back* is not a fault of Jackson's crew as much as of Lindsay-Hogg and the original camera operators.

supply because fake mismatched shots of his Rhodes playing[6] appear more often than for the Beatles. Another example involves a "Twenty Flight Rock" run through on January 23: the film shows Billy playing the Rhodes (matching the audio) but alternately splices in footage of his entry for the day and dancing (Jackson 2021[7]). Thinking about the credit Preston is given for lifting the Beatles' collective spirit is, then, an occasion to reconsider the complexity of his contributions and their context.

Preston's Black American presence—in an almost exclusively white British studio space[8]—is a visible and aural reminder of the music that shaped the Beatles, the very past to which they were trying to get back. Preston's "lift" becomes an entry point into thinking about the Beatles' indebtedness to Black musical traditions that precede his 1969 recordings with the band. The Beatles were jamming informally on some of these songs in those sessions; at the same time, they made each other laugh—and compose—with the kind of wit and wordplay inherited from and shared with their Black idols. Table 4.1 lists all songs in which Preston joined the Beatles in playing in January 1969, divided almost equally between covers and originals (by either the Beatles or Preston himself).

In this chapter, we continue to use specific dialogue and scenes from *Get Back* as occasions for exploring the Beatles' indebtedness to specific Black musicians, but we do so with particular attention to humor. Though we don't treat every single instance of sampling from, or references to, Black musicians, our analysis takes us back to well-known rhythm and blues heroes such as Chuck Berry and Little Richard. We also discuss Lord Kitchener and Mighty Sparrow, understudied calypso influences from the Beatles' pre-fame era. The Caribbean musical associations lead to Desmond Dekker, the latter an influence even more contemporaneous to the filming of what becomes *Let It Be* and eventually *Get Back*. Following a brief consideration of the mid-1960s Detroit sound that includes Stevie Wonder, the Supremes, and Smokey Robinson, Preston returns, and we offer a fuller treatment of his contributions. Like the Beatles, we go back to their beginnings, focusing on the wordplay and wit that characterize multiple Black musical genres from which the Beatles sampled.

---

[6] See, for example, Episode Three (0:32:37-46) in Jackson (2021).
[7] Available in Episode Two (1:39-44-40:11).
[8] The exception is a woman of color named Betty Rodrigues, an EMI Studios cook, who is shown bringing a tray into the studio in *Get Back* (2021).

Wit and Wordplay: Signifyin(g) in Black Discourse
(a Brief Introduction)

The Beatles' (and Lennon's in particular) penchant for punning has long been attributed to an affinity for *The Goon Show*, Lewis Carroll, Stanley Unwin, and Edward Lear (considered in some of the chapters in this collection). But we argue that the band's Black musical forerunners are an understudied influence on the lads' collective sense of humor, especially when it comes to wit and wordplay.

Wordplay is a powerful discursive strategy in African American vernacular, including and especially music, as Henry Louis Gates, Jr. established in his seminal contribution to literary theory, *The Signifying Monkey* (2014), first published in 1988. The central image of that book's title is the master of the game: Monkey is a trickster who uses punning as a strategy of resistance, especially to take a competitor or authority figure down a notch (or several). Monkey's doublespeak involves Western culture's master speech tropes, which Gates Signifies on as "the master's tropes," including comparison via metaphor and irony (2014, 57). Monkey tropes these tropes, claiming them in distinctive ways, such as over-the-top boasting, and for subversive ends. In a similar way, Signifyin(g) also involves meta-textual references and references to previous texts, especially in order to debunk their authority.

Signifyin(g), while competitive, also builds community, especially through the use of call and response. Along these lines, repetition, rhyme, and meter contribute to the poetry of Signifyin(g), underscoring the reliance on musical forms that accompany wordplay (Gates 2014, 56–70). Think of Muhammad Ali's "float like a butterfly, sting like a bee," one of the boxer's most iconic refrains. Issued during the same year he met the Beatles, 1964, the sung-spoken mantra was bolstering and goading—while claiming space and agency in a country hostile to Black people. Via Kimberly W. Benston's pun, Gates also likens Signifyin(g)'s "trope a trope" to Ali's rope-a-dope strategy, one the boxer introduced via sung-spoken putdowns outside of the ring and then implemented once he was there (2014, 57). Understanding the poetry and musicality of Signifyin(g), then, further invites us to treat music and lyrics together: when we talk about the wisdom of wordplay and wit from the Beatles' Black sources, the sung word, often made witty and ironic through sound, is crucial. The role of repetition in African American rhetorical speech—both sacred and secular—as an inspiration for the "compound flow" existing on multiple levels of Black musical grooves is well established in Tim Hughes's essay on Stevie Wonder's "Living for the City" (2008, 260–2).

Humor need not be central to Signifyin(g)'s use of repetition. Just before Preston makes his first entrance on January 22, Lennon asks the others if they heard Dr. Martin Luther King, Jr.'s 1963 "I Have a Dream" speech (likely replayed on television the night before); "just like a poem, just like Tennyson," he enthuses (Jackson 2021[9]). John continues to refer to the speech with multiple non sequitur outbursts of "I had a dream this afternoon," as in during Billy's "Don't Let Me Down" solo on the Rhodes (Jackson 2021[10]). Such non-contiguously repeated motifs are, though, a big part of Lennon's droll humor. Throughout January 1969, Lennon repeatedly jokes for the camera, "practicing" his simple introduction to the "Rock and Roll Circus" performance in exaggerated trickster form.[11]

The Beatles have long tried to demonstrate the depth of their fascination with Black music, citing various epiphanies. Little Richard's screams made Lennon's hair stand on end and inspired career-long imitation attempts by McCartney; the lyrics that Little Richard "woo"-ed around were full of double entendre, often sexual. Berry's lyrics were memorably influenced by country and western music and punctuated by his bluesy guitar's running commentary, but a fascination with words was also shaped by Berry's exposure to "canonical" poetic traditions learned from his schoolteacher mother. Thus, when Lennon calls Berry a "rock poet" in the famous *Rolling Stone* interview with Jann Wenner in December 1970 (qtd. in Wenner 2000, 140), the former Beatle was recognizing something significant about Berry. The insight is applicable to the many other Black artists to whom John and the other Beatles were listening during their youth (such as Fats Domino, Bo Diddley, and Larry Williams) and during the 1960s (such as Smokey Robinson and Nina Simone).[12]

Understanding rock and roll's roots in Black culture thus involves recognizing the subversive discursive strategies that characterize Signifyin(g). Doublespeak unsettles the balance of power, especially when a speaker Signifies on canonical

---

[9] Full quote available in Nagra roll 419A.

[10] Available in Episode Two (1:31:30).

[11] Despite Lennon's incessant wordplay, parodies of lyrics, and overall silliness, Harrison may have the funniest line in *Get Back*. On January 7, one of several disagreements about finalizing the location for an end-of-month performance—George always resolute in not wanting to leave London to face an audience—occurs. In this exchange, director Lindsay-Hogg pushes an amphitheater in Libya; McCartney muses about being forcibly ejected from the Houses of Parliament. Michael then unknowingly recaptures the 1963–66 theme of the Beatles as saviors by suggesting a hospital, playing "for kids with broken legs," then asking "What about an orphanage—how does that grab you guys? … What's the biggest charity in the world?" Harrison quips, "Don't they say that charity begins at home?" (Jackson 2021; see Episode 1 (1:07:15+)).

[12] Lennon's characterization of Chuck Berry is parallel with Dylan's prior praising of Smokey Robinson's poetry, almost to the point of showing an anxiety of influence.

texts or agreed-upon definitions and standard usage of certain words, subverting meaning and issuing a critique.[13] As deeply ironic genres, hip-hop and rap are characterized by Signifyin(g), but the attendant tropes are also available in earlier genres of popular music shaped by Black people in the U.S. and the Caribbean. These genres converge, filtered through the Beatles in *Get Back*.

One *Get Back* story suggests the relationship between power (im)balances and musical Signifyin(g). When the first germs of "Get Back" appear to Paul, strumming his Höfner bass early on the January 7,[14] George joins in with his Les Paul and adds a jazzy, dissonant #9 chord (combining both C-sharp and a C-natural above the root, A[15]) as a snide touch to the chorus. George plays it more forcefully with wah on his Les Paul on the 9th and 10th.[16] Annoyed, bossy Paul says "we should try to get away from" that chord, which he recognizes from an earlier Beatle song (likely "Taxman") that he can't place. In response, John plays a bit of Jimi Hendrix's "Purple Haze," indicating the chord's frequent presence in Black music. Paul says the chord is "passé," but George, who doesn't want to give it up, says, "it's just a chord, like all the others, [good] for different occasions." Sulking and contributing to his growing feelings of worthlessness through numerous slights like this one, George abandons the #9 and reverts to the simple tonic triad that John has been playing all along. Enter Preston: when Billy appears, his Fender Rhodes quickly brings the #9 chord into the same spot George had used it, and Paul never complains. With a trickster's mediation—although not intentionally upsetting the power balance—Billy is clearly authorized where George cannot be.[17]

"The One After 909": Chuck Berry Rhymes and Trickster Rockers

In Jackson's *Get Back*, the Beatles are shown working on "The One After 909" as early as the second day of filming on January 3. If you had to pick one song that encompasses the month's get-back themes, it might be this one, a "Lennon-McCartney Original" reprised from the pre-fame early days and lead-composed by a fifteen-year-old Lennon. As Walter Everett frames the situation, "With the

---

[13] A recent example is Childish Gambino's "This Is America." This 2018 song exposes the exploitation and victimization of Black men in America using a phrase that often celebrates the country's "exceptionalism."

[14] Available in Episode 1 (1:03:08+); see also Nagra roll 51A [Beatles 2000d, disc 1].

[15] Available in Episode 1 (1:05:38).

[16] Available in Episode 1 (1:54:02 and 2:16:59+, respectively).

[17] Thanks to Cameron Greider for pointing out Preston's use of the chord in an early-2022 conversation.

Beatles steeped in memories of their earliest compositions, many of which are demonstrated in these sessions, 'The One After 909' makes its first recorded appearance since March 1963" (1999, 225–6).

The best-known version of "909," the one ending up on the *Let It Be* LP, was mixed from the recording of the January 30 rooftop performance to which Preston "adds the gliss-ful keyboard" (Everett 1999, 226). On the 26th, Paul had played a glissando on piano in "Shake, Rattle and Roll" while Billy played his Lowrey, laughing along (Jackson 2021[18]). (The keyboard glissando reprises the hilarious spot in the Beatles' 1965 Shea appearance, wherein John's "I'm Down" solo features numerous elbow glisses on the Vox Continental, leading Paul to spin in glee.) In "909," the Rhodes glissando adds a humorous touch; although Preston began rehearsing "909" on the 28th, the stop-time gliss had never been part of the song until the following day, requested by Paul: "that'd be great, 'One After 909,' with [Little] Richard [glissandi]."[19] Billy immediately demonstrates on Hammond that he understands Paul's suggestion, which Preston adopts forevermore. Along with Preston's own history with Little Richard, "909" contains the Beatles' beginnings and their last live performance, resulting in circular loops of musical memory.

Especially because of its origins, "The One After 909" is a tune in which the Beatles' early rhythm and blues influences, namely Chuck Berry, are palpable. McCartney identifies the song as one of those that he and Lennon wrote when they "used to sag off every school day" by going back to the McCartney house at 20 Forthlin Road (qtd. in Everett 2001, 28). When Everett quoted that remembrance, he was working from Cott and Dalton's transcription, but McCartney's recollection is now audible (and paired with visuals) in Jackson's *Get Back*. Jackson's edit, however, excludes McCartney's qualifier: "we hated the words to 909." Everett explains the irony of that disdain:

> McCartney did not think the 'station' / 'location' rhyme, along with other aspects of the text, were sophisticated enough to record and release, but this rhyme seems to be in the best Chuck Berry tradition. Although he "hated the words to 909," Paul managed to borrow its line "c'mon, baby, don't be cold as ice" in [an] April 1960 recording of an E-major blues. … The composition of "The One after 909" was essentially finished by the time two rehearsal performances were taped in the same April 1960 sessions.
>
> (2001, 29)

---

[18] Available in Episode Three (0:11:38+); the same footage is repeated for the control-room playback on January 27th (0:19:38).
[19] Available in Nagra roll 1141B [Beatles 2002h, disc 19].

Early in the *Get Back* sessions, as detailed below, the Beatles find they have a newfound affection for the song's lyrics.

Chuck Berry was the OG rock trickster, using his pioneering rhythm & blues to channel teenage rebellion in entertaining, trenchant lyrics. In "Roll Over Beethoven" (covered in numerous early-Beatles stage shows and preserved on *With the Beatles*), Berry kids the long-dead classical composer by telling him that the new style of rock and roll should have him turning over in his grave. The song carries a deeper essence: the songwriter's phonetic parallelism of "o-ove" in both "roll over" and "Beethoven" is a strong rhythmic emulation of sexual accent. The syncopated "O," articulated in an offbeat anacrusis and then sustained but accented on the following strong beat, in successive instances, comes off as a sexual grunt. The "o-ove" rhythm is the same with which Berry humps his guitar onstage. He is almost literally fucking Beethoven while insisting he roll over to become Berry's "bottom." Perhaps crude, but it's the trickster at work. Berry is ever-present through January 1969 in the Beatles' covers of several of his songs. Harrison also encourages Lennon's lap-slide solo on the Hawaiian" Höfner in "For You Blue" by chanting, "Go, Johnny, Go!," thereby quoting the chorus of Berry's "Johnny B. Goode" (Jackson 2021).

In his analysis of the "definitive" 1963 recording of "The One After 909," Everett expands on the Berry allusions, musically present in Harrison's "lead-guitar double-stopped bent-note train whistle," which resembles "Berry's double-stopped imitation of a Dopplerbent car horn in 'Maybellene'" (2001, 79). The use of the key of B Major is also singular in "909," present elsewhere in the Beatles' cover catalogue only when they covered Berry's "Memphis."[20] Everett also explains the "clever rhyme of 'station' and 'location'" as reminiscent of "many such unusual locutions presented by Berry and [which] points forward to such unexpected Lennon rhymes as 'reason' / 'pleasin' in 'Please Please Me'"; the latter is a rhyme Everett connects to Fats Domino's "What's the Reason I'm Not Pleasing You?" (2001, 79). The motoring quality of Berry's songs—in semantic content about driving cars and in the rhythm itself—is yet another dynamic at work in "The One After 909," a song whose trains are vehicles familiar to the Quarry Men's skiffle roots and Liverpool's own Lime Street Station. Lime

---

[20] The key of B major is unusual in both guitar- and piano-based rock literatures. Berry's songs are often based on less usual "flat" keys (such as "Roll Over Beethoven" in E-flat). On January 26, when Lennon (on bass) asks McCartney what key "The Long and Winding Road" is in, he erupts at the composer's response, "What key? E-flat? Fucking hell! Must be mental!" Available in Nagra roll 493A [Beatles 2002a, disc 2].

Street—a terminal for travelers from throughout England and Scotland—is the workplace of sex worker Maggie Mae in the Liverpool folk song and skiffle number covered on January 24 in *Get Back* (Jackson 2021[21]). The first minutes of the film also show the Beatles on January 3 rehearsing Lead Belly's train-based "Midnight Special,"[22] a song that had been a skiffle standby for Lonnie Donegan and others in the late 1950s.[23]

The Berry context for the "station"/"location" rhyme adds profundity to what is visualized in Jackson's *Get Back*. On the second day of filming (January 3), the band reprises "The One After 909" in an especially smiley, spunky run-through, and the pair of rhyming words are reconsidered when the band assesses the worth of the song.[24] Lennon reminds everyone that he wrote it when he was "about fifteen," adding that he "always meant to just change the words." Both McCartney and Harrison are encouraging: "It's great" from Paul and "It's all working. Keep them" from George. McCartney continues to rediscover the wit of the song, laughing as he speaks the lyrics and concludes, "I never sort of knew what it was about before. I mean so she's on a train. And he sort of—" to which Lennon interjects: "Goes to the station and misses it." McCartney continues, still laughing, "But he goes back and finds it was the wrong number, so ..." Harrison dryly offers the punchline: "Wrong location," prompting Lennon's equally dry explanation: "To rhyme with station, you know?"—all the while McCartney leans back, chuckling in appreciation, "That's great" (Jackson 2021).

Everett's earlier observations render the band's bemused reassessment of "The One After 909" significant: they seem to appreciate the very things they liked about Berry's songs, finding the humor present in their own Berry-esque lyrics. As the Beatles themselves point out, the out-of-reach "she" of their "909" dupes the guy—a theme Berry so memorably bequeathed to rock and roll in his "Maybellene." It's a theme present in mid-1960s Beatles songs, such as "Ticket to Ride," "Day Tripper," "Norwegian Wood (This Bird Has Flown)," "You Won't See Me," and "For No One." The Beatles have recently received more and more credit for representing women's independence, but Berry's Maybellene was driving herself out of reach a decade before.

[21] Available in Episode Two (2:11:15).
[22] Available in Episode One (0:30:20).
[23] For more on the Lead Belly-Donegan-Beatles triangulation, see Kapurch and Smith (2023).
[24] Available in Episode One (0:29:14); see also Nagra roll 17A [Beatles 2000c, disc 1].

"I've Got a Hard-On": Introducing Sexual Wordplay with Little Richard

"Is that one called 'I've Got a Feeling'?" asks George following a run-through on the very first day of the *Get Back* sessions (Jackson 2021[25]). "It's called 'I've Got a Hard-On,'" responds John in deadpan. Seated right next to Lennon, Paul adds, laughing, "Everybody had a hard-on." Lennon starts to sing that line in place of the song's title lyric while McCartney adds, still laughing in anticipation of his own joke and looking toward George and Ringo, "Except for me and my monkey." That stops Lennon's playing altogether; he laughs facing McCartney (and the camera), a moment of pure amusement (Jackson 2021). From the film's beginning, Jackson's edit wants viewers to know that the Beatles hadn't lost their ability to joke with each other. Indeed, *Get Back* includes frequent instances of the Beatles' riffing on their own lyrics, with funny meta-textual references that work like inside jokes shared among friends—even as their four-way friendship is suffering under the weight of the cameras and the attendant pressure to compose new songs for a looming concert whose location was constantly debated.

The hard-on line parallels the more familiar "Everybody had a wet dream," delivered with a straight face in the song proper. The banter also involves what is likely a dig at the Maharishi Mahesh Yogi, the Beatles' spiritual guru from the previous year's sojourn in Rishikesh, India. The monkey phrase derives from the Maharishi, whose favorite saying led to the *White Album* song, "Everybody's Got Something to Hide Except Me and My Monkey." At the beginning of the day on January 25, as George plays "Dehra Dun" on an unseen ukulele, Paul mentions his home movies from Rishikesh, taken during the Beatles' retreat. McCartney tells the others that he had re-watched them the night before, laughing about having filmed copulating monkeys, footage that Jackson edits into *Get Back* (Jackson 2021[26]). Why do John and Paul exclude the monkey and his owner from being the possessors of hard-ons? That answer is available in another *White Album* song, "Sexy Sadie," commonly understood as a critique of the Maharishi's sexual (mis)conduct related to young women at the meditation camp. The exception, then, might suggest the Maharishi's impotence, or perhaps the chastity that Lennon supposed the guru ought to have endorsed.

---

[25] Available in Episode One (0:15:24); see also Nagra roll 3A [Beatles 2000a, disc 1].
[26] Available in Episode Two (2:14:28–2:20:05; Paul's laughter occurs at 2:18:55).

In 1969, the Beatles were adding to a longer repertoire of their own sex puns, including the repetition of "tit tit tit" in "Girl" (hidden from producer George Martin) and "fish and finger pie" in "Penny Lane." And those schoolboy jokes have become inside jokes shared among fans, too, doublespeak that exists if you know to listen for it. But the use of sexual puns has a more interesting musical legacy rooted in rhythm and blues and calypso, whose rebellious, often titillating qualities were part of these genres' initial appeal in the 1950s. While sex jokes abound in rock-lyric double entendres, an outrageous early example exists in Little Richard's "Tutti Frutti." Ann Powers capitalizes on the fact that the song originated as "Tutti Frutti, good booty," celebrating gay anal sex, before being toned down for mass marketing (2017, 129). Like Berry, Richard hovers over the *Get Back* project, from conversations with Preston about Richard's whereabouts to covers of several of his songs.

Little Richard's impact in the Beatles' music is well documented. In addition to the covers the band released on their records, the Beatles frequently credited him, along with other rhythm and blues pioneers. Little Richard also distinguished himself, consistently reminding everyone about the credit he deserved, boasting to be "the architect of rock and roll" in as frequently heard a refrain as was Ali's claim, "I'm the greatest." The two surviving Beatles acknowledged their debt when Little Richard died in 2020. On Twitter, Starr praised him as "one of my all-time musical heroes," and on his blog, McCartney gave a vivid tribute: "Little Richard came screaming into my life when I was a teenager. I owe a lot of what I do to Little Richard and his style; and he knew it. He would say, 'I taught Paul everything he knows'. I had to admit he was right." The Beatles have been much less vocal and specific, however, about the influence of calypso, another Black-originating musical genre circulating in the Beatles' pre-fame Liverpool soundscape.

The Beatles Are Bugs: Sex Puns, Calypso, and Lord Kitchener

Calypso, like rhythm and blues, is also characterized by wit and wordplay, especially when it comes to sexual puns. Beatles historians acknowledge that the group's primary initial exposure to calypso musicality arrived through the Trinidad-born Liverpool club owner and early influential mentor, Harold Phillips, better known by his calypsonian sobriquet of Lord Woodbine.

As the leader of one of Britain's first steel bands and a calypso singer, Woodbine was a musical role model; he also provided performance opportunities to the Beatles beginning in 1958. All of this meant that Caribbean music became a part of their creative DNA at an early age (McGrath 2010, 3–5; Lewisohn 2013a, 174–5; Kapurch and Smith 2023). This exposure occurred at various clubs in the Liverpool 8 (which included the city's historically Black district) and the Jacaranda club, known as the "Jac," near Lennon's art school and McCartney's Institute for Boys. The Jac's house band was All Caribbean Steel Band, which Woodbine formed in 1955 and often fronted. Drawing on James McGrath's biographical work on Woodbine, Kapurch and Smith explain,

> the Jac and L8 clubs afforded their exposure to steel-band music, especially that of Woodbine, who sang calypsos, played pans and guitar, and wrote his own songs. For the Beatles (excluding Starr who joined later), Woodbine was a model of professional musicianship and an object of admiration because he was a singer-songwriter. Such was their intrigue that Lennon and McCartney (and sometimes Harrison) were "briefly dubbed "Woodbine's Boys." Woodbine, reflecting on his time with pre-fame Beatles in a 1998 interview, gave an honest assessment: "'There was nothing to pick them out from any of the other groups hanging around Liverpool then. … They were just boys wanting to play music, living off their dole money which they pooled. John Lennon did all the singing. As a singer myself, I didn't think he sounded that good then." Ever humble himself, Woodbine wasn't the one who dubbed the Beatles his "boys"; the nickname came from witnesses, retained in the cultural memory of Black people in Liverpool, including Woodbine's daughter.
>
> (Kapurch and Smith 2023)

The young Beatles, according to L8 clubgoers who witnessed them trying to play the steel band's pans, were teenage boys: presumptuous and often unkempt. But Woodbine was patient with them, sympathetic to their musical ambitions: "Woodbine's patience with the lads owed to his generosity and artistic sensibilities; he was 'bohemian, free, left wing, incautious.' Lennon's sense of humor was particularly appealing to Woodbine, who remembered: 'John could make jokes which had the whole room laughing. … But he would always keep a straight face. I liked that'" (Kapurch and Smith 2023).

A central connective element here is the inherently artful wordplay of calypsonians. It is also important to recall that "Calypso Rock" was the first song that John Lennon wrote, by his own recollection, though no trace of the 1957 composition survives (Lewisohn 2013a, 116, 152). Understanding what appealed to the pre-fame Beatles, especially Lennon, about calypso requires more context: in this era, as far as the international recording industry and mainstream audiences were concerned, the calypso that crossed over was often stripped of its subversive qualities. Harry Belafonte's 1956 *Calypso* LP (RCA), which topped the American charts for a remarkable thirty-one weeks, was the genre's flagship release.[27] With its commercial dilution of the artform (Rohlehr 1990, 533) and less heavily accented vocal articulation, Belafonte's album thrust calypso into a short-lived novelty limelight that overshadowed its authentic performers, complicating the process of being widely heard on their own creative terms as West Indian wordsmiths.

Hearing the title of Lennon's "Calypso Rock" might seem funny now, but the former genre should not be a punchline; the degradation of calypso happened after many white singers appropriated the style in the late 1950s. The Beatles, however, were exposed to calypso firsthand by Woodbine and the other Caribbean musicians regularly playing at the Jac in the last years of the 1950s. It's true that members of the Jac's house band were often asked to play the commercial hits, such as "Day O (Banana Boat Song)" and "Yellow Bird," (both recorded and performed by Harry Belafonte with titular variations). But the members of Woodbine's All Caribbean Steel Band (and later the Royal Caribbean Steel Band) were innovative musicians, who wrote their own music and re-worked other songs.[28] From them, Lennon, McCartney, and Harrison would have heard the genre's sexual puns and other subversive wordplay.

The importance of sexually oriented humorous wordplay in calypso has a lengthy tradition dating back at least to the 1920s according to music historian Gordon Rohlehr. He links its heightened profile and popularity in Trinidad in the 1940s and the post-Second World War era to the presence of American marines on the island and the need for calypsonians to create easily digestible entertainment that could pragmatically coexist with the genre's typical political

---

[27] Belafonte's *Calypso!* album became the first by a solo artist to sell a million copies in America (Sylvester, Alfonso & Baldwin McDowell 2013, 207; Bilby 2004; Alleyne 2008, 253). Temporal context is especially important here since the LP was still in its popular music infancy in the 1950s and the format was consistently outsold by the 45 r.p.m. single in America until the mid-1960s. Peculiarly, despite the many references to Belafonte's million-selling success with this 1956 LP, in 2022 it remained certified by the RIAA (Recording Industry Association of America) only as a gold record signifying sales of over 500,000 copies rather than the platinum certification of over a million copies. In addition, the RIAA's certification of *Calypso!* occurred in March 1963, some six years after its release, suggesting that further clarification is required on its statistical status. The release was added to America's National Recording Registry in 2018 (Harvey 2018, 15).

[28] See references to David Bedford's interviews with members of the Royal Caribbean Steel Band in Kapurch and Smith (2023).

preoccupations (1990, 460–1). In its multiple thematic guises, calypso ultimately functioned as a social mirror reflecting the positives and negatives surrounding its audiences. Internationally distributed calypso recordings from the late 1950s both coincided with the formation and initial compositional efforts of the Beatles, bearing testament to the poetic artistry of two of Trinidad's key genre exponents, Lord Kitchener[29] (d. 2000) and the Mighty Sparrow.[30]

The first volume of Lord Kitchener's *Calypsos Too Hot to Handle* was one of only two records Lennon had in his possession by the end of the 1950s (Lewisohn 2013b, 797). Lennon's calypso record included Kitchener's "Muriel and the Bug," which appeared on at least two of his 1956 releases, one of which was a four song EP (Extended Play) 45 r.p.m. disc (although a 1962 re-release states on the printed label that the recording was first issued in 1954). Apart from the song's suggestive content, there is the intriguing confluence of the scene-stealing bug and the very name of the Beatles (and roughly coincident with the group's formation and more direct adaptation of Buddy Holly's "Crickets" name), raising the possibility of an artistic connection transcending their basic entomological similarity. In Kitchener's bawdy tale, a bed bug elicited screams of panic as he "found himself into Muriel's treasure / That bug is really clever to find that area," as we learn in the chorus. The idea in the song's concluding verse that the bug apparently succeeded where many men previously failed adds a layer of comical irony and continues a theme in calypso lyrics (e.g., in Sparrow's "The Lizard") in which the animal world wreaks erotic havoc on women to the salacious delight of male calypsonian narrators.[31] The totality of the risqué chronicle colorfully

---

[29] Kitchener (né Aldwyn Roberts) was so named, possibly in 1944, by veteran calypsonian Growling Tiger after "the famed British field marshal and war minister" (White 1993, 5), though some sources place Kitchener's adoption of his stage name a year earlier ("Music" 1957, 59). The sobriquet of "Lord" was awarded by his fans and Kitchener was based in England between 1948 and 1962, establishing a club in Manchester in 1958 (Mason 2000). Typically, calypsonians adopt performance monikers symbolizing power that may also be connected to their respective artistic idiosyncrasies. Given the long-term class prejudice against calypso in Trinidad and the critical contexts of slavery, forced migration and British colonial oppression, adopting a grandiose title also became an act of sociopolitical resistance asserting individual worth.

[30] Sparrow (Slinger Francisco) is credited with imbuing the calypsonian's creative mission with a degree of prestige and credibility, often interweaving social commentary with salacious lyricism in the best poetic tradition (Mason 1998, 27, 40–1).

[31] Such narrative strategies interfacing with the animal/creature worlds were also employed in R&B recordings such as Big Mama Thornton's 1953 hit "Hound Dog," mediated and composed by the white duo of Jerry Leiber and Mike Stoller. However, in that particular instance, the protagonist denigrates her erstwhile lover, disengaging from the relationship rather than engaging in metaphoric erotic interplay. The fact that this song became a hit when covered in 1956 by Elvis Presley does nonetheless underscore the rock world's many borrowings from Black music, parallel to Lennon and McCartney's assimilation of such influences.

told during a mere three minutes provides an object lesson in storytelling compression and focus of the type that the Beatles would apply and refine.

Kitchener's frequent use of sexual situation humor and wordplay can be illustrated by a few more selected recordings with relevance to the Beatles. On the Kitchener record that Lennon owned, "My Wife's Nightie" (circa 1956–), Kitchener's illicit lover "Cynthia" made off with his wife's nightgown, placing the protagonist in a seemingly hopeless dilemma, yet the perilous situation is transformed into comedy by the tone of his vocal delivery. (The coincidence that the song's lover shares the name of John Lennon's first wife is intriguing.) In "Kitch Take It Easy" (1953, 1956, 1962), the act of consummation is perennially delayed by an indecisive lover, so that in this case the lyrical humor arises from the absence of sex rather than through artful allusions to it. Lord Kitchener's 1954 British 78 r.p.m. release, "My Wife Went Away with a Yankee," evidences the American appropriation of Trinidad's women at the expense of local men, including calypsonians, marginalized by the economic power of the Yankee dollar. The memorable words of the pragmatic wife portrayed in the song assert in the chorus, "I have made up my mind to go / You can't support me on calypso."

Before the Beatles' ode to the doctor that tricked Harrison and Lennon into taking acid, one of Kitchener's many poetic conceits was utilizing medical scenarios, with the vital administration of euphemistically cloaked sexual relief as the ultimate remedy to an existing malady. In 1963's "Dr. Kitch" (a.k.a. "The Needle"), Kitchener comically and metaphorically inserted himself into the narrative as an unqualified "physician" reluctantly persuaded out of sheer necessity to apply an "injection" at the woman's insistence. The chorus revolved around the alternate insertion of said "needle," its repeated withdrawal and reinsertion, the screams accompanying the ongoing friction, and the calypsonian's triumphantly prurient claims that the woman could not cope with the size of the needle. Similarly, Kitchener sang "Gee Me the Ting" in 1982 (with the calypsonian now accompanied by digitally programmed drums and synthesizers as well as the traditional band with horns). The song involves a role reversal: Kitch's protagonist is the afflicted party in search of urgent remedy, hilariously soliciting immediate medical/sexual supplication from "Audrey" and requesting her compliance with some anonymous doctor's explicit instructions. While this latter recording occurred long after the dissolution of the Beatles, it exemplified extension of the thematic approach exploited in "Dr. Kitch" wherein the wordplay and debauched innuendo are amusingly constructed upon pre-established diagnosis of the need for erotic satisfaction, accompanied by farcical portrayal of the remedial act.

"Instrumental Duel": Echoes of Calypso Competition

During a discussion surrounding playback of the song "Get Back," Glyn Johns characterizes the band's playing (now with Preston) when he suggests an "instrument duel" (Beatles 2021, 136). In addition to their eyeball-to-eyeball songwriting technique in the early days, the generative nature of competition in Lennon and McCartney's collaboration is well-established in Beatles lore. George Martin famously observed, "It was like a tug of war. Imagine two people pulling on a rope, smiling at each other and pulling all the time with all their might. The tension between the two of them made for the bond" (qtd. in Shenk 2014).

John and Paul's songwriting intimacy left George to develop on his own while still in the shadow of the Lennon-McCartney partnership, a point John and Paul nearly acknowledge in a private conversation recorded by a microphone hidden in a flowerpot during 1969 filming. Assessing the reasons for George's departure from the studio, Lennon reasons, "It's a festering wound that we've allowed to—and yesterday we allowed it to go even deeper, and we didn't give him any bandages. And when he is that far in, we have egos" (Jackson 2021). Keeping the beat that glued the egos together was Starr, who seldom if ever jockeyed for attention, happy to lead-sing one song per album. These were usually Lennon-McCartney compositions, but Starr wrote *Abbey Road*'s "Octopus's Garden," a nautical follow-up to "Yellow Submarine." "Octopus's Garden" is about escaping into the loving embrace of an eight-armed underwater creature—two arms to hold each Beatle. *Get Back* offers a glimpse of this song's compositional process in a scene in which Starr receives help from Harrison.

Prior to Preston's arrival, *Get Back* shows the band struggling to compose and collaborate on new songs as a concert date looms in a location that is yet to be decided and no one can agree upon. But they were also aware that pressure yields creativity, an insight reflected in McCartney's comment: "The best bit of us—always has been and always will be—is when we're backs against the wall." This dialogue was included in the promotional trailer for *Get Back*, indicating how Jackson's film would build tension in the re-edit of the original footage. Harrison and his vaulting ambitions are also on display throughout the film: he wants to impress, but then bows out, rescinding his work from consideration. In retrospect, the Beatles (as a whole) appear reluctant to fully embrace competition in 1969; this is especially true when you consider the blatant competition on display during rap battles two decades later. Rappers bested each other, often with braggadocio and insult, exemplifying the legacy of the Dozens, one of the key illustrations of Signifyin(g) as language game (Gates 2014). Still, as a phenomenon prior to rap and hip-hop, the Beatles remain an entry point into seeing competition as an occasion for wit and wordplay, which is particularly true in the musical sparring of two famous calypsonians, Lord Kitchener and Mighty Sparrow.

During calypso's heyday, the late 1950s, the jury was still out about whether calypso or rock would be the next big thing. Against this backdrop emerged an ongoing creative duel pitting the epic artistry of Kitchener and Sparrow, the former genre's leading practitioners, against all other calypsonians; this dynamic duo arguably raised calypso's standards of lyrical witticism, double-entendre, and humorous narratives especially where such involved eluding censorship in placing sexual innuendo in the public domain, either on record or in live calypso tent performances.

As both calypsonians signed international recording contracts involving a series of high-profile labels (e.g., Kitchener on Decca and RCA, Sparrow on RCA and Warner Bros.), as well as lesser known independent imprints, their work became readily accessible to wider audiences. Still, it is often suggested that many of their performative and lyrical subtleties were occasionally lost in cultural translation, contrasted with Belafonte's more commercial delivery (Jose 1969).[32] In his own words, Kitchener "tried to make calypso more intelligent" throughout his career (White 1993, 5). His process involved elevating the genre's literary allusive and metaphorical substance, something the Beatles are credited for doing with rock—although their poetics were also allied to major sonic transformations altering the aural textures of popular music. The successes of Kitchener and Sparrow challenged artists in other fields of popular music to improve their own levels of lyrical (and rhythmic) expression, with the Beatles being among the many likely beneficiaries of this artistic contest.

Although the Beatles seem to abandon their interest in calypso proper, the genre's practitioners were active in the late 1960s, their music still circulating in the vicinity of the Beatles. Sparrow's 1968 single "Mr. Walker" (in which the protagonist suitor is speaking to the female love object's father) was released in England on the Epstein-founded NEMS label. Sparrow's 1956 Trinidad Carnival

---

[32] Although the writer does not specifically mention Belafonte, a *Variety* magazine review of a calypso concert that took place in New York's Madison Square Garden (Jose 1969) seemingly vacillated between recognizing the poetic clarity of communicated meaning in Sparrow's double-entendre lyrical performances and obstacles presented by the peculiarities of his accent. Further, a review of a compilation of Sparrow's early recordings (Lewis 2007, 169–70) notes that the calypsonian imparts "a passing jab at Harry Belafonte for commercializing the genre."

Road March song "Jean and Dinah" (occasionally also known as "Yankees Gone") provided biting social commentary on the presence of the American military base and the ways in which its foreign occupants eroded romantic opportunities for local men with the island nation's women (van Koningsbruggen 1997, 55). Following the consequent rise in the rates of sex workers and the eventual end of the American occupation that began in the 1940s (van Koningsbruggen 1997, 53), Sparrow's "Jean and Dinah" gleefully declared "The Yankees gone and Sparrow take over now." Thus, the song made the calypsonian an agent for sexually based cultural revenge after being dislocated by American men, and this placed the singing protagonist in the dichotomous position of capitalizing on pervasive immorality, filling an exploitative void left by the U.S. Marines. The song portrayed a major shift in relationship power dynamics that was simultaneously personal and political, but which also served humorous entertainment purposes even as it reaffirmed the nation's male hegemonies. It's additionally notable that Sparrow's reign as a leading calypsonian begins with this licentious tale (Dudley 2003, 161), establishing many of his wordplay tactics.

It is curious that the Beatles' "Ask Me Why" (1963) shares an entire lyrical line with the Mighty Sparrow's "Teresa" (1959): "I love you, I'm always thinking of you," further suggesting that the poetic interrelationships between pop and calypso may yet be more pervasive than generally acknowledged. Somewhat oddly, a 1964 *Variety* magazine noted that success of the Beatles' records in Trinidad had resulted in the sudden formation of numerous fan clubs, "leaving calypso in the back seat … in the land of Calypso!" (Jones 1964, 2, 54). The Beatles' musical memory of calypso is another faded memory, much less preserved than their recollections about rhythm and blues.

At first glance, calypso is not obviously preserved in the *Get Back* sessions since they don't cover or sample any calypso. And yet, these sessions have long been characterized by the Beatles' competition with each other. Although that competition was formerly thought to have been evidence of the band pulling apart, the *Get Back* film shows the productive aspects of that process.

"Ob-La-Di, Ob-La-Da": Name Checking Desmond Dekker

Revisiting calypso alongside *Get Back* makes for some intriguing coincidences that arise via the reprisal of "Ob-La-Di, Ob-La-Da," a song with a connection to an emerging Caribbean genre and that lifts the name of one of its practitioners.

In 1969, the song's function is an amusement, an occasion for wordplay, which is immediately ironic considering the stressful recording sessions that took place during the previous year, when McCartney's perfectionist impulses nearly killed the song. Rob Sheffield offers a vivid description of 1968: "Paul is driving everyone batty with a song he's convinced is a hit, … which John dismisses as 'granny music shit.' Paul lashes them through it, night after night, trying to nail the ska offbeats" (2017, 191). At some point, though, Lennon has enough, storming out and back into the studio (re-entering stoned) and "bangs on the keys in a rage, speeding up that jingle-jangle intro … You listen to [the song], a lighthearted ode to family life beloved by children of all ages, you're hearing John beat on the piano, pretending it's Paul's skull" (Sheffield 2017, 192).

Perhaps because it was an occasion for so much tension, "Ob-La-Di, Ob-La-Da" provides joking fodder for the Beatles on two January 1969, dates: the 3rd (Jackson 2021[33]) and the 24th.[34] *Get Back* represents the Beatles' initial riffs on "Ob-La-Di, Ob-La-Da," with Paul singing the opening lines in falsetto while enthusiastically stamping his foot to keep time. John joins him, adding, "Doris had another in the bog" followed by more nonsense lyrics about Charlie having another "another" in the "back of town," concluding "Lordy Lordy did they have a bag of fun." John then replaces the standard refrain with the repetition of "oh my god"—and the song falls apart. The film's edit goes to the aforementioned "Midnight Special" singalong with everyone, including Ringo, joining in. A few minutes later in the film, as the band prepares for "Don't Let Me Down," John complains, "'Ob-La-Di' is back," before announcing, "Desmond had a sparrow in his parking lot." Days later, after a Lennon-and-McCartney eyeball-to-eyeball run-through of "Two of Us," they order lunch; John asks for "sparrow on toast" while Paul orders "boiled testicle" (Jackson 2021). Of course, Lennon's bird jokes are not references to the aforementioned calypsonian Mighty Sparrow; they are, however, an example of Lennon's humor in the delayed-repetition motif since he also asked for "Oscar Wilde on toast," itself another incongruously noncontextual comment that took place on January 23.[35]

Lennon's alterations render the song a vehicle for playing with words. This is another irony given the title's origins: "ob-la-di, ob-la-da" was certainly not nonsense language for Jimmy Scott. The title was a phrase used by this Nigerian conga player, who contributed his musicianship to the Beatles' song; a take that

---

[33] Available in Episode One (0:29:55); see also Nagra rolls 14A and 15A [Beatles 2000b, disc 2].
[34] Available in Nagra roll 438A [Beatles 2001d, disc 2].
[35] Available in Nagra roll 1023B [Beatles 2002f, disc 1].

includes Scott appears on *Anthology 3* (Beatles 1996b). "Ob-la-di, ob-la-da" was "insider" speech in Scott's family that he then shared with audiences in call and response in the Soho clubs where he played—and McCartney frequented. Scott even reassured an anxious McCartney with this phrase; the Beatle then lifted it, refusing to compensate Scott. Scott maintained legal claims on the song until McCartney agreed to pay Scott's bail—in exchange for dropping the issue. This appropriative postcolonial milieu is also instructive to a reading of the song's use of "Desmond," as well as its musical features (Kapurch and Smith 2023).

"Ob-La-Di, Ob-La-Da" might be heard as a response to the then-nascent reggae sound and a pastiche of the jauntier rhythmic aspects that provided commercial danceability. Although the latter can possibly be traced to several rocksteady or early reggae records (most of which still emerged from Jamaica in the mid-to-late 1960s), a probable touchstone is Desmond Dekker's "007 (Shanty Town)" that debuted on the British singles chart in July 1967, the year prior to the release of the Beatles' "Ob-La-Di, Ob-La-Da." As one of the first reggae singles to reach Britain's top 20, it is likely that Dekker's hit had notable impact on shaping mainstream perception of the genre on that side of the Atlantic, thereby possibly influencing the Beatles. By the summer of 1968, American singer Johnny Nash debuted with the single "Hold Me Tight," recorded in Jamaica and eventually peaking at number five in both Britain and America (Alleyne 2012, 193). Although the romantic subject matter of Nash's record sharply contrasted with Dekker's rude-boy criminal narrative in "007," both recordings share a broad radio-friendly similarity, driven by prominently layered rhythm guitar and keyboards arriving on the backbeats and underpinned by solid drum and bass foundations.

The Beatles' 1968 recording of "Ob-La-Di, Ob-La-Da" runs at a faster pace than the aforementioned Dekker and Nash songs, echoing the intensity of ska, the other crucial reggae forerunner. Heard in this context, the Fab Four recording sounds slightly anomalous given reggae's propensity at the time to exploit slower rhythms during and after the mid-1960s rocksteady transitional phase (Alleyne 2012, 236). It is clear from the Beatles' 1964 recording of "I Call Your Name" that the ska phrasing established by Jamaican guitarist/arranger Ernest Ranglin (based in Britain in that year during a residency at Ronnie Scott's jazz club in London) had become at least a marginal element in the group's vocabulary (DiPerna 2021, 60). The narrative tone of "Ob-La-Di, Ob-La-Da" and the whimsical nature of its lyrics are well-suited to lightweight musical accompaniment, but the recording comes across as a pop-flavored, pseudo-reggae treatment that references the genre without doing justice to it, notwithstanding (or possibly because of) the commercial character of the Dekker and Nash hits.

"Ob-La-Di, Ob-La-Da" is a prototype for the style in which many pop artists would later exploit reggae-related rhythms alloyed to (sometimes semi-humorous) situational narratives such as in 10cc's 1978 hit "Dreadlock Holiday" or in later solo work by Paul McCartney on 1974's "Jet" single (Alleyne 2001, 22–3, 28).[36] In such cases, also including the Eagles' "Hotel California" (1977), the affected unnatural vocal articulation on several syllables to mirror the expression of reggae singers magnifies an absence of authenticity, drawing attention to the artificial nature of the work, whether it is intended as homage or humor. As Emerick has noted (2006, 246), McCartney's dissatisfaction with the rhythmic character of the track as he searched in 1968 for "a Jamaican reggae feel" contributed to the friction within the group over the recording process and underscored the inorganic nature of the result. With "Ob-La-Di, Ob-La-Da" and its jocular disposition, the Beatles undertook a cultural excursion, a sort of transient Tropical Mystery Tour counterbalancing (for example) the darkly contemplative "While My Guitar Gently Weeps" on the same *White Album* (and on the same opening side of the vinyl version). Nonetheless, the very coexistence of the musical tangent highlights another example of a Beatles' Black musical debt interwoven with their characteristic witticism.

The eccentric character of "Ob-La-Di, Ob-La-Da" was mirrored in a series of frequently awkward cover versions on singles, all released in 1968. These included the British chart-topping recording by the Marmalade (from Scotland), a peculiar rendition by American soul singer Arthur Conley (best known for his 1967 hit "Sweet Soul Music"), and efforts by British-based reggae acts the Bedrocks and Joyce Bond. The Conley 45 is, in fact, played for the Beatles by Michael Lindsay-Hogg on January 13.[37] It is perhaps unsurprising that none of the covers by Black artists were major hits as those records embodied the simultaneous cultural and commercial paradoxes of copying a white act appropriating Black musical influence. This replicative scenario would be repeated years later when reggae acts reinterpreted recordings by the Police whose white pseudo-reggae fusions (presented on their second album as *Reggatta De Blanc* in 1979) ironically found

---

[36] Also relevant is Linda McCartney's 1977 reggae single, "Seaside Woman," released under the pseudonym, Rikki and the Red Stripes. "Red Stripe" is a Jamaican beer, and the band's full name is a trope on Rikki and the Red Streaks, a Liverpool beat band from the Cavern era that is given a shout out by Lennon on January 22 in *Get Back*'s Episode Two (1:21:30) (Jackson 2021); see also Nagra roll 416A [Beatles 2001b, disc 1].

[37] Available in Nagra roll 127A [Beatles 2001a, disc 1].

far wider audiences than the artists that inspired the group's commercially exploitative engagement with the music (Alleyne 2001, 24–7[38]; Alleyne 2013).

It is also notable that the white performative studio spaces occupied by the Beatles remained devoid of a Black British creative presence, with UK soul and pop considered to be second-rate substitutes at that time for the genuine American article (and this circumstance is loaded with greater irony in the first episode of Jackson's *Get Back* documentary with the prominent references to media coverage of anti-immigrant fascism).[39] Consequently, when the Beatles needed direct input from a Black performer, they capitalized on the availability of seasoned American keys player Billy Preston whose pre-existing connection to the group is also referenced at the beginning of this chapter.

"All the Soul": Getting Back to Billy Preston

"Coming from the north of England, it doesn't come through easy, you know, all the *soul*," confesses McCartney after Preston adds a particularly piquant contrapuntal riff on the Rhodes to "Let It Be" (Jackson 2021[40]). This self-consciousness recalls McCartney's earlier pun during a recording session of "I'm Down" in 1965, when he called the Beatles' music "plastic soul" (Beatles 1996a). Paul's self-deprecating humor acknowledges issues related to authenticity and race, as well as class. The latter implies the Beatles' working-class North, long considered unsophisticated in comparison to "the unsuspecting South," to borrow a phrase in *A Hard Day's Night* (1964). Said in response to Preston, McCartney's comment may also suggest something about the sophistication that the Beatles (and the Mods in general) found so compelling about the fashionable, stylish Black Americans of Motown and other labels, including U.S. singers better known in England, such as Bettye LaVette.[41]

---

[38] Two Various Artist compilations, *Reggatta Mondatta: A Reggae Tribute to the Police* (1997) and its *Volume II* companion (1998), were both released on the Ark 21 label, run by former Police manager Miles Copeland. Thus, the cover song process in this instance seemed far from being commercially spontaneous.

[39] Interestingly, the multiracial Hot Chocolate band (later known only as Hot Chocolate) that achieved huge commercial success in the 1970s released its debut single on Apple Records. The 1969 pop-reggae cover version of the Plastic Ono Band's "Give Peace a Chance" made no chart impact, but it indicated some peripheral Beatles awareness of domestic Black musical activity. Underlining this chapter's Caribbean references, Hot Chocolate's visual presence and songwriting were spearheaded by Jamaican-born singer Errol Brown and Trinidad-born bassist Tony Wilson.

[40] Available in Episode 3 (0:25:58).

[41] For more on the relationship between LaVette and the Beatles, see Kapurch and Smith (2023).

The Beatles' debt to Motown and Stax—seen not only in their early covers but in continual borrowings of the labels' musical approaches, techniques, and even specific motifs—is documented in Walter Everett's essay, "Detroit and Memphis." Motown artists are mentioned, and its songs performed, throughout January 1969. At one point in *Get Back*, Lennon says if they could sing like Stevie Wonder, "Two of Us" would have a looser vibe (Jackson 2021[42]). The Beatles' penchant for invoking the style of Black artists is heard elsewhere during these sessions; on the 26th, Paul wished that "The Long and Winding Road" could sound like Ray Charles.[43] On the 28th, George wished the same for "Something," again referencing Atlantic-then-ABC Paramount artist Charles.[44]

Considering Motown's corporate and popularity ambitions, the label hardly stands as a testament to Signifyin(g), and yet elements of its humor were catchy enough to be applied by others. Examples include a cantankerous verse in the Supremes' "Back in My Arms Again," wherein Diana Ross complains of her backing singers Mary Wilson and Florence Ballard: "How can Mary tell me what to do when she's lost her love so true? And Flo, she don't know, 'cause the boy she loves is a Romeo." We hear the anger in the repetitive strongly clipped accents of beats illustrating Mary's insolence (Mary wags her finger at Diana here in performance). This harshness contrasts with the ironically argumentative line featuring Ross's soft cooing on "Flo" and "know." McCartney seems to refer to this finger wagging in "You're Going to Lose That Girl," with its Motown-inspired vocal arrangement, in *Help!* Later on, the Motown label released Preston's work in 1979–83, although apart from one hit single his recordings for the label failed to mirror the pop success of its 1960s heyday.[45]

The characterization of Billy-as-cheer and the Beatles-as-grumps-needing-creative-inspiration has long been central to the standard story about the *Get Back*-turned-*Let It Be* sessions. Frequently asked about his time with the Beatles, Preston himself added to that narrative, once saying, "They were kind of despondent. They had lost the joy of doing it all" (qtd. in Pareles 2006). The emotional nature of Preston's intervention in an interpersonal dynamic is ingrained in Beatles mythology, especially via the *Anthology* project beginning

---

[42] Available in Episode 2 (2:02:59+).
[43] Available in Nagra roll 494A [Beatles 2002a, disc 2].
[44] Available in Nagra roll 541A [Beatles 2003b, disc 2].
[45] His 1979 single with Syreeta, "With You I'm Born Again" (not written by Preston), reached number four on the *Billboard* Hot 100 on April 19, 1980, maintaining that position for four weeks following a protracted twenty-week ascent. No other singles during his tenure at Motown were hits, and his albums were not major sellers for the label.

in 1995. McCartney called Preston—very much the pro sideman—a "whiz kid," complimenting his expert ear and quick skill, albeit pejoratively, and attributed Preston's positive effects to the fact that Billy had been "an old mate" (Beatles 2000, 318). But it was Harrison who took ownership of inviting Preston, later detailing calls to inquire if "Billy was in town" and requesting that the keys player "come into Savile Row" (Beatles 2000, 318). Perhaps Harrison remembered it this way for a reason: George, ever the "younger brother," and Billy often champion each other in earnest when others have lost interest. On the 29th, for instance, John and Paul repeatedly express an interest in breaking for lunch; Preston alone continues to support George with extended, fast bluesy organ runs, also trying on the Rhodes in "Let It Down," a Harrison composition the group would reject.[46]

The degree to which Harrison is responsible for Preston's initial presence at the studio was in question after *Get Back*. Harrison is seen and heard praising Preston's playing in Ray Charles's then-current London show—"the best jazz band I've seen is Ray Charles's band"—on day one, January 3, well prior to Preston's arrival (Jackson 2021[47]). But Jackson maintains he found no evidence of Harrison's invitations. Still, Harrison's *Anthology* statements prove memorable: "I knew the others loved Billy anyway, and it was like a breath of fresh air. It's interesting to see how nicely people behave when you bring a guest in, because they don't really want everybody to know they're so bitchy" (Beatles 2000, 318). Harrison goes on to compare his invitation of Preston to his earlier decision to bring Eric Clapton into the *White Album* sessions. Note also that Harrison had apparently invited others to the January 1969 sessions, including the Hare Krishna devotee, Shyamsunder Das, whose presence at Twickenham is an occasion for Paul and John to reprise banter from *A Hard Day's Night*: Lennon asks, "Who's that little old man?", to which McCartney responds, "clean though" (Jackson 2021).

Preston's harmonious participation contributes a "lift" to the Beatles partly through the texture and tonal emphases of his organ and piano performances, elevating songs such as "Dig a Pony" and "Let It Be" to an inspirational level and bringing out the fun aspect of "The One After 909." When Preston first arrives, John explains that "every number's got a piano part, and normally we overdub it, you know, but this time we wanna do it live …. and that means having somebody

---

[46]   Available in Nagra roll 1140B [Beatles 2002h, disc 19].
[47]   Available in Episode 1 (0:42:45).

in, so if you'd like to do that, and then you'd be on the album" (Jackson 2021[48]). Preston does contribute some backing vocals and is even caught playing a Fender Bass VI at one loose point in "Old Brown Shoe" rehearsals on the 27th (Jackson 2021[49]). His principal performance, however, is on the keyboards: the Fender Rhodes electric piano and both Lowrey and Hammond organs. Sometimes Preston is filmed playing the Blüthner grand piano, but he was never recorded (outside of the Nagra rolls) on that instrument.

The pervasively positive effect of Preston's presence infuses the sessions with greater warmth and purpose as the Beatles quickly recognize his catalytic effect. During January 22 playbacks, George says, "it's much better since Billy came; he's doing the fills which … anytime there's a space in it" he fills it in.[50] At the start of the following day, John enthuses when asked if he has other songs to work on: "with a decent band, like [with] Billy, I'd do 'On the Road to Marrakesh.'"[51] This was a song that John then envisioned as played by a "big '30s orchestra" (Jackson 2021[52]). Preston's keyboard can, though, add a textural problem new to the Beatles; on the 22nd, after George has Billy double his double-stopped descent in the "Don't Let Me Down" verses, John says that Billy needs to get out of George's way.[53] More often, an issue arises from the simultaneous use of two keyboards occupying the same middle register: on the 26th, following a control-room playback of "The Long and Winding Road" (the take chosen for release), George says that Billy's tremolo-laden Rhodes and Paul's grand piano compete for space. George Martin counters, "your Leslie guitar contributes, too. I mean, it is a bit in the same range as the electric piano with the vibrato" (Jackson 2021[54]). The eventually overdubbed string arrangement, by bolstering the bass register, covers this sin. Despite the "problem," Harrison will have Preston join other keyboardists in much of the "wall of sound" texture of *All Things Must Pass*, a couple of whose songs—such as the aforementioned "Let It Down"—Preston learns in January 1969.

[48] Available in Episode 2 (1:26:50+); see also Nagra roll 420A [Beatles 2001b, disc 2].
[49] Available in Episode 3 (0:24:04); see also Nagra roll 509A [Beatles 2000c, disc 2].
[50] Available in Nagra roll 426A [Beatles 2001c, disc 1].
[51] Available in Nagra roll 1020B [Beatles 2002e, disc 2].
[52] Available in Episode 2 (1:58:54+).
[53] Available in Nagra roll 427A [Beatles 2001c, disc 1].
[54] Available in Episode 3 (0:17:40); see also Nagra roll 498A [Beatles 2002b, disc 1].

After playing "I've Got a Feeling" with Preston, Harrison affirms, "Electric piano is such a great sound" (Jackson 2021[55]).[56] Harrison also bypasses Lennon, who initially suggests they should compile tapes that Preston can audition to familiarize himself with the songs during the Beatles' first extended rehearsal/ jam session. Instead, Harrison recognizes Preston's remarkable ear, proposing, "He'd probably pick them up much quicker hearing us just rehearsing" (Jackson 2021[57]). On the 22nd, John introduces Billy to Yoko by saying, "he's gonna be on our show on the fucking piano, right, because he's a groove!"[58] Punctuating his approval after they run through "I've Got a Feeling," Lennon tells Preston, "You're in the group!" (Jackson 2021[59]).

Growing more and more enthusiastic, Lennon responded to the immediate and tangible positive effect of Preston's keyboards on the collective sound with the enriched color and rhythmic animation, as well as the band's improved mood and chemistry. According to Lennon in a private control-room conversation with Lindsay-Hogg, "We've got Billy now; ... he's the guy, and that solves a lot" (Jackson 2021[60]). Preston's involvement leads to Lennon's explicit recommendation that Preston become "the fifth Beatle," proposing to call the band "The Beatles and Co.," an idea seconded by Harrison but nixed by McCartney because "it's bad enough with four" (Jackson 2021[61]). At the end of the day on the 27th, compliments for Preston's playing on the released take of "Get Back" come from both Martin ("you were good, Bill!") and Johns ("Bill, you were just great!").[62]

At several points during the month, one Beatle or another raises the question of their next single. At the end of the day on the 23rd, John suggests they rush-release "Get Back" (which would be their next A-side, released that May). At this time, however, Lennon is proposing a B-side devoted to what he references as "Part 2,"

[55] Available in Episode 2 (1:29:25+).
[56] Given this chapter's emphasis on wit and wordplay, it's somewhat ironic that Billy Preston's first major American hit was the instrumental "Outa-Space" (1973) which actually displaced lyrical interaction from the song's recorded space with its effervescent clavinet vamps, winning a Grammy Award for Best Pop Instrumental Performance. That recording was also originally the B-side to "I Wrote a Simple Song"(first issued in 1971) that only reached number 77 on the *Billboard* Hot 100 on February 12, 1972, before "Outa-Space" was promoted to A-side status and peaked at number 2 on July 8. In the following year, a print advertisement for his then current A&M Records single "Will It Go Round in Circles" proclaimed that Preston was "The #1 R&B Instrumentalist of 1972" ("Billy Preston" 1973).
[57] Available in Episode 2 (1:27:22).
[58] Available in Nagra roll 423A [Beatles 2001b, disc 2].
[59] Available in Episode 2 (1:29:28).
[60] Available in Episode 2 (1:35:48+).
[61] Available in Episode 2 (1:59:00); see also Nagra roll 438A [Beatles 2001d, disc 2].
[62] Available in Nagra roll 523A [Beatles 2003a, disc 1].

indicating an instrumental jam with Preston which was not to materialize.[63] The following day, John and George tell Paul how they freed Preston from his Capitol recording contract. Not only would this permit the Beatles to credit Billy on "Get Back," but it would allow him to become an Apple artist; Paul says, "He's sort of had a couple of groups together, and he's had records out, and stuff, you know, but he's never sort of done his thing, and I listened to him playing piano yesterday aft; I think he is more like Ray Charles, an album artist." Instead of Preston having to play C&W "shit" like Charles, John wants Billy to have the "prestige and power to play what he likes." As for George, Preston's tight band plays "funkier than jazz" (Jackson 2021[64]). Over the next two years, Preston released two critically acclaimed albums on Apple—*That's the Way God Planned It* and *Encouraging Words*—and several singles, but his first real hits were with A&M, which signed Harrison upon Apple's dissolution.

In Jackson's *Get Back*, the most "Billy-centric" sequence is from 1:17:30 to 1:19:43 in episode 3. The film has already introduced Lennon's fascination with King's "I Have a Dream" speech, demonstrated just prior to Preston's January 22 arrival. King's motif infuses a series of musical exchanges that Preston drives and that will eventually result in "I Want You (She's So Heavy)." In Preston's hands this song is clearly based in the civil-rights speech. Just after lunch on the 29th, Lennon and Preston are equal partners as they repeatedly sing in unison over the group jam, "I had a dream, a very good dream, yesterday" (Jackson 2021[65]), in a cadence that transmogrifies into the *Abbey Road* epic. Alongside this jam on the 27th, Preston takes the lead in an improvisation *not* presented in *Get Back*. With the four Beatles sometimes accompanying and sometimes not, Preston sings, "I told you before, get out of the door ...." above his own jazzy gospel organ or piano playing.[66] This lyric returns in Lennon's "I Found Out," but the music leads elsewhere—to "I Want You." During these sessions, George asks numerous times whether Billy's jam had been recorded the previous day (one must always keep distinct the lower-quality Nagra tapes recorded for the film soundtrack and the high-fidelity multitrack recording that was done very sporadically for potential record release). George never gets a response. Peter

---

63   Nagra roll 436A [Beatles 2001d, disc 2] contains Preston's instrumental jam; the conversation about it is captured in roll 438A [Beatles 2001d, disc 2].

64   These conversations are excerpted in Episode 2 (1:58:54+) in Jackson (2021); see also Nagra rolls 436A and 438A.

65   Available in Episode 3 (1:17:26).

66   Available in Nagra rolls 510A [Beatles 2002c, disc 2] and 511A [Beatles 2002d, disc 1].

Jackson's decision to not include much of this material could be seen as a choice to maintain the authority and legitimacy of the Lennon-McCartney authorship.

As Beatles devotees familiar with the bootlegs have long known, Preston contributed much more to the shaping of individual songs than audiences are allowed to see during the eight hours that aired on Disney+. Here are just two examples of what the film excludes: (1) a run-through of "Let It Be" from January 27 that demonstrates very well how Preston's syncopated legato playing helps glue the ensemble together,[67] and (2) Preston's many Rhodes riffs for "Oh! Darling" on January 23 that end up in Lennon's eventual piano part for the song as recorded.[68] Preston's solo piano playing, so admired by McCartney, was indeed captured on film but did not make Jackson's eight-hour edit. With excellent soulful piano work, Preston demos four post-Charles-like, funky gospel songs that will appear on his own two Apple albums: "Everything's All Right" (*That's the Way God Planned It*), "I Want to Thank You" (*That's the Way God Planned It*), "You've Been Acting Strange" (*Encouraging Words*), and "Use What You Got" (*Encouraging Words*). Interestingly, in regard to a texture-related point discussed above, all of these tracks will be produced by Harrison with both Preston's piano and overdubbed organ parts, heard simultaneously along with bass, drums, guitar by the likes of Harrison (who also contributed Moog and sitar parts) and Eric Clapton, backing singers, and sometimes Stax-like horns.

A viewer of Lindsay-Hogg's *Let It Be* (1970) and Jackson's *Get Back* (2021) cannot adequately focus on Preston's beautiful playing on the rooftop (and in other *Let It Be* songs) because the cameras themselves do not allow such appreciation. But Preston's influence on the Beatles is immense; the R&B nature of the covers they perform with him contrasts with the largely rockabilly and otherwise Appalachian repertoires they enjoin before his appearance, increasing from a 37 percent representation of Black artists (among all artists) covered before Preston's arrival to 53 percent afterwards. Billy's presence seems to make the Beatles want to be an R&B oldies band on the 24th and 26th especially (see appendix). Preston's his Rhodes work on "Stand By Me" is especially fine, as is his twelve-bar boogie medley of Chuck Berry and Larry Williams songs. He changes the Beatles' orientation in the blues; most of their January twelve-bar jamming is squarely in the major mode (as was 1967's "Flying"), but Preston brings a stronger

---

[67] Available in Nagra roll 504A-2 [Beatles 2002c, disc 1].
[68] Available in Nagra roll 1030B [Beatles 2002g, disc 1].

minor-pentatonic language to this format; this point has been anticipated with discussion above regarding the #9 chord of "Get Back." Despite his soul and gospel roots, Preston also adds some Nashville "slip-style" keyboard work landing on downbeats in both John's verse and the Paul/John duet verse of "I've Got a Feeling"; this happens right off the bat on the 22nd.[69] The next day, Preston adds a country-styled right-hand tremolo to his Rhodes solo in "Get Back."[70]

Get Back does not do justice to the many dimensions of Preston, but it's true that his cheer, which is often remarked upon, is indeed part of the equation. Joyful service is an attitude cultivated in the Black Church, but it is especially palpable at Preston's church, both during his time there and still today.[71] Kapurch and Smith have documented the vital role Victory Baptist Church in Los Angeles played in shaping Preston's musicianship, revealing numerous ways that his music reflects this background. At Victory, Preston honed his keys playing, especially on the Hammond B3, the instrument with which he is most closely associated. The church's music ministry continues to reflect a philosophy that shaped Preston's approach: music is joyful noise that serves the Lord. The church's motto, "To Serve the Present Age," is another goal Preston fulfilled with his music, whether he was playing gospel music in church or secular songs with rockers like the Beatles and the Stones (Kapurch and Smith 2023).

At Victory Baptist Church, as in the Black Church generally, the delivery of wisdom through wordplay and wit is prized. This is exemplified in affirmation-inducing sermons, nourished and guided by the musicians' accompaniment. Broadly speaking, "Musicians in the Black Church support and respond to singers, often improvising on the spot." Victory's musicians are especially "gifted in the art of responding to [the present-day pastor's] sermons, offering musical phrases that match or anticipate [his] message, sometimes picking up spoken fragments and turning that speech into song" (Kapurch and Smith 2023). The uses of Signifyin(g) through musical and verbal hyperbole, along with vivid metaphors that elicit responses from the congregation, are discursive techniques born out of the devastation of slavery and ongoing structural disenfranchisement. Black Americans have sustained themselves in a country that oppresses them, developing a rhetoric of joy and uplift to survive as a community; for members

---

[69] Available in Nagra roll 428A [Beatles 2001c, disc 2].
[70] Available in Nagra roll 1026B [Beatles 2002f, disc 2].
[71] On September 11, 2022, Victory Baptist Church burned down, the result of arson. We have chosen to maintain references to the church in the present tense because the community that nourished Preston's artistry remains intact.

of the Black Church (and Victory), this is the body of Christ to which individuals belong and that renders them a collective (Kapurch and Smith 2023).

This chapter stated at the outset that Preston brought a long-perfected understanding of exactly what touch of soul was required in a particular setting. On January 28, he plays solo on the Blüthner grand a draft of one never-released song that might be titled "Unless You Have a Song," a gospel blues.[72] In retrospect, the performance seems like an audition for John Lennon's neo-gospel song, "God." In the opening doo-wop section of the latter, Lennon lays down a foundation in the piano's lower register, and Preston adds a contrafactum in high-register third and fourth hand, quoting the high-register gospel-styled piano riffs from Ketty Lester's "Love Letters."

Preston's professional soulful playing and ability to represent personal spiritual uplift aren't disconnected from each other. So, when John observes that Billy is giving the Beatles a "lift," Lennon unknowingly recognizes an artistic and historical legacy in his appreciation of Preston, one that involves the many other Black musics that the Beatles were sampling and getting back to, often in a lighthearted if not downright humor-inspired atmosphere.

[72] Available in Nagra roll 540A [Beatles 2003b, disc 2].

Table 4.1 January, 1969, performances involving Billy Preston.

Song Title	Model Artist (if cover)	Model's U S Pop / Soul chart debuts and peak positions (if cover)	Beatle instrumentation [excluding references to Mal Evans, George Martin, and Heather See]	January date(s) in Nagra rolls; Rooftop [R] / Let It Be LP [L] / single [45] / Get Back [G] appearance
Save the Last Dance for Me	The Drifters	5 Sep 60 #1 / 3 Oct 60 #1	BP Rhodes, 2 gtrs, bs, dms	22 [G]
Twenty Flight Rock	Eddie Cochran	[1957]	BP Rhodes, 2 gtrs, bs, dms	23 [G]
Maybelline	Chuck Berry	20 Aug 55 #5 / 6 Aug 55 #1	BP Rhodes, 2 gtrs, bs, dms	24
You Can't Catch Me	Chuck Berry	[1956]	BP Rhodes, 2 gtrs, bs, dms	24
Brown-Eyed Handsome Man	Chuck Berry	— / 20 Oct 56 #5	BP Rhodes, 2 gtrs, bs, dms	24
Short Fat Fannie	Larry Williams	24 Jun 57 #5 / 24 Jun 57 #1	BP Rhodes, 2 gtrs, bs, dms	24
Green Onions	Booker T. & the M.G.s	11 Aug 62 #3/25 Aug 62 #1	BP Rhodes, 2 gtrs, bs, dms	24
Bad Boy	Larry Williams	[1959]	BP Rhodes, 2 gtrs, bs, dms	24
Sweet Little Sixteen	Chuck Berry	17 Feb 58 #2/24 Feb 58 #1	BP Rhodes, 2 gtrs, bs, dms	24
Around & Around	Chuck Berry	[1958]	BP Rhodes, 2 gtrs, bs, dms	24
Almost Grown	Chuck Berry	30 Mar 59 #32 / 13 Apr 59 #3	BP Rhodes, 2 gtrs, bs, dms	24
School Day	Chuck Berry	6 Apr 57 #4 / 13 Apr 57 #1	BP Rhodes, 2 gtrs, bs, dms	24 [G]
Stand By Me	Ben E. King	8 May 61 #4 / 15 May 61 #1	BP Rhodes, 2 gtrs, bs, dms	24 [G]
Where Have You Been (All My Life)	Arthur Alexander	26 May 62 #58 / —	BP Rhodes, 2 gtrs, bs, dms	24

(continued)

Song	Artist	Chart info	Instrumentation	Ref
Rip It Up	Little Richard	7 Jul 56 #17 / 30 Jun 56 #1	BP Lowrey, gtr, pno, bs, dms	26
Shake, Rattle and Roll	"Big" Joe Turner	14 Aug 54 #22 / 8 May 54 #1	BP Lowrey, gtr, pno, bs, dms	26 [G]
Kansas City	Little Richard	11 May 59 #95 / —	BP Lowrey, gtr, pno, bs, dms	26 [G]
Miss Ann	Little Richard	24 Jun 57 #56 / 24 Jun 57 #6	BP Lowrey, gtr, pno, bs, dms	26 [G]
Lawdy Miss Clawdy	Lloyd Price	— / 17 May 52 #1	BP Lowrey, gtr, pno, bs, dms	26
Blue Suede Shoes	Elvis Presley	7 Apr 56 #20 / —	BP Lowrey, gtr, pno, bs, dms	26 [G]
You Really Got a Hold on Me	The Miracles	8 Dec 62 #8 / 29 Dec 62 #1	BP Lowrey, gtr, pno, bs, dms	26
The Tracks of My Tears	The Miracles	17 Jul 65 #16 / 10 Jul 65 #2	BP Lowrey, gtr, bs, dms	26
Agent Double-O-Soul	Edwin Starr	7 Aug 65 #21 / 31 Jul 65 #8	BP Lowrey, gtr, bs, dms	26
Bring It on Home to Me	Sam Cooke	23 Jun 62 #13 / 23 Jun 62 #2	BP Rhodes, 2 gtrs, bs, dms	27
The Walk	Jimmy McCracklin	24 Feb 58 #7 / 10 Mar 58 #5	BP Rhodes, 2 gtrs, bs, dms	27
Hava Nagila	[trad]		BP Rhodes	27
Sticks and Stones	Ray Charles	27 Jun 60 #40 / 27 Jun 60 #2	BP pno, gtr, dms	28
Rainy Day Women, # 12 and 35	Bob Dylan	16 Apr 66 #2 / —	BP Rhodes, 2 gtrs, dms	28
God Save the Queen	[trad]		BP Rhodes, gtr, bs, dms	30 [G]
[12-bar jams]			BP Rhodes, 2 gtrs, bs, dms; BP pno, slide gtr, bs, dms, Yoko voc; BP Lowrey, pno, bs, dms	23, 26, 27
I've Got a Feeling			BP Rhodes, 2 gtrs, bs, dms	22 [G], 23 [G], 27 [G], 28 [G], 30 [R, L, G]
Don't Let Me Down			BP Rhodes, 2 gtrs, bs, dms	22 [G], 27 [G], 28 [G], 30 [R, G]

Dig a Pony	BP Rhodes, 2 gtrs, bs, dms	22 [G], 28, 30 [R, L, G]
Get Back	BP Rhodes, 2 gtrs, bs, dms [also attempted with lap slide]; BP to organ on 28	23 [G], 24, 27 [4, L, G], 28, 30 [R, G]
The Long and Winding Road	BP Rhodes, pno, gtr, bs, dms; BP moves to Hammond on 27 and back to Rhodes on 29; BP to organ and back to Rhodes on 31	23, 26 [L, G], 27 [G], 28, 29, 31 [G]
Let It Be	BP Rhodes, pno, gtr, bs, dms; BP moves to Lowrey on 26 and to Hammond on 27th; to Lowrey on 31	23, 26 [G], 27 [G], 29, 31 [L, 4, G]
[Can You] Dig It	BP Rhodes, lap slide, gtr, bs, dms; BP moves to Lowrey, PM from bs to pno and JL from lap slide to bs on 26	24 [G], 26 [L, G], 28, 29
The One After 909	BP Rhodes, 2 gtrs, bs, dms; BP to organ and pno on 29	28, 29, 30 [R, L, G]
For You Blue	BP Rhodes, lap steel, gtr, prepared pno, dms	29
Oh! Darling	BP Rhodes, 2 gtrs, bs, dms; PM moves from bs to pno on 27	23 [G], 27 [G]
Old Brown Shoe	BP bs, gtr, pno, dms; BP moves to Rhodes on 28th; to pno and GH moves from pno to gtr on 28th	27 [G], 28 [G]

(continued)

Song	Instrumentation	Recording dates
Something	BP organ, 2 gtrs, bs, dms	28 [G]
On the Road to Marrakesh [> Child of Nature]	BP organ, 2 gtrs, dms	28
All Things Must Pass	BP organ, 2 gtrs, bs, dms	28, 29
I Want You (She's So Heavy)	BP pno, 2 gtrs, dms, maraca; BP to organ on 28 and to Rhodes on 29	28 [G], 29 [G], 31
Let It Down	BP organ, gtr, bs, dms; BP moves to Rhodes	29
Love Me Do	BP organ, 2 gtrs, bs, dms	28
Lady Madonna	BP Rhodes, gtr, pno, bs, dms	31
12-Bar Rocker	BP Rhodes, 2 gtrs, bs, dms	22
"Freakout" Jam	BP Rhodes, slide gtr with feedback, dms, Yoko vocal	23 [excerpt in G]
I Told You Before [> I Found Out]	BP on Lowrey, gtr, bs, dms; BP pno solo	26 [G], 27
Everything's All Right	BP grand pno	23
I Want to Thank You	BP grand pno	23
You've Been Acting Strange	BP grand pno	23
Use What You Got	BP grand pno	23
Unless You Have a Song	BP grand pno	28

References

Alleyne, Mike. 2001. "White Reggae: Cultural Dilution in the Record Industry." *Popular Music & Society* 24, no. 1: 15–30. http://dx.doi.org/10.1080/03007760008591758.

Alleyne, Mike. 2008. "Globalization and Commercialization of Caribbean Music." *Popular Music History* 3, no. 3: 247–73.

Alleyne, Mike. 2012. *The Encyclopedia of Reggae: The Golden Age of Roots Reggae.* New York: Sterling.

Alleyne, Mike, "Reggae in the Material World: The Police Revisited." (Paper presented at the International Reggae Conference, Kingston, Jamaica, February 14–16, 2013).

Beatles. 2000. *The Beatles Anthology.* San Francisco: Chronicle Books.

Beatles. 2021. *The Beatles: Get Back.* London: Apple and Callaway.

Bilby, Kenneth. 2004. Calypso as a world music. Newsletter—*Institute for Studies in American Music* XXXIV, no. 1 (Fall): 4–5. https://ezproxy.mtsu.edu/login?url=https://www.proquest.com/scholarly-journals/calypso-as-world-music/docview/1845865398/se-2?accountid=4886 (accessed March 25, 2022).

"Billy Preston." *Billboard (Archive: 1963–2000)*, April 07, 1973, 7. https://ezproxy.mtsu.edu/login?url=https://www.proquest.com/magazines/billy-preston/docview/1505953819/se-2?accountid=4886.

Caulfield, Keith. 2014. In 1956, Belafonte ruled the first weekly albums chart. *Billboard* 126, no. 10 (March 22): 60. https://ezproxy.mtsu.edu/login?url=https://www.proquest.com/trade-journals/1956-belafonte-ruled-first-weekly-albums-chart/docview/1513232791/se-2?accountid=4886 (accessed March 25, 2022).

Di Perna, Alan. 2021. "All Hail The King of Ska Guitar!: The Life and Times of Jamaican Guitar Legend Ernest Ranglin." *Guitar World*, July: 56–60.

Dudley, Shannon. 2003. "Calypso Awakening / Lord Invader: Calypso in New York." *Revista De Música Latinoamericana* 24, no. 1 (Spring): 161. https://ezproxy.mtsu.edu/login?url=https://www.proquest.com/scholarly-journals/calypso-awakening-lord-invader-new-york/docview/222857928/se-2?accountid=4886.

Emerick, Geoff, and Howard Massey. 2006. *Here, There and Everywhere: My Life Recording the Music of The Beatles.* New York: Gotham.

Everett, Walter. 1999. *The Beatles as Musicians: Revolver through Anthology.* Oxford: Oxford University Press.

Everett, Walter. 2001. *The Beatles as Musicians: The Quarry Men through Rubber Soul.* Oxford: Oxford University Press.

Everett, Walter. 2002. "Detroit and Memphis: The Soul of *Revolver*." In *Every Sound There Is: The Beatles' Revolver and the Transformation of Rock and Roll*, edited by Russell Reising, 25–57. Aldershot, England: Ashgate.

Gates, Jr., Henry Louis. 2014. *The Signifying Monkey: A Theory of African-American Literary Criticism.* 1988. 25th anniversary edition. Oxford: Oxford University Press.

A Hard Day's Night. 1964. Richard Lester, dir. United Artists.

Harvey, Steve. 2018. National recording registry adds 25 titles. *Pro Sound News*. 05, https://ezproxy.mtsu.edu/login?url=https://www.proquest.com/magazines/national-recording-registry-adds-25-titles/docview/2082464429/se-2?accountid=4886 (accessed March 25, 2022).

Hughes, Tim. 2008. "Trapped within the Wheels: Flow and Repetition, Modernism and Tradition in Stevie Wonder's 'Living for the City.'" In *Expression in Pop-Rock Music: Critical and Analytical Essays*, edited by Walter Everett, 239–65. New York: Routledge.

Jackson, Peter, dir. 2021. *The Beatles: Get Back*. Disney+.

Jones, Brunell. 1964. Miscellany: Bellydancers & Beatles Tops in Land of Calypso. *Variety* (Archive: 1905–2000). May 13, https://ezproxy.mtsu.edu/login?url=https://www.proquest.com/magazines/miscellany-bellydancers-beatles-tops-land-calypso/docview/1014822776/se-2?accountid=4886 (accessed March 24, 2022).

Jose. 1969. "Vaudeville: Concert Reviews—A Calypso Spectacular." *Variety* (Archive: 1905–2000), July 30, 67. https://ezproxy.mtsu.edu/login?url=https://www.proquest.com/magazines/vaudeville-concert-reviews-calypso-spectacular/docview/1014860852/se-2?accountid=4886.

Kapurch, Katie, and Jon Marc Smith. 2023. *Blackbird: How Black Musicians Sang the Beatles into Being—and Sang Back to Them Ever After*. University Park: Penn State University Press.

Lewis, D. N. 2007. The Mighty Sparrow: First Flight—Early Calypsos from the Emory Cook collection. *ARSC Journal* 38, no. 1: 169–70, 176, 140. Retrieved from https://ezproxy.mtsu.edu/login?url=https://www.proquest.com/scholarly-journals/mighty-sparrow-first-flight-early-calypsos-emory/docview/220897483/se-2?accountid=4886.

Lewisohn, Mark. 2013a. *Tune In—The Beatles: All These Years, Vol. 1*. New York: Three Rivers Press.

Lewisohn, Mark. 2013b. *Tune In—The Beatles: All These Years, Vol. 1; Extended Edition*. New York: Little Brown.

Mason, Peter. 1998. *Bacchanal! The Carnival Culture of Trinidad*. Kingston: Ian Randle Press.

Mason, Peter. 2000. "Lord Kitchener." *The Guardian*, February 12. https://www.theguardian.com/news/2000/feb/12/guardianobituaries (accessed March 24, 2022).

McGrath, James. 2010. "Liverpool's Black Community and The Beatles." *Soundscapes—Journal on Media Culture* 12. http://www.icce.rug.nl/~soundscapes/VOLUME12/Interview_McGrath.shtml.

Music: BWI's Lord Kitchener Inked by Jolly Joyce. 1957. *Variety* (Archive: 1905–2000). March 20, https://ezproxy.mtsu.edu/login?url=https://www.proquest.com/magazines/music-bwls-lord-kitchener-inked-jolly-joyce/docview/1014788619/se-2?accountid=4886 (accessed March 25, 2022).

Pareles, Jon. 2006. "Billy Preston, 59, Soul Musician, Is Dead; Renowned Keyboardist and Collaborator: [Obituary]." *New York Times*, June 7, 2006. https://www.nytimes.com/2006/06/07/arts/07preston.html.

Powers, Ann. 2017. *Good Booty: Love and Sex, Black & White, Body and Soul in American Music*. New York: Dey St.

RIAA. "Gold & Platinum." https://www.riaa.com/gold-platinum/?tab_active=default-award§Harry+Belafonte#search_section (accessed March 25, 2022).

Rohlehr, Gordon. 1990. *Calypso & Society in Pre-Independence Trinidad*. St. Augustine, Trinidad: Rohlehr.

Sheffield, Rob. 2017. *Dreaming the Beatles: The Love Story of One Band and the Whole World*. New York: HarperCollins.

Shenk, Joshua Wolf. 2014. "The Power of Two." *The Atlantic*. July/August. https://www.theatlantic.com/magazine/archive/2014/07/the-power-of-two/372289/.

Sulpy, Doug. 2001. *The 910's Guide to The Beatles' Outtakes, Part Two: The Complete Get Back Sessions*. Jackson, NJ: The 910.

Sulpy, Doug, and Ray Schweighardt. 1997. *Get Back: The Unauthorized Chronicle of The Beatles' Let It Be Disaster*. New York: St. Martin's Press.

Sylvester, Meagan, Fabien Alfonso, and Heather Baldwin McDowell. 2013. "An Era Revisited: Trinidad & Tobago's Indigenous Calypso Music—First Recordings, First Live Performances, First Music Publishing, and First Recordings on Film from 1900–1950." *ARSC Journal* 44, no. 2 (Fall): 201–16. https://ezproxy.mtsu.edu/login?url=https://www.proquest.com/scholarly-journals/era-re-visited-trinidad-tobabos-ingigenous/docview/1473702354/se-2?accountid=4886 (accessed March 25, 2022).

van Koningsbruggen, Peter. 1997. *Trinidad Carnival: A Quest for National Identity*. London: Macmillan.

Wenner, Jann. 2000. *Lennon Remembers*. London: Verso.

White, Timothy. 1993. Lord Kitchener Still Rules Calypso. *Billboard* (Archive: 1963–2000). January 30, https://ezproxy.mtsu.edu/login?url=https://www.proquest.com/magazines/lord-kitchener-still-rules-calypso/docview/1505979509/se-2?accountid=4886 (accessed March 25, 2022).

Discography

Beatles. 1996a. *Anthology 2*. Apple/Capitol.

Beatles. 1996b. *Anthology 3*. Apple/Capitol.

Beatles 2000a. *Day By Day: The Complete Get Back Sessions, as Recorded by Camera A, Vol. 1: January 2nd, 1969 [two discs]*. Japan: Yellow Dog Records YDD 001/2.

Beatles 2000b. *Day By Day: The Complete Get Back Sessions, as Recorded by Camera A, Vol. 2: January 3rd, 1969 [two discs]*. Japan: Yellow Dog Records YDD 003/4.

Beatles 2000c. *Day By Day: The Complete Get Back Sessions, as Recorded by Camera A, Vol. 3: January 3rd, 1969 [two discs]*. Japan: Yellow Dog Records YDD 005/6.

Beatles 2000d. *Day By Day: The Complete Get Back Sessions, as Recorded by Camera A, Vol. 7: January 7th, 1969 [two discs]*. Japan: Yellow Dog Records YDD 013/14.

Beatles 2001a. *Day By Day: The Complete Get Back Sessions, as Recorded by Camera A, Vol. 15: January 13th, 1969 [two discs].* Japan: Yellow Dog Records YDD 029/30.

Beatles 2001b. *Day By Day: The Complete Get Back Sessions, as Recorded by Camera A, Vol. 20: January 13th, 1969 [two discs].* Japan: Yellow Dog Records YDD 039/40.

Beatles 2001c. *Day By Day: The Complete Get Back Sessions, as Recorded by Camera A, Vol. 21: January 22nd and 23rd, 1969 [two discs].* Japan: Yellow Dog Records YDD 041/42.

Beatles 2001d. *Day By Day: The Complete Get Back Sessions, as Recorded by Camera A, Vol. 22: January 23rd and 24th, 1969 [two discs].* Japan: Yellow Dog Records YDD 043/44.

Beatles 2002a. *Day By Day: The Complete Get Back Sessions, as Recorded by Camera A, Vol. 29: January 26th, 1969 [two discs].* Japan: Yellow Dog Records YDD 057/58.

Beatles 2002b. *Day By Day: The Complete Get Back Sessions, as Recorded by Camera A, Vol. 30: January 26th and 27th, 1969 [two discs].* Japan: Yellow Dog Records YDD 059/60.

Beatles 2002c. *Day By Day: The Complete Get Back Sessions, as Recorded by Camera A, Vol. 31: January 27th, 1969 [two discs].* Japan: Yellow Dog Records YDD 061/62.

Beatles 2002d. *Day By Day: The Complete Get Back Sessions, as Recorded by Camera A, Vol. 32: January 27th, 1969 [two discs].* Japan: Yellow Dog Records YDD 063/64.

Beatles 2002e. *Get Back Camera B Rolls, Vol. 13: January 22nd and 23rd, 1969 [two discs].* UK: Unicorn Records UC-122/23.

Beatles 2002f. *Get Back Camera B Rolls, Vol. 14: January 23rd, 1969 [two discs].* UK: Unicorn Records UC-124/25.

Beatles 2002g. *Get Back Camera B Rolls, Vol. 15: January 23rd and 24th, 1969 [two discs].* UK: Unicorn Records UC-126/27.

Beatles 2002h. *Get Back Camera B Rolls: January 25th-31st, 1969 [twenty-four discs].* UK: Unicorn Records UC-S001-S024.

Beatles 2003a. *Day By Day: The Complete Get Back Sessions, as Recorded by Camera A, Vol. 33: January 27th and 28th, 1969 [two discs].* Japan: Yellow Dog Records YDD 065/66.

Beatles 2003b. *Day By Day: The Complete Get Back Sessions, as Recorded by Camera A, Vol. 35: January 28th, 1969 [two discs].* Japan: Yellow Dog Records YDD 069/70.

Lord Kitchener. 1954. "My Wife Went Away with a Yankee." Melodisc 1300.

Lord Kitchener. 1956. *Calypso Time* (EP). Melodisc EPM7-67.

Lord Kitchener. 1963. "Dr. Kitch." Jump Up JU 511.

Lord Kitchener. 1982. "Gee Me the Ting." Charlie's Records CRD 010.

Mighty Sparrow. 1956. "Jean and Dinah."

Mighty Sparrow. 1959. *King Sparrow's Calypso Carnival.* Cook 00920.

Mighty Sparrow. 1968. "Mr. Walker." NEMS 56-3558.

Preston, Billy. 1971. "Outa-Space." A&M AM-1320.

Preston, Billy. 1972. *Music Is My Life.* A & M.

Part Two

Playing Solo

5

Madcap Laughs: The Evolution of John Lennon's Humor

Jeffrey Roessner

"It's a laugh a line with Lennon."

A Hard Day's Night

"I'm crying, I'm crying, I'm crying, I'm crying."

"I Am the Walrus"

Lennon the leader. Lennon the songwriter. Lennon the confessor. Lennon the thief. Lennon the fat Elvis. Lennon the abuser. Lennon the satirist. Lennon the truth-teller. Lennon the Dylanite. Lennon the artist. Lennon the savior. Lennon the Lost Weekender. Lennon the househusband. Lennon the baker. Lennon the father. Lennon the martyr. With his steady accumulation of roles and identities, and despite his devotion to naked confession, John Lennon remains an elusive character, brimming with complexity and self-contradiction. Unlike his songwriting partner, Paul McCartney, who repeatedly took on the guise of characters in his songs, Lennon's most consistent mask was his own face. He, not Lucy, had kaleidoscope eyes. But amidst this play of identity, one character trait did remain consistent: Lennon the comic.

Laughter is not one thing, of course, and it rarely serves a single purpose. And that's particularly true for Lennon, who brandished his wit as a personal and social tool throughout his career. His comic sensibility ranged from unbridled joy and surreal humor to the intense emotions registered in lyrics that include frequent references to both laughing and its seeming opposite, crying. As tropes of romance, both fit comfortably within pop music formulas. But Lennon's use of them evinces a psychological complexity that moves beyond cliché. Self-presentation repeatedly evokes emotional duplicity, or a surface emotion and a hidden, genuine feeling that he asserts and then often complicates or retracts.

Frequently driven by shame and fear of humiliation, that dynamic underscores the defensive armor of laughter he deployed on stage, in interviews, and in lyrics. He used it to bond his bandmates to him, aggressively assert authority, mock weakness and deformity, and attack those who he thought had insulted him. Theorists have linked such themes—especially of concealment and the obsession with size/status—to the personality traits of professional comedians, who also exhibit the kind of anxiety and depression that feature in Lennon's work. Still, as Lennon embraced an aesthetic of authenticity in the later 1960s, he broadened his notion of laughter to include childlike play and communal joy. He even began to reckon with his aggression and ultimately found in himself the qualities of those he had savagely mocked.

Playing the Fool

In the famous interview scene from *A Hard Day's Night*, a reporter asks Ringo, "Are you a mod or a rocker?" to which Ringo deadpans, "I'm a mocker." It's a classic line—but one that should most certainly have come not from the genial and ingenuous Starr, but from the wry mouth of John Lennon. Indeed, a large portion of Lennon's humor is grounded in mockery, some of which is taking the piss, as the English say, and some of which shades to cruelty. No matter whether it's served warm or cold, infectious humor was a key element of The Beatles' appeal, and Lennon was at the center of it.

Reflecting on the Beatles' failed January 1962 Decca audition, Peter Doggett notes, "Certainly any producer listening to [Lennon's] mock-Peter Sellers contributions to ensemble pieces like 'Three Cool Cats' might have reckoned that he had more of a future as a comedian than as a frontline singer" (Doggett 2005, 25–6). While disparaging Lennon's vocal contributions, Doggett underscores the central role of the group leader's wit. Indeed, in an interview right before his death, Lennon himself said, "Part of me would sooner have been a comedian. I just don't have the guts to stand up and do it, but I'd love to be in Monty Python rather than the Beatles" (UK Film 2019). Humor was not only crucial for the band's identity, but also a direct reflection of Lennon's comic sensibility.

The attractive side of Lennon's wit is on evidence at almost every turn. He displays surreal humor throughout his books, delighting in puns and comic wordplay, and in interviews, in which he indulges in absurd put-ons, à la the famous interview scene in *A Hard Day's Night*. If you're looking for a brief sonic moment that epitomizes this side of the Beatles' appeal—all the thrilling joy, all the gleeful madness—the bridge of "Yellow Submarine" serves well. McCartney's paean to life beneath the waves, with its sing-along chorus and Ringo's deadpan delivery, extolls the counterculture fantasy of communal escape, with perhaps a wink to marijuana as the choice vehicle of deliverance. Engineer Geoff Emerick noted that the carnival-like atmosphere of the session—with instruments and effects scattered across the studio and everyone jumping in to participate— seemed "straight out of a Marx Brothers movie" (Emerick 2006, 120). During the song's bridge, Lennon takes command, barking his garbled directives and ordering "full speed ahead." Employing Abbey Road's echo chamber to enhance the nautical atmosphere, Lennon remained there "to repeat Starr's lines, Goon-style, throughout the final verse" (MacDonald 2007, 207). Then, right before we roll back to the chorus, he offers his maniacal shout, "Ah-ha!" It's the purest expression of unhinged freedom ever committed to record. That brief second tells us why we want to be on his submarine: as the captain, he rallies the Beatle crew and they joyfully follow his lead.

Lennon was also adept at turning his mockery on himself. While refusing to be taken for a fool, Lennon could adroitly play the fool for his own ends. As John Morreall notes, our laughter often "expresses feelings of superiority over other people or *over a former state of ourselves*" [italics mine] (Morreall 2020). Repeatedly undercutting his own pretense, Lennon loved buffoonery, consistently playing the clown with his gang. In an early interview, the Beatles are asked to introduce themselves and their roles in the band. In a bit of lilting mockery that drips with condescension, George Harrison says, as though speaking to children, "I'm George and I play a guitar" (Beatles 1963a). Lennon follows and at first seems to strike the same tone: "I'm John and I, too, play a guitar." Then he dryly adds, "Sometimes I play the fool." Harrison goes for the obvious, while Lennon is three steps ahead comedically, his pun slicing through any pretension.

Such self-deprecating wit was an essential part of Lennon's arsenal, and it remained with him throughout his life. Even as late as the *Playboy* interviews from 1980, he happily skewered the Beatles. He greets his interviewer at the door with an improvised verse to the tune of "Eleanor Rigby": "Here's David Sheff, come to ask questions with answers that no one will hear" (Sheff 2000, 114). In the same interview—remember, this is *Playboy*—he advises readers as an aside, under his breath, "This Beatles talk bores me to death. Turn to page 196" (Sheff 2000, 92). Such self-abnegation fits well with Lennon's comic deflation of pomposity or pretense, as when he asserts that, despite the outcry of fans after their breakup, the Beatles were "only a rock group that split up, it's nothing important" (Lennon 1971b). As disarming as Lennon's wit could be when turned on himself, however, he often had his laugh at the expense of others.

The Rapier Wit

From the Beatles' inception, Lennon brought maniacal energy and an acid tongue to the proceedings—traits not easily tamed as manager Brian Epstein groomed the Beatles for success. Lennon wanted fame and attention enough that he was willing to compromise in many ways to achieve them. He donned the fashionably cut suits and went along with a sanitized stage act: no smoking, eating, or swearing during the sets, and nice tidy bow at the end—choices he later lamented as selling out (Lennon 1971a). But as the early recordings of the Beatles' late 1962 stint in Hamburg reveal, he wasn't above undermining their performance for a lark. When McCartney delivers the syrupy "Till There was You," he's met with parody at every turn, with Lennon sarcastically (drunkenly?) echoing the lines. Trouble starts in verse two when McCartney croons, "There were robins [Lennon: 'There were robins'] in the sky [Lennon: 'in the sky']" (Beatles 1977). After Lennon parodies "never saw them winging," McCartney laughs through the beginning of the next line. Gamely carrying on as the mockery continues *for the rest of the song*, McCartney seems to want to be part of the joke rather than the butt of it. (And to his credit or detriment, depending on how you view the material, the mockery didn't stop McCartney from formally recording such confections with the band.)

That brand of derision remained central to Lennon's character. During the Beatles 1963 Christmas show, Lennon mocked emcee Rolf Harris from backstage as he was attempting to perform a comedy routine. As Harris delivered his lines, Lennon's voice boomed over the speakers, "I dunno about that, Rolf" and "Well, of course, you could say that. But, then again, I dunno, Rolf. Maybe you're just making it up" (Brown 2020, 97). Harris played along as the audience laughed, but he was reportedly so angry that afterwards he "barged his way into the Beatles' dressing room and shouted, "If you want to fuck up your own act, do it! But don't fuck up mine!" (Brown 2020, 97). Lennon doesn't seem concerned that such ridicule would undermine a performance, even with his own band. Later, in 1968, fed up with McCartney's overwrought approach to "Ob-La-Di Ob-La-Da,"

Lennon and Harrison again turned to parody, faintly echoing McCartney's rhymes "ring" and "sing" in absurd falsetto. When Desmond lets the children "lend a hand," the background chorus unhelpfully adds, "arm, leg." During the *Get Back* sessions, too, Lennon openly mocks Harrison's demo of "I Me Mine" and he later hams it up for the camera by dramatically lip-synching along with McCartney's performance of "Let It Be"—or "Ark the Angels Come," as Lennon introduces it on the album (Jackson 2021).

Along with seeming bonhomie and good-natured ribbing, Lennon's mockery could be small and mean, the dark, cutting edge never far from view. "There was a lot of chippiness about John," Indica Books owner and Beatle friend Barry Miles noted: "An awful lot of his 'rapier wit' would have been just old-fashioned rudeness if it had come from anyone else" (Miles 2002). From an early age, Lennon mocked weakness and affectation, and cruelly imitated the physically and mentally challenged. He repeatedly pulled grotesque faces and pretended to be physically deformed. Indeed, Mark Lewisohn indicates that Lennon did his spastic routine on stage for many years, through the mid-1960s (Lewisohn 2017). Fans have assembled collections of these images and clips, in which he puts his tongue in his cheek and contorts his jaw, shoving his face into the camera lens, as though it's one more performance ("Lennon Face" 2018). (Cementing Lennon's reputation as a nascent punk, Johnny Rotten pulled similar wild-eyed faces for the camera during the Sex Pistols musical assault in the 1970s.) It's no wonder that Brian Epstein feared Lennon would tell the crowd to "rattle yer fuckin' jewelry" at the Royal Command Performance in 1963 (Norman 2008, 330).

Lennon seemed to have no brakes, regardless of the size or significance of the venue. After appearing on *The Ed Sullivan Show* in 1964, the band travelled to Washington, D.C., for their first concert appearance in America. The fans were at fever pitch—and there was Lennon, pulling faces and stomping his weirdly canted leg across the stage. Commenting on these antics during the Beatles ascent in England, Norman notes that "Amazingly, no one among the thousands present was offended, indeed no one even seemed to notice when, in place of the regulation bow, he responded with a toothless village-idiot leer, stomping one leg on the stage as if it were malformed and clapping his hands with both sets of fingers curled into 'spassie' claws" (Norman 2008, 330). As Norman and Lewisohn both note, incredulously, Lennon escaped criticism for insensitive behavior utterly taboo in contemporary culture (Lewisohn 2017).

Such aggressive humor, unfortunately, also came out in homophobic taunts. As Brian Epstein prepared to release his 1964 autobiography *A Cellarful of Noise*,

Lennon reportedly suggested he call it "Queer Jew," and later said it should have been titled "A Cellarful of Boys" (Norman 2008, 363). Antagonism toward the homosexual manager seems part of a larger macho defensiveness on Lennon's part. In 1963 Lennon took a now infamous holiday in Spain alone with Epstein and rumors swirled about their possible affair while away. When DJ and friend Bob Wooler made a remark about the alleged tryst, a drunken Lennon proceeded to assault him: "He called me a queer so I battered his bloody ribs in" (Coleman 1985, 189). Lennon makes a humorous but slightly embarrassed reference to the incident during the *Get Back* sessions, when he responds to George Martin's suggestion that he needs to tune his guitar: "I've had some wine, you know. Remember Bob Wooler!" (Jackson 2021). Recording "Baby, You're a Rich Man" in 1967, Lennon added another snide swipe at Epstein by singing along to the chorus: "Baby, you're a rich fag Jew" (MacDonald 2007, 258). In some scrapped takes, he also reportedly took "wicked shots at Paul, Ringo, and Mick [Jagger]" (Spitz 2005, 686). With this literal record of caustic parody, it's no great leap to the unmasked aggression of "How Do You Sleep?" from 1971, with its barbed assault on McCartney ("The only thing you done was 'Yesterday'").

Man, He Was Mean

To contemporary ears, Lennon's cruelly volatile "humor" likely strikes us as immature, a hyper-masculine reaction to anguish he hadn't found a way to express, and it doubtless served as a psychological prop. One early explanation of humor is called the "superiority theory," and Lennon could be exhibit A. Though now discredited as an analysis of *why* things are funny, the superiority theory aptly describes one social function of humor (Lintott 2016, 348). Grounded in ridicule, laughter at misfortune both undergirds our sense of the inferiority of others and shores up our own identity. Not only are we laughing at the expense of fools, but we're in fact banking the psychological profit in ego strength (Kaufman and Kozbelt 2009, 84). The superiority theory also implies an important protective function of humor, as it's directed at misfortune in ways that elicit "amusement rather than outrage, tears or compassion" (Bicknell 2007, 458). Lennon's first wife Cynthia notes his long-standing fixation with disability. "In our student days he'd mocked the disabled and drawn ghoulish cartoons of cripples. For some reason disability terrified him, though he could never admit it. It made him feel inadequate and guilty" (C. Lennon 2005, 188).

Jokes provide an antidote to such uncomfortable feelings, a ready escape from facing what terrifies us, and Lennon fully indulged. In every assertion of superiority, especially through humor, we find both malice and defense. As Lennon himself famously noted, "Part of me suspects I'm a loser and part of me thinks I'm God Almighty" (Sheff 2000, 223). Behind every defiant Lennon declaration, there's a whisper of insecurity. Behind every parodic assault on McCartney, there's a fear—he's getting more attention (especially from young women), he's writing better melodies, he's getting the A-sides of the singles. In many ways, Lennon weaponized humor, and it was an essential means for securing his role as leader of the band and ensuring fealty: after all, who wants to be on the receiving end of the rapier wit?

The unsavory elements of Lennon's wit have increasingly evoked criticism: how can we account for the shifting response? Working out an ethical theory of humor, Jeanette Bicknell explains how previously acceptable jokes can later come to be seen as insensitive. In the terms of her argument, the moral problem with telling racist, sexist, or homophobic jokes "lies either in the failure to take account of vulnerability in others, or in the decision to exploit such vulnerability for the sake of humor" (Bicknell 2007, 463). Crucially, our awareness of that vulnerability—and the vulnerability itself—depends on context. We don't mind laughing at lawyer jokes because we don't perceive that group as particularly at risk. But "the perception of who is vulnerable and what should or should not be made fun of, changes over time" (Bicknell 2007, 464). Since the 1960s, LGBTQ+ activism, along with critiques of ableism, has increased awareness of systemic oppression experienced by both queer and disabled populations. Lennon's jokes were mean and harmful back then, but they immediately read as unfunny and rankly offensive today. For example, when 1964 concert footage of Lennon's "spastic" routine re-surfaced in 2015, many contemporary viewers were offended at the mockery, in marked contrast to his reception more than half a century ago (Tonkin 2015; Lewisohn 2017).

Hiding in the Light

Regardless of the era from which we judge Lennon's jokes, especially his abusive taunts, his aggressive wit mirrors the obsessions of many comedians. In their study of the psychology of comics, Fisher and Fisher outline several persistent themes in their routines. They note that "Comics are fascinated with size" and are "acutely tuned into the relative magnitude of objects" (Fisher and Fisher 1981, 35). Note how often Lennon employs language of size and scale. In "You've Got to Hide Your Love Away," the shame is connected to feeling "two foot small"—a Freudian slip if there ever was one, as he shrivels with humiliation. And smallness is frequently countered with its opposite: inflation. In a 1963 interview, reflecting on the Beatles' career path, he says, "You can be big-headed and say, 'Yeah, we're gonna last ten years.' But as soon as you've said that you think, 'We're lucky if we last three months'" (Beatles 1963b). His 1971 *Rolling Stone* interview is rife with references to sizable egos and oversized effects: he sympathizes with Ono's plight at having to deal with the "the most bigheaded, up-tight people on earth" and talks about a "big scandal," "big announcement," "big egos," "big bastards," and "bigger drugs" (J. Lennon 1971a). In fact, he uses the word "big" or a variation of it *35 times* in Part 1 of the interview alone. As for lyrics, we know Sexy Sadie is going to get hers yet no matter how "big" she thinks she is. "Hey Bulldog" ruminates on measuring happiness, innocence, and solitude. Feeling child-like, the singer assaults the "big man" who is secretly "frightened of the dark."

Lennon is a complicated man, and he often turns the aggression back on himself, as though he's shooting in a hall of mirrors. Recall the take-down of heartless, pompous "Bungalow Bill," in which Yoko Ono sings the line "Not when he looked so fierce" as *the mother*—a role that Lennon gives her symbolically (in "Julia") and literally (calling her "mother"). So who is the hard-headed Saxon son who needs protection? Who is the "big man" frightened of the dark? It sounds a lot like John Lennon.

Along with that obsession over inflation and deflation, Lennon exhibits another key theme of comedians: concealment. Fisher and Fisher devote a section of their study to discussing concealment and the unconscious, considering Freudian theory and speculating that "when an individual tells jokes that permit the concealed expression of repressed, forbidden impulses, the gratification he obtains from such venting results in pleasure and laughter" (Fisher and Fisher 1981, 84). We can easily see that dynamic at work in Lennon's lyrics, where images of hiding and the fear or thrill of exposure recur. In "I'll Cry Instead," he tells us, "Don't wanna cry when there's people there / Get shy when they start to stare." He concludes by hiding himself away, while threatening to return and wreak vengeance on all those hapless girls. Repeatedly, Lennon offers lyrics infused with a stunning degree of self-consciousness, raising questions about his psychological investment in self-display and self-revelation. Beatles historian Mark Lewisohn claims to have deduced the precise date when Lennon started doing his "spastic" routine, connecting it to a particularly concentrated moment of display "after or before a school speech day" (Lewisohn 2017). Lewisohn goes on to note that "when John Lennon pulls these faces, a lot of that is when he's feeling self-conscious …. [T]here was an element of it that was him being self-conscious about the camera being on him, or in some way it's a reflection of [being] crippled inside" (Lewisohn 2017). Lennon wanted it both ways for a good bit of his career: to stand on the stage and demand to be looked at, but at the same time to consistently deflect personal attention. The comic hides in the light—and Lennon worked under one the biggest spotlights in popular culture—which cast a large public shadow containing many demons.

The Tears of a Clown

Perhaps unsurprisingly, the underside of aggression is vulnerability: Lennon's assaults were often driven by his fear of exposure and shame, which he dramatizes repeatedly in his lyrics. Early Lennon songs frequently associate laughter, and being laughed at, with humiliation. In "I'm a Loser," after the dramatic opening declaration, his first statement is "I'm not what I appear to be." Such self-consciousness at being looked at becomes an obsessive trope in his lyrics. Before landing on the refrain in "You've Got to Hide Your Love Away," he claims he has turned to face the wall and, with people everywhere staring at him, "I can see them laugh at me and I hear them say …." It's an odd twist of phrase that he "sees" rather than hears them laughing, but it accords perfectly with the humiliation of being exposed for who you really are. By the third verse, he's underscoring the mortification of "hearing them, seeing them," making clear that the subject of the song is not any kind of love, but the constant fear of public inspection. Ashamed for exposing this inner side—the love he's carefully guarded from sight—the best advice he gets or can give is to repress the painful emotional display and move on.

When Lennon turns his face to the wall in "You've Got to Hide Your Love Away," we understand the implication: in his shame, he's hiding his tears. Laughter is often bound intimately with pain, and as Lennon mocks others, so he expects them to return the same. He dramatizes shame repeatedly in his relationship songs, where the anguish is doubled by not only being frustrated, but also being ridiculed. In "You Can't Do That," after warning the girl that she better knock off her flirting, Lennon invokes the specter of public ridicule by the crowd: "But if they'd seen you talking that way / they'd laugh in my face."

In "Norwegian Wood," his hoped-for assignation collapses around him. The woman tells him she works in the morning and starts to laugh: once again, the joke is on him—apparently justifying his vengeful burning of her house. That's what you get for laughing at me.

If aggression helps hide the vulnerable, shameful parts of the personality, we might also note that aggressive humor has been correlated with depression and anxiety, themes that arise repeatedly in the Lennon oeuvre (Kaufman and Kozbelt 2009, 84). For Lennon, sorrow is laughter's twin, and in his lyrics we as often find him crying as laughing. Tears are a stylized convention in popular music, of course, and Lennon and McCartney fully buy into the lovelorn trope. Thirty original Beatles songs refer to some version of "crying" or "tears," including many signature Lennon tracks such as "If I Fell," "Girl," "I'm a Loser," and "Because" (Forrest). Katie Kapurch has argued persuasively that the investment in crying reflects an essential melodramatic theme in the Beatles' catalog, and helps cement their connection to female fans by signaling empathy and intimacy (Kapurch 2016, 208). And with Lennon in particular, the tears could never remain a cliché for long, as they quickly become part of the intense psychological drama he stages in verse.

The apotheosis of these doubled strains—the funny and the sad—occurs in one of Lennon's most celebrated tracks, "I Am the Walrus." Perhaps unsurprisingly, the song's avant-garde sonic collage, production tactics, and surreal lyrics have gotten most of the critical attention. But the piece has an unsettling, melancholic undertow from its launch, starting with the un-homed, descending chord sequence that pulls us in. While the song is driven by a pulsing rhythm, the verse ultimately gives way to a pensive, legato bridge as he waits in the garden for the sun, only to be greeted (surprise?) by the English rain. As we might expect, Lennon clinches the chorus with the title "I Am the Walrus," repeated a total of four times in the lyric. But we shouldn't miss the song's real confession—"I'm crying"—which he repeats six times, prompting the question: what is the song's true refrain? Amidst the weeping, actual laughter does appear on the track. But when it arrives, it's a grotesque chorus in the final verse. After Lennon asks his rhetorical "Don't you think the joker laughs at you?" we hear the jeering response, "ho ho ho, hee hee hee, ha ha ha"—as though all Lennon's fears of being laughed at have come incarnate. The track externalizes the ridicule he previously confronted in his head, and we lurch between laughing and crying as he attempts to sort out his confusion—who is he? The eggman? The walrus? He? Me? She? *Everyone?*

Such confusion was part of a reckoning for Lennon in the mid-1960s. So much change and loss occurred for him, it's no wonder that he was cracking under psychological strain. The Beatles famously played their final official concert in August 1966—that part of his public performing life was essentially over. Their manager and steadying force Brian Epstein died a year later. Meanwhile, Lennon's marriage to Cynthia was in free fall, helped along by the appearance of a slight Japanese performance artist called Yoko. And he had begun a heavy regimen of LSD, sequestering himself in his Kenwood estate over an hour from EMI Recording Studios and far indeed from the London avant-garde art scene, which McCartney was busily embracing. The turmoil and the effects of the hallucinogenic drugs precipitated a crisis and a quest and ultimately a profound personality change that, among other things, reshaped his humor.

Changing His Scene

In his earlier lyrics, Lennon had hinted at a hidden, darker side of his personality beneath his veneer of humor. But by 1967, a startling confessional unmasking begins. On *Sgt. Pepper*'s "Getting Better," he offers the unflattering admission that he was an angry young man who was mad, mean, cruel, and beat his woman. This is no pop singer wearing a frown—no, this is another level of aggression and violence. At this point, though, such honesty still came draped in all the Beatle charm McCartney could muster. A jaunty melody and harmony-laden chorus assured us that all that bad stuff was in the past, and things were so much better now, and about to get even better still. Just you wait!

But Lennon was busy making other plans. Was it the drugs, the meditation retreat with Maharishi in early 1968, the chaotic and stunning world of violence and assassination that spring, the full merger with Yoko Ono and the end his first marriage, or a stew of all of it mixed together that led to the dramatic shift in his personality? Whatever the complex etiology of the change, a new Lennon emerged. The single most public declaration of the shift was, of course, the infamous full-frontal nude cover of Lennon and Ono's *Unfinished Music No. 1: Two Virgins* album. The hiding and concealment that are central to the surprise of humor were gone, replaced by the full Lennon. Total honesty and total communication, that was the aim. Lennon would out-McCartney McCartney with his avant-gardism, and he would out-Dylan Dylan with his confessions. Things just got *real*.

The effect on Lennon's humor was complex. On the one hand, LSD perhaps contributed to the abrupt end of Lennon's spastic routines, which were never to be seen again (Lewisohn 2017). But the embrace of the real and the end of concealment also meant that the brakes were finally off. It turns out he had only just begun to deal with the aggression that drove his wit. Seemingly unfeeling in his ridicule of others, Lennon himself would not be mocked. It's difficult to imagine, for example, McCartney or Harrison ever daring to undercut a Lennon vocal performance. With newly unleashed fervor, Lennon let loose. In "Sexy Sadie," the biggest indictment against the Maharishi— or any guru—is the swindle: "You made a fool of everyone," he sings in a line immediately repeated in case you missed the point. And then in grand Lennon style, the lyric turns threatening as he warns, "You'll get yours yet …. no matter how big you think you are." In his confessional outing, he's no longer turning his face to the wall at being taken for a fool—he's owning the emotion and lashing out. With his Liverpool brashness, when Lennon turned on you, he turned hard. The clown has his day, seeking revenge with a cutting, vindictive candor that is so extreme it veers into comedy. As Rob Sheffield observes,

> every line is funny—not the words themselves, but the deadpan vocal, the dry consonants, the blue notes, the self-mocking falsetto at the end, the way he rolls the 'x' in 'sexy' around in his mouth, as if it's a toothpick he's about to spit …. The sarcasm dripping out of John's mouth is the meanest and funniest recorded evidence of his nasty streak.
>
> (Sheffield 2017, 239)

For his turn, the main character in "The Continuing Story of Bungalow Bill" comes in for savage mockery of his pseudo-machismo and cavalier drive to kill for sport. This era also gives us the composition of "Mean Mr. Mustard," another enemy, set up for ridicule for his tart flavor, his rudeness, the smallness of his world. In May 1968, the suffer-no-fools attitude comes out in full force during the press conference for the launch of Apple Corps. Explaining the alternative business model for the company, Lennon glares at the gathered reporters: "we want to set up a system whereby people who just want to make a film about anything don't have to go on their knees in somebody's office … probably yours" (Lennon and McCartney 2018). As he adds the tag, provoking laughter and applause in the room, you can sense his tongue edge along his teeth in utter contempt. Three months of meditation in India had not dulled the blade. This is indeed the same Lennon who plotted lyrically against Sadie, Bungalow Bill, and all the other frauds who mistook *him* for the fool.

In their analysis of the personality of comedians, Fisher and Fisher suggest, "If one applies Freud's paradigm to the comics, one might expect that they would have repressive attitudes toward sexual and hostile material" (Fisher and Fisher 1981, 86). In Lennon's earlier work, such impulses were clearly present but partially disguised, concealed within the tropes of romance and heartbreak. The girl in "Run for Your Life" must flee because of jealousy, not because the singer is coming to terms with his rage. Even the desperate plea in "Help!" turns into a realization that he needs the girl like he never done before. By 1968, though, the repressed returns with a vengeance. The *White Album* gives us Lennon's most salacious sex song, "Happiness Is a Warm Gun," as well as his unchecked howl of despair, "Yer Blues"—which is of course nothing less than the slowed down, un-popified, uncensored version of "Help!" In the embrace of authenticity, Lennon became fiercely aggressive and overtly sexual and suicidal. Paradoxically, that freedom also opened another side to his laughter.

Doing the Best That He Can

The multifaceted Lennon never remains stuck in one register for long. The *White Album* period gives us "Sexy Sadie" and "Bungalow Bill"—finger-pointing lyrics, to borrow a phrase from Dylan—that lashed out, threatened, and belittled. But in that same period of withering scorn, we begin to see a softening of Lennon's humor as the *White Album* records the tussle between conflicting elements of his personality, the vindictive and the winsome. In early 1968, he had already begun to sketch a new lyrical register in "Across the Universe," where the "pools of sorrow" mingle with "waves of joy." But ultimately it's the "sounds of laughter" that invite him to a transcendent love. In this era, he embraces a lightness and sweetness in ways that had not been so eloquently expressed before. In "Dear Prudence," over a lovely descending finger-picked guitar line, he urges the reclusive young woman to "come out and play" and asks her to "let me see you smile again." Lennon acknowledges that play doesn't have to mean concealment, instead offering a joyful openness as the antidote to hiding.

Although he never fully sands down the sharp edges of his caustic humor, Lennon offers a glimpse of laughter as a communal experience. As both the 1960s and the Beatles come to a close, we find him celebrating ecstatic laughter, suggesting that he hadn't completely abandoned the utopian impulses of earlier songs such as "The Word" and "All You Need Is Love." *Abbey Road*'s "Sun King"—like "Across the Universe" before it—evinces a Romantic belief in transformation and transcendence. The lush, multi-tracked harmonies offer a glistening sheen that pours like honey from the speakers: as the Sun King arrives, "everybody's laughing" and "everybody's happy." The final section presents a grab-bag of words from various Romance languages, reinforcing the universalism in this paean to imminent bliss. But still, the lads do manage to sneak in another naughty bit of Liverpool slang, "chicka ferdy," a local expression that McCartney suggests means "f*** off" (McCartney 2020). Once again, an in-joke pulls the band together. But significantly, laughter itself has become a communal experience of joy. In this ecstatic moment, no one is subject to ridicule and "everybody" takes part. Without being defensive or controlling, Lennon offers a vision of transcendental laughter, bigger than all the insecurities that plagued him.

A complex man with extraordinary insight and troubling flaws, Lennon repeatedly displayed the tension between the various elements of his humor. On his second solo album, *Imagine* (1971), he returns to the savage mockery of McCartney in "How Do You Sleep?" But on another track from the same album, he professes sympathetic identification with those "crippled inside," reflecting an awareness of his emotional stuntedness and perhaps of his own earlier cruelty. He offers the song in the second person, as advice to "you," but within the context of the album's confessional bent, the personal implication seems clear. The first verse employs language that directly alludes to "I'm a Loser." In that song, though he smiles and acts "like a clown," behind the mask, he wears a frown. In the first verses of "Crippled Inside," he also references wearing a mask and hiding behind a false smile, suggesting that he's once again chiding himself. The opening lines also reference the disguise of a suit and tie—the very outfit he donned as a "happy Beatle" for Brian Epstein. The slur against looking cute could be another shot at his bandmate Paul, but just as easily reads as self-recrimination for having sold out and cleaned himself up at Epstein's behest. The punch of the song, though, is Lennon's jaunty insistence that emotional disfiguration is the one thing *you can't hide.*

Lennon had been obliquely sharing his insecurity for years, hiding in plain sight in song after song about his disguises. "Crippled Inside" marks an important step toward self-awareness, unfolding from his embrace of complete honesty and the aesthetics of authenticity that he had announced, nakedly, in 1968 (Kapurch and Everett 2020, 209–11). Just as he had earlier acknowledged that he might be the nowhere man ("Isn't he a bit like you and me?"), he uses "Crippled Inside" to turn his former derision and cruelty toward physical disability back on himself. His disfigurement is emotional, of course, but nonetheless debilitating: we recall that he suffered repeated traumatic losses, with his mother and father abandoning him, in childhood, to his Aunt Mimi, and the subsequent death of his mother, his best friend Stu Sutcliffe, his manager Brian Epstein—not to mention the dissolution of his marriage and his band. In this context, his turn to primal scream therapy in the early 1970s seems nearly inevitable.

How far did Lennon go in his journey to deal with those demons? Quite a distance, it seems, judging by the hopeful optimism of his last official lyric pronouncements, on *Double Fantasy* (1980). "Beautiful Boy," for instance, offers key insight into his maturity. On the one hand, a heart-melting expression of love for Sean and a vow to take care of him, the song—like almost everything in Lennon's catalog—can be read as a message to himself, an attempt to self-soothe in a frightful, disorienting world. There's joyous hope anticipating Sean coming of age, yes, but there's also reassurance to himself that the monsters can be kept at bay and that "daddy's here." To paraphrase Wordsworth, in this song the man becomes father to himself, finally supplying the comfort that he missed from his own absent parents. Intriguingly, we also find Lennon taking on the optimistic persona of his old bandmate. In "Getting Better," from *Sgt. Pepper's Lonely Heart's Club Band* (1967), McCartney avers that it's getting better, to which Lennon sardonically replies, "It can't get no worse." Over a decade later, in "Beautiful Boy," Lennon assumes McCartney's role, insisting that "every day in every way it's getting better and better." Any trace of mockery or satire has subsided, replaced by tender caretaking of both others and himself.

****

The tension between the aggressive and the vulnerable, the cutting and the shy, the mockery and the inviting love, underpins a good bit of John Lennon's appeal. McCartney might express sadness or heartbreak, but we rarely feel that he's truly anguished. Think McCartney's "For No One" versus Lennon's "Yer Blues," for example—two brilliant songs with wildly distinct "sad" sensibilities. The seams in Lennon's character reveal his charisma, his exuberant joy, his just-say-yes to life resilience, but also his streaks of anxiety, depression, even loneliness. Those traits are part of what made him a complicated riddle that fans and critics still want to solve. And nowhere do we find a more complicated expression of this mystery than in his comedy. Lennon had employed humor to deflect criticism and assert control and aggressively uphold his defenses. But there is often a delicious thread of joy present, stitched not far under the surface. As he evolved artistically, fully embracing his aesthetic of authenticity, he also broadened his sense of laughter—inviting everyone to come out to play.

References

The Beatles. 1963a. "Beatles Greetings." Track 1, disc 1 on *Live at the BBC*. Apple. 1994.

The Beatles. 1963b. "Beatles Interview: Manchester Dressing Room 8/28/1963." By the BBC. August 28,1963. http://www.beatlesinterviews.org/db1963.0828.beatles.html.

The Beatles. 1977. "Till There Was You." *Live! at the Star Club in Hamburg, Germany; 1962*. Lingasong, vinyl LP.

Bicknell, Jeanette. 2007. "What Is Offensive about Offensive Jokes?" *Philosophy Today* 51(Winter 2007): 458–65.

Brown, Craig. 2020. *150 Glimpses of the Beatles*. New York: Farrar, Straus and Giroux.

Coleman, Ray. 1985. *Lennon*. New York: McGraw-Hill.

Doggett, Peter. 2005. *The Art and Music of John Lennon*. Baltimore: Omnibus.

Emerick, Geoff. 2006. *Here, There and Everywhere: My Life Recording the Music of the Beatles*. New York: Gotham Books.

Fisher, Seymour, and Rhonda L. Fisher. 1981. *Pretend the World Is Funny and Forever: A Psychological Analysis of Comedians, Clowns, and Actors*. Lawrence Erlbaum.

Forrest, Adam. 1998. "The Beatles Lyrics Machine." The Internet Beatles Album, October 1998. https://www.beatlesagain.com/btlyrics.html.

Jackson, Peter, director. 2021. *Get Back*. Part 2. Apple Corps Ltd. 2 hrs, 53 min.

Kapurch, Katie. 2016. "Crying, Waiting, Hoping: The Beatles, Girl Culture, and the Melodramatic Mode." In *New Critical Perspectives on the Beatles: Things We Said Today*, edited by Kenneth Womack and Katie Kapurch, 199–220. London: Palgrave Macmillan.

Kapurch, Katie, and Walter Everett. 2020. "'If You Become Naked': Sexual Honesty on the Beatles' *White Album*." *Rock Music Studies* 7, no. 3 (2020): 209–25.

Kaufman, Scott Barry and Aaron Kozbelt. 2009. "The Tears of a Clown: Understanding Comedy Writers." *The Psychology of Creative Writing*. Cambridge: Cambridge University Press.

Lennon, Cynthia. 2005. *John*. New York: Three Rivers Press.

"The Lennon Face." 2018. September 2, 2018. https://imgur.com/a/ZV1Vk6w#kvoKP1T.

Lennon, John. 1971a. "Lennon Remembers, Part One." Interview by Jann Wenner. *RollingStone*, January 21, 1971. https://www.rollingstone.com/music/music-news/lennon-remembers-part-one-186693/.

Lennon, John. 1971b. "Interview of John Lennon with Yoko Ono: St. Regis New York, 2 East 55th Street, Manhattan, New York City, October 1971." Track 7, disc 1 on *The Beatles Tapes from the David Wigg Interviews*. Recorded October 1971. Polydor, compact disc.

Lennon, John and Paul McCartney. 2018. "John Lennon and Paul McCartney - Americana Hotel – 14 May 1968." YouTube video, 12:21, posted by John C Stoskopf, June 10, 2018, https://www.youtube.com/watch?v=LmuqczpRW7M.

Lewisohn, Mark. 2017. "Birth of the Beatles." Interview by Rohan Silva. *Medium*, February 16, 2017. https://medium.com/workandlife/birth-of-the-beatles-153d6fe02341.

Lintott, Sheila. 2016. "Superiority in Humor Theory." *The Journal of Aesthetics and Art Criticism* 74, no. 4 (Fall 2016): 347–58.

MacDonald, Ian. 2007. *Revolution in the Head: The Beatles' Records and the Sixties*. Third Edition. New York: Owl Books.

McCartney, Paul. 2020. "You Gave Me the Answer—Slang Words." Paul McCartney. August 28, 2020. https://www.paulmccartney.com/news-blogs/news/you-gave-me-the-answer-slang-words.

Miles, Barry. 2002. "John, Paul, George and … Barry," interview by Mick Brown, Miles. October 16, 2002. http://barrymiles.co.uk/biography/john-paul-george-and-barry/.

Morreall, John. 2020. "The Philosophy of Humor." *The Stanford Encyclopedia of Philosophy*. Edited by Edward N. Zalta. August 20, 2020. https://plato.stanford.edu/archives/fall2020/entries/humor/.

Norman, Philip. 2008. *John Lennon: The Life*. New York: Ecco.

Sheff, David. 2000. *All We Are Saying: The Last Major Interview with John Lennon and Yoko Ono*. New York: St. Martin's Griffin.

Sheffield, Rob. 2017. *Dreaming the Beatles: The Love Story of One Band and the Whole World*. New York: Dey St.

Spitz, Bob. 2005. *The Beatles: The Biography*. Boston: Little, Brown and Company.

Tonkin, Sam. 2015. "Fans of John Lennon shocked by video footage in new documentary that shows him mocking disabled people during Beatles concert." *Daily Mail*, September 20, 2015. https://www.dailymail.co.uk/news/article-3242759/Fans-John-Lennon-left-shock-video-footage-new-documentary-1960s-shows-mocking-disabled-people-Beatles-concert.html.

UK Film. 2019. "John Lennon's Last BBC interview—December 6th, 1980." YouTube. March 18, 2019. 2:07. https://www.youtube.com/watch?v=0CU6jqMyiJg.

6

"Shall We Dance? This Is Fun!": Paul McCartney's Popular Song Pastiches

David Thurmaier

"If I'd have to choose anyone," announced Paul McCartney, "I'd be very happy to be thought of as a channeller of Nat King Cole or Fats or Fred" (McCartney 2021, 299). Unlike the other Beatles, sometimes characterized as acerbic and witty (John), deadpan and self-deprecating (George), or an everyman (Ringo), McCartney is known more for his earnestness than his humor. Yet McCartney can be humorous, often as a result of his unintentional character traits and musings. For example, his song lyrics that have no obvious meaning, such as "Oklahoma was never like this" from "Press," have become subjects of discussion and unintentional humor due to McCartney's sincere, head-scratching explanations.[1]

McCartney treats humor in witty and clever ways through his many pastiches of the American and British popular song traditions. McCartney's penchant for recreating song styles and recognizable nuances from music of earlier eras is, on the one hand, compelling musically, but it also illuminates how McCartney presents himself as an artist through pastiche, defined by Richard Dyer as "a kind of imitation that you [the viewer, listener, etc.] are meant to know is an imitation" (Dyer 2007, 1). Or, as Fredric Jameson puts it, pastiche is characterized by "the imitation of a peculiar or unique, idiosyncratic style" (Jameson 1993, 16–17). Pastiche, which is usually more celebratory and reverential to source

---

[1] As McCartney stated in a 1986 interview from the magazine *Sound on Sound*, "'Oklahoma was never like this'. That can mean whatever you want it to mean. To me, when you're writing songs, you often get a line you assume you're going to edit later, you're going to knock it out and put something sensible in. But every time I came to that line, I couldn't sing anything else—just the scanning, the way it sang. People would have understood it if it was 'Liverpool was never like this', but it wouldn't have sung the same. It's a symbol for the provinces, the sticks, the out of the way places. The line just wouldn't change, and when you meet such resistance from the lyrics themselves, you have to give in." http://www.muzines.co.uk/articles/press-to-play/1668/.

material than is parody, is a common technique employed in music of the past and present, particularly prominent in modernist classical music, as well as twentieth-century popular music. In fact, given today's diffuse and flattened cultural landscape where all music of the past is easily available with a few clicks and the blending of styles and influences is encouraged, one could argue all current music exhibits traits of pastiche.

My chapter examines several of McCartney's popular song pastiches musically (i.e., analysis of musical structure and techniques) as well as intertextually (i.e., lyrically and stylistically) with a focus on highlighting unintentionally humorous moments, contextualized through McCartney's own statements and performances. Such pastiches often subjected McCartney to scorn and disdain (including by his former bandmate Lennon), but they are so competent that they illuminate McCartney's unique sense of humor, available in his musical expressions (e.g., scat singing, spoken asides, vocal histrionics) and textual references. In the end, what may appear on the surface as a throwaway musical number often reveals salient musical and historical aspects about its composer.

Antecedents

Before analyzing McCartney's extensive use of pastiche, examples in different genres of music can serve as models for understanding how and why he uses this technique. For pastiche to be effective and to make sense, contemporary usage must be built upon markers, styles, genres, and themes from the past. In classical music, composers inhabit a complicated space with those from the past, often eschewing earlier music while inevitably borrowing from or referring to it. Some works harbor obvious ties to the past, whether through the use of genres, like symphonies, or by evoking particular musical movements or styles. An example of the former can be found in the symphonies of Gustav Mahler (1860–1911), a composer who straddled Romanticism and Modernism in significant ways. Mahler adhered to the general form and structure of a symphony (i.e., four movements with specific tempo and formal models), but greatly expanded—or "maximalized" as Richard Taruskin describes it—the genre of a symphony, enriching it with unusual instruments (e.g., mandolin, guitar) and influences from outside "traditional" classical music (e.g., folk music, Jewish Klezmer music; Taruskin 2009, 8–9). In this way, Mahler comments on the genre of a symphony in ways that let the listener know intent (i.e., he is writing a symphony) but then transforms the genre into something his own through its "maximalist" expansion.

Another classical music example more akin to McCartney's pastiches occurs in the neoclassical music of Igor Stravinsky (1882–1971). In his *Pulcinella*, "inspired by" the music of the Baroque composer Giovanni Pergolesi, Stravinsky orchestrates and rearranges extant selections in ways that modernize them, yet clearly reveal their earlier origins.[2] A paradoxical listening experience is thus formulated: we *know* the music sounds like it comes from the Baroque era, but it does not sound "quite right"; it is evident that the music must have been written in the twentieth century because of the way the instruments are used, scored for, or arranged. For one cognizant of the stylistic musical markers of the Baroque period, hearing Stravinsky's arrangements can be humorous, as when one shares an inside joke. The music still *sounds* like Stravinsky, even though he did not compose the source material. Though McCartney composes his own source material intended to sound old, his pastiches also always *sound* like him.

From the popular music realm, Stephen Sondheim's musical *Follies* (1971) teems with pastiche numbers. In fact, the entire musical creates two different worlds both in its plot and music. A brief explanation of the plot: living performers from a much earlier era reunite at the theater where they used to perform, now set to be demolished. Throughout the course of the musical, we learn of the performers' missed opportunities, failed love relationships, longings for what might have been, and eventual acceptance of their current state. Sondheim's music for *Follies*, which he called "an orgy of pastiche," imitates music from notable composers of the Golden Age of American Popular Song (e.g., Porter, Gershwin, Rodgers, etc.). A prescient clue about how Sondheim uses pastiche is given in his own definition of the term: "pastiches are fond imitations, unlike parodies or satires, which make comment on the work or the style being imitated" (Sondheim 2010, 200). The songs thus imitate and comment on the past, as Stravinsky and Mahler do, but they also spur a contemporary comment on the style. In the case of *Follies*, despite there being many laughs and fond remembrances, the more poignant moral is one can never recapture the past.

Another popular music example is Frank Zappa and The Mothers of Invention's first album, *Freak Out!* (1966). Zappa would be known for pastiches and parodies throughout his career, but instances on this album are noteworthy

---

[2] There have been debates about the source of Stravinsky's materials for *Pulcinella,* but Eric Walter White argues that all the music comes from extant published scores of Pergolesi's music (White 1985, 283).

because they comment on rock music from less than a decade prior. On "Go Cry on Somebody Else's Shoulder," Zappa composes a doo-wop song complete with all the gestures and musical traits identifiable with the style: the buffo bass and falsetto background singers, the dramatic opening, the archetypal chord progression and melodic structure, the reverb and production qualities. One may be fooled into thinking that this was a song from the 1950s if not for the lyrics plainly *not* from that period (e.g., "You cheated me baby/And told some dirty lies about me"). Zappa evokes a clear musical model, puts a contemporary spin on it, and offers commentary on the often-ridiculous things that happen in teenage relationships. And along the way, the exaggerated sung gestures and unexpected lyrics engender humor in listeners. McCartney acknowledged that *Freak Out!* influenced *Sgt. Pepper's Lonely Hearts Club Band*, so Zappa's pastiches may have been influential on multiple levels.[3]

As these examples show, humor in different forms grows out of pastiches; for Mahler, irony emerges from his symphonies, with their blends of different musics that often comment on each other and the symphonic genre as a whole. In Stravinsky's music, past and present musical and stylistic markers engage in a lively dialogue, with those in the present chuckling at the clever asides and inside jokes at the expense of the past. For Sondheim and Zappa, direct attempts to create songs that clearly sound from an earlier era mix with sharp and humorous lyrics, accentuated by musical touches straight out of the past. McCartney's pastiches borrow elements from all these other artists in that they sometimes mix styles and have an ironic side (especially lyrically), they engage with music of the past in a way that offers commentary, and they often seem like "relics from a different age" with their vocal mannerisms, endearing and earnest lyrics, and musical arrangements that solidify the relationship between the past and present.

McCartney and Pastiche in the Beatles

In McCartney's case, what past do his pastiches imitate? McCartney shared with the other Beatles (and continues to project) an affinity for American and British pre-Second World War popular song. Evidence of this love abounds in

---

[3] This connection became particularly humorous since Zappa's 1968 album *We're Only in It for the Money* spoofed *Sgt. Pepper*. https://lemonwire.com/2017/04/21/revisiting-frank-zappas-anti-sgt-pepper-album/.

the band's story as told by its own members, from songs Julia Lennon and Jim McCartney played and taught their sons, to crooner songs like "Red Sails in The Sunset" that the pre-fame Beatles performed in Hamburg and Liverpool, to solo projects like Ringo Starr's *Sentimental Journey* and McCartney's *Kisses on the Bottom*, and George Harrison's fervent interest in Hoagy Carmichael.[4] For kids growing up during and after the Second World War, genres that predated rock and roll influenced their musical tastes and development. McCartney is clearly the Beatle most interested in this music (later purchasing catalogs of noted popular song composers like Harold Arlen) as revealed both in interviews and in musical productions like concerts and recordings. To his biographer, McCartney remarked that he "grew up steeped in that music-hall tradition" (McCartney and Miles 1997, 23). In fact, some of his earliest compositions (e.g., "When I'm Sixty-Four") were outgrowths of this popular song influence.

To understand McCartney's pastiches and their humorous traits, it helps to identify the musical elements involved in a popular song from the pre-Second World War period. Let us consider a song performed by one of McCartney's favorite performers, Fred Astaire (who will return later in this chapter). Now probably known best as a dancer, Astaire also had a successful recording career as a singer between 1926 and 1943. He scored a #1 hit with "Cheek to Cheek" in 1935, a song specifically written for him by Irving Berlin. The song is cast in AABA (verse, verse, bridge, verse) form, which is the Beatles' preferred form for many of their songs.[5] In "Cheek to Cheek," Astaire is accompanied by a small jazz orchestra, with muted trumpets, strings, piano, guitar, saxophones, and percussion. The lyrics describe how life's problems and even enjoyable activities (e.g., fishing, mountain climbing) all pale next to dancing "cheek to cheek" with the narrator's partner. Astaire sings the song dryly but with a sly enthusiasm, scooping his notes up and down ("hea-ven"), with an earnestness that is even more apparent in the song's appearance in the movie *Top Hat*. Harmony in the verses of "Cheek to Cheek" is simple and repetitive but takes on a darker hue in the bridge (B) when it turns to a minor chord on the words "dance with me,"

---

[4] For more on Harrison's use of American popular song, see David Thurmaier, "George Harrison and the Influence of Popular Song" in *New Critical Perspectives on the Beatles*, edited by Kenneth Womack and Katie Kapurch (New York: Palgrave Macmillan, 2016), 139–55. Harrison's interest in Carmichael and his music, whose life and musical style parallel his own *even* though they never met, shares a resemblance to McCartney's fondness for Fred Astaire and his era.

[5] We can also use the acronym SRDC, coined by Walter Everett, to describe the form in a similar way: statement, restatement, departure, and conclusion (Everett 2001, 132). Also see Drew Nobile, "Form and Voice Leading in Early Beatles Songs," in *Music Theory Online* 19, no. 3 (2011) for discussion of SRDC-B form.

and the melody sustains the same note. The contrast in harmony is essential for understanding how McCartney comments on this music, as the "B" sections of his pastiche songs often contain the most interesting chords and melodic ideas. In short, "Cheek to Cheek" can serve as a key model for McCartney's pastiches, with respect to instrumental arrangements, harmony, lyrics, form, and melody.

"Your Mother Should Know"

In addition to the aforementioned musical characteristics, McCartney's pastiche songs almost always have common lyrical and performance features. Though the music may provoke humor amusement to one who understands the musical games being played, it is in these areas where McCartney's sense of humor— intentional and unintentional—rises to the surface. The lyrics contain at least two consistent markers: sentimental and often-dated language that clearly evokes an earlier time and characters that strive to overcome odds or a challenge to end up in a better place. A salient example comes from 1967's *Magical Mystery Tour*, "Your Mother Should Know." This song is less a musical pastiche (i.e., only the Beatles play on it, without any of the typical musical instruments or gestures found in earlier eras, like the clarinets on "When I'm Sixty-Four") than a lyrical one, where McCartney honors the time period and songs from when "your mother was born" (in his case, the 1910s–20s). The nostalgic lyrics and danceability of the song were put to good use at the end of the film *Magical Mystery Tour*, when the four Beatles concluded the movie with it produced as a dance number.

Not only do the lyrics remind listeners of older eras and songs, but McCartney's vocal delivery and performance also designates "Your Mother Should Know" as a kind of pastiche. McCartney holds back his rock voice (i.e., rough and strained, such as on early Beatles songs like "I'm Down") and sings in a sweeter, innocent voice befitting a crooner from the 1930s–40s. McCartney had an impressive ability to change his vocal timbre and style to suit a song's mood, adding believability to what he sings. In this case, the smooth vocal timbre and the background vocals from the other Beatles are performed such that the performance hearkens back to earlier periods. McCartney's playful use of the "da" syllable over the last verse conjures up images of dancers from the 1920s or 1930s. As a result, "Your Mother Should Know" is unintentionally humorous, engendering a positive feeling in its sentimentality (or perhaps the opposite, for cynical listeners). The song's pastiche qualities heighten when one considers the song in its context either on the British EP or the American LP. On the EP, "Your Mother Should Know" comes between "Magical Mystery Tour" and "I Am the Walrus," and on the LP it comes between "Blue Jay Way" and "I Am the Walrus." In both cases, McCartney's pastiche is sandwiched between two psychedelic songs brimming with experimentation (musically and lyrically), rendering it as earnest and sincere, and clearly *not* of its time. If a pastiche piece should offer commentary on what it imitates, "Your Mother Should Know" serves to remind listeners of the Beatles' interest in and love of popular song, which existed long before the wooly psychedelic days of Summer 1967.

"Honey Pie"

Yet still another interpretation of McCartney's use of pastiche is available in relation to "Your Mother Should Know," "When I'm Sixty-Four," and other songs about to be discussed. Could McCartney be assuming the role of a character, perhaps resembling one of the old stars in Sondheim's *Follies*, in order to look back on a "golden" era? If so, what was he trying to say about those earlier times, especially those before his birth? I have chosen 1968's "Honey Pie" to serve as a model for several of the next section's excursions into McCartney's first decade as a solo artist and to act as a formative song for the blending of music, lyrics, and performance techniques. "Honey Pie" from *The Beatles*, first appeared as a demo on the Esher sessions recorded at George Harrison's house in May 1968. The song represents McCartney's attempt to write a Fred Astaire song. In his recent book *The Lyrics: 1956 to the Present*, McCartney explains that "Fred [Astaire] is a bit of an inspiration to me, and sometimes, when I'm thinking, I'll pretend to be him to get that 'little' voice .... I was definitely thinking of Fred and the whole world of the silver screen when I was writing 'Honey Pie'" (McCartney 2021, 299).

"Honey Pie" asks the listener to decide whether to take the song seriously on its own merits, or to hear it as a pastiche. Critical opinion has faced this challenge as well, as opinion about "Honey Pie" is mixed. Ian MacDonald points out the song's "consummate writing and performing pastiche," but then bemoans its "air of faintly smarmy pointlessness" (MacDonald 2005, 320). Walter Everett calls the song "McCartney's compulsively obligatory vaudeville number" that (somewhat less positively) "blatantly attempted to recapture the sound of the 1920s" (Everett 1999, 189). And John Lennon laughed and shared that he "[didn't] even want to think about that" when the interviewer brought up songwriter credits for "Honey Pie" during his *Playboy* interview in 1980. Yet the song works so well *as* a pastiche because the music, lyrics, and performance are done at such a competent level.

"Honey Pie" reflects the definition of pastiche from the *Oxford Dictionary of Music*: an "imitation ... a work deliberately written in the style of another period or manner" (Kennedy, Kennedy, Rutherford-Johnson 2012). In the case of this *White Album* song, that period is the 1920s. The grandiose, dramatic introduction of "Honey Pie" recalls the verse section of popular songs often forgotten or not used in typical performances (i.e., only the chorus is normally performed) but which serves to set the stage for the story ahead. Because Astaire was on McCartney's mind for inspiration, let us consider Astaire's other chart-topping hit from 1932, his take on Cole Porter's "Night and Day." That classic song begins with a verse, which is perhaps better viewed as an introduction, sometimes excised from recordings; its first line includes onomatopoeia, "Like the beat, beat, beat of the tom tom," followed by other similarly constructed lyrical schemes that provide examples of the persistent thought of a lover embodied by a ticking clock, raindrops, and a voice repeating "you"; these examples then lead to the title of the song (and the beginning of the chorus), which conflates the images of the title, "Night and Day." As in "Night and Day," the lyrics in "Honey Pie" begin with concrete images about a character, tell the listener key facts, and then pause to begin the song proper.

Also like "Night and Day," "Honey Pie" begins with a rubato introduction that introduces the main character, a "working girl" from the North of England. Accompanied only by freely played piano and guitar, McCartney speak-sings the introduction, and subjects his voice to studio technology to evoke a scratchy phonograph record with his announcement about the girl hitting "the big time." The drama heightens at the end of the introduction when the tempo slows with each word deliberately enunciated and pronounced for effect. The chord progression also leads to a *caesura* (break or pause) on a prolonged dominant chord, creating the need for a resolution in the lyric, "This is what I'd say," which requires the music to continue.

After the introduction, other pastiche elements emerge in lyrics and music. The song title, "Honey Pie," is a term of endearment from past eras and specifically evokes vaudeville, a comedic, theatrical genre combined with music popular in the 1920s. McCartney's lyrics tell the story of a man whose girlfriend, an actress, has found success and even fame in America—but he wants her to return home (presumably England). The speaker is lazy, however, and does not want to go after her, so he waits for her return. The turns of phrase and journalistic style are effective in portraying different scenarios and images, in a way more sophisticated than many comparable songs that limit the focus to love. Instead, "Honey Pie" involves a rags-to-riches story, referencing the movies and Hollywood and immigration, boat ride to and from America (McCartney cleverly notes the ability of the wind to send the woman's boat back and forth across the ocean). Save for the endearing nickname, the lyrics outline a love story and exhibit less pastiche influence, whereas the performance style and music display more pastiche traits.

How does McCartney create a pastiche in the recording and musical performance of "Honey Pie" and his other Beatles pastiches? Most often, it is a result of collaborations between McCartney and George Martin on the musical arrangements. First, McCartney's vocal style is carefree and loose, with some slight swoops and slides around the pitch, as if singing live in a dance hall swept up by the motion of the music (like Astaire in "Cheek to Cheek"). He includes some syllabic vocalizing in unison with the instrumental lines at the end in falsetto, ending in a high range befitting the conclusion. The instrumentation of "Honey Pie," with McCartney on piano, Harrison on bass, Starr on drums, and Lennon on lead guitar with additional woodwinds (saxophones and clarinets), displays a swing tempo and feel, with accents on two and four. The regular, metrical performance by the guitar and drums (played with style-appropriate brushes) suggests the 1920s in their sound, even supported by rhythmic "hits" that clearly imitate the style (i.e., when McCartney sings "ti-ti-ti"). Martin, familiar with American and British popular song having scored many arrangements for artists like Matt Munro and others, orchestrated the woodwinds with gestures that came right out of a 1920s jazz band and accentuated McCartney's musical conception. Although the critical reception (noted earlier) was mixed, "Honey Pie" is highly effective—as a song *and* a pastiche.

But what of the criticism, or at the very least the observation, that McCartney was playing a character in "Honey Pie"? As Everett argues, "If the song remains light and fluffy, it is more than well-crafted and authentic in all of its elements; the words have just the right tone and engender a warm nostalgia—despite the composer's staged distance—as surely as does "When I'm Sixty-Four." (Everett 1999, 190). Or, as McCartney defends "Honey Pie," "It's not a parody, it's a nod to the vaudeville tradition that I was raised on" (Miles 1997, 497).

Further refining the definition of pastiche, Dyer states something "works as pastiche if you know what it is imitating," and "it facilitates an experience of the imitated work" (Dyer 2007, 60). In this case, familiarity with musical styles and lyrical topics of the 1920s enhances appreciation of the obvious and subtle touches in the song. Moreover, it provides an entry into what a 1920s vaudeville song sounded like, and McCartney achieves this through expert attention to detail.

But if the composer playing a character, is he "distant," or are we truly meant to be transported to the 1920s? I would argue the opposite on both counts supported by the song's context. First, this song was released in 1968 on a Beatles album rife with a panoply of diverse styles and kinds of songs, from the electronic music of "Revolution 9" to song snippets like "Why Don't We Do It in the Road" to surf music ("Back in the USSR") to folk songs McCartney has attached a political message ("Blackbird"). McCartney's pastiche on "Honey Pie" is clearly intentional, yet one does not forget that he is the singer and composer because precedent for such style songs had been set on earlier albums. We are also not intentionally transported back to the 1920s, but rather approach that time period from the present as though looking through a scrapbook or photo album—or hearing a scratchy record in a bit of nostalgia, hence McCartney's assertion that the song is not a parody but a "nod" to tradition. He is not playing a character, but instead leading an invented one on a nostalgic journey. "Honey Pie" may not appeal to every listener, but it does evince smiles and chuckles at the "McCartneyisms" expected by 1968, reaffirming his love for older styles of music and his unabashed (and unparalleled) ability to comment upon works of the past.

McCartney's Solo Pastiches (1970–79)

"Suicide"

With "Honey Pie" as a foundational McCartney pastiche, let us turn to a chronological analysis of songs from his early solo and Wings period that further this genre. The song "Suicide," briefly excerpted on McCartney's first solo album *McCartney* (1970) after the song "Hot as Sun/Glasses," received its first official release in the McCartney Archive series in 2011. Despite its peculiar title (for the ever-optimistic McCartney), this song has a fascinating history that further displays McCartney's passion for pastiche, as well as his ironic sense of humor. Originally written as a teenager, again highlighting McCartney's lifelong fascination with early popular song, "Suicide" was performed briefly during the Beatles' "Get Back" sessions (in a particularly hammy version with vocal accompaniment from Lennon) but was first performed as a more complete demo during the *One Hand Clapping* sessions in 1974 (Perasi 2013, 21). McCartney filled out the song further in 1977 and performed it yet again on the Parkinson TV show in 1999. What makes McCartney return to "Suicide" throughout his career, and what makes it a pastiche? Could it be that McCartney keeps trying to make it into a successful song, or that he loves the song and sees it as a fun set piece?

"Suicide" is a pastiche partly because of its genesis and the story surrounding it, and partly because of the music and lyrics. McCartney recalled that when he was a teenager writing songs like "When I'm Sixty-Four," he wrote another one as a "bit Rat Pack, smoochy, with words like 'When she tries to, run away, uh-huh ...' Boom! And stabs from the band, y'know?'" (Du Noyer 2015, 194). That song turned out to be "Suicide" and was intended for Frank Sinatra, written in a Vegas style, over the top in both lyrics and music. The gist of the story is Sinatra once requested a song from McCartney, and he suggested "Suicide," which did not entice the crooner as intended; Sinatra thought McCartney was "taking the piss" (i.e., mocking or joking about him), and did not record it (Du Noyer 2015, 195). But this story also highlights McCartney's love of Sinatra's music, and if the song had different lyrics, it may have been a hit for Ol' Blue Eyes.

Lyrically, the humor (such as it is) of "Suicide" resides first in the absurdity of the title, which is a metaphor for the speaker's view of unbalanced behavior in a relationship. Lyrics in the first verse illuminate the pitfalls of the man not being a good partner, where "suicide" is the expected outcome (i.e., a breakup, or death of the relationship). Moreover, with the title word being used in such a nonchalant manner, sung in an exaggerated fashion as a normal word in the chorus and bridge, McCartney disarms and steers listeners away from the literal meaning of the word.[6] The dark humor, in which a serious topic becomes humorous through sound, is echoed in other McCartney songs, such as "Maxwell's Silver Hammer." Apart from the constant use of the word in the song's title, the rest of the lyrics cobble together various nonsensical images and scenarios (e.g., riding in a parade) that depict the foibles of love.

---

[6] This is not the first time McCartney used "suicide" in a song; in "That Means a Lot," an unreleased Beatles song from the *Help!* sessions, the bridge starts with the lyric "love can be suicide."

Whereas the lyrics adopt a dark humor that clearly turned off Sinatra, the music of "Suicide" is wonderfully evocative of early Sinatra swing music, notably arranged by Nelson Riddle. One example is the song "Saturday Night (is the Loneliest Night of the Week)" by Sammy Cahn and Jule Styne, first recorded by Sinatra in 1950, rerecorded with Riddle in 1959. A staple of Sinatra's Vegas shows, "Saturday Night" features many of the same musical traits as "Suicide." McCartney's imitation starts with a rubato section in which he sets the tone of the song, with a combination of jazz chords and progressions befitting popular song (e.g., II-V-I, half-diminished chords). On top of the music, McCartney vocalizes in a scat-like style, with "doo-de-doo-de-doo" syllables that center around his smooth middle register. "Suicide" adopts a regular tempo at the first verse, and then locks into a swinging quarter-note pulse. Though much slower than many Riddle-arranged Sinatra songs (especially on their earliest collaborations), one can envision a jazz band accompaniment complete with horns punctuating the accents for McCartney's song. The curvy contour of the bass and melodic lines, often moving by step or half-step, accentuates the late-night atmosphere of the song, and recalls cabaret music heard at smoky nightclubs before the advent of rock music. Extending the pastiche idea even further, at the end of each chorus ("I'd call it suicide") McCartney vocalizes with the piano an arpeggiation of diminished chords that slip into a "da da da" motif leading back to the next verse.

In sum, the combination of the slinky chords, the vocalizing, the buildup toward the climax of each chorus (with the refrain containing the title), and McCartney's overly dramatic piano playing all contribute to an effective—and catchy—pastiche of Sinatra's 1950s style. The lyrics, though containing some darkly amusing moments, do strike a sour note and may be responsible for the song's disuse. In contrast to "Honey Pie," which has a charm and evinces smiles with its lyrics and musical inside jokes, "Suicide" falls short of a truly effective pastiche on account of its lyrics. With less problematic lyrics, "Suicide" would have made an effective original composition alongside covers recorded for 2012's *Kisses on the Bottom*, especially since McCartney kept returning to it for many years.

"Gotta Sing, Gotta Dance"

Another "show" or big band number in a similar vein—unreleased and seemingly dropped quickly—is 1973's "Gotta Sing, Gotta Dance" from the *James Paul McCartney* TV special. This song could almost be a sequel to "Suicide," another piano-based song with some cringeworthy lyrics and numerous lyrical and musical gestures plucked out of the big band era. But "Gotta Sing, Gotta Dance" ramps up the pastiche elements to another level with its actual big band arrangement. The song, described by Chip Madinger and Mark Easter as "insufferable," "shtick," and the "lowpoint" of the TV special, was apparently written for model and singer Twiggy, but she never performed it (Madinger and Easter 2000, 180–1).[7] Instead, McCartney and Wings do a full-on dance number complete with choreography intended to evoke the early jazz era.

"Gotta Sing, Gotta Dance" begins with another rubato section, with McCartney speak-singing images and phrases redolent of the past like "stick-in-the-mud," "polish my tonsils," and "put on my dancing shoes." The narrator of the song is "unable" to stop singing and dancing due to numerous interruptions like a train whistle and an ocean liner. The musical arrangement, though elaborate, features an everything-but-the-kitchen-sink approach, with several style changes—a tap-dance routine, an exaggerated cabaret bit, a typical show tune—all mashed together while McCartney dances and acts out each style accordingly. Though the song proper has an attractive melody and harmonic structure befitting a song from the 1920s or 1930s, McCartney's pastiche is less effective in its musical execution because the production swallows the song and emphasizes the abrupt style shifts. Instead of provoking humor, as in "Honey Pie," or even the dark humor of "Suicide," "Gotta Sing, Gotta Dance" ends up more kitsch than pastiche.

"Suicide" and "Gotta Sing, Gotta Dance" are clearly examples of pastiche, but they were excluded from official album releases, so they did not participate chronologically in McCartney's trajectory of recalling earlier genres in his commercial music. The final two songs I will discuss are eminently more successful as pastiches, as songs, and as enduring contributions to the McCartney catalog.

"You Gave Me the Answer"

"You Gave me the Answer," from 1975's *Venus and Mars*, packs some of the same musical, lyrical, and production elements observed in McCartney's pastiches with the Beatles into a compact and attractive composition that became a key

---

[7] Twiggy did release an album of standards called *Gotta Sing, Gotta Dance* in 2009, but oddly the McCartney song does not appear on it.

number in Wings' live shows during 1975–76. The inclusion of "You Gave Me the Answer" on *Venus and Mars* and in concerts suggests that McCartney felt comfortable including a tribute to the 1920s–30s alongside rock numbers like "Rockshow" or "Listen to What the Man Said." In addition, he thought highly enough of the song to feature it on the "B" side of the "Letting Go" single, presenting a contrasting pair. Moreover, McCartney made his debt to Fred Astaire apparent since Astaire was the dedicatee in concerts; the instrumentation could have been lifted from one of his records, and McCartney's vocal timbre even mimics Astaire's vocal quality throughout with its sound processing.

Considering "You Gave Me the Answer" in the context of its release, one may again wonder why McCartney recorded such a song at this time, in 1975. Perhaps he was thinking of his father Jim, who was in ill health (and would die in 1976) and wanted to pen a tribute to the music he heard growing up. In many ways, "You Gave Me the Answer" can be heard as a sequel to "Honey Pie" in its lyrical and musical content, as well as the overt Astaire inspiration. The lyrics are straightforward and charming, with an elegant sheen depicted in lines that refer to a crowning by the aristocracy, having tea, and mutual love and respect between the characters. McCartney also intersperses amusing spoken directions and remarks in the instrumental break like "shall we dance?" and "this is fun." The musical arrangement is particularly authentic to the period, featuring muted trumpets, clarinets, and a striking bassoon solo performed in unison with McCartney's vocalizations. The song is even cast as a quick two-step similar to Astaire songs like "I'm Putting All My Eggs in One Basket." McCartney has not indicated if he modeled his Astaire pastiches on particular songs, but it is clear he knows the style well and can pinpoint and highlight all the traits necessary to perform a set piece. This pastiche works well because it is both an imitation and an update of the older style, and McCartney's acute attention to detail results in a charming and humorous composition that plays up his most enduring attributes like positivity and hope.

"Baby's Request"

One final composition, "Baby's Request" from 1979's *Back to The Egg*, is the last pre-rock pastiche McCartney recorded for some time, and for that reason serves as a capstone and culmination to the genre that would only reappear on 2011's *Kisses on the Bottom*. "Baby's Request" was originally conceived as a song for the Mills Brothers after McCartney heard them while vacationing in France in the late 1970s. The Mills Brothers were a vocal quartet especially popular in both the United States and UK during the Second World War, but they still performed into the 1980s as an oldies act. A misunderstanding ensued when the group expected McCartney to pay them to record the song, which he did not do (Benitez 2010, 95). Even so, the Mills Brothers were a suitable inspiration for "Baby's Request," which shares similarities to some of their hits like "Till Then" (1944) and "Nevertheless (I'm In Love With You)" (1950).

"Baby's Request" also has a promotional video that indicates some idea of the effect McCartney envisioned for the song. Filmed in Camber Sands, a beach in East Sussex (South East England), the video depicts a wartime regiment complete with a NAAFI (Navy, Army, and Air Force Institute) "Refreshment Van." The uniformed soldiers rest, while listening to a band—the members of Wings—performing on a makeshift stage. The scene is a throwback to a mellow beach-party movies of the early 1960s, especially since some of the bandmembers (sans Macca) are not playing their normal instruments (e.g., Linda McCartney is "playing" bass). Paul then emerges from a car and starts singing after Laurence Juber's improvised jazzy guitar introduction. Not much else happens in the video other than a straight performance and McCartney miming and strolling around the stage and audience area. But by setting the video in wartime, McCartney ties the song to its intended performers (The Mills Brothers) and situates the music during the Second World War when that song style was popular. On another level, the song also evokes the Beatles' 1950s and 1960s with romantic beach songs sung in the movies (think of Elvis). The retro visual experience of the video heightens the pastiche, as the viewer understands what styles are suggested.

As for the music and lyrics of "Baby's Request," McCartney made a statement by including a discernable pastiche as the last track on a largely rock (and even punk at times) album, again stressing his musical diversity and ability to shift from style to style. As Perasi describes the song, "Baby's Request" is a "little gem with alluring images and the old times atmosphere of a small night club" (Perasi 2013, 185). One of those "alluring images" begins the song, painting an impressionistic scene about the moon and stars going to sleep. McCartney's speaker is at a club listening to a band late at night (as depicted . in the first lines), and keeps asking the band to play the couple's favorite song (hence the title, "Baby's Request"). This song must be an old one, as the speaker mentions having heard the song before, but now the couple's life situation is different (e.g., they are empty nesters). Once again, McCartney sets up a nostalgic scenario in the lyrics, which are analogous to the Mills Brothers' songs mentioned earlier; "Till Then," for example, is a song of romantic longing (similar to "Honey Pie," with its references to "oceans we must cross") and steeped in nostalgic language yearning for better days.

Like the backward-looking lyrics, the music and instrumentation of "Baby's Request" are nostalgic too, with the jazzy electric guitar flourishes and slow swing feel. In addition, the song's structure displays a sophistication found in popular song composition contemporaneous to the time the song imagines. "Baby's Request" is written in an AABA form (with intro, solo, and outro) like other McCartney pastiches; the chord progressions contain myriad chords more associated with jazz than rock (e.g., strings of seventh chords and chromatic passing tones) and the vocal melody is soaring and wide, over an octave. In other words, "Baby's Request" would have been perfect for either a crooner like Bing Crosby or Fred Astaire, or for the rich vocal harmonies of the Mills Brothers. Instead of adding humorous touches like vocal asides and clear references to what was dated language at the time of writing, "Baby's Request" sounds like a serious attempt at writing a pre-war popular song that indicates McCartney's full growth as a pastiche writer. In lieu of either using dark humor that a listener (even Sinatra!) may not understand (i.e., "Suicide") or writing an over-the-top set piece (i.e., "Gotta Sing, Gotta Dance"), McCartney owns his predilection for memorializing the past, which is now his own past. "Baby's Request" is a highly effective pastiche song that closes *Back to the Egg*, which also marks the end of the band Wings, with elegance at the close of the 1970s.

Conclusion

This examination of Paul McCartney's pastiches reveals several salient factors related to his development as a composer and performer. First, his love of pre-war popular song has been a recurring lifelong interest, beginning with "When I'm Sixty-Four" and "Suicide" written as a teenager, performances of "Till There Was You" and originals like "Honey Pie" in the Beatles, and culminating in songs throughout the 1970s with Wings that showcased his compositional prowess. Second, these pastiches show an increased sophistication and attention to detail (i.e., "You Gave Me the Answer," "Baby's Request"), and a confidence in his material to place these songs on rock albums and even release them as singles.

No doubt McCartney was aware of the brickbats he might get thrown at him for his "granny music shit," but he forged ahead and released them anyway.[8] We must also consider how these songs work as pastiches, as imitations of previous styles, and in what ways they communicate with the past. Delving into songs by influences McCartney has identified as significant to his own development (e.g., Sinatra, Astaire) sheds light on how he may have modeled the pastiches, whether on specific songs or by showcasing general performance traits. In this way, we gain insight into how McCartney's influences shaped his songwriting, whether through vocal histrionics (i.e., Little Richard) or his affection for music of the past (rock or popular song). And finally, to the point of this collection, these pastiches demonstrate different types of humor perhaps not always associated with McCartney. His humor is not uproarious or cutting, but rather witty, urbane, and for those who understand the models used for pastiche, inside jokes that illuminate his musical (and sometimes lyrical) sophistication.

Leonard B. Meyer writes that "A knowledge of style is indispensable for criticism because ... to appreciate fully what something *is*—to comprehend its significance—is to have some notion (however informal or unformulated) about what it *might have been* .... The road actually taken is invariably understood partly in terms of those not taken" (Meyer 1989, 31–2). In McCartney's pastiches, he takes the road of writing updated, stylized songs designed to pay tribute to or hearken back to an earlier age, instead of making mere allusions to the past by reciting names of past artists in lyrics or referring to older acts merely in interviews. McCartney's pastiches are snapshots of his musical and historical mind at specific points in time, thus allowing us to understand more deeply his rich musical legacy.

References

Benitez, Vincent P. 2010. *The Words and Music of Paul McCartney: The Solo Years*. Santa Barbara, CA: Prager.

Du Noyer, Paul. 2015. *Conversations with McCartney*. New York: Overlook Press.

Dyer, Richard. 2007. *Pastiche*. London: Routledge.

Emerick, Geoff. 2006. *Here, There, and Everywhere: My Life Recording the Beatles*. New York: Gotham Books.

---

[8] Comment made by Lennon as noted in Geoff Emerick, *Here, There, and Everywhere: My Life Recording the Beatles*. (New York: Gotham Books, 2006), 246.

Everett, Walter. 1999. *The Beatles as Musicians:* Revolver *through the* Anthology. Oxford: Oxford University Press.

Everett, Walter. 2001. *The Beatles as Musicians: The Quarry Men through* Rubber Soul. Oxford: Oxford University Press.

Hoesterey, Ingeborg. 2001. *Pastiche*. Bloomington: Indiana University Press.

Jameson, Frederic. 1993. *Postmodernism, or, The Cultural Logic of Late Capitalism*. London: Verso.

Kennedy, Joyce, Michael Kennedy, and Tim Rutherford-Johnson, eds., 2012. *The Oxford Dictionary of Music*.

MacDonald, Ian. 2005. *Revolution in the Head: The Beatles' Records and the Sixties*. Chicago: Chicago Review Press.

Madinger, Chip and Easter, Mark. 2000. *Eight Arms to Hold You: The Solo Beatles Compendium*. 44.1 Productions.

McCartney, Paul. 2021. *The Lyrics: 1956 to the Present*. New York: Liveright.

McCartney, Paul and Miles, Barry. 1997. *Many Years from Now*. New York: Henry Holt.

Meyer, Leonard B. 1989. *Style and Music: Theory, History, and Ideology*. Philadelphia: University of Pennsylvania Press.

Perasi, Luca. 2013. *Paul McCartney: Recording Sessions (1969–2013)*. Milan, Italy: L.I.L.Y. Publishing.

Sondheim, Stephen. 2010. *Finishing the Hat*. New York: Knopf.

Taruskin, Richard. 2009. "Mahler: Maximalizing the Symphony." In *Music in the Early Twentieth Century*. New York: Oxford University Press.

Thurmaier, David. 2016. "George Harrison and the Influence of Popular Song." In *New Critical Perspectives on the Beatles*, edited by Kenneth Womack and Katie Kapurch. New York: Palgrave Macmillan. 139–55.

Walter White, Eric. 1985. Stravinsky: The Composer and His Works. Berkeley: University of California Press.

7

"I Was So Young When I Was Born": George Harrison and the Mansion of Mirth

John Covach

The nineteenth-century Indian spiritual teacher Ramakrishna once remarked: "The jnani says: 'This world is a "framework of illusion." But he who is beyond knowledge and ignorance describes it as a mansion of mirth'" (M 1942, 523).[1] Some eighty years later, an American reporter asked the Beatles: "Are you going to get a haircut at all while you're here?" John Lennon, Paul McCartney, and Ringo Starr answered together: "No!" George Harrison then piped in: "I had one yesterday" (Badman 2000, 81).[2] At first glance, there is no reason to interpret Harrison's quick response to a reporter's question as having much to do with Indian thought or spirituality. The Beatles were, of course, well-known for their quick wit and comedic outbursts and Harrison was no exception in this regard. Graeme Thomson observes that "Harrison gravitated toward a very English kind of humorous eccentricity designed to undercut the pomp and prattle of authority figures," noting that George was a fan of the *Goon Show* and later loved *Monty Python's Flying Circus* from the time it debuted in 1969. (Thomson 2013, 316).[3] Beatles producer George Martin was fond of recounting how, in response to advising the group at a 1962 recording session that if there was something they didn't like they should tell him, Harrison quipped: "Well, for a start, I don't like your tie." Martin writes that he soon learned that this "was typical Beatles humour" (Martin 1979, 126).

---

[1] Cited by Kinsley 1974–5, 116. This remark is dated September 14, 1884.
[2] This press conference was held in New York on February 7, 1964. Badman does not transcribe John, Paul, and Ringo answering "no," but this is clearly audible in video of the event, widely available on the internet.
[3] Bill Harry notes that both Harrison and Lennon were admirers of well-known English performer George Formby, whose songs often featured humorous lyrics (Harry 2003, 179). Harrison claims that "he wasn't that much of an influence on me," though there are accounts describing how much he loved the Formby songs. See Kahn (2020, 511–13) and Thomson (2013, pp. 333, 376, and 383).

There is, however, an element of detachment in Harrison's joking that perhaps sets it apart from his bandmates. In the case of the 1964 press conference, Harrison seems immediately to identify the hostility in the question and defeats this mild attack by ignoring its obvious criticism: he answers as if the reporter is earnestly asking him about his last haircut and not commenting disapprovingly on his hairstyle. His remark to Martin similarly takes Martin's remark literally while gently testing, as Thomson suggests, any assertion of authority or control. In both cases, Harrison quickly sizes up the situation and, rather than reacting with anger or irritation, responds playfully. Harrison would not be exposed to Indian philosophy until 1965 and would not begin to study it in depth until late 1966. But these early instances suggest that Indian ideas of detachment from the material world, and in this case that such detachment could take the form of playfulness, would find a welcome resonance in Harrison's personality when he became seriously engaged with the Vedic tradition in the late 1960s, and especially in the 1970s and 1980s.

This chapter will explore the role of humor in Harrison's music with an emphasis on the role of playfulness. Along with songs devoted to innocent romance ("You Like Me Too Much," "I Need You," "I Want to Tell You"), Harrison was certainly capable of writing angry, dismissive, accusatory, and impatient lyrics, beginning with "Don't Bother Me" (impatient) and continuing through "Think for Yourself" (angry, accusatory), and "If I Needed Someone" (dismissive). The lyrics of "Love You To" are even accusatory and focused on concerns of the material world in spite of the track's use of Indian musical elements.[4] These songs, however, are all from the first few years of Harrison's songwriting (1963–66). With "Taxman" (1966), Harrison's writing—at least in some of his songs—initiates a turn toward detached playfulness and this playfulness extends through the remainder of Harrison's career, becoming an important element in his writing during his years as a solo artist. In addition, Harrison's playfulness extends beyond the lyrics and is a factor in the musical dimensions of his work, depending for its effectiveness on the listener's ability to detect incongruities of musical style and content that can be either coordinated

---

[4] Susan Shumsky (2022, 78) provides an interesting interpretation of these lyrics in terms of Indian philosophy, though it seems unlikely Harrison had studied Indian spirituality in great depth at the time this song was recorded (April 1966); his knowledge of Indian *music* was much more advanced during this period, with his added focus on the *philosophy* coming later in 1966. In this sense, the lyrics to "Love You To" are much more akin to those of "Think for Yourself" from *Rubber Soul* (1965) than to those of "Within You Without You" from *Sgt. Pepper* (1967). For a detailed consideration of Harrison's engagement with both Indian music and spirituality, primarily during the Beatles years, see Covach (2023).

with the lyrics or independent of them. And when Harrison begins to produce music videos to support his singles in the 1970s, playful humor is often a central element in the video dimension, even at times when there is nothing particularly humorous in the lyrics or music.

Līlā in Indian Philosophy

Humor and playfulness had been a part of the Beatles' experience with Indian philosophy almost from the beginning. Reflecting on meeting the Maharishi Mahesh Yogi in 1967, Paul McCartney remarks that they "saw that Maharishi was on one of his voyages round the world ... There he was, just a giggling little swami who was going around the world to promote peace ... So when he came around again and somebody said there was a meeting, we all went. 'Oh, that's that giggly little guy. We've seen him. He's great'" (Miles 1997, 400).[5] This dimension of Indian spirituality would have a marked effect on Harrison. In his overview of play in Hindu spirituality, David R. Kinsley writes that "an important theme in Hindu philosophy and mythology is *līlā*, the idea of divine sport, play, or dalliance. In the mythology of nearly every major Hindu deity it is explicitly stated or implicitly suggested that play is an important or essential aspect of divine activity" (1974–5, 108). Kinsley goes on to emphasize the role of *līlā* in divine creation: the world arises not out of necessity nor as a result of any form of causation, but rather as a "divine reflex or divine amusement" (Kinsley, 109). William S. Sax writes, "the idea is that God's creation of the world is motivated not by any desire or lack but rather by a free and spontaneous activity" (Sax 1995, 4).[6] While the finer points in such theological consideration are central to Kinsley's and Sax's concerns, for this chapter it is enough to note the centrality and ubiquity of the idea of playfulness in Hindu thought; no serious student of Indian philosophy and culture could be unaware of it, and Harrison was a dedicated follower of this tradition, at least after 1966. Further, there is the idea, as expressed in the Ramakrishna remark cited above, that for the enlightened person—someone who has realized a oneness

---

[5] See Shumsky (2022, 141–7), for a discussion of the relationship between McCartney's "Fool on the Hill" and the Maharishi Mahesh Yogi. This discussion appears in a chapter entitled "The Giggling Guru."

[6] Sax (1995) provides a collection of essays devoted to a wide variety of instances of *līlā* in South Asian philosophy, spirituality, devotional practices, and drama. See also Dimock (1989).

with Brahman—the entire material world is a kind of divine amusement, a "mansion of mirth."[7] The enlightened master understands the world around him as a vast panoply of cosmic playfulness. Strangely enough, this is the point at which Indian philosophy and *Monty Python's Flying Circus* meet—a place where *A Hard Day's Night* and Ramakrishna find significant common cause.[8] As Sax puts it, "God is playful" (Sax 1995, 3) and as Ananda K. Coomaraswamy summarizes, "the best and most God-like way of living is to 'play the game'" (Coomaraswamy 1941, 98–9).

As suggested above, "Taxman" provides a good starting point for considering the use of humor in Harrison's music. The song is clearly critical of the British government, but the lyrics are not so much angry as humorous, poking fun at the tax laws and political leaders.[9] These lyrics turn especially playful during the central bridge section in which the words "street," "seat," "heat," and "feet" are rhymed as line endings. These lines start out sensibly enough: if one drives a car, one can expect to pay taxes on the roads ("street"). But if one even tries to sit down, they can expect a tax on the "seat." It is typical to pay taxes on the "heat" one uses, but who can imagine paying taxes on their own "feet"? What makes these lyrics so playful is that they participate in a kind of songwriting game in which the listener comes to understand, as the song unfolds, that each line must end with the same rhyme but at the same time that the sense of the lyrics must be maintained. Among American songwriters of the first half of the twentieth century, Cole Porter was certainly one of the many who delighted in such wordplay; his "Where Is the Life That Late I Led" from the 1948 musical *Kiss Me Kate*, for instance, provides a ready example of this particular rhyming game: the rhyming syllables change but the game extends across two lengthy verses, rhyming "Becky-weckio" with the "Ponte Vecchio" and "Fedora, the wild Virago" with her "gangster sister from Chicago," among others. A more likely direct influence on the Beatles, however, would have been the Coasters' 1961 single "Little Egypt." The Beatles were great fans of the Coasters and they likely knew the record. Written by Jerry Leiber and Mike Stoller, "Little Egypt"

---

[7] In his discussion of this point, Heinrich Zimmer (1951, 571) cites another passage from Ramakrishna: "This very world is a mansion of mirth: Here I can eat, here drink, and make merry" (M 1942, 139).
[8] It is worth noting that the film *Help!* presents a woefully caricatured image of Indian spiritual practice, including human sacrifice, to comedic ends. Strangely enough, had it not been for this theme in that film—no matter how stereotyped and false—Harrison might never have come to embrace Indian music and thought. See Covach (2023) for a fuller discussion.
[9] Harrison (2017, 90) notes that the song was written when he realized he was giving most of his money away in taxes. John Lennon remarks that he "threw in a few one-liners" when Harrison asked for help with the song (Sheff 1981, 134).

employs words that rhyme with "show" at the end of each line in its three verses. As the lyrics unfold, the playfulness of telling the story of a belly dancer who eventually ends up as a housewife, while simultaneously maintaining the same end rhyme, is central to the humor.[10] However much one might be tempted to view the "Taxman" lyrics as angry, this comedic bridge section seems to defeat such an interpretation. It is the best early example of Harrison's songwriting playfulness. Though written before he had any significant exposure to Indian philosophy, it reflects the fundamental spirit of *lila*: play in the world around us.

Like "Taxman," "Savoy Truffle" offers another instance of humorous lyrics, though in this case the songwriting "game" is very different. Appearing on *The Beatles*, "Savoy Truffle" takes its lyrics from a chocolates box, motivated by Eric Clapton's cavities and love of candy. As early as "Tomorrow Never Knows" (1966), John Lennon had used preexistent or "found" texts as the basis for his lyrics, in this case paraphrasing from Timothy Leary's *The Psychedelic Experience* (Leary, Metzger, Alpert 1964). Lennon would later use a circus poster as the basis for the lyrics to "Being for the Benefit of Mr. Kite" and a daily newspaper for his verses in "A Day in the Life," both songs appearing in 1967 on *Sgt. Pepper's Lonely Hearts Club Band*. Harrison would first use a preexistent text by lifting passages from the *Tao Te Ching* for the lyrics to his "The Inner Light" in early 1968. By the time Harrison got to "Savoy Truffle," then, the use of preexistent texts for lyrics was an established practice within the Beatles. The previous uses of this practice by Lennon and Harrison, however, had not engaged humor in any way; the difference in "Savoy Truffle" was the addition of the playfulness element. Clapton loves chocolates but eating them causes him pain; Harrison gently teases him with the names of various kinds of candy found in the box, noting that the Savoy Truffle is the most dangerous of the bunch.

Humor and Listener Competency

During the same period in which Harrison wrote "Taxman" he also wrote two other songs with playful lyrics: "Piggies," which would appear on *The Beatles* in 1968, and "It's Only a Northern Song," which was proposed for *Sgt. Pepper* but rejected, ultimately appearing on the *Yellow Submarine* soundtrack in 1969.

---

[10] The story line in McCartney's "Ob-La-Di, Ob-La-Da" from *The Beatles* may also owe something to "Little Egypt." Molly, a singer with the band, eventually ends up married, a homemaker and mother.

In the case of these two songs, the humor in the lyrics is reinforced by humor in the music itself. In "Piggies," Harrison casts the upper class as pigs who are willing to eat their own, a dark theme made somewhat lighter by the humor in the characterizations ("in their starched white shirts," etc.) and the exaggerated choral singing on the last verse, not to mention the pig snorting sounds used throughout.[11] The music employs a chamber ensemble of strings with harpsichord—instrumentation meant to suggest a high-society gathering—and passages that imitate the style of high-brow eighteenth-century classical music. "Only a Northern Song," by contrast, is a song about being a (not very good) song.[12] The lyrics detail certain musical aspects that might sound like mistakes—the "chords are going wrong" and the "words are not quite right." As these lyrics unfold, elements in the musical accompaniment also sound like mistakes: consider the solo brass instruments in the first two verses, for example, or the cacophonous instrumental passage after the bridge—all clearly "wrong" musical elements that then permeate the remainder of the track. If "Taxman" set its sights on the government and "Piggies" zeroed in on the upper classes, "Only a Northern Song" makes the songwriter and the band the target, offering a track full of unlikely clams and wrong notes.[13] Taken together, this trio of songs constitute the beginning of a string Harrison songs that engage humor and playfulness that would extend well into his post-Beatles solo career.[14]

In the case of "Piggies" and "Only a Northern Song," the humor depends partly on the lyrics and partly on the listener's ability to detect certain musical elements. In "Piggies" the listener needs to be able to identify the classical music references to appreciate the full comedic effect, which lies in the ironic use of this musical style. In "Only a Northern Song," she must detect the elements that sound wrong musically within a single style. This kind of ability to detect both

---

[11] Harrison (2017, 124) describes the song as "a social comment" and is at pains to point out that the word "piggies" here has no relationship to the derogatory use the term to refer to police. See also Kahn (2020, 425), where he reinforces this distinction. Jonathan Gould (2007, 524) suggests a connection to George Orwell's *Animal Farm*.

[12] Harrison remarks that the song is a joke "relating to Liverpool," but also refers to the song's publisher, Northern Songs Ltd., "which I don't own" (2017, 96). In 1968 Harrison would move his publishing to his own company, Harrisongs.

[13] Ian Inglis considers "Only a Northern Song" to be the Beatles' first postmodern song while also claiming that "Harrison's lyrics mock both the listener and himself" (2010, 10)—an interpretation that perhaps privileges bitterness over playfulness.

[14] Another trio of songs from about the same time mark Harrison's first sustained engagement with Indian music: "Love You To" (1966), "Within You Without You" (1967), and "The Inner Light" (1966). Of these, only "Within You Without You" employs original lyrics dealing with Indian spirituality. The other two songs are discussed elsewhere in this chapter. For a fuller discussion of Harrison's songs from the Beatles years, see Covach (2017).

congruities and incongruities of musical style and content is often referred to as "stylistic competency" and these skills are central in how the music itself can participate in the humor, either in conjunction with the lyrics or separately.[15] "Blue Jay Way" from *Magical Mystery Tour* offers another instance of incongruity, in this case between the lyrics and the music. The lyrics offer a straightforward narration of someone waiting for friends to arrive after they have been delayed en route and the humor resides in the banality of the lyrics. The music, however, includes an Indian-influenced drone, drums, a swirling, somewhat psychedelic organ, melodic interjections on cello, and a sometimes-menacing vocal melody with Leslie-modulated background vocals, all without a hint of humor. If one perceives humor in the song overall, it is in the playful juxtaposition of these unlikely lyrics with the generally earnest trippiness of the music; if the lyrics were different—perhaps employing some "found" text, for instance—one would not likely guess that there had ever been any humorous aspect to the track.[16] In "Only a Northern Song," the incongruities of lyrics and music work in tandem to elicit an amused response; in "Blue Jay Way" it is the incongruity between the lyrics and music in general, along with the content of the lyrics in general, that create the humor.

Humor in the Solo Music

While the songs on Harrison's first post-Beatles solo album, *All Things Must Pass* (1970), generally do not engage humor, the album does feature two clearly humorous instances, both found on the third LP of this three-record set (sides Five and Six). "It's Johnny's Birthday" is a patently playful and carnivalesque birthday greeting to John Lennon lasting less than a minute. "Thanks for the Pepperoni" is an otherwise non-comedic instrumental jam on a standard 1950s twelve-bar-blues chord progression that borrows its title from a line on a Lenny

---

[15] See Covach (1990; 1995) for fuller discussion of both theories of humor and stylistic competency and how these can be used to elicit a humorous response in listeners.

[16] Gould (2007, 454) describes the song as "darkly funny" and points out that the lyrics "Please don't be long" can also be heard as "Please don't belong"; he sees this second meaning as a "plea for non-attachment" and relates this wordplay to the lyrics of Lennon and McCartney's "It Won't Be Long," in which this shift in meaning is obvious. Inglis (2010, 9–10) takes this second meaning as resonating with "contemporary advice attributed to Timothy Leary—'turn on, tune in, drop out.'" These interpretations seem to allow the earnestness of the music to drive the interpretation of the lyrics—a tendency that tends to diminish the humor, though it does retain an element of playfulness.

Bruce comedy album.[17] The first songs employing humor in Harrison's post-Beatle solo career can be found on his 1973 *Living in the Material World* release. Remarking on the album's second track, "Sue Me, Sue You Blues," Harrison writes: "I wrote it during the big suing period and it's vaguely based on the Square Dance type of fiddle lyric: 'You serve me and I'll serve you/ Swing your partners, all get screwed'" (Harrison 2017, 252). On one level, such lyrics could be understood as expressions of bitterness, and as Harrison points out, they were indeed prompted by bitter legal (and probably at times personal) exchanges. But Harrison takes a step back from all that: instead of emphasizing the anger, he instead invites us to imagine the lawyers as square dancers, going through the steps in a kind of courtroom do-si-do as he plays the role of the square-dance caller. From this perspective, such legal wrangling seems absurd and Harrison seems to delight in the playfulness facilitated by this kind of comic detachment. The cultural incongruity of casting skyscraper-dwelling lawyers as dancers in a rural barn-dance tradition only amplifies the absurdity and adds to the fun. The humor in this song resides primarily in the lyrics. The music supports the lyrics but is not comedic, though if considered in absence of the lyrics, the sing-song melodic quality of the verses might indeed hint at humor.

The main focus of the title track "Living in the Material World" is on the spiritual realization, influenced in part by A.C. Bhaktivedanta Swami Prabhupada, that while we are in these material bodies in the physical world, we are ultimately not these bodies. Harrison also notes that "It's almost a comedy song with a few jokes in case you didn't notice!" (Harrison 2017, 276). As it turns out, the comedy is not so much in the lyrics as it is in how the music "comments" on the lyrics. At 1:12 in the track Harrison begins a verse recounting how he met John and Paul, the band later picking up "Richie" (Ringo) on a tour, and noting that the four became "caught up" in the material world. Harrison himself mentions these particular lyrics as part of the comedy, but taken on their own they seem to chronicle how the Beatles got onto the wrong path, allowing themselves to get sucked into worldly illusion: it is hard to see where the joke is. But as Harrison sings the line about "Richie," the music is briefly interrupted by a Ringo-esque drum fill (1:27–1:30). To match this light-hearted musical interjection, Harrison adds a flute interruption in the parallel structural position in a later verse (4:34–4:36), just after mention of

---

[17] The track is "Religion Inc." from Bruce's 1959 comedy album, *The Sick Humor of Lenny Bruce*. The routine lampoons organized religion and the line "thanks for the pepperoni" occurs as an aside during a telephone call to Italy. Bruce, of course, is among the many figures included on the *Sgt. Pepper* cover along with Indian guru Paramahansa Yogananda and Yogananda's gurus, Babaji, Lahiri Mahasaya, and Sriyukteshwar.

Humor primarily in the lyrics

"Taxman" (1966), "Savoy Truffle" (1968), "Sue Me, Sue You Blues" (1973)

Humor in both the lyrics and music

"Piggies" (1966/1968), "Only a Northern Song" (1966/1968)

Humor primarily in the music

"Living in the Material World" (1973)

Humor in the lyrics, music, and performance

"Miss O'Dell" (1973)

Figure 7.1 Humor in George Harrison songs through 1973.

Krishna, a divine figure often represented playing the flute. If "Sue Me, Sue You Blues" provided an instance of humor created by the lyrics (though supported by the music) in a manner much like "Taxman" and "Savoy Truffle," "Living in the Material World" serves as an example of how the humor can reside primarily in the music, though in immediate interaction with the lyrics.

Harrison recorded several other tracks during his solo years that engage humor, including "His Name Is Legs" from *Extra Texture* (1975) and "Soft Hearted Hana" from *George Harrison* (1979). Perhaps the most delightful of these is "Miss O'Dell," which originally appeared as the B-side to the 1973 single, "Give Me Love (Give Me Peace on Earth)," and was subsequently re-released on the 2006 remastered edition of *Living in the Material World*. The music lightly spoofs Bob Dylan while the lyrics are comically mundane and reminiscent of "Blue Jay Way." Harrison breaks into laughter throughout the track, seemingly barely able to deliver the vocal at times, making the thoroughly playful intent of the song unmistakable. In this case it is not only the lyrics and music that are humorous, but also the performance itself that elicits an amused response. Figure 7.1 summarizes the ways in which an amused response is elicited in the songs discussed above.

Humor in the Music Videos

Video adds a new dimension of playfulness to Harrison's creative expression in 1974 with the release of the promotional video in support of the single "Ding Dong, Ding Dong" from the *Dark Horse* album.[18] This was not the first time a

---

[18] Mike Carrera (n.d.) provides a very useful online collection of Harrison videos with informative commentary.

Harrison song had been presented on video or film, however: "I Need You" had been featured in the 1965 film *Help!*, "Blue Jay Way" had appeared in *Magical Mystery Tour* of 1967, and "Only a Northern Song" had appeared in the 1968 animated film, *Yellow Submarine*. None of these included very much in the way of humor or comedy. Aside from mugging for the camera during "I Need You" (Lennon mostly), a few small details and some comic jumping around reminiscent of *A Hard Day's Night* during "Blue Jay Way," and a healthy portion of psychedelic whimsy during "Only a Northern Song," the visual elements do not elicit much of an amused response.[19] In many ways, the humor in "Ding Dong, Ding Dong" is a continuation and extension of Harrison's previous practice. The song itself is upbeat and optimistic. Engaging the theme of temporality, the song's chorus whimsically employs the melody played by clock towers that ring out the time of day. Like "Savoy Truffle" and "The Inner Light," the lyrics are drawn from a preexistent source, in this case carvings in his Friar Park estate (Harrison 2017, 300). The verses that begin "ring out the old" are drawn from Alfred Lord Tennyson's poem "Ring Out, Wild Bells," published in 1850. In the original handwritten lyrics, Harrison has drawn a guitar and written "Lord Tennyson Ernie Ford," combining the names of the English poet with American country and Western singer Tennessee Ernie Ford (Harrison 2017, 301). In addition to the Tennyson lines Harrison uses in the song, the lines beginning "yesterday today was tomorrow" are also a found text, engraved elsewhere at Friar Park. Harrison was unsure of the original source of these lines, commenting, "maybe Sir Frank Knows?" (2017, 300), referring to the estate's original owner, the eccentric Sir Frankie Crisp. These lines, as Harrison uses them anyway, are more playful than humorous, reflecting the spirit of fun with which the song is saturated.[20] While the song's music and lyrics elicit a mildly humorous response, it is in the video dimension that the primary focus of the humor emerges.

After Harrison appears walking through the forest during the song's introduction, the video cuts (0:24) to him seated, playing a Gibson ES-5 hollow-body electric guitar through a tweed-covered amplifier while wearing a leather

---

[19] The comic details in the "Blue Jay Way" segment include Harrison playing on a keyboard that has been drawn on the ground next to a sign that reads "2 Wives and a Kid to Feed" and a recurring image of a bare male torso with "Magical Mystical Boy" written across it. Harrison delivers the vocal with a serious demeanor throughout, never cracking a smile or even a grin. Harrison also provided music for the 1968 film *Wonderwall*, but as soundtrack music it falls outside of consideration here.

[20] By contrast, Tennyson's full poem was part of *In Memoriam A.H.H*, an elegy to a friend.

jacket with slicked-back hair. This begins the personal history aspect of the video and this shot is meant to suggest the 1950s; the guitar, the amp, and the fashion all align with this period in rock history. At 0:49 the shot changes: now Harrison is wearing an early-era Beatles suit, donning a Beatlemania-era wig, and playing his Rickenbacker electric twelve-string. There is no guitar amp in the shot initially but soon a Fender solid-state amp is shown and a turban-clad man sits to Harrison's right. All of this suggests the mid-1960s. The third version of this shot appears at 1:47: Harrison is clad in his *Sgt. Pepper* outfit holding a baritone horn, his Epiphone Casino is propped up against the Fender amp while the figure behind him to the right is playing sitar. To the right of the shot we can begin to see a large photo of Paramahansa Yogananda and Sriyukteshwar—an image that will eventually move to the center of the shot.[21] This third version suggests 1967. In the fourth version of the shot (2:15) Harrison is playing his red Gibson Les Paul, suggesting the late 1960s. The figure on the right is now wearing what looks like an eye patch over his nose and a new figure is present behind Harrison to his left, wearing a green wig. The Yogananda-Sriyukteswar picture has moved closer to the center of the shot and by the end of the shot is in the center behind Harrison, as his Les Paul is now sitting next to his Casino (with a Fender Stratocaster added to the bunch) while he plays a dobro and sports a green velvet suit and a hat emblazoned with a dollar sign, all suggesting the early 1970s and perhaps also hinting at the Beatles-breakup struggles over money. The fifth version of the shot is similar to the fourth except that now Harrison plays the dobro with a slide until the shot shifts at 2:53 to show him playing a Zemaitis acoustic 12-string and wearing a shirt featuring the Om symbol. There are figures in the background, including the man with the green wig, a pirate, and a figure moving their arms up and down alternately, perhaps suggesting an Indian god. Most of these background figures make their way to the front of the shot at 3:11 (they were also seen at 1:18). Interspersed with these personal history shots there is a sequence of shots in which a pirate flag is replaced with a flag displaying the Om symbol (1:14, 2:34, 3:27). At 1:21 Harrison appears in the Beatles suit standing in front of the Friar Park clock tower, as the camera pans upward to the sky, he is then seen clad in his *Dark Horse* overcoat and furry

[21] Harrison's enthusiasm for Yogananda's *Autobiography of a Yogi* (1998), first published in 1946, has been well documented. See Covach 2023.

boots (1:29) and then at 1:31, wearing only the furry boots with a small acoustic guitar covering his private parts.[22]

The target of the humor in this sequence of shots is Harrison himself—his own musical, professional, and spiritual history. His attention to detail—the particular guitars he plays, the changing fashions and hairstyles, the engagement with Indian music and spirituality—all of these elements are presented in an exacting yet playful manner.[23] He pokes fun at each of the eras of his history as he follows the lyrics' injunction to ring out the old. As the Om flag replaces the pirate flag, he rings in the new. These video images greatly amplify the playful and whimsical quality of the music and lyrics, creating a humor that includes music, lyrics, and text. And of course, the generally broad comedy of the costumes (or lack thereof) and the comic antics of the background figures make the comedic intent abundantly clear. Following Coomaraswamy's characterization, Harrison seems to be fully "playing the game" in the spirit of *līlā*.

Harrison made three videos to support tracks from his 1976 album, *Thirty-Three & 1/3*. The music of "This Song" is upbeat but taken alone gives little indication of comedic intent. Like "Only a Northern Song," the lyrics refer to the song itself, but in this case they arise from Harrison's experience in a copyright infringement claim filed against him over "My Sweet Lord."[24] Clearly meant to elicit an amused response, the lyrics state that they "don't infringe on anyone's copyright" and later that the singer's "expert" tells him "it's okay," among other references to the litigation. In what is probably a Beatles reference (and as such, a playful copyright nod to McCartney), the lyrics state that when it comes to this song we'll "let be," following this by informing us that the song is "in E." A later Beatles reference refers to "Carry That Weight" from *Abbey Road* by wondering if the song's riff could be "one more weight to bear." In a song prompted by a copyright infringement case, then, Harrison chose to reference a string of other songs. Probably taking its cue in part from the courtroom scene in the Rolling Stones' 1967 video for "We Love You"—a video that followed on the heels of legal problems Mick Jagger and Keith Richards were experiencing at the time but that cast the scene as a re-enactment of the Oscar Wilde trial—Harrison's

---

22 As the camera pans upward, one can briefly read the inscription on the theme of time's passing that would be the basis of Harrison's "Flying Hour," a track co-written with Mick Ralphs and eventually rejected for inclusion on 1981's *Somewhere in England* album. The inscription reads: "Past is gone, thou canst not that recall/ Future is not, may not be at all/ Present is, improve the flying hour/ Present only is within thy power."

23 Babiuk (2015) provides a detailed study of instruments used by the Beatles, including Harrison's guitars from his Beatles days.

24 See Clayson (2003, 353–6), for discussion of the court case, the song, and the video.

video also takes place in a courtroom. The video narrative roughly follows courtroom proceedings, with Harrison being led in in handcuffs, testifying on the stand, addressing the jury, and ultimately being led out again in handcuffs. There is a steady stream of gags throughout from the judge wearing headphones, to the musical experts all lined up in a row, each with a badge reading "expert," to a court stenographer who enthusiastically plays the piano licks on the court transcribing machine until later in the video she is seen playing a Fender Rhodes electric piano. In many ways, this is all a clear extension of "Sue Me, Sue You Blues" taken into the video realm. Ultimately, the lyrics tell us, the reason for the song is "you," and while that "you" may be the listener, it seems more likely that the "you" referred to here is God ("My Sweet Lord").[25] The comedy in "This Song" is broad and constant and provides an example of the lyrics and video providing the humor while the music plays it straight, a variation on the interaction of elements that can be found in "Ding Dong, Ding Dong."

A second song from *Thirty-Three & 1/3*, "Crackerbox Palace," provides a strong narrative in the lyrics that then direct the sequence of images in the video; it is directed by Monty Python's Eric Idle and filmed at Friar Park.[26] While the lyrics begin with a humorous line (as quoted in the title of this chapter), the remainder of the lyrics do not engage humor to any significant degree. Instead, they use "Crackerbox Palace" as a metaphor for life in the material world. As the verses unfold, the narrator moves from birth and infancy with promises of faithful love and devotion, to childhood and adolescence with its pressures to conform within society, and finally to adulthood with its ups and downs. Accordingly, the video opens with Harrison singing from a baby carriage while being pushed by a nurse; he then appears in the school uniform and short pants of a child or young teenager; and lastly as an adult sitting on his bed, at one point flanked by lingerie-clad women. Along the way we are treated to singing and dancing gnomes, menacing policemen, and a cast of carnivalesque characters led by a vampire. At 2:47 Harrison appears seated in half lotus position with the cast of characters surrounding him, singing "know that the Lord is well and inside

---

[25] See Inglis (2010, 61–2) for an interpretation taking the "you" as the listener.

[26] As mentioned above, Harrison was a great fan of Monty Python. He and Idle would go on to write "The Pirate Song" in 1975 for Idle's *Rutland Weekend Television* series. In 1978, Harrison made a cameo appearance in Idle's spoof of the Beatles, *All You Need Is Cash*. While Harrison's involvement in filmmaking is beyond the scope of this chapter, it is worth noting that Harrison provided the funding for Python's 1979 film, *Life of Brian*, which takes a light-hearted, though indirect, approach to the life of Jesus. See Thomson (2013, 317–18; 319–23).

of you."[27] In this video, then, the music is not humorous, the lyrics are mostly serious, but the video is filled with playful images meant to elicit an amused response. "When We Was Fab" from the 1987 album *Cloud Nine* provides a similar instance: though the lyrics provide some clever references songs by other artists such as Bob Dylan and Smokey Robinson, and the singing incorporates a reference to "I Am the Walrus," the lyrics and music mostly play it straight. The video, however, is filled with gags and humor, including appearances by Ringo Starr and reputedly Paul McCartney.

Finally, "True Love" from *Thirty-Three & 1/3* is Harrison's version of a song written by Cole Porter that was featured in the 1956 film musical starring Bing Crosby and Grace Kelly, *High Society*. The song is a beautiful ballad with no humorous content whatsoever in the lyrics or music. Eric Idle also directs the video for this track, filmed at Friar Park. The scene for the video is set in the late nineteenth century, perhaps the 1890s, and Harrison is seen in period costume singing the song to a romantic interest as they drift lazily down a stream in a small row boat. The gag, besides the silly costumes and comically exaggerated gestures, is that the pair have a guardian angel (mentioned in Porter's bridge) and that Harrison's beau sneaks off to be with that angel instead of with him. The comedy here is whimsical and not nearly as developed as in the videos discussed above. Harrison would return to this kind of simple humor in the video for "Blow Away," a single from the 1979 album, *George Harrison*. The video is directed by Neil Innes, who had been a member of the Bonzo Dog Doo-Dah Band, worked with Monty Python, and written the songs and starred in the 1978 Rutles movie, *All You Need Is Cash* (he also played the nurse in the "Crackerbox Palace" video). The lyrics and music are not meant to be humorous; the music is bright and the lyrics optimistic, but there is no intention to elicit an amused response. Innes' video, by contrast, features Harrison singing the song in various humorous visual situations—at times mugging for the camera, dancing and striking poses with the guitar, and singing next to a giant toy bird, while seated in a giant duck, and then astride a giant bobbing-headed dog. This playful silliness is juxtaposed to scenes of open sky, clouds, and shoreline vistas shot from above. These two videos employ humor only in the video dimension and do so in a relatively elementary fashion.

---

[27] Harrison describes how he got the title of the song from a conversation he had with the manager (the "Mr. Greif" mentioned in the lyrics) of comedian Lord Buckley, who Harrison admired. Harrison states clearly that he means "Crackerbox Palace" to be "the world" in these lyrics (Harrison 2017, 358). The primary meaning of "Lord" here is God, but Harrison likely also relished the secondary reference to Lord Buckley.

Harrison's cover of "Got My Mind Set On You," released as a single and included on the *Cloud Nine* album of 1987, presents an interesting case: the song was written by Rudy Clark and recorded by James Ray in 1962 and two videos were made for it. There is little humorous content in the music or lyrics and in the first video released, there is no humorous content; like the videos for "Faster" (from *George Harrison*) and "This Is Love" (from *Cloud Nine*), humor plays no role in the lyrics, music, or video. But the second video version of the song is humorous. It features Harrison playing guitar in a spacious and wood-trimmed great room with fireplace. As he sings, the room seems to come alive to the rhythm of the music. Stuffed animal heads on the wall sing along and a stuffed squirrel plays the sax solo on a pipe, while a book and drawers open and close to the beat of the music. At one point a stunt double for Harrison bounds out the chair and does acrobatic flips around the room. Of all the videos discussed here, it is perhaps the most delightfully playful. But the fact that there can be two video versions employing the same studio recording that elicit such different responses underlines the crucial role video can play in shaping our experience of a song. Figure 7.2 summarizes the use of humor in the Harrison videos discussed above.

"Ding Dong, Ding Dong" (1974)—lyrics and music mildly humous, video humorous

"This Song" (1976)—humorous lyrics, non-humorous music, humorous video

"Crackerbox Palace" (1976)—mildly humorous lyrics, non-humorous music, humorous video

"When We Was Fab" (1987)—mildly humorous lyrics, non-humorous music, humorous video

"True Love" (1976)—non-humorous lyrics and music, humorous video

"Blow Away" (1979)—non-humorous lyrics and music, humorous video

"Got My Mind Set On You" (1987)—non-humorous lyrics and music, humorous video/non-humorous video

"Faster" (1979) and "This Is Love" (1987)—non-humorous lyrics, music, and video

Figure 7.2 Humor in select George Harrison videos after 1973.

Harrison and *Līlā*

That any song's lyrics or music are humorous, or that the video for a song is humorous, does not mean that such a song or video invokes Indian spirituality. Indeed, most humorous songs and videos in the West have little intended connection to *līlā*. In the case of Harrison, the role of humor in his songs and videos becomes a significant element because it is consistent with his own often-articulated spiritual values—values that lie at the core of much of his music. In his discussion of the lyrics to "I Me Mine," for instance, he focuses on the "ego and eternal problem" as it is understood in Advaita Vedanta (Harrison 2017, 156). Echoing the lyrics of "Within You Without You," Harrison writes that one must merge the little "I" into the big "I," citing Vivekananda, one of his favorite writers on Indian spirituality. In the poem "Samadhi," another Harrison favorite, Paramahansa Yogananda, describes this merging of individual consciousness with universal consciousness in deep meditation as follows: "The tiny bubble of laughter becomes the sea of mirth itself" (Yogananda 1949, 196). A central element in moving away from thinking about the personal self and merging into the universal self is in achieving detachment from the material world. This is where *līlā* enters the picture: if one can "play" in the world as Coomaraswamy suggests, not motivated by any desire or lack, as Sax remarks, but rather engage in a free and spontaneous manner, then one can view the world as a "mansion of mirth," as Ramakrishna puts it. Humor with detachment is *līlā*, but humor with malice is not, since any malice serves only to amplify the ego—the small 'i'—and reinforce attachment. While Harrison was capable of angry, dismissive, accusatory, and impatient lyrics, especially in his early career (as mentioned above), his humor was not malicious. Even when the humor is pointed, as in the frustration over legal and contractual battles that inspired "Sue Me, Sue You Blues" and "This Song," Harrison dispenses with any anger and bitterness, as if to say, "it really doesn't matter in the end, and it's all kind of funny—absurd even— when you think about it." That's the sense of detachment that characterizes Harrison's use of humor. Indeed, it's humor that provides an answer to living in the material world: "let go and have fun with it."

References

Babiuk, Andy. 2015. *Beatles Gear: All the Fab Four's Instruments from Stage to Studio*, Ultimate Edition. Milwaukee: Backbeat Books.

Badman, Keith. 2000. *The Beatles: Off the Record*. London: Omnibus Press.

Carrera, Mike. n.d. "George Harrison: Music Videos." *The Daily Beatle*. Accessed November 1, 2022. http://webgrafikk.com/blog/george-harrison-music-videos/

Clayson, Alan. 2003 [1996]. *George Harrison*. London: Sanctuary.

Coomaraswamy, Ananda K. 1941. "Līlā." *Journal of the American Oriental Society* 61 (2): 98–101.

Covach, John. 1990. "The Rutles and the Use of Specific Models in Musical Satire." *Indiana Theory Review* 11: 119–44.

Covach, John. 1995. "Stylistic Competencies, Musical Humor, and 'This Is Spinal Tap.'" In *Concert Music, Rock and Jazz since 1945: Essays and Analytical Studies*, edited by Elizabeth Marvin and Richard Hermann, 402–24. Rochester, NY: University of Rochester Press.

Covach, John. 2019. "George Harrison: Songwriter." In *Part of Everything: The Beatles' White Album at Fifty*, edited by Mark Osteen, 177–96. Ann Arbor: University of Michigan Press.

Covach, John. 2023. "George Harrison's Road to India." In *Speaking Words of Wisdom: The Beatles and Religion*, edited by Michael McGowan, 43–67. University Park: Penn State University Press.

Dimock, Edward C. Jr. 1989. "Līlā." *History of Religions* 29 (2): 159–73.

Gould, Jonathan. 2007. *Can't Buy Me Love: The Beatles, Britain, and America*. New York: Three Rivers Press.

Harrison, George. 2017. *I Me Mine*, extended edition. Guildford, England: Genesis Publications, Ltd.

Harry, Bill. 2003. *The George Harrison Encyclopedia*. London: Virgin Books.

Inglis, Ian. 2010. *The Words and Music of George Harrison*. Santa Barbara: Praeger.

Kahn, Ashley, ed. 2020. *George Harrison on George Harrison: Interviews and Encounters*. Chicago: Chicago Review Press.

Kinsley, David R. 1974–5. "Creation as Play in Hindu Spirituality." *Studies in Religion* 4 (2): 108–19.

Leary, Timothy, Ralph Metzger, Richard Alpert. 1964. *The Psychedelic Experience: A Manual Based on the Tibetan Book of the Dead*. New York: University Books.

M [Mahendranath Gupta]. 1942. *The Gospel of Sri Ramakrishna*. Translated by Swami Nikhilananda. New York: Ramakrishna-Vivekananda Center.

Martin, George. 1979. *All You Need Is Ears*. New York: St. Martin's Press.

Miles, Barry. 1997. *Paul McCartney: Many Years from Now*. New York: Henry Holt and Co.

Sax, William S., ed. 1995. *The Gods at Play: Līlā in South Asia*. New York: Oxford University Press.

Sheff, David. 1981. *The Playboy Interviews with John Lennon and Yoko Ono*, edited by G. Barry Golson. New York: Playboy Press.

Shumsky, Susan. 2022. *The Inner Light: How India Influenced the Beatles*. New York: Permuted Press.

Thomson, Graeme. 2013. *George Harrison: Behind the Locked Door*. London: Omnibus Press.

Yogananda, Paramahansa. [1946] 1998. *Autobiography of a Yogi*, Thirteenth Edition. Los Angeles: Self-Realization Fellowship.

Yogananda, Paramahansa. 1949. *Whispers from Eternity*, first version. Los Angeles: Self-Realization Publishing House.

Zimmer, Heinrich. 1952. *Philosophies of India*, edited by Joseph Campbell. Princeton: Princeton University Press.

8

George Martin, Parlophone Records, and Great Britain's Funnymen

Kenneth Womack and Ed Zareh

From their first moments in the world's consciousness, the Beatles became known for their witty, unbridled senses of humor. Whether it was their hilarious mock-Shakespearean turn on *Around the Beatles* or their wisecracking press conference in the Pan Am Lounge, comedy lived and breathed in their collective psyche. Their unquenchable yen for humor finds its roots, at least in part, in the zany British comedy of the 1950s, followed closely on its heels by the so-called "satire boom" in the early 1960s. Both movements owe a debt—as do the Beatles themselves—to the efforts of George Martin, their future visionary producer, in fashioning a home for Great Britain's funnymen at one of the world's most powerful and influential record companies.

In 1955, Martin was promoted to serve as A&R Head at Parlophone Records, the lowest rung of the vaunted EMI Group. At age twenty-nine, Martin was the youngest executive in EMI's history, although his tenure was destined to be short-lived if he couldn't establish a new income stream for the struggling label. Out of sheer desperation to save Parlophone—and his own livelihood—Martin discovered his saving grace in the zany world of British comedy. As Martin later observed, the time was right for British comedy: "I hit upon the idea of making the kind of records that other people weren't making. And nobody was making comedy records in Britain. Stan Freberg and Bob Newhart were making comedy records successfully in America, but nothing much was happening in England" (Hanly 2012).

Early Years

Comedy and tragedy are often thought of as siblings, the two extremes of the human psyche. Many of our greatest comic minds suffered and endured painful and difficult childhoods. In *The Struggle to Be Strong*, psychologists Al Desetta and Sybil Wolin point out that there is good reason for this crucial link. Humor acts as a key to resilience—essential to surviving trauma and thriving thereafter (Desetta and Wolin 2000, 242–4). As with his future client John Lennon, Martin's early life underscores this primal aspect of humanity.

Born in 1926, Martin spent much of his childhood steeped in the privation of an economically depressed England. Abuse, either physical or emotional, seems thankfully absent from the Martin home. But Martin's experience with poverty was profoundly traumatizing. During the Depression, his father Henry was unemployed for eighteen months. He finally landed a job selling newspapers on a streetcorner. Years later, Martin would recall with some shame the pity he felt watching his father standing out in the cold, trying to scrape together a living. It was a sinking feeling he resolved to avoid for himself. Thankfully, young George had his mother Bertha's influence to buoy him. He was six when his family finally acquired a piano from a relative. "A piano then was what the television has become now, not simply a piece of furniture, but a focus of family gatherings," he later remarked. He was drawn to it immediately. By the age of eight, Martin had coaxed piano lessons from his mother—"eight of them to be exact" (Martin with Hornsby 1979, 11). Blessed with perfect pitch, he taught himself to play after that, imitating various Chopin pieces by ear. He had decided early on that piano and the arts would be his ticket out of his unfortunate circumstances of birth.

Martin's life-trajectory was fueled by ambition, but he often chose comedy as the vehicle by which to propel himself towards success. In grammar school, he would join the Quavers, a drama club with a taste for comedy. Together, they would perform mostly Noel Coward comedies. In this troupe, young George would not just continue his education in the arts—supplementing his love of music and the piano—but he would discover and internalize a creative code of values that would define him and his work. In short, he was "a theater kid." Like many young people in school drama clubs, Martin was exposed to, and became, a cherished breed of creative individual. School drama kids are collaborative, inclusive, and introspective. They are taught to be group-minded, finding something for everyone to do, and encouraged to channel social dynamics into creative expression. They learn to interact together for the good of the show. Working together, they focus on the larger production at hand. Individual performance is important, as always, but it is secondary to the good of the production as a whole. Hence, the phrase, "there are no small parts, only small actors." This unspoken ethical creed would become a foundation upon which he would build. Years later, when attempting to decide which chap should be the Beatles' front man (and which of the Liverpudlians should act his sidemen), he would conclude that they should remain a foursome. "Why not take them as they were?" (Martin with Hornsby 1979, 124). It was a decision that would make any high school drama club teacher proud.

Even still, young George dreamt about a career in aviation. But his parents, always influential, loving, and supportive, held decidedly different views about the course of his future: "While I had been at school, my parents were always trying to impress on me the importance of a job with security. I had always been good at mathematics and drawing, so now my mother suggested: 'Why don't you go in for architecture?'" Meanwhile, his father, Harry, had different plans in mind: "Why don't you go in for the Civil Service? You'll never get chucked out of a job then." As Martin recalled, "To him that was, understandably, paramount, having suffered so much unemployment, but in both of them there was the feeling that they wanted me to do better than they had, an 'Our George is going places' mixture of parental pride and ambition" (Martin with Hornsby 1979, 17).

As with so many young men of his day, Martin's ambitions quickly shifted to the omnipresent military effort that galvanized the nation. After passing the entrance exam, he joined the War Office's nonuniformed ranks as a temporary clerk grade three. Never straying very far from the sound of music, Martin continued to tickle the ivories with his dance band by night. Indeed, by this point, George Martin and the Four Tune Tellers netted a tidy sum for their gigs—especially in contrast with his meager earnings as a clerk. But after eight months, during which he mainly provided tea service and worked in the mail room of the War Office's Easton Square headquarters in London, he strolled into the recruiting office at Hither Green and, without first telling his parents, volunteered to join the Royal Navy. His reasoning, like many would-be recruits, was fairly simple: "It was inevitable I was going to be conscripted before long. The Army didn't appeal to me because I wanted to fly, but I didn't particularly want to go into the Royal Air Force because everyone was doing that. I thought it would be different to join the Fleet Air Arm." Like so many young men, he later admitted to being inspired to join the Fleet Air Arm after hearing the awe-inspiring story of its success at the Battle of Taranto, which enjoyed national headlines in November 1940 for its crippling air attack on the Italian fleet using aerial torpedoes. On yet another occasion, he put it even more bluntly, saying that he "didn't want to be a poor bloody infantryman" (Martin 2003, 18).

A fortnight stay in Greenwich for officer's training proved to have a lasting influence on Martin's future, with both positive and negative implications. On the one hand, young George relished the company of the older commissioned officers with whom he enjoyed formal dinners in the station's exquisite Painted Hall, nicknamed "the Sistine Chapel of the UK" for Sir James Thornhill's elaborate murals. In addition to being schooled in the finer aspects of tableside etiquette, Martin began to self-consciously refine his unsharpened North London accent with the posh tones of the gentlemen-officers whom he chose to emulate. Years later, Martin would confess to having long been concerned about the all-too-overt "cor blimey" aspects of his lower-class comportment. He would recall having first heard his recorded voice at age fifteen and recoiling at its unpolished sound. But those evenings among the officers in the Painted Hall would inspire him to pursue a decidedly different path. Tall, lean, and fair-haired, Martin began to take on the full appurtenances of a civilized and cultured Englishman.

A Wartime Comedic Mindset

As Martin would soon discover, comedy was a slippery concept during a war-footing, when a populace is largely united under threat from a common enemy. A cultural premium is placed on loyalty to higher powers. Allegiance to one's government, devotion to "God and country" are demanded—and readily offered up. Comedy at home becomes base, and devolves to common denominator appeal, wherein physical humor, slapstick, and innocent puns are all safe territory. Sexual innuendo becomes the outer limit of acceptable taste. Criticism is largely reserved for the bad guys. Satire, comedy's sharpest weapon, is to be inflicted exclusively upon the enemy. So injurious was British satire that Churchill's government employed it as a weapon of war. The BBC's German Service broadcast comedy satirizing the Third Reich overseas "to reach ordinary Germans in World War II. Its aim was to break the Nazi monopoly on news" and to demoralize Hitler's supporters (Moorehead 2019). The overarching goal of all wartime comedy involved the maintenance of the existing order at home, the fortification of the domestic power structure, and the ultimate destruction of the threat of a competing outside force.

When he was demobilized in 1947, Martin prepared to enter civilian life with precisely this mindset. In retrospect, it fully prepared him for navigating the uncertain world of life as a music student at London's Guildhall, followed by a wholly unexpected career at a failing record label. When he joined Parlophone's ranks in September 1950, EMI was something of a boarding school for adults. Its mission was clearly stated, like a school motto. Its departments were well-defined silos, like houses. Its corporate hierarchy was strictly set, like grades or levels. Although he was used to the rank-and-file order and the self-discipline of the military, Martin was understandably surprised to discover that the attitudes and culture of the largest producers of music in Great Britain had very little in common with the community spirit of the Quavers drama society of his youth. It was quite the opposite. The EMI Group was a competitive enterprise run by ambitious individuals whose behind-the-scenes maneuvering and backbiting would leave Martin with a bad taste in his mouth for years. Thankfully, he was resilient. He would survive and thrive at EMI in spite of the company culture there, not because of it. In fact, he would reject and dispense with as much of the corporate mindset as he possibly could during his years at EMI. And he would do it by sticking to the creative values he internalized in the theater, by relying on his intuition and by developing, sharing, and commodifying his sense of humor.

Martin was initially thrilled with his new job at EMI, where he would serve as assistant to Oscar Preuss, the longtime head of Parlophone records. What Martin failed to realize was that, even in those first few months, he was being groomed to take over Preuss's job. Martin could hardly believe his luck. But what seemed like a stroke of good fortune soon lost its luster. If Martin knew precious little about Parlophone at the time, he could hardly be blamed. "I had no idea what EMI stood for," he later admitted. "I didn't know what it was" (Martin 2003, 24–5). At EMI House, Parlophone was then regarded as the "third label"—a lower rung specializing in light orchestral works, jazz, and dance-band recordings, as well as a stepchild of sorts to Columbia, EMI's commercial juggernaut, and HMV, the blue-chip "His Master's Voice" label. The EMI Group actually held a fourth label among its subsidiaries—Regal-Zonophone, which produced Salvation Army recordings. Parlophone had been founded in Germany by the Carl Lindström Company before the outbreak of the First World War. In honor of the Swedish-born Lindström, Parlophone's logo featured a distinctive capital L as its moniker, which is often mistaken for a British pound sign.

Martin's early years at Parlophone were marked by a series of frustrating starts and stops—he was, quite literally, learning the record business as a form of on-the-job training. He was forced to learn the rudiments of recording artistry as a sheer means of survival in a business that he barely understood. Years later, he would look back on a key collaboration with fledgling comic Peter Ustinov, whom he met via his work with the London Baroque Ensemble, as an early success. Ustinov enjoyed a reputation in the early 1950s for being the *enfant terrible* of British actors. Anxious to capitalize on his friend's notoriety, Martin recorded Ustinov's tongue-in-cheek "Mock Mozart," a three-minute mini-opera in which the actor sang all of the soprano, alto, and tenor parts. "For those days," Martin later reflected, "that was pretty adventurous. We didn't have multitrack recording, of course, so in order to produce the four-part ensemble he had to sing with himself" (Martin with Hornsby 1979, 44). To accomplish this end, Martin instructed his technical engineer to dub Ustinov's voice from one tape onto another, mixing each recording as the process moved forward. In those pre-multitrack days, Martin recognized that the recording was certain to suffer generational loss as the tape deteriorated from successive recordings. Indeed, with each new pass, the signal to noise ratio worsened ever more perceptibly. The resulting record was an unusual release by any standards.

And not surprisingly, it had been met with institutional scorn. At a monthly EMI meeting, Martin was summarily accosted for his experimental foray with Ustinov: "What do you think you're up to, George?" a colleague brusquely inquired. "It doesn't make sense. No one's ever made a record like this before." As it happened, Martin had the last laugh when he learned that the Oxford Street record shop had sold all 300 copies of "Mock Mozart." "I was flying by the seat of my pants," he later admitted regarding the making of Ustinov's record. "I mean, I was doing things I wanted to do, hoping that the public would like them." By the time that EMI managed to press additional copies, the demand for Ustinov's confection had dried up. But for Martin, the lesson was clear and lasting: there was a commercial appetite, no matter how modest at the moment, for his experimental adventures—and especially in terms of good old, tried, and true British comedy. It was also confirmation of Martin's growing belief about a coming shift in his profession. "When I came to working as a producer, up to that time people had been making records as faithfully as they could, reproducing the original sound. What they were doing was making photographs. I said, 'Let's paint, instead of having photographs'" (Hanly 2012). With "Mock Mozart," Martin's paintings were beginning to come into more vivid relief.

In December 1954, when Preuss announced his retirement from EMI, Martin was flabbergasted to find himself in the running for his mentor's job. When he learned that he would be promoted to head of Parlophone Records, he was genuinely shocked to have been selected, later remarking, "I thought that someone would come in and be put above me, so I was shaken to the core when they said I could have the job" (Lewisohn 2013, 261). He soon came to realize there was a catch: Parlophone's finances were a shambles, thanks to historically ineffectual record sales. Indeed, an administrative plan was already in place to mothball Parlophone and redeploy its dearth of revenue-generating artists, rendering Martin's possible career as studio head stillborn. His lucky break suddenly felt akin to a boarding school prank. With nothing to lose, he decided to settle in and make a go of it.

If he were to save Parlophone from the scrapheap, Martin had little hope beyond expanding the label's record sales. When he assumed the role of A&R Head, several of his most successful artists had been lured away by Decca Records, EMI's chief competitor. He could hardly blame them. As Martin himself reasoned, Decca was "a very good and powerful label" in comparison with Parlophone, "a tinpot little label" that was now being "run by a man who was little more than a music student." Yet for all of his self-doubts, Martin clearly understood the magnitude of the new opportunity that Oscar's retirement had afforded him. He readily admitted that it had been "quite adventurous" of EMI's Chairman Sir Joseph Lockwood to appoint "a fairly brash young man without much experience in the record business" like himself as Parlophone head. "But for me, it was an unbelievable chance," he wrote. "I was boss of a whole record label. I was on my own" (Martin with Hornsby 1979, 63).

In his first act as label head, Martin took stock of Parlophone's position: "I had to maintain allegiance to the artists we already had—Jimmy Shand, who was our biggest seller, Eve Boswell, Ron Goodwin, Jack Parnell, Johnny Dankworth, Humphrey Lyttleton." But more importantly, he quickly recognized that to leave his mark on the business—to set Parlophone on an even more powerful, possibly even uniquely different course—he needed to "get between the cracks" of the other labels in EMI's stable (Hanly 2012). Not surprisingly, Martin instinctively shifted his attentions toward comedy. He was proud of his work on Ustinov's "Mock Mozart," and while EMI had bungled the opportunity, in his mind, of netting additional sales, he sensed a significant consumer appetite for clever, well-made comedy records. In fact, with the rise of the Angry Young Man movement in literature and the arts, his timing simply couldn't have been better. Ustinov was hardly alone in the brave new world of British comedy. The trick was discovering the next shining star.

Striking Comedy Gold at Parlophone

At Parlophone, where Martin felt like the captain of a sinking ship, beset by pirates planning his demise, he plotted a new course. Stressed over the fading fortunes of the label and unsure about whom he could really trust at the company, he decided to go out to the show. In early 1957, he attended a two-man revue called *At the Drop of a Hat* at the tiny New Lindsey Theatre near Notting Hill Gate. The show featured actor and singer Michael Flanders and composer, pianist, and linguist Donald Swann. *At the Drop of a Hat* took place on an empty stage, save for Flanders, who suffered from polio, in a wheelchair, and Swann seated behind the piano. Their repertoire consisted of fiendishly witty introductory comments and one hilarious song after another. For his part, Martin was simply bowled over by their performance. After a little persuasion, he succeeded in talking them into selling him the rights to record the show.

And he did so in just the nick of time. On January 24, 1957, Flanders and Swann shifted *At the Drop of a Hat* to the Fortune Theatre in London's West End, and the comedy duo struck gold. The show ran at the Fortune for a remarkable 808 performances before moving to New York City in 1959. Excited by the opportunity to attach Parlophone to Flanders and Swann's hit revue, Martin recorded the duo live at the Fortune for five consecutive nights, later editing the material together to create a seamless whole. Rushed into stores, *At the Drop of a Hat* gave the struggling label some sorely needed success on the British charts. Perhaps Martin would find a way to get between the cracks and score some surefire hits for Parlophone after all.

Reflecting back on those heady days in 1957, Martin felt that "it was a good time for comedy," reasoning that Parlophone's sudden bout of success could be attributed to radio enjoying its second wind in the face of television's initial onslaught. "Comedy records succeeded because sound dominated in the days before television got its grip on people." At that point, television was still "black and white, with very few stations and a limited number of hours of transmission per day. Radio was still king and listeners had aural imaginations: people could picture in their own minds what was going on." Martin shrewdly recognized that he had a genuine knack for bringing mental images to life. And perhaps more than that, he had a powerful talent for bringing them to fruition in the studio. He was also willing to work long hours to see a project through. As he later observed, "It was enormously hectic, but I was very keen, and I did so desperately want

Parlophone to be a big label. I worked all the hours, and it was worth it because I thought I was doing something really worthwhile" (Martin 2003, 47).

Flush with the excitement of Flanders and Swann's success, Martin wasted little time in turning his efforts back to an old friend from his early years at EMI. Back in 1953, Martin had recorded *Jakka and the Flying Saucers*, a space fantasy play for children. Written by lyricist Ken Hare and with Ron Goodwin as its composer, the play included a wide range of whimsical voices and songs in a fairly limited story about a space-boy, Jakka, who trolls about the sky on a space-scooter accompanied by his five-legged space dog. One of the play's characters was voiced by Peter Sellers, who had made his start in radio on Ted Ray's weekly radio show *Ray's a Laugh*, later emerging as a member of the BBC Home Service's burgeoning radio program *The Goon Show*. Martin looked back at *Jakka and the Flying Saucers* with a sense of embarrassment: "It was a complete disaster, and I blush to think of it." While the record "sold 10 copies," he couldn't shake the memory of one sound in particular. In Sellers' hilarious impression—the record's only genuine bright spot—"the voice of God came out remarkably like Winston Churchill." As always, Martin's ear was fine-tuned for comedy, and Sellers had it in spades (Martin 2003, 48).

In June 1955, he seized the opportunity to work with Sellers yet again—this time, in the company of fellow Goon Spike Milligan. With Martin's full attention, they pitched the idea of recording a parody of "Unchained Melody," which had been a smash hit in the UK the previous year. In fact, four different cover versions of the song by Al Hibbler, Les Baxter, Jimmy Young, and Liberace had simultaneously settled into the British top 20. As far as Sellers and Milligan were concerned, it was ripe for the pickings. For Martin, it was his chance to finally produce a record under the Goons moniker. But his hopes were just as quickly dashed at EMI's monthly supplement meeting, when Martin excitedly played the finished record for "the assembled EMIcrats, one of whom said: "Well, of course, if we're going to put out that particular version of 'Unchained Melody,' we'll have to get permission from the copyright owners, because you are distorting the song a bit." As it happened, Martin and the two Goons weren't merely distorting the song "a bit"—they were lampooning the thing to high heaven, complete with madcap voices and a ukulele. Martin was truly flummoxed at EMI's reticence, arguing that they were going to be paying a copyright anyway in order to record the song. As Martin later wrote, "My view was 'Issue first, and ask questions afterwards'"—a practice that would come back to haunt him time and time again. But on this occasion, EMI contacted the publisher, who rejected the song in short order, declaring that they would never grant permission for their "gorgeous opus" to be defiled in such a heinous fashion. For his part, Martin was decidedly bitter about the turn of events, as were the Goons, who left Parlophone for Decca. Not long thereafter, the Goons released "I'm Walking Backwards for Christmas," one of their biggest hits, as well as a standout moment in Milligan's career (Martin with Hornsby 1979, 89–90).

But as it turned out, all was not lost. A few years later, Martin managed to cajole Sellers back into the studio, where they recorded a single, "Boiled Bananas and Carrots" b/w "Any Old Iron." Sung tongue-in-cheek in mock-Cockney tones, "Boiled Bananas and Carrots" found Sellers in high-flying style remaking the old Harry Champion music-hall tune. In contrast with the unfortunate *Jakka and the Flying Saucers*, Sellers' single enjoyed modest sales. On the strength of "Boiled Bananas and Carrots," Martin pitched the notion of making an album with Sellers to the EMI brass. In spite of having relative autonomy as Head of Parlophone, Martin needed the approval of the managing director and EMI record division in order to undertake a long-player, which was still considered a major label decision at the time. Once again, Martin's enthusiasm was crushed during a monthly marketing meeting. For Martin, it was like Ustinov all over again. "A single is one thing, but making an album?" the marketing team asked. "Who is going to listen to a whole half-hour of that stuff?" Never one to remain daunted, Martin hatched a compromise—a bit of necessary "argy-bargy"—with EMI's top brass: in exchange for a limited production budget, he and Sellers would cut a 10-inch LP as opposed to the standard 12-inch long-player (Martin 2003, 48). The result would be cheaper both for the consumer and in terms of the EMI Group's manufacturing costs. More importantly for Martin, he would be able to showcase Sellers' talents in long-playing form.

The eventual album, which Martin entitled *The Best of Sellers* to needle his EMI colleagues for their preemptive doubts about the project, consisted of one sidesplitting comedic confection after another. At times, the album even required Martin to engage in physical comedy, as with "A Drop of the Hard Stuff," in which Sellers and Martin simulated an extended fight scene. With no other means at their disposal to generate the necessary sound effects, Martin, Sellers, and the engineers "piled a heap of chairs and tables and music stands in the middle of the studio. Then, as Peter was doing his Irish bit, a chair was kicked away, and a music-stand was sent hurtling across the floor. Bedlam ensued." Joining in the mêlée, Martin found himself on the unhappy receiving end of a flying chair, courtesy of Sellers. Listeners can even hear his shriek of pain on the record. "I really hurt my shin," Martin later recalled, when "Peter got carried away" with their stage-fighting (Martin with Hornsby 1979, 88). As with his deployment of sound effects, Martin soon discovered that he could accent Sellers' hilarious timing through well-placed, carefully honed incidental music. In such instances in his early career, Martin opted to work under pseudonyms. After trying out the exotic-sounding "Lezlo Anales," he toyed with "John Chisholm," the name of his father-in-law, before settling on "Graham Fisher," a moniker that he drew directly from the name of a childhood chum from his Bromley dramatic society days with the Quavers (Lewisohn 2013, 279).

The Satire Boom

What followed for Martin was a slew of successful comedy records, many featuring Sellers and his colleague Spike Milligan from the Goons comedy troupe, who came to view Parlophone as their home label. It is difficult to overstate the influence of the Goons' comedy influence in the 1950s. With the Second World War decidedly won, comedy standards and tastes began to shift. Britons were safe from the existential threat of the Nazis, but they had paid—and continued to pay—a steep price. Poverty, rationing, and rebuilding persisted into the 1950s. The public's taste for satire grew steadily as the primary means by which to channel their discontent. As Britons' penchant for discontent was mighty, so then did it fuel a massive demand for satire. The emergent British Satire Boom during this era was the result—a pervasive public reexamination of civil society itself, the public institutions that had seen the populace through the war, and the those that needed reform. Nothing was off limits, and the more outrageous the critique, the better. At its height, the satire boom became most closely associated with the intelligentsia, generally hailing from Cambridge and Oxford—namely, Peter Cook, John Bird, John Fortune, David Frost, and Bernard Levin, among others.

The Goons leapt into this comic void, filling the need for levity, observational wit, and criticism. Years later, writing in a 1973 *New York Times* book review of Milligan's *Goon Show Scripts*, Lennon attempted to introduce his favorite comedy troupe to his adopted homeland. "For Americans who never heard of it," he wrote, "*The Goon Show* is difficult to describe. Call it pure radio and pure comedy with a good dollop of the Marx brothers veering off into the empyrean of pure surrealism" (Lennon 1973, 446). The group was considered absurdist and subversive, mixing ludicrous plots with surreal humor, puns and catchphrases. They employed musical interludes as transitions. Teamed with fledgling BBC Radiophonic Workshop, Goons' material was supported by arsenal of bizarre sound effects, which were new and unique to listeners in the post-war era. The Goons created a new comedy vocabulary and sonic language as they savaged everyday life in post-war Britain. No subject was off limits: politics, art, show biz, diplomacy, the police, even the vaunted British class system. All were fair game. The public adored them. And they cast a long cultural shadow that would influence generations of Britons.

The British comedy boom of the 1950s was a boon to Martin and to Parlophone. Martin delighted in working with each of the Goons—Sellers, Milligan, and Harry Secombe—on individual comedy records. For Martin, these records not only represented a lucrative cash cow for his label, but also marked a return to the spirit of fun and collaboration he experienced working on comedic plays in the Quavers drama society. He merrily participated in the production of these records, playing instruments, creating new sound effects, and even performing as a voice actor when needed.

In short, Parlophone was reinvented from the inside out thanks to Martin's affiliation with members of the Goons. Parlophone both fed and fed off of the British Comedy boom, contributing a slew of new material and reaping the rewards of healthy record sales. Martin took special pride in the trailblazing success of *Songs for Swingin' Sellers*, which filled Martin with a well-earned sense of vindication. "After *The Best of Sellers* had proved such a success—to the private chagrin of the EMI people who had said it would be a waste of time—those same people now asked me to do another record," Martin wrote. "It was a kind of accolade, which recognized Parlophone as the label for humorous people" (Martin 1979, 88–9). Thanks to comedy, the repositioning of Parlophone put the label in an excellent fiscal position. The bottom line grew fat enough that Martin was able to reinvest the label's profits. At this key juncture, he made a series of deft decisions that would benefit Parlophone well into the future. Recognizing full well the importance of sound effects on the Goons' radio show, Martin rose to the challenge of creating a similar level of quality for the production of their records. He invested in new technology, upgrading the equipment in the studio, while also learning to master the techniques behind creating cutting-edge new sounds.

Meanwhile, Up in Liverpool …

Perhaps most significantly, Martin's alignment with the satire boom afforded him with the opportunity to produce hit records that left their mark across the whole of the UK. The fruits of his labors had attracted legions of devoted listeners, including members of the Beatles—Lennon, most notably—who would cite Martin's records as key influences upon the direction of his musical art. Indeed, the Beatles' and Martin's shared affinity for spoken-word comedy would prove to be a central aspect of their world-beating partnership.

While Martin had been busy riding the comedy wave in London, 200 miles to the north, in Liverpool, two young boys were allowing that same wave to wash over them, absorbing surreal ideas, adopting outlandish attitudes, and internalizing wacky, brilliant, anti-authoritarian points of view. Although they hadn't met yet, by the early 1950s Lennon and Paul McCartney were avid Goons fans. "I was 12 when the *Goon Shows* first hit," Lennon recalled, "16 when they finished with me. Their humor was insane" (Lennon 1973, 446). Lennon cited the Goons, along with Lewis Carroll and Elvis Presley, as one of the three primary inputs on the Beatles' collective psyche. Similarly, McCartney and his younger brother Mike had taken to quoting Goon lines so often they came to be known as the "Nurk Twins." Their delighted school friends delighted in the McCartney boys' performances, and bestowed upon them the gooney honorific in reference to Fred Nurke, a lovable bungling Goon Show character. Paul and Mike would recite lines from the show so often that their grade school chums bestowed upon them the gooney honorific. Years later, Lennon and McCartney would resurrect the name Nerk Twins for a one-off pub performance at the Fox and Hounds during a Caversham holiday (Lewisohn 2013, 831).

In point of fact, both John and Paul so loved the Goons that each boy—independently of each other—had managed to negotiate the installation of a hardwire from the radio in the family living room up into their bedrooms so that they could listen to the Goons at night. Neither boy could tolerate the idea of missing a single moment and insisted on drifting off to sleep with gooney voices echoing in their heads. The power of late-night programming, it seems, is hardly a trivial matter. No less than Lorne Michaels, the esteemed creator of *Saturday Night Live*, has observed that nocturnal experience leaves a powerful mark on our psyches. "It's closer to the edge of the subconscious, more dangerous. Interesting things happened there, breakthroughs sometimes" (Hill and Weingrad 2014, 44).

Meeting the Beatles

Thanks to their shared sense of humor, Martin enjoyed his own breakthrough of sorts—and during one of the strangest moments across his long and storied career. It all started with a meeting with Beatles manager Brian Epstein in February 1962, courtesy of Sid Colman, General Manager of EMI's Ardmore and Beechwood publishing arm. In Martin's memory, Sid said to Brian, "Why don't you go 'round and see George Martin at Parlophone? He deals in unusual things. He's had a big success with the most unlikely recording acts. I'll give him a ring and make an appointment, if you like." Indeed, it was well-known around EMI during this period that Martin was open to artists of all stripes. As Bernard Cribbins later remarked, "George Martin was the chap they sent all the weirdies to" (Martin with Hornsby 1979, 122).

Things were awkward from the moment that the Beatles arrived for their first session at EMI Studios that June. Staffer John Skinner later recalled the band's arrival in front of Abbey Road. "They pulled into the car park in an old white van," he reported. "They all looked very thin and weedy, almost undernourished. Neil Aspinall, their road manager, said they were the Beatles, here for a session. I thought, 'What a strange name.'" As Aspinall set up the band's gear, EMI personnel did a series of double-takes as they watched the Beatles amble into the studio in their matching suits and, even more conspicuously, with their long hair and halting Scouser accents. "Good God, what've we got 'ere?" balance engineer Norman Smith muttered to himself up in the control room. For their part, the Beatles were transfixed by the prospect of arriving at the studio—*any* studio— as artists with an actual recording contract to their name. McCartney vividly recalled that Number 2 had "great big white studio sight-screens, like at a cricket match, towering over you, and up this endless stairway was the control room. It was like heaven, where the great gods lived, and we were down below. Oh God, the nerves" (Lewisohn 2013, 655–6).

By all accounts, this first meeting between Martin and the Beatles was going nowhere fast. During the recording of four preliminary numbers, the boys were not themselves. Martin had a lot to say about them—none of it was good. Their equipment was a shambles, their songs were no good, and their drummer couldn't keep the beat. When they had completed the session, the Beatles joined the production team upstairs, where Martin launched into an extended monologue about the recording studio and, eventually, the quality of their performance. "He was giving them a good talking to," engineer Ken Townsend later recalled. Martin had clearly grown exasperated with the band's seeming lack of studio professionalism. According to Smith, the Beatles remained mute for the duration of Martin's remarks. "They didn't say a word back, not a word," Smith recalled,

> They didn't even nod their heads in agreement. When he finished, Martin said, 'Look, I've laid into you for quite a time, you haven't responded. Is there anything *you* don't like?' They all looked at each other for a long while, shuffling their feet, then George Harrison took a long look at George [Martin] and said, 'Yeah, I don't like your tie'.
>
> (Lewisohn 2013, 670)

After the formality of Martin's lengthy diatribe, the room lapsed into an awkward silence. This was EMI, after all, the studio where technical personnel wore crisp white lab coats, while administrative types like Martin donned coats and ties. At first, Martin didn't register the joke. He would later remember being especially pleased with the tie that he had chosen that day—a black number featuring a red horse motif. Harrison briefly felt as if he might have crossed a line with his deadpan attempt at humor, later recalling that "there was a moment of ohhhhh, but then we laughed and he did too. Being born in Liverpool you have to be a comedian." Once everyone had joined in the merriment, the floodgates of the Beatles' penchant for humor and self-deprecation opened wide up. As Smith remembered, Harrison's moment of levity "cracked the ice, and for the next 15 to 20 minutes the Beatles were pure entertainment. When they left, George and I just sat there saying, 'Phew! What do you think of that lot then?' I had tears running down my face" (Lewisohn 2013, 670).

It is impossible to say—given everything that was to happen, not to mention the improbability and impact of the journey that they would share together—how significant Harrison's one-liner may truly have been in establishing a foothold, no matter how slight, for them with the Parlophone head. "I did think they had enormous talent," Martin would later allow, "but it wasn't their music, it was their charisma, the fact that when I was with them they gave me a sense of well-being, of being happy. The music was almost incidental. I thought, 'If they have this effect on me, they are going to have that effect on their audiences.'" In short, he was absolutely charmed by them, by their personalities far more than their music at this stage. As Martin later remarked, "You actually felt diminished when they left." For the Beatles' part, the Scousers from Liverpool were understandably intimidated by the 36-year-old Martin—the tall fellow with the posh accent, a real educated type. "We hadn't really met any of these London people before, these people who talked a bit different," McCartney later remarked. "George Martin was very well spoken, a little above our station, so it was a little intimidating, but he seemed like a nice bloke." Harrison agreed, later observing that "we thought he was very posh—he was friendly but schoolteacherly, we had to respect him, but at the same time he gave us the impression he wasn't stiff—that you could joke with him" (Lewisohn 2013, 670–1).

The Biology of Laughter

While he had scarcely given the session a second thought before June 6th came to pass, Martin could hardly think about anything else after they left the studio that night. "It was love at first sight," he later wrote. "John, George, and Paul— I thought they were super. They had great personalities, and they charmed themselves to me a great deal" (Lewisohn 2013, 671). Although it is impossible to know exactly what was said during that golden quarter hour of comic hilarity, it is unthinkable that Lennon did not have at the ready the quirky character voices and reliable bits he'd pinched from the Goons as a kid—and would pull out at a moment's notice throughout his life. Indeed, to perform those very bits for the man who had originally recorded them would have proven too great a temptation to resist. For his part, Martin would have instantly recognized the references and find himself flattered. There are few things creative people enjoy more than having their own work referenced by a true fan. But what Martin discovered among the Beatles that day was more than fandom. It was closer to meeting one's own progeny. The comedy language his records had captured years earlier had found their way into the minds of the bright young lads standing before him. They were speaking his language. From then on, Lennon recalled, "our studio sessions were full of the cries of Neddie Seagoon!" (Lennon 1973, 446), referring to Secombe's Goon alter-ego. The Beatles' new producer would return the favor by regaling the boys with stories about his recording sessions with the likes of Sellers and Milligan.

With Martin, the Beatles enjoyed a partnership founded not merely on their considerable talents as songwriters and musicians, but the shared biology of comedy itself. Laughter is magical stuff. A sudden release of endorphins bathes the brain, lungs engage, oxygenating the blood, heartrate quickens, body temperature increases, and after 15 or 20 minutes, facial muscles start to cramp and ache. There are many physiological benefits to laughter, similar to a good workout. But the psychological and emotional impacts are far more profound. Laughter reduces stress, relaxes the muscles, revitalizes the blood, and builds the bonds of trust within a group. Individuals like Lennon, who control laughter by making jokes, exert an outsized social influence in groups. And when those feel-good endorphins stop coming, we feel a mild sense of withdrawal. As Martin presciently recalled after the Beatles' departure, we miss the people who make us laugh (Newport Academy 2018). For Martin and the Beatles, humor would provide the foundation for a partnership for the ages, with the studio emerging as a workshop of infinite possibilities.

References

Desetta, Al, and Sybil Wolin, eds. 2000. *The Struggle to Be Strong: True Stories by Teens about Overcoming Tough Times*. Minneapolis: Free Spirit.

Hanly, Francis, dir. 2012. *Produced by George Martin*. BBC.

Hill, Doug, and Jeff Weingrad. 2014. *Saturday Night: A Backstage History of Saturday Night Live*. San Francisco: Untreed Books.

Lennon, John. 1973. Rev. of *The Goon Show Scripts*, by Spike Milligan. *New York Times* (September 30): 446.

Lewisohn, Mark. 2013. *Tune In: The Beatles—All These Years, Volume 1*. Boston: Little, Brown.

Martin, George, with Jeremy Hornsby. 1979. *All You Need Is Ears*. New York: St. Martin's.

Martin, George. *Playback: An Illustrated Memoir*. 2003. Guildford: Genesis Publications.

Moorehead, Kristina. 2019. "How Britain Fought Hitler with Humor." *BBC Culture* (August 30): www.bbc.com/culture/article/20190829-how-britain-fought-hitler-with-humour.

Newport Academy. 2018. "Why Laughter Is Good for Mental Health." *Newport Academy* (March 20): www.newportacademy.com/resources/mental-health/laughter-good-for-you/.

9

Yoko Ono's Avant-Garde Humor

Stephanie Hernandez

As the 1993 episode of *The Simpsons*, "Homer's Barbershop Quartet," unfolds into a semi-roman-à-clef retelling of the Beatles' story, Barney, the John Lennon-inspired character, finds a girlfriend, who Principal Skinner refers to as "the Japanese conceptual artist." She is dressed in all-black, complete with a beret, and is instantly recognizable as Yoko Ono. When they stop in for a drink at Moe's "Cavern," she orders "a single plum, floating in perfume, served in a man's hat" ("Homer's" 1993). In 2019, twenty-six years later, Ono included this as an item in her *Yoko Ono: One More Story* exhibition at the Reykjavik Art Museum. Her inclusion of this piece shows an awareness of, and an appreciation for her reputation in popular culture as the conceptual, eccentric woman who helped bring the avant-garde to the mainstream.

In headlines that stretch back to the early 1960s, and forward to the present day, Ono has recurrently been referred to as avant-garde: the catch-all term for "experimental artist." With a career that was first established in the early 1960s, Ono has come to represent many things in popular culture; some good, some bad, but overall—eccentric. It's undeniable that she has (mistakenly) been blamed for breaking up her husband's band, an idea that, according to Carolyn Stevens, is deeply rooted in misogyny and racism: "she is best (or perhaps worst) known as the woman—a Japanese woman—who broke up the Beatles" (Stevens 2018, 115). This chapter aims to analyze the far more significant and underappreciated aspect of Yoko Ono's legacy, her avant-garde humor. In a 1999 episode of ITV's The South Bank Show about Ono and her art, social critic Camille Paglia insinuated that Yoko didn't have an adequate sense of humor ("Yoko Ono" 1999). Paglia claimed that Ono "stripped away from John Lennon his brilliant sense of British humor. The surrealistic kind of writing and prankster-ism that came out of Lewis Carroll via Oscar Wilde. Yoko thought it was silly, she never understood it" ("Yoko Ono" 1999). It is Paglia who doesn't understand Ono's absurdist and surrealist sensibilities (she does have a song called "Cheshire Cat Cry," by the way). Perhaps Yoko's humor is underestimated because she often appears serious, but this is one of her ultimate sleight of hand tricks. Through a prism of Dadaism, Surrealism, and Fluxus, I make a case for Yoko's art as comedic artistry by sketching a lineage of Yoko Ono's unique aesthetic of humor through an analysis of her book *Grapefruit*, as well as her late 1960s peace campaign with John Lennon.

Dadaism, Surrealism, Fluxus

Ono's humor can be seen through many lenses, but the most prominent ones include the aesthetics of Dadaism, Surrealism, and Fluxus. Each of these moments in Western art history are interconnected, and Ono transformed them into her own style which created her unique brand of humor. Dada has a complex history that originated in the early twentieth century. It is characterized by "the reduction of poetry to phonetics, of music to elemental sound, and of art to planes, angles, colours and simplicity of line" (Bigsby 2018, 9). A notable character of Dada is Marcel Duchamp, who branded the art style with his *Readymades*; "retinal art" created by taking ordinary objects such as a urinal or a bicycle wheel, repositioning the item, and declaring it art. Demonstrating the essence of Dada, in his *Dada Manifesto* (1918), figurehead Tristan Tzara wrote, "Dada applies itself to everything, and yet it is nothing, it is the point where the yes and the no and all the opposites meet, not solemnly in the castles of human philosophies, but very simply at street corners, like dogs and grasshoppers" (Motherwell 1951, 251).

In 1924, André Breton inaugurated Surrealism into the fore with his *Manifeste du Surrealism*, in which he wrote, "I believe in the future resolution of these two states—outwardly so contradictory—which are dream and reality, into a sort of absolute reality, a *surreality*" (Breton 1992, 89). Surrealism is often seen as a byproduct of Dada, but without the characteristics of being disruptively "anti-art." Breton's statement indicates that surrealism is a space where the imagined can be believed. It is characterized visually by the dream-like paintings of Salvador Dalí or René Magritte, and is seen as a manifestation of the deepest part of the unconscious mind. Working through the repressed feelings from society and the onslaught of war, surrealism allowed for a manifested reality through the imagination.

The artistic "movement" that Ono is most associated with, Fluxus, emerged in the late 1950s, and was essentially Neo-Dadaism in collaboration with Futurism. In his *FLUXMANIFESTO on Fluxamusment* (1965), George Maciunas wrote, "anything can substitute for art and anyone can do it ... the value of art-amusement must be lowered by making it unlimited, mass-produced, obtainable by all and eventually produced by all" (Maciunas 2011). It is characterized by the experimental "sound music" of John Cage; his most famous piece 4'33" was composed in 1952 and instructs a pianist to sit at the piano and play nothing (Kotz 2001, 57). The music is instead made from the elemental sounds of the concert hall: coughs, the whirring of air conditioning, doors opening and closing, etc. In collaborating with Cage, Ono also demonstrated an interest in this kind of auditory experience. That being said, she never felt completely immersed into Fluxus. As with many moments in her life, "Ono felt alienated by a certain stuffiness and elitism in the scene" (Zoldaz 2015).

Ono began studying poetry and music at Sara Lawrence in 1952, and subsequently became involved in the underground circles of New York's artistic scene. She was steeped in a cocktail of avant-garde inspirations, as well as their tongue-in-cheek approach to creativity. While it is necessary to see that Yoko is operating in the tradition and spirit of these artistic styles, she is also an innovative multi-media artist in her own right, as evidenced by *Grapefruit*.

Grapefruit

Full of Ono's artistic directives, *Grapefruit*, was originally published independently in Tokyo with a limited number of 500 copies in circulation. In 1964, she published the small book with her own press, Wunternaum, which, according to Ono, "has the roots in Wunderbaum. I wanted to publish my work from 'another world'" (Kellein 2008, 147). *Grapefruit* was published again in 1970 by Simon & Schuster, this time featuring an introduction by John Lennon, which reads simply: "Hi! My name is John Lennon. I'd like you to meet Yoko Ono." The name of the book is an autobiographical pun, as Yoko stated in "To the Wesleyan People," the grapefruit "is a hybrid of lemon and orange" (Kellein 2008, 147). Yoko believes herself to also be something of a grapefruit as she lives a hybrid, part-Japanese, part-American life. The book is written in a manner of plain poetics, occasionally playing with typography and in a free-flowing style reminiscent of her poetry professor at Sarah Lawrence, Alastair Reid (Allen 2022).

The Simon & Schuster publication of *Grapefruit* is divided into nine sections: Music, Painting, Event, Poetry, Object, Film, Dance, Architecture Pieces, On Films. Here, I offer a selection from Music, Painting, and Event to discuss how Ono's avant-garde humor came to fruition.

Grapefruit: "VOICE PIECE FOR SOPRANO"

"VOICE PIECE FOR SOPRANO," dated 1961, is from the Music chapter. The piece begins with the directive "Scream," followed by a numbered list of three instructions to perform that action "against" three objects: the wind, wall, and sky (Ono 1970a). One of Yoko's most prominent contributions to popular culture is that of her scream-singing. It's a running joke in sitcoms, parodies, and comics that often reduce her music to wailing. "VOICE PIECE FOR SOPRANO" is an early example of how Ono regards screaming as not only a piece of music, but also a medium through which one can express feelings that are resonant enough to stand up against the sky. In Ono's feminist anthem, "Sisters, O Sisters" (1972), she sings, "It's never too late / To shout from our hearts." This lyric indicates a central tenet of Ono's thinking: shouting is rebellious, inherently political, and has the power to transform society. Of course, there is also an element of catharsis in Yoko's screaming. "Scream from the Heart: Yoko Ono's Rock and Roll Revolution" suggests that, retrospectively, we can apply the theories of Arthur Janov to "VOICE PIECE FOR SOPRANO" and Yoko's scream-pieces (Brown 2014, 119). In 1970, Janov published his study, *Primal Scream: Primal Therapy: The Cure for Neurosis*, which called for the use of screaming as a form of psychotherapy to cure the neurosis created by a repressive society.

Demonstrated in recorded songs such as "Why" (1970b), Ono's approach to scream-singing can be both lyrical, as in shouting the word "why?" or sonic, as in making spontaneous vocalizations. The fact that Yoko's screams are caught in a space somewhere between being vocals and noise indicated her interaction with the popular Cagean concepts of "noise" or "sound" music. Yoko believed in Cage's idea that "sound is everywhere," but she refrained from acquiring his skepticism (Herwitz 1988, 792). While Cage showed an acute interest in silence as music, Yoko went to the other end of the sound music spectrum, using screams to bombard the senses. Avant-garde musician Morton Feldman once said, "John Cage was the first composer in the history of music who raised the question by implication that maybe music could be an art form rather than a music form" ("Thomas Moore" 1983). If Cage was the first to question this idea, Ono is the artist who continues to interrogate it throughout her work.

A quick search for "Yoko Ono Screaming" on YouTube will bring up a video of Yoko performing "VOICE PIECE FOR SOPRANO" at the Museum of Modern Art (*Yoko Ono Screaming at Art Show!* 2010). It has over 6 million views, and upwards of 28,000 comments that range from positive to negative and everything in between. What is abundantly clear is that people derive a sense of entertainment, sometimes pleasure, from her screaming, even when it is confrontational. In her piece "The Unfinished Music of John and Yoko," Tamara Levitz writes, "[Yoko's] voice is not beautiful, lyrical, or accompanimental ... it forces an awareness of Yoko's very real existence, as it relates imaginatively with listeners' own inner sounds and the emotions attached to them" (Levitz 2005, 223). The Internet, especially via social media, is its own echo chamber of inner sounds and emotions, allowing users to display their own feelings toward Yoko in the various comment sections under her work.

Participatory Internet culture also allows users to edit videos in any way imaginable. People have used the video of Yoko screaming to create a spinoff of "Rickrolling." This Internet prank involves the unexpected inclusion of Rick Astley's "Never Gonna Give You Up," which is edited into another video. The term used for the Ono spinoff is "Yokorolling." It follows the same method, but instead of Astley, it is Ono performing "VOICE PIECE FOR SOPRANO." Although this audiovisual editing is out of Ono's hands, it demonstrates a key part of her legacy in the public sphere: she's a woman who screams. Her screams have often been parodied in television shows, such as in *The Power Puff Girls* "Meet the Beat-Alls" episode where covert villainess Moko Jono communicates in Ono-esque screeches (2001). The Cartoon Network children's show introduced a new generation to Ono and the avant-garde ideas purported by her "VOICE PIECE FOR SOPRANO."

Grapefruit: "PAINTING TO BE STEPPED ON"

In "PAINTING TO BE STEPPED ON," Ono is clearly playing with the visual medium. Although she has labelled it a "PAINTING" there is no actual paint involved unless the artist previously completed a painting. Instead of relying on paint spread by a brush, the piece relies on the particles that cover the soles of shoes. "PAINTING TO BE STEPPED ON" fits nicely into the tradition of Dada since the piece opens creativity to anyone who has a canvas and time. Dada, in its conception, was a reaction against the early twentieth-century European society that had an elitist bias toward art; Dadaists aimed to "taunt the bourgeoisie" (Bigsby 2018, 5). In leaving a finished painting on the ground to be stepped on, Ono shows an irreverence regarding the original piece and the expectations associated with the viewing of a painting; the standard museum rule is "don't touch." This represents the principle of Dada as a mockery of the established ideas of "high art."

Dada and Fluxus were also concerned with breaking the barrier between art and the audience. Yoko epitomized this in "PAINTING TO BE STEPPED ON" since it shifts the onlooker's role from observer to performer. Ultimately, the piece reveals a distinct facet of her personality, one that involves minimalism and collaboration. Ono has always operated in a network of artists, and she also has continued to create pieces that work on a global scale. This forms an essential idea in her later efforts, such as the "IMAGINE PEACE TOWER" in Reykjavik, Iceland, which invites people from all over the world to make a wish on a light beam. In the "World Wide Recorder Concert" episode of the Comedy Central television show *South Park*, a Yoko-Ono character works with Kenny G to organize the world's largest recorder concert with over 4 million children in participation (2000). Caricaturing Ono, the character she inspired becomes increasingly angry when the 4 million children can't seem to play in unison and therefore sound awful. This joke works on many levels, especially considering Yoko's concept of music, but, overall, the representation of Ono depicts participatory collaboration as one of her fundamental principles. In "PAINTING TO BE STEPPED ON," Ono shows that she finds beauty in both the extremely ordinary and the idea of total collaboration, collecting footprints from around the world.

Grapefruit: "SMOKE PIECE"

From the Event section of *Grapefruit,* Yoko Ono's "SMOKE PIECE" instructs the reader to smoke anything and everything, including your "pubic hair" (Ono 1970a). In the 1950s and 1960s, smoking formed a major part of Western culture, mainstream, and counterculture. Tobacco cigarette advertisements were frequently seen on the television and in newspapers, and beatniks experimented with smoking marijuana. Yoko uses "SMOKE PIECE" as a mirror reflecting society's preoccupations back onto itself, commenting on the collective addiction and asking the question: to what length will one go to get their fix?

In creating the image of smoking pubic hair, she conscribes her humor onto the body. More specifically, she calls attention to the part of the body most often hidden from public view. The lower region, according to Mikhail Bakhtin, is the first of the "three main acts in the life of the grotesque body: sexual intercourse, death throes, and the act of birth" (Bakhtin 1971, 353). This aspect of Ono's humor reappears elsewhere in Ono's oeuvre since she is constantly toying with seriousness and the unexpected, especially when focusing on the body. Consider her feature film *Bottoms* (1967), which is essentially a montage of naked bottoms, or the *Two Virgins* (1968) album cover, for which she posed nude with John Lennon, or the 1981 cover of *Rolling Stone* on which a nude John Lennon embraces a clothed Yoko Ono. All of this nude-body imagery is not only sexually liberating, but it's also very surrealist, bringing to light the repressed conversations surrounding the human body, both its anatomical functions and its socially derived symbolism.

A survey of popular Surrealist works of visual art reveals a widespread interest in pubic hair. In Salvador Dalí's *Surrealist Object Functioning Symbolically*, "several accessories (pubic hairs glued to a sugar lump, an erotic little photograph) complete the object" ("Salvador Dalí" 1931). Another figurehead of surrealism, René Magritte, depicts pubic hair on multiple levels in his painting *The Rape (Le viol)* (1934). Méret Oppenheim's *Object (Le déjeuner en fourrure)*, or "Breakfast in Fur," features what was to many a shocking reference to women's pubic hair (1936). The surrealist convention of using pubic hair, then, was not atypical in the art that Ono and her contemporaries actively took interest in. Her emphasis on pubic hair in "SMOKE PIECE" is connected to not only the surrealist preoccupation with the repressed, but also the 1960s ideals of sexual liberation.

In popular culture, Ono's preoccupations with the body reach comedic heights when parodied. Referring back to the same Simpsons episode that opened this chapter, when Yoko and Barney play the group their newest tape, "Revolution 8," the tape unwinds to the sound of the Yoko character monotonously repeating "number eight," immediately followed by Barney burping on a loop ("Homer's" 1993). While burping is a straightforward expression of bawdy humor, it also illustrates Bakhtin's concept of the grotesque as the belching becomes a rhythmic part of the song, and Ono's art, once again, originates in the body.

Peace Campaign

When Ono and Lennon married in March of 1969, they immediately set out to promote their shared ideas of peace in a world ravaged by the Vietnam War. During their honeymoon, they ran a promotional campaign to "sell" the idea of peace as a product, like "soap," which John Lennon explained they would sell "until the housewife thinks that there's peace or war, that's the two products" ("BED PEACE" 2012). Employing the tactics of Fluxus "happenings," a collaborative piece of performance art, Yoko and John became global spokespeople for peace through their *Bed-Ins* and *Bagism*.

The *Bed-Ins* happened as part of John and Yoko's honeymoon, referenced in the lyrics to the Beatles' "The Ballad of John and Yoko." The couple provided the press an all-access pass to come see the newlyweds in bed for ten hours a day. Under these circumstances, they were using sex as bait to hook the public's attention. The headline of John and Yoko in bed together is sexy, guaranteed to pique the public's interest whether they approved of the antics or not. In her piece "Unbosoming Lennon: The Politics of Yoko Ono's Experience 1992," Kristin Stiles writes that the *Bed-Ins* "subverted conventional as well as radical politics by fusing the public art-event, the happening or 'Be-In,' with the private events of the human body. In this way, Lennon and Ono returned politics to the bedroom" (Stiles 2016, 149). Using the bed as a platform, the couple showed how the inherently personal (the private space of a bedroom), can be an origin of the peaceful revolution. In other words, change begins with the self. The iconography surrounding the couple are signs reading "BED PEACE" and "HAIR PEACE," a play on words that relate to Ono's *Grapefruit*, in which she labels her instructions as "pieces," such as "LAUGH PIECE," or "COUGH PIECE." During interviews from the *Bed-Ins* in Amsterdam and Montreal, John and Yoko explained that they decided to undertake the *Bed-In* as a happening because anyone can buy into, and therefore promote peace simply by staying in bed, peacefully ("BED PEACE" 2012). This links back to Maciunas' Fluxus idea of "Non-Art Reality: to be grasped by all peoples, not only critics, dilettantes and professionals" ("George Maciunas" 1963).

The *Bed-In* is one of the many zeniths in the careers of John and Yoko and has a lasting legacy in the public consciousness. The song written and performed by the couple at the Montreal *Bed-In*, "Give Peace a Chance," was also performed as part of the Moratorium to End the War in Vietnam in Washington D.C. (1969). With lyrics that mock over-intellectualization, and make the anti-war message clear, echoes of "Give Peace a Chance" are still heard in global peace marches to this day. Further resonating in popular culture, the *Bed-In* has been referenced by artists ranging from Oasis ("Don't Look Back in Anger"), to Jhene Aiko and Childish Gambino ("Bed Peace"). The images from the *Bed-In* show John and Yoko at their most revolutionary and have become classic iconography of the couple.

Other artists have also used Ono and Lennon's *Bed-In* imagery in unique ways. The album cover of Japanese pop duo Puffy AmiYumi's *Nice* (2003) portrays a *Bed-In* with their own slogans to promote the album. In 2006, Billie Joe Armstrong (of Green Day) and his wife, Adrienne Armstrong, posed for pictures in bed with a sign overhead reading, "Haz el amor y no la guerra" ("make love not war" in Spanish). In a 2007 episode of *Gilmore Girls*, music aficionado Lane Kim attends her own baby shower while in bed (on bed rest), accompanied by her long-haired husband who joins her to sing a punk-style version of the lullaby "Mockingbird." While the song choice may have been a nod to the marital bliss exemplified by Carly Simon and James Taylor's mid-70s rendition of "Mockingbird," the overall effect links back to John and Yoko. Surrounded by a group of partygoers, the visuals are immediately recognizable as referring to Ono and Lennon's *Bed-In*. These examples illustrate how imagery of the couple's *Bed-In* is constantly re-purposed not only to sell products, but also to continue portraying peace and love. In that way, the *Bed-In* image has become like that of a Duchampian *Readymade*, one that can constantly be repositioned while maintaining its credence as art.

Originally, *Bagism* was an artistic concept of Yoko Ono's which called for a person to get inside a bag. There are many variations of the piece which include getting naked inside the bag or having sex inside the bag, but the mechanics stay the same. As a byproduct of the *Bed-In*, John and Yoko decided to add *Bagism* to their peace-promotion portfolio. At their *Bagism* press conference in Vienna, the couple welcomed the media from inside their bag. This left the interviewers bewildered, and many requested that the couple come out of the bag. Yoko explained how the bag facilitates "total communication" removing the fixation on "what sort of face you have or what sort of taste you have in your clothes, etcetera ... those things usually disturb and lock the mind of people, and they can't communicate totally" (*John and Yoko "Bagism" Protest (March 31, 1969)* 2019). In entering the bag, all stereotypes are left behind. What remains is the Bagists' message. *Bagism* can also be seen as a Fluxus happening, or one of Yoko's Event pieces. As a piece of performance art, *Bagism* demonstrates the legacy of Dada as it is stripped of all pretense; it's two people in a bag, and anyone can do it.

When defending the concept of *Bagism* at the press conference, Lennon said, "Yoko and I are quite willing to be the world's clowns [...] if by so doing it will do some good" (Fawcett 1980, 51). In a later interview shown in the film *24 Hours: The World of John and Yoko*, Yoko espouses similar thoughts, saying "Everything needs a smile ... We might stop the war by being jolly. When you're happy and you're smiling, you don't want to kill somebody, do you?" (Morrison 1969). These statements reflect Yoko's sentiments on peace promotion: it *has* to originate from a place of happiness or whimsy in order to work. In turn, Ono used her sense of humor to advocate for peace.

Conclusion

Throughout her career, Yoko Ono has pioneered the avant-garde in multiple mediums, including writing, performance art, music, and activism. She is an accomplished woman even without her collaborations with John Lennon, but her highly publicized relationship with the Beatle did give her a platform to bring the avant-garde to the masses. By operating within the artistic innovations of Dadaism, Surrealism, and Fluxus, Ono has created her own creative aesthetic that moves through a range of emotions, but her humor is the praxis that she used to establish herself in the public eye. Her conceptualism, her screaming, her global spirit of collaboration, her fascination with the body, and her tenacity for "happenings" to promote peace all contribute to the multi-faceted ways in which Ono's legacy has thrived in popular culture. Echoed in the repeated references to her in cartoons, music, and sitcoms, Yoko's eccentricities define her presence in the public consciousness. The seriousness that Yoko exudes is a bodily form of smoke and mirrors, tricking culture critics like Camille Paglia into believing that she doesn't have a satisfactory sense of humor. Hidden behind the sincerity of her face, however, Yoko is laughing with those who are "in" on her avant-garde jokes.

References

2shellrock. *John and Yoko "Bagism" Protest (March 31, 1969)*. June 1, 2019. https://www. youtube.com/watch?v=AIlgx1t3hSM.

Allen, Austin. 2022. "'My Beautiful Never-Nevers': Yoko Ono's Poetry Revisited." *Los Angeles Review of Books*, April 4, 2022. https://lareviewofbooks.org/article/my-beautiful-never-nevers-yoko-onos-poetry-revisited/.

Bakhtin, Mikhail. 1971. *Rabelais and His World*. Translated by Helene Iswolsky. Cambridge: MIT Press.

The Beatles. 1969. "The Ballad of John and Yoko." Apple Music.

Bigsby, Christopher W. E. 2018. *Dada & Surrealism*. Volume 2. New York: Routledge.

Brown, Shelina. 2014. "Scream from the Heart: Yoko Ono's Rock and Roll Revolution." In *Countercultures and Popular Music*, edited by Sheila Whiteley and Jedediah Sklower, 171–86. Surrey: Ashgate.

Breton, André. 1992. "Excerpt from the First Manifesto of Surrealism (1924)." In *Art in Theory 1900–1990: An Anthology of Changing Ideas*, edited by Charles Harrison and Paul Wood, 87–92. Oxford: Blackwell Publishers.

Dalí, Salvador. 1973. *Surrealist Object Functioning Symbolically*. Assemblage. 47.5 x 28 x 10 cm. Dalí Theatre-Museum, Girona.

Fawcett, Anthony. 1980. *John Lennon 1940–80: One Day at a Time*. New York: Grove Press.

"George Maciunas." Accessed May 18, 2022, http://georgemaciunas.com/exhibitions/flux-labyrinth-fluxus-gag/fluxmanifesto-fluxamusement-1965/.

GrandmasterofWin. *Yoko Ono Screaming at Art Show! (Original)*. September 11, 2010. https://www.youtube.com/watch?v=HdZ9weP5i68&t=11s.

Herwitz, Daniel A. 1988. "The Security of the Obvious: On John Cage's Musical Radicalism." In *Critical Inquiry* 14, no. 4 (Summer, 1988): 784–804. http://www.jstor.org/stable/1343672.

"Homer's Barbershop Quartet." 1993. *The Simpsons*. September 30.

Janov, Arthur. 1970. *Primal Scream: Primal Therapy: The Cure for Neurosis*. New York: Dell Publishing Co.

Kellein, Thomas. 2008. "Coughing Is a Form of Love: A Portrait of the Artist as a Young Philosopher." In *Yoko Ono: Between the Sky and My Head*, edited by Thomas Kellein. Köln: Buchhandlung Walther König.

Kotz, Liz. 2001. "Post-Cagean. Aesthetics and the 'Event' Score." In *October* 95 (Winter, 2001): 55–89. http://www.jstor.org/stable/779200

Levitz, Tamara. 2005. "The Unfinished Music of John and Yoko." In *Impossible to Hold: Women and Culture in the 1960s*, edited by Avital H. Bloch and Lauri Umansky, 217–39. New York and London: New York University Press.

Maciunas, George. 2011. "*Fluxus Manifesto (1965)*." In *Fluxus and the Essential Questions of Life*, edited by Jacquelynn Bass, 22–3. Chicago: University of Chicago Press.

Magritte, René. 1934. *The Rape (Le viol)*. Oil on canvas. 73.3 x 54.6 cm. The Menil Collection, Houston, TX.

"Meet the Beat-Alls." 2001. *The Power Puff Girls*. February 9.

Morrison, Paul, dir. 1969. *24 Hours: The World of John and Yoko*. TV Short.

Motherwell, Robert. 1951. "Tristan Tzara: Dada Manifesto (1918)." In *The Dada Painters and Poets: An Anthology*, edited by Robert Motherwell. 249–51. Cambridge: The Belknap Press of Harvard University Press.

Ono, Yoko. 1970a. *Grapefruit*. New York: Simon & Schuster.

Ono, Yoko. 1970b. "Why." *Yoko Ono/Plastic Ono Band*. Apple Music.

Ono, Yoko. 1972. "Sisters, O Sisters." *Some Time in New York City*. Apple Music.

Ono, Yoko. 2012. *BED PEACE starring John Lennon & Yoko Ono (1969)*. June 23. https://www.youtube.com/watch?v=mRjjiOV003Q.

Oppenheim, Méret. 1936. *Object (Le déjeuner en fourrure)*. Fur-lined teacup. Museum of Modern Art, New York.

"Salvador Dalí." Accessed May 28, 2022, https://www.salvador-dali.org/en/artwork/catalogue-raisonne-sculpture/obra/49eab9bd42ece411947100155d647f0b/object-functioning-symbolically.

Stevens, Carolyn S. 2018. "Yoko Ono: A Transgressive Diva." In *Diva Nation*, edited by Laura Miller and Rebecca Copeland, 115–32. Berkeley: University of California Press.

Stiles, Kristin. 2016. "Unbosoming Lennon: The Politics of Yoko Ono's Experience 1992." In *Concerning Consequences: Studies in Art, Destruction, and Trauma*, 134–56. Chicago and London: The University of Chicago Press.

"Thomas Moore." Accessed May 20, 2022, https://thomasmoore.info/interview-morton-feldman/#:~:text=John%20Cage%20was%20the%20first,music%20in%20a%20historical%20sense.

"Will You Be My Lorelai Gilmore?" 2007. *Gilmore Girls*. February 27.

"World Wide Recorder Concert." 2000. *South Park*. January 12.

"Yoko Ono." 1999. *The South Bank Show*. December 5.

Zoldaz, Lindsay. 2015. "Yoko Ono and the Myth That Deserves to Die." *Vulture*, May 13, 2015. https://www.vulture.com/2015/05/yoko-ono-one-woman-show.html?regwall-newsletter-signup=true#_=_

Part Three

Playing in Context

10

Bug Music: Beatle Memes in 1960s American Sitcoms

Matthew Schneider

Though the Beatles had (in Ringo's words) "conquered France ..., Spain and Italy," as their plane approached Idlewild Airport on the early afternoon of February 7, 1964, "we were worried about America" (*Anthology* 116). Any misgivings the four might have had were unfounded: by early April, Beatle songs held twelve positions on the Billboard Hot 100, including the top five—a domination of the American popular music charts they would sustain through the end of the decade. But the Beatles' influence on American entertainment went far beyond music. Their arrival in February was breathlessly awaited nationwide, and when they returned for summer tours in 1964–6 the Beatles were front-page news in every city they played. Even when they were not on American soil, the Beatles maintained their hold on the public by furnishing comic fodder for television, especially the classic situation comedies of the mid- to late-1960s. The *Dick Van Dyke Show*, the *Patty Duke Show*, *Gilligan's Island*, *The Munsters*, *The Addams Family*, *F Troop*, *Get Smart*, and *Bewitched* built episodes (and, in the case of *The Monkees*, an entire series) around the epiphenomena of the Beatles and Beatlemania. A 1965 episode of the animated prime-time sitcom *The Flintstones* coined a succinct phrase describing both the Beatles and the hysteria they ignited: "bug music." American sitcom writers ran with this concept, naming fictional groups after insects: The Love Bugs, The Mosquitoes, The Honey Bees, The Gnats, The Termites, The Bedbugs.

In the early 1960s, comics would have called insect-named groups a running gag or shtick. That this can be traced, though, to early news reports about British Beatlemania in the fall of 1963 makes this recurrent gag a *meme*, evolutionary biologist Richard Dawkins's term for an idea that spreads from mind to mind in a manner analogous to the transmission of a gene. Casting the "British Invasion" of

America by the Beatles as a pest infestation helped dissipate the cultural anxiety aroused by the group's sudden dominance of the nation's social landscape. In an era when few American households had more than one set, television audiences were overwhelmingly adult, and situation comedies both created and reflected the sensibilities of the Beatles' fans' parents: the "Greatest Generation," born between 1901 and 1927. The journalists, entertainment executives, and cultural commentators from this demographic cohort fashioned the "meme-pool" from which sitcom writers drew a remarkably consistent set of Beatlesque tropes: pop groups with crazy names, long hair, shouts of "yeah, yeah, yeah," the "special relationship" between Britain and America, the capriciousness of sudden musical fame and Ringo as the lovably simple recipient of history's luckiest break. As the Beatles evolved from moptops to avatars of late sixties counterculture, these memes evolved as well. The purpose of these comic memes, though, remained consistent from the earliest notices of Beatlemania through the group's dissolution at the end of the tumultuous decade: to help Americans adjust to the massive societal transformations effected by the Beatles' establishment of rock music as the predominant art form of the second half of the twentieth century.

Memes as Infectious Ideas

In the Internet age, memes are typically stock photos, screencaps from films or television, or celebrity images which have been doctored by humorous captions and then spread through email or social media. In this chapter, I use meme in the sense originally articulated by Richard Dawkins in *The Selfish Gene* (1976) to explain in evolutionarily valid terms the production and spread of cultural information. Just as a gene is the unit through which genetic information is transmitted from one individual to another, a meme is a unit of cultural transmission, "analogous to genetic transmission in that, although basically conservative, it can give rise to a form of evolution" (Dawkins 2016, 189). Preserved in speech, texts, rituals, and gestures, memes are replicable phenomena transmitted from individual to individual through imitation:

> Examples of memes are tunes, ideas, catch-phrases, clothes fashions, ways of making pots or building arches. Just as genes propagate themselves in the gene pool by leaping from body to body via sperms or eggs, so memes propagate themselves in the meme pool by leaping from brain to brain in a process which, in the broad sense, can be called imitation. If a scientist hears, or reads about, a

good idea, he passes it on to his colleagues and students. If the idea catches on, it can be said to propagate itself, spreading from brain to brain.

(Dawkins 2016, 192)

Dawkins's concept—further developed in his 1982 book *The Extended Phenotype*—has been taken up by thinkers outside of biology, such as the American philosopher Daniel Dennett, who wrote that memes constitute "a new way of thinking about ideas in which everything from wearing clothes to deconstructionism 'obeys the law of natural selection' jumping from brain to brain via 'habits of communication'" (Dennett 1990, 128).

Though subject to evolutionarily selective pressures, memes—like genes—do not necessarily contribute to the survival of their hosts but survive based on their ability to replicate. And just as genes are visible only in the "characteristic effects which they tend to produce in their gene vehicles (organisms)," memes are "carried by meme-vehicles, namely pictures, books, sayings (in particular languages, oral or written, on paper or magnetically encoded, etc.)" (Dennett 1990, 129). To both Dawkins and Dennett, humanity's capability for material reproduction of memes is one of our species' distinguishing characteristics. "We live, today," writes Dennett, "awash in a sea of paper-borne memes, breathing in an atmosphere of electronically-borne memes," and "memes now spread around the world at the speed of light" (Dennett 1990, 131). Like their genetic counterparts, these memes must struggle with competing memes for reproductive fidelity in the meme-carrying organism. Thus, Dennett argues,

> each meme-vehicle is a potential friend or foe, bearing a gift that will enhance our powers or a gift horse that will distract us, burden our memories, derange our judgment. We might compare these airborne invaders of our eyes and ears to the parasites that enter our bodies by other routes. There are the beneficial parasites such as the bacteria in our digestive systems without which we could not digest our food, the tolerable parasites, not worth the trouble of eliminating, such as all the normal denizens of our skins and scalps, and the pernicious invaders that are hard to eradicate such as fleas, lice, and the AIDS virus.

(Dennett 1990, 130)

Big Crawly Things: American Media Discover the Beatles

The Beatles' punning name, combined with their having crossed an ocean carrying a plague of frenzy that infected teenagers in early 1964, furnished sitcoms with a set of memes they would use to poke fun at pop music's transformation of American culture through the end of the decade. These memes appeared in and were spread by American media in their first notices about the Beatles in mid-November 1963.

Time and *Newsweek*, the United States' two major weekly newsmagazines, ran stories on the Beatles and Beatlemania in Britain on November 15 and 18, respectively; both stories viewed the new craze with amused dismissiveness, an attitude that carried over to the earliest television news reports. The Huntley-Brinkley Report on Monday the 18th concluded its half hour with Edwin Newman's four-minute segment introducing viewers to "the hottest musical group in Great Britain," the Beatles, "not a collection of insects but a quartet of young men with pudding-bowl haircuts" who "emerged from [Liverpool's] cellar night clubs" to sell "two-and-a-half million records and earn $5000 a week." In his trademark deadpan, Newman (born in 1919) described the Beatles' fans as "compulsive screamers" and explained that the Beatles' Britishness may be the key to their success: "at last the British juvenile has someone immediate to identify with, not some distant American rock and roll hero." Over recorded audio from their November 16, 1963 show in Bournemouth, Newman demonstrated how the Beatles' "Mersey sound" could barely be heard over their fans' screams, punning that the "quality of Mersey is somewhat strained." Alarmingly, Newman continued, "the Beatles may bring their Mersey sound to the United States, to which it may be rejoined, 'show us no Mersey'" (Newman 1963).

Newman's mordant response to British Beatlemania established the pattern that nearly all mainstream American media followed from November 1963 to the end of the year, demonstrating how memes form and are dispersed. On November 19, the day after Newman's segment for NBC, CBS News's London correspondent Alexander Kendrick filed a four-minute report from the Beatles Fan Club's London headquarters that faithfully matched Newman's tone. "Yeah, yeah, yeah, those are the Beatles, those are," said Kendrick, "and this is Beatleland, formerly known as Britain, where an epidemic has seized the teenaged population." With an air of bemused detachment, Kendrick reported that "the Beatles sound like insect life, but it's spelled B-E-A-T, beat, and these four boys from Liverpool, with their dish-mop hairstyles, are Britain's latest musical, and, in fact, sociological phenomenon" (Kendrick 1963). Inserted in Kendrick's piece were excerpts from an interview filmed by reporter Josh Darsa after the Beatles' Bournemouth show on Saturday, November 16. "What are Beatles?" Darsa asks, to which Paul replies, "You know those little crawly things? We're big crawly things." When Darsa asks, "What has occurred to you, as to why you've succeeded?" Paul responds, "I don't know, really. As you say, the haircuts—we didn't think they were a gimmick, but everyone else said, 'ho, what a gimmick!'" (Kendrick 1963).

Kendrick's segment aired on the CBS Morning News on Friday, November 22, and was scheduled to show again on that day's evening news. But the assassination of President Kennedy that afternoon pushed mention of the Beatles off the airwaves for the next three weeks. Finally, on December 10, the CBS Evening News with Walter Cronkite aired Kendrick's piece, which was seen by Ed Sullivan, who phoned his friend Cronkite for information (as Cronkite remembered it) "about those kids you just had on the air—what do you call them? The bugs, or the beetles, or something" (Crandall 2014). After "I Want to Hold Your Hand" rose up the American pop charts in December, on January 3, 1964 another sardonic member of the Greatest Generation, talk show host Jack Paar (born in 1918), played a clip of the Beatles performing "She Loves You," ending with the now famous "yeah, yeah, yeah." As the camera returns to the bow-tied Paar, he stares expressionlessly and deadpans "It's nice to know that England has finally risen to our cultural level" before assuring his viewers that "science is working on a cure for" the teenage hysteria aroused by the group (Paar 1964).

As Beatlemania surged across North America in the first month of 1964, the Greatest Generation's cynicism was so overwhelmed by memetic teenage excitement that when the Beatles played on Paar's rival Ed Sullivan's show, Ed could not resist twitting Paar by announcing that the boys had dedicated their performance to Jack's fifteen-year-old daughter Randy. Throughout the spring and summer of 1964, the Beatles saturated American radios and record players, and the Beatles' music, merchandise, and personalities were so ubiquitous that even old-timers like Sullivan and Paar found themselves succumbing to memetic Beatle fever. For his October 4, 1964 show Sullivan put a Beatle wig on puppet mouse Topo Gigio, who sang "She Loves You, yeah, yeah, year" before altering his customary sign off from "Kiss me goodnight, Eddie" to "kiss me goodnight, Ringo!" Having been already scripted and mostly filmed prior the sudden onrush of American Beatlemania in late 1963 and early 1964, though, sitcoms were slower to react. When the 1964–65 television season began in the fall, however, the attitudes and the memes of infectious insect swarms and crazed teenagers of the early news reports returned, persisting through most of the rest of the decade. Gags which played on the Beatles' punning name were the first and most widespread of these memes, suggested by the association between Beatlemania and infestations, plagues, and epidemics.

Entomology: Insects, Rock Gnats, Mosquitoes, Love Bugs, Honey Bees, and Termites

One of the first sitcoms to feature an insect-named group was the animated ABC series *The Flintstones,* in the episode "The Hatrocks and the Gruesomes," which aired on January 22, 1965. Steering a middle course between the Baby Boomers' glee and their parents' skepticism, the episode pokes gentle fun at the Beatles while acknowledging the attractiveness of their novelty. Jethro Hatrock, a hillbilly from Arkanstone, visits the Flintstones en route to the World's Fair. Prior generations of Hatrocks and Flintstones had feuded in Arkanstone, but Jethro and his extended family are friendly when they arrive—too friendly, in fact, as they overstay their welcome. Fred Flintstone schemes with his best friend Barney Rubble and their neighbors the Gruesomes (a macabre family modeled on *The Addams Family* and *The Munsters,* both of which premiered in the fall of 1964) to send the Hatrocks their way. It finally dawns on Fred that the only thing the Hatrocks cannot stand is "bug music" ("Hatrocks" 1965). Wiring the Flintstones' radio to a microphone in the Rubbles' house, Fred and his wife Wilma and Barney and his wife Betty don Beatle wigs and—with Fred playing a stone guitar—sing through the radio "I said, yeah, yeah, yeah, he said yeah, yeah, yeah, she said yeah, yeah, yeah," shaking their heads and shouting "whee" at the end of each phrase. Granny Hatrock exclaims that the "bug music" is "giving me the horrors!" as Jethro shoots the radio with his rifle. The music does not stop, so the Hatrocks seek refuge among the Gruesomes, only to find Weirdly Gruesome and his family also in Beatle wigs, singing the same song. The Hatrocks flee only to turn back for Arkanstone when they see a billboard advertising "Bug Music with the 4 Insects" at the World's Fair ("Hatrocks" 1965). Though the Beatles and Beatlemania irritate the older generation, the episode suggests, they are inescapable, so the parents had just as well get used to them.

Depicting the Beatles and their music as the latest salvo in an ongoing generational conflict—to which parents will eventually have to surrender—recurred in many mid-sixties American sitcoms. The Standells—a Los Angeles band who would become famous for their 1968 hit "Dirty Water"—made something of a career for themselves by portraying Beatle-like groups in no less than three sitcoms, beginning with "Bugged by the Love Bugs," episode 16 of Bing Crosby's short-lived sitcom *The Bing Crosby Show,* which aired on January 18, 1965. In stage suits resembling the velvet-lapeled gray jackets the Beatles wore in their February 11, 1964 concert in Washington D.C. and in the finale of *A Hard Day's Night,* the Standells play a Mersey-beat tinged number titled "I Won't Come Back to You" before backing Crosby on "Kansas City," enabling Crosby—who plays the exasperated father of two teenage girls—to effect a truce between jazz and rock "n" roll ("Bugged" 1965). Two months later, the Standells, appearing this time under their own name, performed "I Want to Hold Your Hand" on *The Munsters* ("Far Out" 1965). Later that year, Sherwood Schwartz's *Gilligan's Island* built an entire episode around an insect-named group in "Don't Bug the Mosquitoes." Exhausted by their fame and mobs of screaming teenage fans, the Mosquitoes are dropped by helicopter on the island for a restful getaway. To get the Mosquitoes to recall their helicopter and thereby effect their rescue, the castaways form two singing groups, hoping to remind the band of the joys of wild acclaim. The four men on the island comprise the Gnats; but all they can do is don shaggy straw wigs and bash away at homemade guitars and drums while shouting "yeah, yeah, yeah" ("Don't Bug" 1965). This does not impress the Mosquitoes; but when Mary Ann, Ginger, and Mrs. Howell, as the Honey Bees, sing "You Need Us," the Mosquitoes sneak off the island, explaining in a note that the castaways will not be rescued, because the Mosquitoes don't need any competition of the Honey Bees' caliber.

As Dawkins noted, memes are—like genes—basically conservative, and so tend to preserve older forms of the type until environmental pressures force a change. As the Beatles continued to dominate American music and popular culture through the mid and into the late sixties, the insect-name meme persisted even after the novelty of the Beatles' name had worn off and the group had established itself as more than just a teenage fad. One of the best illustrations of the endurance of the insect meme is from 1967, when the Beatles had established they were no longer just the latest craze. In "That's Show Biz," episode 23 of season 2 of *F Troop,* Sergeant O'Rourke hires a band called the Bedbugs to play the troop's upcoming regimental ball. The general and his wife, O'Rourke tells his friend Corporal Agarn, love to dance the waltz, and the Bedbugs come highly recommended from a successful saloon gig in Dodge City. O'Rourke changes his mind, though, when the Bedbugs (led by future Little Feat co-founder Lowell George) arrive and can only play a loud, fast, electrified version of "Tales from the Vienna Woods." Certain that the general will not approve, O'Rourke tells the Bedbugs that they will be paid off and are free to return to Boston. Agarn sees the Bedbugs as his way to wealth and resigns his commission to become their manager. Their first performance at the Fort Courage saloon is a flop, though, so Agarn takes them to the Hekawi, the local native tribe, whose chief assures them that the Bedbugs will be a big hit "on the teepee circuit" ("That's Show Biz" 1967). To get Agarn to return to F Troop, the captain and Sgt. O'Rourke use a similar ploy to that employed by the castaways of *Gilligan's Island*. With the help of Wrangler Jane, the captain's girlfriend, O'Rourke and a few other members of F Troop form a rival insect-named band, the Termites. Arriving at the Hekawi camp in a horse-drawn wagon, The Termites—sporting shaggy wigs—sing "Lemon Tree," prompting the chief to declare "Termites are in, Bedbugs are out." Agarn, his dreams of show biz glory dashed, returns to F Troop, but becomes suicidal after receiving a letter from the Bedbugs, who went to England after being dropped by the Hekawi. Agarn reports, "They're a big hit in Liverpool, a smash in London; they gave a command performance for the Queen, and now it looks like they're going to be knighted!" ("That's Show Biz" 1967).

Multiplying Memes: Sudden Fame, Hair, and the Barrier of a Common Language

The Bedbugs' reversal of the Beatles' transatlantic triumph highlights another Beatle meme of mid-1960s sitcoms: England and America as countries separated by the barrier of a common language. Early news reports about the Beatles in late 1963 frequently highlighted their English accents, their unique hairstyles, and their cheeky wit, characteristics that Americans had been primed to treasure via a wave of British entertainment that had begun in the 1950s. "Though Americans might find the Beatles achingly familiar," wrote the author of the *Time* piece on the Beatles of November 15, 1963, "they are apparently irresistible to the English" (*"The New Madness"* 1963, 64). Ed Sullivan introduced the Beatles as "four youngsters from Liverpool" (Sullivan 1964) and Newman, Kendrick, and Paar all commented on the Beatles as an Anglo-American artistic and sociological product, the latest in a long line of cultural exchanges between two great English-speaking peoples.

As Steven Stark has written, the Beatles' conquest of America was part of "a wave of Anglophilia [that] had been sweeping the U.S. since the late 1950s and early '60s" (Stark 1997, 17). While *My Fair Lady* and *Camelot* broke box office records on Broadway, *Lawrence of Arabia* (directed by Englishman David Lean) and *Tom Jones* (directed by Englishman Tony Richardson) won Best Picture Oscars in 1962 and 1963. Early- to mid-1960s sitcoms were also swept up in this wave of Anglophilia, featuring characters modeled on the exaggerated British comic types played by actors like Margaret Rutherford and Terry-Thomas. *Bewitched*, for example, which debuted on ABC in September 1964, featured the recurring characters Aunt Clara, played by American actress Marian Lorne in a style reminiscent of Margaret Rutherford's absent-minded English ladies, and Dr. Bombay, portrayed by Welsh actor Bernard Fox with Terry-Thomas style bombast. *The Patty Duke Show* featured its eponymous star as both the Brooklyn teenager Patty Lane and her identical Scottish cousin Cathy, who loved classical music and spoke with a received pronunciation English accent.

When the Beatles burst onto the American scene in February 1964, pop music became, as Michael Bracewell has written, "the principal cultural currency of Englishness in America" (Bracewell 1997, 82). Among the first to capitalize on this new currency were Chad and Jeremy, who sported Beatle haircuts and whose September 1963 minor hit "Yesterday's Gone" rode the Beatle wave to number 21 in the United States in July 1964. In "The Redcoats Are Coming," which aired on *The Dick Van Dyke Show* on February 10, 1965, the duo—renamed Freddie and Ernie—have to spend the night in the suburban home of television writer Rob Petrie and his wife Laura (Dick Van Dyke and Mary Tyler Moore) when the hotel they were going to stay in is besieged by screaming teenage girls. In addition to singing three of their songs on the show, the duo flash instances of the dry British wit that American audiences had come to associate with the Beatles. Walking into the Petries living room, Jeremy points to a plush recliner and asks, "Do you know what we call this in England?" "No, what?" replies Rob. "A chair!" he intones with a hard American "R" ("Redcoats" 1965). The very next week, Chad and Jeremy, this time named Nigel and Patrick, guest-starred on *The Patty Duke Show* in an episode titled "Patty Pits Wits, Two Brits Hits." At the show's open, Chad and Jeremy are performing "Summer Song," their biggest hit in the United States, at what appears to be a school assembly, on a stage flanked by the US flag and the Union Jack. In a flashback, the episode tells how Patty, to help Nigel and Patrick succeed in the music business, tricks her cousin Cathy into playing a record by the duo on the classical music program she hosts on her high school's radio station. Being played on the radio earns Nigel and Patrick a recording contract, and they repay Patty by playing a free concert at Brooklyn Heights High School. All this proves, says Patty at the end of the episode, "that if you've got British pluck, a lot of talent, and long hair, nothing can stop you!" ("Patty" 1965).

In mid-1960s sitcoms, there was no better exemplar of British show-biz pluck than the Beatles' young manager Brian Epstein. The "No Biz Like Show Biz" episode of *The Flintstones*, which aired September 17, 1965, features Fred and Barney dreaming of pop music fame for their children Pebbles and Bamm-Bamm after seeing a televised interview with Eppy Brianstone, manager of The Termites and "the world's most famous teenage impresario" ("There's No Biz" 1965). Of course, Eppy speaks with an English accent and wears an ascot. Englishness as a crucial component for pop music success was also manifested by *The Monkees'* Davy Jones. In "The Success Story" (October 17, 1966), episode 6 of season 1, Davy and the other Monkees find themselves having to scramble for money in anticipation of a visit from Davy's upper-class English grandfather, to whom Davy had boasted that he had become a "huge success" in the United States ("Success" 1966).

Even as late as 1967, the Beatle-derived meme of British musical prowess found its way into *My Three Sons*, arguably the unhippest sitcom of the 1960s. Jeremy Clyde (this time without his partner Chad Stuart) appears as English folk musician Paul Drayton in "The Liverpool Saga." Chip, the middle of the three sons, has a rock group, and when a neighboring teenage girl tells him of an English exchange student who has just come to town from Liverpool, Chip is determined to recruit him to the band. When his bandmates ask Chip what Paul plays, Chip does not know, but assures them that "he's English and he's from Liverpool. What more do you want?" ("Liverpool" 1967). But Paul from Liverpool disappoints the band when he pulls out his acoustic guitar and plays a fingerpicked version of "Greensleeves." All works out in the end, though, when Paul, sitting in with Chip's group on a rock version of "Greensleeves," helps them win a battle of the bands, demonstrating yet again England's might in the world of rock music. That canny talent scouts like Epstein—as he had done with the Beatles—could make teen sensations out of ordinary folks was another common meme of 1960s sitcoms. *The Addams Family* and *The Munsters*, both of which premiered in the fall of 1964, built episodes around the sudden ascension of one of their characters to pop music fame. In "Lurch, the Teenage Idol," Gomez Addams is convinced that his butler Lurch (played by Ted Cassidy) has what it takes to be a pop star. Though record producer Mizzy Bickel tries to put Gomez off by explaining that he only handles "standard groups like the Polecats, the Zombies, and the Head Splitters," after hearing Lurch grunt while playing the harpsichord, Bickel declares "I'm going to make him the biggest thing in the music business" ("Lurch" 1965). Bickle is true to his word, and soon the Addams' family home is mobbed by teenagers screaming for Lurch. Life imitated art when Cassidy—as Lurch—appeared on *Shindig* on October 30, 1965, singing and dancing to "Do the Lurch," a record he had cut with Capitol producer Gary Paxton. In "Will Success Spoil Herman Munster?", Herman rockets to stardom when his recording of "Dem Bones" hits number three on the top forty. In a dream sequence, Herman's wife Lily worries that she will lose him to rock and roll stardom, as she envisions him, playing an electric guitar and dressed like Marlon Brando in *The Wild Ones*, flanked by go-go girls, singing "Love, love you baby, and all that other groovy junk! / Be my swingin' baby, I'll be your ever-lovin' punk!" before fading out to repeated shouts of "Yeah, yeah, yeah!" ("Will Success" 1965).

Boy, You're Gonna Carry That Weight: Ringo as Punchline

American sitcoms for the most part did not individually characterize the four or five members of their made-up groups, who—like the Beatles—came off as indistinguishable in their matching hairstyles and stage suits. The exception to this rule, though, was Ringo. Likely because he was both the comic protagonist and butt of most of the jokes in *A Hard Day's Night* and *Help!*, Ringo was singled out by sitcom writers and the doleful, hangdog character he projected in the Beatles' films mined for its comic possibilities. In his naivete, guilelessness, and childlike charm, *The Monkees'* Peter Tork plays the Ringo of that group, throughout the run of the series but especially in "The Case of the Missing Monkee." Like Ringo in *Help!*, in this episode Peter is abducted by a mad scientist, from whom he must be rescued by his bandmates ("Case" 1967). In "Monkees Manhattan Style," the band's misadventures start when Peter is invited to a gambling den called "The Millionaire's Club" mirroring Ringo's invitation to Le Cirque in *A Hard Day's Night* ("Monkees Manhattan" 1967). Peter is especially Ringo-like in the first season finale, which follows the Monkees for a backstage look at their Phoenix concert in January of 1967. Throughout the episode Peter snaps photos with a Pentax single-lens reflex camera, the same model Ringo uses during the "parading" sequence of *A Hard Day's Night*.

The sitcoms' special focus on Ringo was jump-started by songwriter/parodist Allan Sherman, who in early 1965 recorded "The Ballad of Ringo Starr," and later that year recorded "Pop Hates the Beatles" for his third album, *Songs for Swingin' Livers*. Sherman had rocketed to nationwide fame in 1962 after President Kennedy was overheard singing "Sarah Jackman," a parody of "Frere Jacques" that appeared on Sherman's album *My Son, the Folk Singer*. The president's endorsement helped make that album the fastest-selling record in American history up to that time. Sherman followed up the success of *My Son, the Folk Singer* with "Hello Muddah, Hello Faddah" in August 1963, and was arguably the most successful American recording artist of the four months preceding the Beatles' arrival. Pushed out of the limelight by the Beatles, Sherman retaliated with "The Ballad of Ringo Starr," a parody version of Lorne Greene's 1964 gunfighter ballad "Ringo," which Sherman sang on *Funnyland*, the pilot of a one-hour comedy variety show that premiered on January 18, 1965.

Spoken, rather than sung (like Greene's original), "The Ballad of Ringo Starr" tells the story of an encounter with a man from Liverpool who sought to prove his mettle as the fastest barber in the west by cutting "the hair of Ringo." The unnamed man is unsuccessful in his quest; but at the end of the song Sherman receives a telegram "collect to me" that reveals that the barber—though he never managed to cut Ringo's hair—did perform the tonsillectomy that delayed Ringo's appearance in the Beatles' 1964 tour of the Netherlands and Australia (*Funnyland* 1965). Later that year, Sherman appeared on the *Dean Martin Show* to sing—with Martin and crooner Vic Damone—"Pop Hates the Beatles," in which the Beatles are derided for wearing out phonograph needles, playing out of tune, failing to stay in England where they belong, and provoking girls to scream. In the song—which is set to the tune of "Pop Goes the Weasel—Sherman mentions only one of the Beatles by name, and of course it's Ringo, the "one with the drum": "It shows you what a boy can become / Without a sense of rhythm!" (Sherman 1964). Sherman had, perhaps, good reason to hate the Beatles: after the British Invasion, he never came close to approaching the wild acclaim he enjoyed in the early sixties. But however resentful its impetus, "Pop Hates the Beatles" offers a complete list of Greatest Generation Beatle memes in a tight three minutes: long hair, cacophony rather than music, hysterical teenagers, and the fervent belief that the group represented Britain's revenge on the United States for the revolution. Sherman ends the song by calling on American parents to re-enact the Boston tea party and throw the boys from Liverpool into Boston Harbor—but not before we "take 'em to a barber!" (Sherman 1964).

Ringo's stagy sobriquet alone might have been enough to single him out for specific attention, like naming the four Mosquitoes of *Gilligan's Island* Bingo, Bango, Bongo, and Irving. Another Ringo-related comic meme, however, arose from the suggestion—widely circulating at the time—that in joining the Beatles shortly before their big break, he had been the beneficiary of the world's luckiest break. *F Troop* exploited this meme through a recurring character named Private Leonard "Wrongo" Starr, around whom the series built episodes in both of its two seasons. Portrayed by Henry Gibson, who a year or so later would become nationally famous for the simplistic "flower child" poems he recited on *Rowan and Martin's Laugh-In*, Wrongo Starr—like his namesake—is slight and soft-spoken, but earnest and childlike. Unlike Ringo, however, the sheepish Wrongo lives under a cloud of bad luck. As he explains to O'Rourke, Agarn, and the captain of F Troop, "Everywhere I go, things go wrong—that's why they call me Wrongo" ("Wrongo Starr" 1966). Of course, in both Wrongo Starr episodes, Wrongo's lack of guile ends up saving the day by foiling the ill intentions of the episodes' villains. In "Wrongo Starr and the Lady in Black," a beautiful young widow comes to town. Her history of having married several soldiers who subsequently died under mysterious circumstances—leaving her as sole heir or life insurance beneficiary—soon comes to light. O'Rourke tricks her into thinking Wrongo has inherited a million dollars; but when she finds this is not true, she leaves town. Gibson reprised his role as Wrongo in the second season episode "The Return of Wrongo Starr." This time, Wrongo is tasked with providing F Troop with dynamite, "a new weapon" ("Return of Wrongo" 1966). Naturally, clumsy Wrongo mishandles his dangerous cargo. But instead of blowing up both himself and the rest of Four Courage, Wrongo emerges as the hero when his bungling attempts to do his duty end up foiling an Apache attack.

The Beatles and the Hippie Menace

As the Beatles' image changed from clean-cut moptops to pioneers of psychedelia and the hippie movement in 1967 and 1968, new memes corresponding to this step in the group's evolution appeared. As mid-1960s sitcoms did in response to their long hair, loud music, and ability to incite teenage frenzy, late-1960s sitcoms saw the Beatles' psychedelic turn as a spur to generational conflict, seizing on George Harrison's interest in Indian folk music and Hindu philosophy and religion to revive early sixties racist tropes of Asian brainwashing, memorably featured in John Frankenheimer's 1962 film *The Manchurian Candidate*. The *Get Smart* episode "The Groovy Guru" pits secret agents Maxwell Smart and Agent 99 against the zombiefied hippie followers of the Groovy Guru. Smart and 99 are dispatched to the "Temple of Meditation and Inner Peace," where they meet the Groovy Guru (played by Larry Storch of *F Troop*), who—like a Bond villain—delineates his evil scheme and demonstrates his mind-control techniques. These techniques include the music of "The Sacred Cows," named by 99 as "the hottest rock and roll group in the country" ("Groovy" 1968). Backed by The Sacred Cows' twangy electric guitars, the Groovy Guru explains that by electronically inserting subliminal messaging into their music, the "swingin' sounds ain't just hip, they're hypnotizing!" which he demonstrates by pointing to a pair of conservative-suited CONTROL agents, glassy-eyed and dancing the frug. As the Sacred Cows play "Kill, Kill, Kill" and neon lights on the wall flash anti-authoritarian slogans ("Rebellion Is Hip", "Obey", "Make Trouble"), Agent 99 finds herself unable to resist dancing, and feels herself succumbing to the lyrics which rhyme "thrill" with "kill," and urge her to "Bump off a square / Yeah, yeah, yeah!" ("Groovy" 1968).

Hippie culture as the potentially dangerous outgrowth of the mass hysteria of Beatlemania also appears as a comic meme in the *Bewitched* episode "Hippie, Hippie, Hooray." Accompanying herself on a psychedelically painted electric guitar, Samantha Stevens' mischievous identical cousin Serena (also played by Elizabeth Montgomery) entertains Darin Stevens' square boss and his wife with "The If'n Song," which tells the advertising executive that he can appeal to the young demographic by never bathing or combing his hair, concluding with the Beatles' signature phrase: "Yeah, yeah, yeah!" ("Hippie" 1968). Though in the psychedelic era the young have escalated the war between the generations by not only wearing their hair long but refusing to wash or comb it, "yeah, yeah, yeah" connects the older generation's fear of the hippie menace back to the Beatles, reifying this group's status as the source of most of the comic memes and tropes stemming from rock and roll music's cultural domination of the 1960s.

Memes as Generational Mediators

By processing the culturally disruptive dimensions of the Beatles and Beatlemania through memetic repetition and comic deflation, sitcoms fulfilled what John Bryant has defined as the function of all formulaic art: providing "a complex mode of fantasy in which recurring patterns of aesthetic conflict (as revealed in plot, character, and imagery) correspond to and help resolve social conflicts perceived by a particular audience" (Bryant 1989, 119). As delighted as teenagers were with the arrival of the Beatles on America's shores, their parents and grandparents—who comprised most of sitcoms' audiences—were wary, even a little alarmed by this latest outbreak of mass hysteria and the seismic shift in generational power it betokened. Acknowledging that the world was undergoing rapid and drastic change, but at the same time enabling the older generation gently to mock emergent realities, the "bug music" memes of American sitcoms mediated between the Greatest Generation's desire for cultural stability and the memetic evolutionary pressures that would sweep that stability away.

References

Beatles, The. 2000. *The Beatles Anthology*. San Francisco: Chronicle Books.

Bracewell, Michael. 1997. *England Is Mine: Pop Life in Albion from Wilde to Goldie*. Hammersmith: Flamingo.

Bryant, John. 1989. "Situation Comedy of the Sixties: The Evolution of a Popular Genre." *Studies in American Humor* 7, no. 2: 118–39.

"Bugged by the Love Bugs." 1965. *The Bing Crosby Show*. Episode 1: 16.Directed by James Sheldon. Written by William Morrow. ABC, January 18.

"The Case of the Missing Monkee." 1967. *The Monkees*. Episode 1: 17.Directed by Bob Rafelson. Written by Dee Caruso and Paul Mazursky. NBC, January 9.

Crandall, Bill. 2014. "Ed Sullivan: "Who the Hell are the Beatles?." *CBS News*, January 17, 2014, /www.cbsnews.com/newyork/news/ed-sullivan-who-the-hell-are-the-beatles/?intcid=CNM-00-10abd1h.

Dawkins, Richard. 2016. *The Selfish Gene*. Fourth Edition. Oxford: Oxford University Press.

Dennett, Daniel C. 1990. "Memes and the Exploitation of Imagination." *The Journal of Aesthetics and Art Criticism* 48, no. 2 (Spring): 127–35.

"Don't Bug the Mosquitoes." 1965. *Gilligan's Island*. Episode 2: 12.Directed by Steve Binder. Written by Sherwood Schwartz and Brad Radnitz. CBS, December 9.

"Far Out Munsters." 1965. *The Munsters*. Episode 1: 26. Directed by Joseph Pevney. Written by Dick Conway. CBS, March 18.

Funnyland. 1965. Directed by Greg Garrison. Written by Sam Bobrick, Bill Idelson, Roger Price, Allan Sherman, and David Vern. NBC, January 18.

"The Groovy Guru." 1968. *Get Smart*. Episode 3: 15.Directed by James Komack. Written by Norman Paul and Burt Nodella. CBS, January 13.

"The Hatrocks and the Gruesomes." 1965. *The Flintstones*. Episode 5: 19. Directed by Joseph Barbera and William Hanna. Written by Alan Dinehart and Herbert Finn. ABC, January 22.

"Hippie, Hippie, Hooray." 1968. *Bewitched*. Episode 4: 21. Directed by William Asher. Written by Michael Morris and Sol Saks. ABC, February 1.

Kendrick, Alexander. 1963. *The CBS Evening News*, December 10.

"Liverpool Saga." 1967. *My Three Sons*. Episode 8:16. Directed by Frederick De Cordova. Written by Freddy Rhea. ABC, December 23.

"Lurch, the Teenage Idol." 1965. *The Addams Family*. Episode 1: 33. Directed by Sidney Lanfield. Written by Phil Leslie. ABC, May 14.

"Monkees Manhattan Style." 1967. *The Monkees*. Episode 1: 30. Directed by Russ Mayberry. Written by Gerald Gardner and Dee Caruso. NBC, April 10.

"The Monkees on Tour." 1967. *The Monkees*. Episode 1: 32. Directed by Bob Rafelson. Written by Dee Caruso, Gerald Gardiner, and Paul Mazursky. NBC, April 14.

"The New Madness." *Time*. November 15, 1963. 64.

Newman, Edwin. 1963. *The Huntley-Brinkley Report*, November 18.

Paar, Jack. 1964. *The Jack Paar Show*. NBC, January 3.

"Patty Pits Wits, Two Brits Hits." 1965. *The Patty Duke Show*. Episode 2: 23. Directed by Bill Colleran. Written by Arnold Horwitt. ABC, February 17.

"The Redcoats are Coming." 1965. *The Dick Van Dyke Show*. Episode 4: 20. Directed by Jerry Paris. Written by Bill Persky and Sam Denoff. CBS, February 10.

"The Return of Wrongo Starr." 1966. *F Troop*. Episode 2: 14. Directed by Gary Nelson. Written by James Barnett and Stan Dreben. ABC, December 8.

Sherman, Allan. 1964. "Pop Hates the Beatles," track 6 on *For Swingin' Livers Only*. Warner Brothers, 1964.

Stark, Steven D. 1997. *Meet the Beatles*. New York: HarperCollins.

"Success Story." 1966. *The Monkees*. Episode 1: 6. Directed by James Frawley. Written by Dee Caruso and Bernie Orenstein. NBC, October 17.

Sullivan, Ed. 1964. *The Ed Sullivan Show*. CBS, February 9.

"That's Show Biz." 1967. *F Troop*. Episode 2: 35. Directed by Hollingsworth Morse. Written by Arthur Julian. ABC, February 9.

"There's No Biz Like Show Biz." 1965. *The Flintstones*. Episode 6: 1. Directed by Joseph Barbera and William Hanna. Written by Alan Dinehart and Herbert Finn. ABC, September 17.

"Will Success Spoil Herman Munster?" 1965. *The Munsters*. Episode 2: 12. Directed by Ezra Stone. Written by Lou Shaw. CBS, December 9.

"Wrongo Starr and the Lady in Black." 1966. *F Troop*. Episode 1: 18. Directed by Charles R. Rondeau. Written by Stan Dreben and Howard Merrill. ABC, January 11.

11

The Beatles and the Birth of British Comedy in the 1960s with *Beyond the Fringe* and *Monty Python's Flying Circus*

Richard Mills

In the early 1960s, *Beyond the Fringe* "rained satire [...] day and night, harder and harder and harder, spreading outwards from London to cover the whole of the British Isles," said Michael Frayn (1987, 7). The Beatles' satirical humor had a similarly profound social impact. For Baby Boomer audiences, *Beyond the Fringe* and the Beatles had the artistic freedom to critique the British establishment. The Fringers' groundbreaking sketches ridiculed British politicians for the first time; before *Beyond the Fringe*, it was unheard of for comedians to mimic politicians. When British Prime Minister Harold Macmillan went to see the show in at the Fortune Theatre, Convent Garden, London in 1962, Peter Cook wandered off script and aimed a series of disparaging jokes at the prime minister, leaving Macmillan no option but to sit there and take it all (Sandbrook 2005, 638). The Beatles presented comparable cheek in their press conferences and interviews, which often became a "comic dialogue between the four Scousers and the middle-class voice[s] of the BBC" (Atkinson 2010, 21).

Picking up where the Beatles left off, Monty Python's absurdism was also the comedy of transgression; both the Beatles and the Pythons were an inextricably wedded to the subversive *zeitgeist* of the 1960s:

> The late George Harrison used to say that he felt the spirit of the Beatles passed on to Monty Python. After all, Python came together in 1969, just as the Fab Four were becoming four fairly fab individuals. Both were groups of men who in a short period of time produced an amazing body of work that came to dominate their particular field, whether music or comedy. And of course, both, in their own way, changed the world.

(McCabe 2003, 6)

The comedy of *Beyond the Fringe*, the Beatles, and Monty Python had a politically enlightening effect merging satire and surrealism, they were in the nonsense tradition of Lewis Carroll, Edward Lear, and *The Goon Show*: taking the real world and turning it on its head.[1] Bearing McCabe's statement regarding an English cultural and social revolution in mind, my chapter discusses the political significance of the comedy of these three 1960s phenomena.

The two predominant styles in British comedy in the 1960s were satire and surrealism, exemplified in *Beyond the Fringe* (1960–4), the Beatles (1962–70), and *Monty Python's Flying Circus* (1969–74).[2] Although the Beatles were musicians first, their surreal and satirical humor places them in a similar artistic context to the Fringers and the Pythons. The art of all three birthed a British comedy that had a "predisposition to treat everything that becomes sacred and unquestionable with reserve, to turn pathos into absurdity, to undermine the dead certainties of the tribe" (Jarniewicz 2010, 77). In this chapter, I argue that the Beatles embody tropes, puns, and subversive humor that are found in *Beyond the Fringe* and Monty Python. Their humor was an indispensable part of their act and it is unlikely that they would have been as successful without their mordant, carnivalesque, and surreal angle on life.

Surrealism and the Bakhtinian Carnivalesque in the Fringers, the Beatles, and the Pythons

Surrealism is central to the work of all three groups. *Beyond the Fringe* surreally riffed on philosophers, no doubt influencing the Pythons who attend the Beyond the Fringe show, Cleese and Idle describing it as the greatest and funniest moment of their lives. The Fringe philosophy sketch combined surrealism and high culture for the reception of a general audience: "Jonathan: Plato, Aristotle [...] were asking questions about life and death that were entirely irrelevant. Alan: I call them not philosophers but para-philosophers. [...] Well you've heard of these chaps—paratroopers—well, para-philosophers are the same, you see.

---

[1] Edward Lear (1812–88) was an English author and poet who was best known for his nonsense children literature. Lear was an influence on John Lennon's books *In His Own Write* (1964) and *A Spaniard in the Works* (1965). His influence was acknowledged by the Beatles in their song "Paperback Writer" in the lyrics "It's based on novel by a man named Lear."

[2] Russ Bestley describes satire as "a mode of social criticism that adopts a scornful, mocking, or sarcastic tone in order to improve, destroy, or increase awareness of the object of its ridicule" (2019, 77). For more on the British satire boom of the 1960s, see Carpenter 2000.

Philosophers with their feet off the ground" (Bennett et al. 1987, 51). Eroticized women[3] and subconscious dream imagery are an essential part of the Pythons' work. Terry Gilliam's cartoons, which often interrupt sketches, are indispensable to the Monty Python team. Flying sheep, giant fish, a huge Bronzini foot, linguistic nonsense all add up to a kaleidoscopic surreal mosaic unlike anything therefore to on British TV. The Beatles work embraced psychedelia in a similar manner to the Pythons, which by its very definition is surreal: that is disparate unrelated dream images from the subconscious. As I will discuss later, "I Am the Walrus" is the acme of the Beatles surreal psychedelic period with its litany of Hare Krishnas, pigs in a sty, policemen in a row, and the kicking of the nineteenth-century Gothic writer Edgar Allan Poe.

The surrealist transgression which ridiculed conformist nine-to-five society is the essence of these three 1960s cultural monoliths. The Beatles, the Fringers and the Pythons predicated their art on a political surrealism that influenced the UK, especially during the counter-cultural pop revolution in the 1960s. Politics is shaped by culture and vice versa. Politics decides where, when, and how money is spent; art on the other hand shapes society's direction. In a Marxist sense, the Base (the economic structure) is affected by the Superstructure (the art and culture): both affect the other. The "straight" society was something that was ridiculed by these three comedy/musician groups. There is a serious dimension to these troupes' art, that is, the "straight" society these long-haired artists interrogated has economist concerns with the dissemination and production of money, whereas these satirical groups impacted on society because they have a more culturalist angle on social formations.

It is impossible to quantify the socio-cultural effect that these groups had on British society in the 1960s. My contention is that the British class system and the aesthetics of British humor were radically changed by these innovative comic artists. It is not an oversimplification to state that nothing was immune to ridicule after the Fringers, the Beatles, and the Pythons. Historically speaking, the consumer boom of the 1960s, the creation of the NHS under a Labour government in 1948, and the access of working and lower-middle class people to higher education meant that pop music and comedy had a new confident

[3] When women did appear in Python, it was nearly always men in drag talking in high squeaky voices, and dressed in dowdy middle-aged women's clothes, which made them look like Pepperpots! the name the Pythons called older women to distinguish them from young attractive fetishized women, played by the only Python woman, Carol Cleveland.

meritocracy that inverted the authority of Church and State. We can broadly refer the 1960s as a period akin to what the philosopher Mikhail Bakhtin called the Carnivalesque[4] since there was a certain comedic tendency characterized by intellectual and satirical surrealism. The 1960s revelers in the UK were better fed, heathier, and better educated. This meant they could comment on the state of the nation, often from the inside of important institutions, such as Oxbridge in the case of the Fringers and the Pythons. The Beatles also issued a critique from the inside, such as their anarchic Liverpudlian accents on the BBC or cheeky request for the Queen Mother to "rattle her jewelry" at the Royal Variety Performance in 1963. The 1960s carnival was a period when Church and State had no control over the revelers; it cleared the ground for new ideas to enter public discourse.

Beyond the Fringe, the Beatles, and Monty Python personify cultural change and cultural spaces where "the laws, prohibitions, and restrictions that determine the structure and order of ordinary life [...] are suspended" (Bakhtin 1965/1984, 122–3). Along these lines, the clown is an embodiment of surrealism and satire, and who uses status inversion "as positive spaces of cultural levelling" (Kohl 2010, 79). Consider, for example, the Rabelaisian sexuality of "Why Don't We Do It in the Road" and status inverting carnival of "Helter Skelter." The Fringers, the Pythons, and the Beatles epitomize the Bakhtinian carnival: "Carnival laughter is the laughter of the people. [...] It is directed at everyone, including the carnival participants [...] This laugher is ambivalent: it is gay, triumphant, and at the same time, mocking, deriding" (Bakhtin 1965/1984, 11–12).

In a Bakhtinian sense, the Beatles, the Fringers, and the Pythons used absurdism and surrealism to comment on society. Their jokes and puns were part of a 1960s satire boom that was inconvenient and irresponsible using sick, bodily humor, surreal puns, and mordant jokes to poke fun at institutions and middle-of-the-road society (see Carpenter 2000). It is difficult to gauge the effect of these satirical artists, but their clowning and humor did make their audiences at least engage with politics. These artists regularly shocked when they confronted taboos, such as the Fringers satirically ridiculing politicians, the Beatles teasing interviewers, or the Pythons writing a sketch advocating cannibalism. The result is the comedy of transgression that is understood within the cultural revolution of the 1960s.

---

[4] To Bakhtin, the Carnivalesque denotes the carnivals of medieval Europe where the authority of Church and State were inverted temporarily; he also saw the Carnivalesque as a literary and comic tendency.

Although these artists didn't have an explicit political ideology, I argue that their blend of satire and surrealism critiqued the rigidity, hypocrisy, and absurdity of the English class-based economic and political system. The comedy of *Beyond the Fringe*, the Beatles, and *Monty Python's Flying Circus* is a mix of clownish satire and surrealism whereby the clown has a definite social function: "The clown [...] lives with the elite and polite society, but does not belong to this company and makes impertinent remarks about it. He questions everything that is regarded self-evident. He looks at things from aside, discovering what is not obvious in the supposedly obvious and what is not definite or not conclusive in the supposedly definitive or conclusive" (Jarniewicz 2010, 76). The Polish philosopher Leszek Kolakowski has also written about the clown figure as an embodiment of satire and surrealism, who has the capacity to turn the world upside down: "the philosophy of the clowns in any epoch unmasks what is most permanent, reveals as contradictory what is indisputable, makes fun of the self-evident truths of the common sense, looks for reason in absurdities [...] because of mistrust towards the stabilized world" (1989, 161–80).

Kolakowski's satirical concept is similar to what theater scholar Richard Weihe terms *Narrenfreiheit* or the fool's liberty (2016, 272), which "allows the clown to speak the truth freely and without risk of punishment," as Matthias Heyman explains elsewhere in this volume (2023, 52). Kolakowski's thesis is a fitting description of the carnivalesque satire and the weaponized surrealism of *Beyond the Fringe*, the Beatles, and *Monty Python's Flying Circus*, as all three belong to a satire boom that changed 1960s England: *Beyond the Fringe* was the first show to ridicule British politicians openly on stage, the Beatles' regional accents and surreal humor were likewise transgressive, ridiculing the Received Pronunciation of the middle and upper classes, and the Python's destructive surrealism stimulated what George Meredith called "thoughtful laughter" (Ives 1998, 140). In other words, 1960s comedy was a very serious business.

That business is reflected in the beginning of the Beatles' relationship with their producer George Martin, who was, in fact, unimpressed with the Beatles' music at their audition in January 1962, but he went on to sign the band because he loved their sense of humor. It is not surprising that Martin loved the Beatles' cheeky humor given their shared love of *The Goon Show* and Martin had recorded comedy albums with Peter Sellers and Spike Milligan. Comedy had, in fact, kickstarted Martin's sucess; EMI put him in charge of EMI's comedy label and "[q]uite suddenly Parlophone had emerged as the home for the premier British comedians of the day" (Womack 2017, 48). Martin recorded the *Beyond the Fringe* show at the Cambridge Theatre in London's West End, and subsequently went on to record them over five times and the result "was a smash hit for Parlophone, ushering in a new era of satirical comedy in Great Britain" (2017, 48). Martin "found himself rather cannily moving about the satire boom's circle" (2017, 49). Martin is a common factor between the Beatles and the Fringers, and it continues to be striking how much he was equally at home in satire and pop circles.

The Beatles are relational to the Fringers and the Pythons because of their sense of absurd subversiveness; music also played a significant role in the success of the Fringers and the Pythons. Dudley Moore won an organ scholarship to Cambridge and his musical satires were an essential part of the huge success of *Beyond the Fringe*. Musical satire was an essential ingredient in the success of the Pythons, too, from satirical songs in the first series of *Monty Python's Flying Circus* in 1969 through their Christ-lite Brian showbiz song on the cross to their triumphant swan song and the O2 in 2014—the O2 show was at least 50 percent song and dance; it was in many ways *Monty Python: The Musical*. The reason for the emphasis on music was that the conception, organization, and writing of the show was largely by Eric Idle—the musical Python. Idle is a singer, songwriter, and guitarist of estimable ability. These three groups deployed music and comedy to make surreal and transgressive art.

The new ideas promulgated by these acts were surrealism, satire and, in the case of the Beatles, the demotic working-class voice used to comic effect. The table below is a time line of British comedy and popular music in the years 1961 to 1974: I end in 1974 as I am defining 1961 to 1974 as the long 1960s. In fact, 1974 seems much more in keeping with current attitudes on dress and sexual emancipation in the 1960s than sepia and far off 1961, where short back and sides haircuts and sober suits, shirts and ties were *de rigueur* for aspiring British men. Uniformity in dress was so ubiquitous in the UK pre-1960s that even a cursory glance at an English soccer match pre-1962 will show the football fans dressed in identical dark suits and ties. The Beatles had to eschew black leather for suits to find success and the Fringers all dressed in conservative business suits. By 1974 in the UK, however, soft drugs were ubiquitous and politicians and footballers sported long hair. It is also appropriate to mention the sexual politics of these performers.

These three groups are male and the casual sexism of their comedy will be addressed in this chapter: here are groups with no women and when women characters are required, the Pythons usually drag up and play women themselves[5]: Terry Jones has written that he was worried that contemporary view of gender "was going to tear us to shreds" (Dobrogoszcz 2014, 7). The Beatles, too, often depicted women as exoticized dream others, such as Lucy in the Sky, although Eleanor Rigby and Lady Madonna are recognizably "real" to contemporary cultural observers. Given the limitations in time and space that a chapter in a book dictates, my ruminations on the birth of British comedy take the readers on a journey in a time capsule that drops us down in 1960s Britain where three all-male groups sliced up the comic empire between themselves.

Table 11.1 (**Comedy and Music in the Long 1960s**) outlines the timeline of my discussion of the Birth of British comedy. As you can see, I trace the birth of British comedy to the performance of Peter Cook's impersonation of the British Prime Minister Harold Macmillan in 1961 ending with the Peter Cook and Dudley Moore's satire of 1960s pop, the LSD Bumblebee. The Beatles' comedy

Table 11.1 Comedy and Music in the Long 1960s

Beyond the Fringe and related	"T.V.P.M" sketch in *Beyond the Fringe* (1961)	"Aftermyth of War" sketch in *Beyond the Fringe* (1961)	"The L.S. Bumble Bee," Peter Cook and Dudley Moore in *Not Only ... But Also* (1967)
The Beatles	*Pop Goes The Beatles* (BBC Radio, 1963)	The Mersey Sound. Written and produced by Don Haworth for BBC-TV, 1963.	The *Yesterday and Today* album cover (Capitol, 1966) "I Am the Walrus" (Parlophone, 1967)
Monty Python's Flying Circus (1969–74)	"The Undertakers" sketch in "Royal Episode Thirteen" (1970)	"The Man Who Speaks ..." sketch in "Royal Episode Thirteen" (1970)	"The Man Who Speaks in Anagrams" sketch in "Blood, Devastation, Death, War and Horror" (1972)

---

[5] The exception who proves the rule is the actor Carol Cleveland, who occasionally played young and desirable women.

is analyzed in interviews, album covers, and songs. The Pythons' carnivalesque comedy is typified in three groundbreaking sketches, which highlight the team's love of grotesque bodily humor and absurd linguistic flights of fancy. These texts personify the birth of British comedy as a profound rumination and commentary on class-ridden British society in a surrealist manner. All three groups use the trope of the fool as status inversion: "Fools represent a topsy-turvy world in which the king is a fool and a fool is a king" (Dobrogoszcz 2014, 63). The tripartite fools on top of the comedy hill in 1960 Britain use comedy to make a statement about society and the absurdity: "The Pythons manage to strip lies, denial, and pretense from every subject they touch—they have no illusions: life is absurd, unpredictable, often cruel, and it always ends in death" (Dobrogoszcz 2014, 20).

The Fringers, the Beatles, and the Pythons poignant critique of British culture begins in 1961 with Peter Cook's cruel parody of Harold Macmillan, Prime Minister of the UK from 1957 to 1963. To this writer, this performance is the ground zero of British comedy where the comedy manifesto was that everybody was a target regardless of position or privilege. This theatrical explosion affected all aspects of English cultural life, not just comedy. The political and cultural ramifications were far reaching, as a new iconoclasm had entered British life. In a similar manner to Cook's exaggerated gargoyle-like and cruel impersonation of Macmillan, we had the Beatles joking and subverting interviewers turning press conferences into subversive stand-up routines. Cook's iconoclasm in Beyond the Fringe was the precursor to David Frost's satire *That Was the Week That Was.*[6]

Beyond the Fringe and Related

Cook's performance of Macmillan is an out of touch Conservative patriarch who capriciously drones in a boring monotone jumping from subject to subject in an eccentric manner. There is something of the medieval carnivalesque about Cook's portrait of Macmillan. Cook's impersonation of Macmillan, or a character clearly meant to represent him, such as Lord Stockton, was a staple of his television performances on British TV for years after *Beyond the Fringe.*[7]

[6] *That Was the Week That Was* or TW3 was a groundbreaking, satirical British television show which ran from 1962 to 1963 before being pulled off the air before the 1964 General Election for fear that its controversial content would sway the result. This was deemed unacceptable as the BBC was supposed to be politically unbiased.
[7] Peter Cook's Macmillan is disguised as Lord Stockton on *Saturday Night Live* (UK, Channel 4, 1986).

In the sketch "T.V.P.M.," a reference to the increasing influence television was having in influencing election campaigns, Cook twitches, groans, and twists his face to represent Supermac as a befuddled grandfather confused by the rapid changes of the 1960s Britain.[8] He begins by mocking Britain's reduced status in world post-Suez: in the years 1957–64, Britain lost what remained of its Empire, and Cook flags up this post-colonial crisis in his monologue:

> I then went on to America, and there I had talks with a young vigorous President of that great country, and danced with his very lovely lady wife. We talked of many things, including Great Britain's position as some kind of honest broker. I agreed with him, when he said no nation could be more honest, and he agreed with me, when I chaffed him that no nation could be broker.
>
> (Bennett et al. 1987, 54)

Cook's post-colonial riff had an unsettling effect on the audience. Michael Frayn attended the show in 1961 and wrote that the Macmillan sketch upset a young Tory couple in the audience:

> The couple in front of me, a perfectly sound pair of young Tories, were right with us, neighing away like demented horses, until the middle of Peter Cook's lampoon on Macmillan, when the man turned to the girl and said in an appalled whisper, 'I say! This is supposed to be the Prime Minister,' after which they sat in silence for the rest of the evening.
>
> (Frayn 1987, 7)

With the benefit of hindsight in the 21st Century, this is a very mild and inoffensive critique, but at the time it was shocking.

The satire had of course reached the North of England and the four Beatles were fans who were taking their iconoclastic cue from the Oxbridge fab four of Alan, Peter, Jonathan, and Dud. John Lennon was a fan of Cook's puns and wordplay, and Peter Cook and Dudley Moore became good friends of the Beatles in the 1960s; Lennon appeared in Cook's and Dudley's hit series Not *Only ... But Also* in a sketch with Cook. Lennon appeared three times in the series: he read his nonsense poetry on the pilot in 1964, the first episode of the first series in 1965, and he famously played Dan, a doorman of club located in a toilet[9] on an episode that aired on 26 December 1966. George Martin, too, was a huge fan of comedy, and when the

---

[8] Supermac was a 1958 cartoon image of Macmillan, which became an enduring nickname. The image by Vicky Weisz first appeared in London's *Evening Standard* on 6 November 1958.

[9] The public toilet on Broadwick Street, London (near to Carnaby Street and Berwick Street) is now a heritage tourist site for Beatles and Peter Cook fans. The lavatorial and bodily humor here is in keeping with Bakhtin's ideas on the Carnivalesque.

Beyond the Fringe team recorded their first album for Parlophone (the soon-to-be Beatles label!), it was only fitting that he was the producer. The Fringers, the Beatles, and the Pythons represented a new British comedy elite. Jerzy Jarniewicz refers to these figures as "clowns": "The clown […] lives with the elite and polite society, but does not belong to this company and makes impertinent remarks about it" (2010, 76). Cook green-lighted this impertinence on stage in 1961; as Frayn contends, "It was the official opening of the Satirical Sixties" (1987, 7).

The Fringers' sketch "Aftermyth of War" (Bennett, Cook, Miller, and Moore 1987, 72) proved to be even more controversial than "T.V.P.M." The Oxbridge fab four turned their satirical sights on the clichés of World War II: Spitfires, British stoicism, stiff upper lips, cheery cockneys, and upper-class poltroons. All four Fringers excel in this piece: Cook is a cockney gardener who is more concerned with his vegetables than the Luftwaffe raging above him; Bennett drags up to play a middle-aged woman who is incredulous that Hitler won't answer her phone call to stop the war; Dudley provides portentous and poignant score for the sketch, but the *coup de grace* is Cook and Miller playing two RAF men. The Cook character urges Miller to lay down his life as a futile gesture to boost the war effort: this is funny, sharp, and genuinely shocking to older audience members for whom the war was fresh trauma only sixteen years hence.

The biopic of Peter Cook and Dudley Moore, *Not Only But Always* (Johnston 2004), depicts the consternation this sketch caused as one middle-aged walked at a pre-West End performance in Brighton. As he left the theater, he interrupted Cook and Miller in mid-flow, acidly observing, "You young bounders don't know the first thing about it" (Johnston 2004). The scene ends with Cook and Miller flabbergasted and mouths agape, staring speechless as the man leaves. Satire may have a limited effect on the economic base, but at this moment the 1960s Superstructure bubbled and hissed with a splash of subversion. There were to be more splashes of iconoclasm with Cook and Moore, the Beatles, and the Pythons. As the long 1960s drew to an end circa 1974, Britain had been changed irreversibly by a tsunami of comedy absurdism from all three groups.

"The L.S. Bumble Bee" (1967) is a song parody by Peter Cook and Dudley Moore from *Not Only … But Also*.[10] So accurate was this fab faux satire, replete with sitars and whimsical hippy lyrics, that Disc Jockeys in the 1960s mistakenly thought the song was an outtake by the Beatles. This hippie counterculture parody shows the extent to which the Beatles, the Fringers, and the Pythons

---

[10] Following Jerry Palmer, Bestley explains parody as consisting "of the imitation (allusion, if not direct quotation or misquotation) of some other text or texts, even if only by using stylistic devices which are typical of the text(s) in question" (2019, 77).

aesthetic and ideas intersected. The song is performed by Pete and Dud dressed in Nehru suits and Peter sporting a hippie moustache. There are seagull screeches at 2:12 in the song, which is a reference to the backward tape loops on the Beatles' "Tomorrow Never Knows" (2017). The surreal lyrics are sharp satire of the Beatles psychedelic period and of the LSD experience where experimenters' senses become jumbled, "Where my hands can see/And my eyes can walk" ("L.S. Bumble Bee," 1967). Dudley Moore conceived the song as a satire of the Beach Boys, but the falsetto John Lennon vocal and the references to creepy crawly insects make the Beatles the parodic target:

> In a letter from December of 1981, Moore offered a bit of insight: "Peter Cook and I recorded that song about the time when there was so much fuss about L.S.D., and when everybody thought that "Lucy in the Sky With Diamonds" was a reference to drugs. The exciting alternative offered to the world was L.S.B.!, and I wrote the music to, in some ways, satirize the Beach Boys rather than the Beatles. But I'm grateful if some small part of the world thinks that it may have been them, rather than us!
>
> (qtd. in Dangerous Minds 2022; see also Cook 2013)

Cook and Moore are often compared as the Lennon and McCartney of British comedy: Cook is Lennon, cruel, caustic reveling in punning linguistic gymnastics, while his more successful and musical sidekick, cute Dudley, is the prodigiously musically talent housewife's choice. They were comedians who were adept at music and, as we shall see, the Beatles were musicians who were equally at home with comedy.

The Beatles

Shooting for The Mersey Sound took place between August 27 and 30, 1963. The film is perhaps most notable for its interviews with the Beatles where they are irreverent, joke and their accents are scouse! Lennon wryly tells the director Don Haworth that fans thought they were German when they returned to Liverpool from Hamburg. What is most significant about these films is the Beatles' humor which carnivalesque working-class status inversion, as Peter Atkinson contends, "The Beatles' working-class accents provided a key signifier in the symbol they became for the beginning of the era known as the sixties. The band's members shared the strong and distinctive Liverpool accent known as 'scouse'" (2010, 16). Regional accents were practically unknown in the British media until the Beatles came to prominence (compare the Beatles' accents to the Oxbridge Fringers and Pythons and the Beatles, for example). These two films were the first signs of the Beatles carnivalesque subversion which in the 1963 to 1965 period were couched in their image as harmless and cheeky boys next door. However, two texts exploded their cozy mop-top image: the Bakhtinian bodily carnivalesque (the etymology of which is goodbye meat!) so-called "Butcher Cover" for their *Yesterday and Today* album (1966) and their surreal attack on the status quo in "I Am the Walrus."

The Butcher Cover of the Beatles' *Yesterday and Today* album was mired in controversy from the moment it first came to the attention of the executives at Columbia Records. The cover picture was taken by the surrealist photographer Robert Whitaker and featured the Beatles dressed in butchers' coats covered in pieces of red, raw meat, draped in strings of sausages, and surrounded by decapitated and mutilated baby dolls. The carnivalesque bodily humor was later described by Lennon as a comment on the Vietnam War. Whether this was the encoded intention of Whittaker and the other Beatles has never been verified. More likely that the grinning Beatles were tired of their lovable mop top image, and the cover was an art statement intended to explode the myth of their boys-next-door image. The Beatles succeeded with this intention: as soon as their American record label Capitol saw the cover, it was goodbye meat! Capitol immediately withdrew the offending album cover and replaced it was an asinine shot of the boys astride a suitcase gazing miserably into the camera.

The Butcher Cover is one of the most subversive artistic acts in the Beatles' career. Their album covers were always well thought out and were aesthetically pleasing, but the Butcher Cover was their most daring. The image of the Beatles laughing and grinning while covered in meat signaled an embrace of the new and the Avant Garde: they were sick of being commodified and standardized mop tops: Beatles for Sale! By 1966 they had morphed into artists who used "sick" comedy to make a socio-political point. To Rabelais, the artist uses fecal matter, bodily organs, and food for status inversion:

> The essence of the grotesque is precisely to present a contradictory and double-faced fullness of life. Negation and destruction (death of the old) are included as an essential phase, inseparable from affirmation, from the birth of something new and better. The very material bodily lower stratum of the grotesque image (food, wine, the genital force, the organs of the body) bears a deeply positive character.
>
> (Bakhtin 1965/1984, 86)

Other examples of such grotesque Rabelaisian humor can be found in two films. The 1964 music video for "I Feel Fine," filmed at Twickenham Studios, has the Beatles crouching on their hands and knees and heartily eating fish and chips. The clip is available on YouTube and shows the Beatles relishing the greasy carry-out meal with their hands. Of course, this is not the most grotesque image of the Beatles and food. In the *Magical Mystery Tour* (1967) film, John Lennon shovels spaghetti onto the plate of the Aunt Jessie character, thereby anticipating (or perhaps inspiring?) the infamous Mr. Creosote sketch in Monty Python's 1983 film, *The Meaning of Life*.

A series of grotesque comic images recur the Beatles' satire of English life in "I Am the Walrus". The song is a series Bakhtinian carnivalesque imagery: knickers being pulled down, semolina pilchard, pigs in a sty, the kicking of Edgar Allan Poe. Ian MacDonald describes the song as "pure linguistic mischief" and pure invective (1994, 234), which, as I will show, links this song with the bodily humor of the Python's Undertaker's sketch and Eric Idle's wordplay in the Ends of Words and Anagrams skits. MacDonald puts the context of Lennon's song in its satirical 1960s countercultural context: "'I Am the Walrus' became its author's ultimate anti-institutional rant—a damn-you-England tirade that blasts education, art, culture, order, class, religion, and even sense itself" (1994, 234). The inspiration for Lennon's song is Bakhtinian grotesque humor: the song's line coming from a playground chant from Lennon's childhood: "Yellow matter custard, green slop pie/All mixed together with a dead dog's eye" (MacDonald 1994, 234). Lennon's two books, *In His Own Write* (1964) and *A Spaniard in the Works* (1965), were also full of this type of punning and comic humor influenced by Carroll and Ogden Nash.[11]

Monty Python's Flying Circus

The Pythons' humor and satirical impulse is in the tradition of the Fringers and the Beatles. Yet unlike the Fringers and *That Was the Week That Was* (1962), the Pythons deliberately avoid writing about and specific political events since they were simply bored with that kind of writing and wanted to do something new: in this way, they were more similar to the Beatles' humor because surreal

---

[11] Frederic Ogden Nash (1902–71) was an American poet known for his unconventional rhyming schemes and ridiculous puns.

humor, puns, and corporeal imagery were the basis of the Pythons' jokes. For instance, the Undertakers sketch from the second series of *Monty Python's Flying Circus* in 1970 is an apotheosis of their work. What turned out to be the most controversial sketch of the Pythons' TV show begins with John Cleese taking his dead mother to an undertaker, who is played by Graham Chapman. Cleese shows the cadaver to Chapman who suggests they can burn her, bury her, or dump her in the Thames. Then, noticing that she is quite young, he yells to his assistant (Eric Idle) that "We've got an eater" (Monty Python 1970). At first the son is outraged at the prospect of eating his mother, but he becomes hungry and finally succumbs to the undertaker's suggestion. Chapman's undertaker ends the sketch by saying that he feels guilty he can always vomit his mother into a ditch. At this point, the audience invade the stage in well-rehearsed mock outrage.

In a manner similar to the medieval carnival Bakhtin observes, Fringe, Beatles, and Python humor was a popular art form. To Bakhtin, "sick bodily humor in the middle ages existed and developed outside the official sphere of high ideology and literature, but precisely because of its unofficial existence, it was marked by exceptional radicalism, freedom, and ruthlessness" (Bakhtin 1965/1984, 78). In any previous decade, the Pythons would not have been able to broadcast the Undertakers sketch. In fact, the BBC only allowed it to air on the condition that the audience interrupt and protest its dark content. After the initial broadcast the BBC also wiped the tape and replaced the Undertakers sketch with "Spot the Braincell" from episode 7 of the second series.

The Undertakers sketch is the finale of "Royal Episode Thirteen," which begins with a special animation sequence, "The Queen Will Be Watching," which mocks its own seriousness. Following this is a sketch featuring the Python crew: Terry Jones plays an interviewer with a series of guests: "the man who says things in a very roundabout way" (Chapman), "the man who speaks only the ends of words" (Idle), "the man who speaks only the beginnings of words," (Cleese), and "the man who speaks only the middles of words" (Michael Palin). After a cacophony of high-pitched syllables, the latter three manage to say "good evening" in unison. Although the speech acts of the Pythons are entirely logical, the collective sound of all three speaking together sounds like a squeaking pre-Oedipal noise. The studio audience reacts with hysterical laughter recognizing unusual, absurd, and ostensibly meaningless discourse.

Fans of this kind of wordplay would no doubt be at home with the nonsense of Lennon's punning in his two books. In the just-discussed sketch, the Pythons demonstrate "speech patterns excluded from official intercourse" and their hysterical nonsense is imbued with the "carnival spirit, [which] transformed their primitive verbal functions, acquired a general tone of laughter, and became, as it were, so many sparks of the carnival bonfire which renews the world" (Bakhtin 1965/1984, 17). The viewer knows the Idle character is called John Smith, but he is referred to "Ohn Ith" throughout (Monty Python 1970). The repetition of "Ohn Ith" transforms the quotidian and boring name into the absurd and unfamiliar.

A couple years later, an episode of *Monty Python's Flying Circus's* third series, "Blood, Devastation, Death, War and Horror" (1972), includes another sketch with similar wordplay and absurd, unfamiliar language.[12] The sketch, "The Man Who Speaks in Anagrams," revolves around Palin interviewing Idle as "Hamrag Yatelrot," the sketch's title character. Idle and Palin discuss Hamrag's work on Shakespeare (Malliwi Rapessheake), including *The Mating of the Wersh, The Two Netlemeg of Verona, Twelfth Thing, The Charmrent of Venice, Themal, and Ring Kichard the Third*. Palin challenges Hamrag, correctly identifying this a spoonerism, to which Hamrag responds, "If you are going to split hairs, I'm going to piss off!" (Monty Python 1972).

Conclusion: The Politics of the Surreal

Dark comedy, cannibalism, linguistic gymnastics, surrealism, and a satire of the staid television chat format show are tropes that recur in these three sketches and are the basis of the humor in *Beyond the Fringe*, the Beatles, and Monty Python. All three collectives have to be understood in the context of the 1960s art, as Arthur Marwick contends: "A large proportion of sixties creative work was deliberately intended to be 'counter-cultural,' profoundly critical of 'bourgeois' or consumerist society" (1998, 318). Although the Fringers and the Pythons were middle-class and the Beatles were aspirational workers' aristocracy who were being streamlined into grammar schools and a bourgeois class, all three groups used their work to critique consumerist society. The Fringers satirized the Second World War, the Prime Minister, and Peter Cook's surreal monologues transcended logic while his subversive thoughts were as whimsical and illusive as butterflies in a hurricane. *Monty Python's Flying Circus* attacked games shows, chat shows, TV interviews, religion, the clichés of TV, and middle-class rituals

---

[12] In the comic spirit of the Pythons, I toyed with changing the name of the author of this chapter to Darrich Sllim!

(who can forget the most awful family in Britain swamped in baked beans and chanting the mantra "Beans!" throughout the sketch).

In the 1960s, surrealist music and comedy seemed to explode (an image not unlike a Python gag). According to Marwick two of the most important constituents of 1960s were "the blurring of boundaries between elite and popular art" (1998: 317). This is true of the Fringers satirizing classical music in a hit West End/Broadway show; Alan, Peter, Jonathan, Dudley's MO was also to bring topical political events into the comedy mainstream. The Fringers were Oxbridge intellectuals bringing deep conceptual ideas into the marketplace: they were popular intellectuals. This description is also fitting for the Pythons, who toyed with philosophy (Greek philosophers versus German Philosophers football match, Karl Marx on a game show, references to Wittgenstein et al. in "The Philosophers Song"). The Beatles brought pop art (Peter Blake's *Sgt. Pepper* cover, Richard Hamilton's *White Album* cover, Stockhausen-esque experimental electronic music with classical orchestration) into the mainstream, too.

It bears noting that the cultural revolution typified by these comedic and musical acts was exclusively white, male, and (with the exception of three-quarters of the Beatles) middle class. British comedy took decades to address this gender divide. It could be argued this sexist chasm wasn't crossed until The Goodness Gracious Me comedy team rose to prominence in the 1990s with 50 percent of cast comprising of women performers. GGM team were Python fanatics, who starred in their own BBC2 series, which ran from 1998 to 2001. The cast were four British Asian actors, Sanjeev Baskar, Kulvinder Ghir, Meera Syal, and Nina Wadia. GGM demonstrates the collision between traditional South Asian culture and British life. This is just one example testifying to the legacy of the Fringers, the Pythons, and the Beatles, who fired up generations of British satirists and surrealists encouraged to enter the carnivalesque comedic sphere.

The Fringers, the Beatles, and the Pythons were always keen to remind audiences that their primary aim was to entertain. But their work demonstrates how art challenges and subverts: as the 1960s recede rapidly in the rear-view mirror, a strange mixture of surrealist images persist: songs being sung at the crucifixion, a petulant Peter Cook mocking the PM, the political surreal pop of "I Am the Walrus", the gross bodily humor of the Butcher Cover and the Undertakers sketch. The legacy of these comedian/musicians is that comedy and satire are a serious business because clowning does get people thinking about politics—even and especially if they are laughing.

References

Atkinson, Peter. 2010. "The Beatles and the Broadcasting of British Cultural Revolution, 1958–63." In *Fifty Years with the Beatles: The Impact of the Beatles on Contemporary Culture*, edited by Jerzy Jarniewicz and Alina Kwiatkowska, 15–29. Lodz: Lodz University Press.

Bakhtin, Mikhail. 1965/1984. *Rabelais and His World*. Bloomington: Indiana University Press.

Bennett, Alan, Peter Cook, Dudley Moore, and Jonathan Miller. 1987. *The Complete Beyond the Fringe*, edited by Roger Wilmut. London: Methuen.

Bennett, Alan, Peter Cook, Dudley Moore, and Jonathan Miller. 1992. *Beyond the Fringe*. Acorn Media.

Bestley, Russ. 2019. "'Anarchy in Woolworths': Punk Comedy and Humor." In *The Routledge Companion to Popular Music and Humor*, edited by Thomas M. Kitts and Nick Baxter-Moore, 76–84. New York: Routledge.

Carpenter, Humphrey. 2000. *A Great Silly Grin: The British Satire Boom of the 1960s*. New York: Oubic Affairs.

Cook, Peter. 1986. *Peter Cook, Lord Stockton: A Life*. Channel 4, UK. https://www.youtube.com/watch?v=ocMUBZ8elDs&t=10s Accessed November 05, 2022

Cook, Peter and Dudley Moore. 1967. *The L S Bumble Bee*, Decca. https://www.youtube.com/watch?v=FQg08-QTT0U Accessed November 02, 2022.

Cook, William. 2013. *One Leg Too Few: The Adventures of Peter Cook and Dudley Moore*. London: Preface.

Dangerous Minds. 2022. https://dangerousminds.net/comments/cook_and_moores_long-lost_beatles_track_the_l.s._bumble_bee. Accessed September 18, 2022.

Dobrogoszcz, Tomasz. 2014. *Nobody Expects the Spanish Inquisition: Cultural Contexts in Monty Python*. London: Rowan and Littlefield.

Frayn, Michael. 1987. Introduction. In *The Complete Beyond the Fringe*, edited by Roger Wilmut, 7–9. London: Metheun.

Heyman, Matthias. 2023. "I Laugh and Act Like a Clown: The Beatles as Paradoxical Clowns." In *The Beatles and Humour: Mockers, Funny Papers, and Other Play*, edited by Katie Kapurch, Richard Mills, and Matthias Heyman, 41–57. New York: Bloomsbury.

Ives, Maura. 1998. "Essay on Comedy and Other New Quarterly Publications." In *A Critical Edition*, 140. London: Bucknell University Press.

Jarniewicz, Jerzy. 2010. "The Beatles—Prophets or Fools of the Counterculture?" In *Fifty Years With The Beatles: The Impact of the Beatles on Contemporary Culture*, edited by Jerzy Jarniewicz and Alina Kwiatkowska, 71–9. Lodz: Lodz University Press.

Johnston, Terry (dir). 2004. *Not Only But Always*. TV film. Company Pictures.

Kohl, Paul R. 2010. "When I Get to the Bottom I Go Back to the Top ... The
    Carnivalesque World of the Beatles." In *Fifty Years With The Beatles: The Impact
    of the Beatles on Contemporary Culture*, edited by Jerzy Jarniewicz and Alina
    Kwiatkowska, 79–87. Lodz: Lodz University Press.

Kolakowski, Leszek. 1989. "Kaplan I blazen." In *Pochwala niekonsekwencji, vol 2*.
    Warszawa: Nowa.

Marwick, Arthur. 1998. *The Sixties: Cultural Revolution in Britain, France, Italy, and the
    United States, c. 1958–1974*. Oxford: Oxford University Press.

MacDonald, Ian. 1994. *Revolution in the Head: The Beatles' Records and the Sixties*.
    London: Fourth Estate.

McCabe, Bob. 2003. "In Which the Pythons Meet the Pythons." In *The Pythons
    Autobiography* by the Pythons. London: Orion.

Monty Python. 1970. "Royal Episode Thirteen." Series 2, Episode 13. *Monty Python's
    Flying Circus*. December 22, 1970. London: BBC1.

Monty Python. 1972. "Blood, Devastation, Death, War and Horror." Series 3, Episode 4.
    Monty Python's Flying Circus. November 9, 1972. London: BBC1.

Sandbrook, Dominic. 2005. *Never Had It So Good: From Suez to the Beatles*. London:
    Little, Brown.

Weihe, Richard. 2016. *Über den Clown: Künstlerische und Theoretische Perspektiven*.
    Bielefeld: transcript Verlag.

Womack, Kenneth. 2017. *Maximum Volume: The Life of Beatles Producer George Martin:
    The Early Years,1926–1966*. Chicago: Chicago Review Press.

12

Pastiche, Parody, or Post-Irony? The Beatles' Influence on Tears for Fears

Mark Spicer

Rock history has many stories to tell about the Beatles' influence. Just as literary critic Harold Bloom (1973) famously argued for the enormous influence of precursor giants like Shakespeare and Milton on post-Enlightenment English-language poetry, we could make a similar claim for the extent of the Beatles' influence on post-1960s Anglophone pop and rock music. The Fab Four's sheer abundance and creativity as songwriters and performers, particularly in their later work from *Revolver* (1966) onwards, set the bar so very high that all subsequent pop and rock musicians have had to confront this huge creative space in the landscape of recorded popular music. I have written elsewhere about groups such as the Electric Light Orchestra (ELO) and 10cc that emerged in the Beatles' immediate wake and who, like Brian Wilson of the Beach Boys, experienced a profound anxiety of influence toward the Beatles (see Spicer 2018; Spicer and Spencer 2023).[1]

In this chapter, I will be telling the story of Tears for Fears, a UK group that emerged in the early 1980s, by which point the Beatles' importance to the next generation of pop and rock musicians had at first seemed to diminish in the aftermath of punk. For a few years there, during the height of the so-called New Wave, it was no longer cool to love the Beatles.[2] Joe Strummer of the Clash captured this prevailing sentiment when he sang in his group's 1979 post-punk anthem, "London Calling": "Phony Beatlemania has bitten the dust."

[1] As Tim Riley (2002, 389–90) aptly puts it, "The arc that went from 1963's *Please Please Me* to 1969's *Abbey Road* and 1970's *Let It Be* had enough thoughtful curves to exert anxiety of influence over generations of bands to come" (see also Reynolds 2011, 177–78).
[2] This is essentially the point made by Rob Sheffield in his "The Ballad of Eighties Beatles vs. Nineties Beatles" (Sheffield 2017, 295–308).

From Graduate to *The Hurting*

Like John Lennon and Paul McCartney, Roland Orzabal and Curt Smith met as teenagers, but where they grew up—the elegant resort city of Bath in the southwest of England—was quite different from the rough-and-tumble northern port city of Liverpool. Still, both boys were from broken homes and were raised primarily by their mothers on council estates; this and other parallels perhaps drew them to one another. Orzabal told *The Quietus* in 2013:

> Curt and I are both the middle of three boys, and in my situation there was domestic violence. There are a lot of people who have difficult childhoods. ... We can all make a big deal that we were council estate kids. But that was the biggest thing that upset me, that my Dad would be physically violent towards my Mum. And it got so bad that in the end she left.
>
> (Wallace 2013)

In 1978, when they were just seventeen, Orzabal and Smith formed a mod-revival band called Graduate with three other members, releasing one album, *Acting My Age*, in 1980, and enjoying modest success in the UK and Europe with the single "Elvis Should Play Ska."[3] Roland and Curt left the group in early 1981, saying they hated traveling from gig to gig in a van with no roadies. They decided to continue as a duo (albeit with a little help from their friends, Ian Stanley on keyboards and Manny Elias on drums), and the name of their new project—Tears for Fears—was inspired by the writings of American psychologist Arthur Janov, particularly his seminal work, *The Primal Scream* (1970), and his then-current book, *Prisoners of Pain* (1980). It is well known, of course, that Lennon himself underwent primal scream therapy with Janov in 1970 in an attempt to exorcise the demons of his troubled childhood, but alas, Roland and Curt at the time could only afford to read his books.[4] Nevertheless, the lyrics to most of the songs on Tears for Fears' debut album, *The Hurting*, released in March 1983,

---

[3] To be clear, that is Elvis Costello referred to in the song's title, not Elvis Presley. The 1960s' style of Jamaican ska was enjoying a huge revival in the United Kingdom during 1979 and 1980, notably through the work of such groups as Madness, the Specials, the [English] Beat, and the Police. "Elvis Should Play Ska" reached only #82 on the UK singles chart, but did make it to the top ten in Spain.

[4] On Lennon's sessions with Janov, see Riley (2011, 497–500). The effect that primal scream therapy had on Lennon the musician can be heard most obviously in several songs from *The Plastic Ono Band* album (released December 1970), especially "Mother," the extended coda of which culminates with him screaming repeatedly the phrase "Mama don't go, Daddy come home."

were influenced directly by Janov's ideas.[5] As Paul Sinclair (2013) explains in his liner notes from the thirtieth-anniversary reissue, "The genius of *The Hurting* is that on one level it's just an album of great, melodic, hook-filled pop songs, ... [but] the basic idea behind Janov's Primal Therapy—the impact that the trauma of childhood has on your character as an adult—was the blood running through the veins of the record."

Orzabal quickly assumed the role of Tears for Fears' primary songwriter, and while he claims that all of the songs on *The Hurting* were written on acoustic guitar, the duo fleshed out the songs and developed their electric arrangements by playing with the new-fangled synthesizers (such as the Roland Jupiter-4 and TR-808 drum machine) and eight-track recording equipment that their "rich friend" Stanley had at his house (Rickett 2014). The album's most well-known song, "Mad World," reached #3 on the UK singles chart in late 1982. Curt Smith sings in the prechorus, "... the dreams in which I'm dying are the best I've ever had"—certainly not your typical lyric for a pop record.[6] In fact, Tears for Fears' debut album to me sounds nothing like the Beatles, if only because the timbral palette and gadgets being used are so new and different from what we hear on the Beatles' songs recorded during the late 1960s.

The Toppermost of the Poppermost, 1980s Style

For their follow-up album, 1985's *Songs from the Big Chair*, Roland and Curt set out to make a record that would be a huge hit on the other side of the Atlantic and they definitely succeeded. The album's cover features a black-and-white photo of the duo staring smugly at the camera yet with notably 1980s hairstyles—very different from the moptops sported by the Beatles in Robert Freeman's iconic black-and-white photo on the cover of their second UK album

[5] Tears for Fears' debut UK single, released in November 1981 and later re-recorded for *The Hurting*, was called "Suffer the Children." Other songs from *The Hurting* with pointed references to Janov in their titles include "The Prisoner," "Ideas as Opiates" (borrowed from the title of one of the chapters of *Prisoners of Pain*), "Start of the Breakdown," "Watch Me Bleed," as well as the title track.

[6] A stripped-down version of "Mad World," recorded by American film composer Michael Andrews and singer Gary Jules for the soundtrack to the 2001 film *Donnie Darko*, replaced the synthesizers and drum machine of the original with a simple piano accompaniment and went on to become the UK Christmas #1 single in 2003—which, as Smith says, "shows you a little bit about the English mentality" (quoted from the 2014 video, *Spotify Landmark: Songs from the Big Chair*, commemorating the thirtieth anniversary of the release of the album).

With the Beatles.[7] Table 12.1 shows the chronology of Tears for Fears' seven studio albums (excluding live albums and greatest hits compilations), along with their respective peak UK and US chart positions. This table confirms that *Songs from the Big Chair* remains Tears for Fears' most successful album by far, reaching #1 in the United States while peaking at #2 in their native England (although I should say that their remarkable 2022 comeback album, *The Tipping Point*, has been giving *Big Chair* a run for its money). Orzabal recounts what he and Smith were thinking about as they wrote and recorded the songs for their sophomore album in 1984: "We were … losing a little bit of our … shoegazing early 80s electronic edge, and we were actually listening to believe it or not Bruce Springsteen's *Born in the USA,* and becoming acutely aware of huge-sounding records" (*Spotify Landmark* 2014).

The first US single from *Songs from the Big Chair,* "Everybody Wants to Rule the World," was indeed a huge-sounding record and reached #1 on the *Billboard* Hot 100 in June 1985. Their follow-up US single from the album, "Shout," released later that summer, also reached #1.[8] While the song's title might remind us of the Beatles' covers of the Isley Brothers' versions of "Shout" and the even-more-famous "Twist and Shout" (the latter of which was itself a US #2 hit

Table 12.1 Chronology of Tears for Fears studio albums

ALBUM TITLE	RELEASE DATE	PEAK CHART POSITION
The Hurting	March 1983	UK #1, US #73
Songs from the Big Chair	February 1985	UK #2, US #1
The Seeds of Love	September 1989	UK #1, US #8
Elemental	June 1993	UK #5, US #45
Raoul and the Kings of Spain	October 1995	UK #41, US #79
Everybody Loves a Happy Ending	September 2004 (US); March 2005 (UK)	UK #45, US #46
The Tipping Point	February 2022	UK #2, US #8

[7] While the hairstyles are certainly different (1980s vs. 1960s), one might argue that Tears for Fears on the cover of their sophomore album were imitating the cover of *With the Beatles* as a form of tribute, through the iconic use of black and white, the poses, and spotlighting the fashionable hairdos of their respective decades. I thank Matt Heyman for pointing this out to me.

[8] Outside of the United States, "Shout" was released as the first single from *Big Chair.* The third single, "Head Over Heels," did not make it to #1 in the US but did reach #5 (in the UK, the song peaked at #12); for an analysis of this song's unusual harmonic design and its connection with "Shout," see Spicer (2017, n. 17).

for the Beatles in 1964), aside from the fact that its chorus is situated right up front—a trick the Beatles often deployed in their hit songs ("She Loves You," for example)—little about "Shout" sounds overtly Beatlesque. "Shout" begins with its signature Emulator drum machine loop before launching immediately into the first statement of the big chorus, set over a dirge-like repeating chord loop of I–♭VI–IV–I. At the time, Orzabal downplayed the idea that "Shout" was just another song about primal scream therapy: "Quite simply, it's about protest. It's about making noise about things, either politically or socially, that disturb you— for instance, nuclear weapons or whatever. When I wrote it, I found it quite therapeutic just to sing those words, 'these are the things I can do without,' and I think that's been part of its appeal."[9]

A Swirl of 1967 Beatles References

After a year-long world tour in support of *Songs from the Big Chair*—during which Roland and Curt performed a few of their US shows without the full band, "by themselves on the stage surrounded by machines" (Holden 1990)—Tears for Fears took a brief hiatus in late 1986 before reconvening in 1987 to begin work on the songs for their next album, *The Seeds of Love*. The album cover shows the duo dressed in sparkly blue and gold jackets—a kind of 1980s retake on the dayglo military uniforms the Beatles wore on the cover of their *Sgt. Pepper's Lonely Hearts Club Band* album—against a painted backdrop of suns, stars, hearts, sunflowers, mountain tops, and other "flower power" imagery. Orzabal tells the story of his initial inspiration for what would become the album's title track and hit single: "I was driving up the M4 from Bath to London and was listening to Radio 4 … and there was a program about a man called Mr. England … he was a gardener … and he was copyrighting or rediscovering all the traditional [folk] tunes that weren't so familiar in other areas of the UK. There was a traditional song called 'The Seeds of Love.' So … in my head the title

---

[9] The Orzabal remarks are transcribed from the 1985 documentary, *Scenes from the Big Chair* (re-released on DVD in 2006). He goes on to say that "initially ['Shout'] was just a chorus, and the idea I had … was that it would be a kind of mantra thing and it would be repeated over and over again." (Despite the 1980s synthesizers and drum machine permeating the surface of the record, this is in fact a case of Roland showing his Beatles influence, since mantra-like repetition was a compositional technique the Beatles were especially fond of in their late work, for example, the infinity codas to "Hey Jude" and "I Want You (She's So Heavy)"; see Samarotto 2012.) Ian Stanley had to convince Orzabal that he had written the chorus of a "worldwide smash" before helping him flesh out the rest of the song.

'Mr. England Sowing the Seeds of Love' was instilled (*Spotify Landmark* 2014). (Mr. Orzabal misremembers the facts here, since it was actually musicologist Cecil Sharp who was collecting the folk songs, and John England was the name of the Somerset gardener who sang the tune to him.[10]) Orzabal goes on to admit, "From now it wasn't very difficult. Once you have a concept, it's just basically plugging in the major version of 'I Am the Walrus' ..."

I will have more to say about this below, yet we should remember that 1987, not coincidentally, marked the twentieth anniversary of the *Sgt. Pepper* album and was also the year that the UK Beatles albums were first released on compact disc.[11] If the Beatles' importance had been waning in the 1980s, then the re-release of their catalogue in this new digital format of the CD, along with all the hype surrounding the twentieth birthday of *Pepper*, re-elevated the Beatles into the public consciousness in a big way. Coinciding with the very month of *Pepper*'s re-release, Margaret Thatcher won a third consecutive term as Prime Minister in the June 1987 general election. It should therefore come as no surprise that a nostalgia for 1967's Summer of Love and the growing dissatisfaction with Thatcher's politics during her final term are both subjects that loom large in "Sowing the Seeds of Love." The title may have been inspired by an old English folk song, yet the song's musical fabric is cleverly constructed by stitching together strategic intertextual references to 1967 Beatles songs, all in the service of enriching the song's overall message.[12]

The single "Sowing the Seeds of Love" was released in August of 1989 and peaked at #5 in the UK and #2 in the United States, scoring Tears for Fears their biggest US hit since "Shout."[13] Clocking in at over six minutes, the form of this song is rather complex, with contrasting verses and choruses interrupted by an extended musical interlude and two different bridge sections (which I am calling bridges because these sections not only provide harmonic and textural contrast to what comes before but each culminates with a big retransition into a subsequent verse or chorus). Continuing the theme of political protest

[10] "The Seeds of Love" is the first English folksong Cecil Sharp ever collected (see Sharp 1916, no. 33).
[11] For a detailed account of the continuing reception and legacy of *Sgt. Pepper's Lonely Hearts Club Band* into the 1980s and 1990s, see Moore 1997, 58–82.
[12] On *stylistic* vs. *strategic* intertextuality in the Beatles' music, see Spicer 2009. As I hope to demonstrate, the strategic intertextual references to 1967 Beatles songs in "Sowing the Seeds of Love" contribute markedly to the song's meaning, much like what the Beatles themselves achieved by the swirl of international quotations during the fadeaway coda of "All You Need Is Love" (Spicer 2009, 354–59).
[13] "Sowing the Seeds of Love" was kept out of the top spot on the *Billboard* Hot 100 by Janet Jackson's "Miss You Much."

expressed in "Shout," in the first verse Orzabal sings about taking a stand and shaking things up, while also referencing the Ecstasy and rave culture pervasive in late-1980s England. In the second verse, Orzabal takes a direct stab at Maggie Thatcher ("Politician Grannie"), claiming that she had no clue as to what most of the British people were feeling about her politics at the time. The line "Kick out the Style, bring back the Jam!" is aimed at their musical compatriot Paul Weller, urging him to abandon the slick pop of his mid-1980s group the Style Council and resurrect his snarling neo-mod group, the Jam, while the reference to a sunflower in the third verse was inspired by a piece of graffiti Orzabal saw on a wall near his house in London that summer (*Spotify Landmark* 2014).

In stark contrast to the snide pessimism of the verses, the big choruses have the duo singing the title lyric of "Sowing the Seeds of Love," recalling the jubilant chorus of the Beatles' own Summer of Love anthem, "All You Need Is Love," the song that serves as their most obvious inspiration here. The overall message of "Sowing the Seeds of Love" is thus tinged with post-punk irony, cleverly evoking 1967's Summer of Love of a means of critiquing British life and politics in the late Thatcher era. This is not unlike what the Beatles themselves had done two decades earlier in their late-period songs with political leanings, such as "Taxman," "Revolution," and especially "Back in the USSR," where the song's title spoofs Chuck Berry's "Back in the USA" and the bridge's lyrics strategically reference the Beach Boys' "California Girls," all for darkly humorous effect at the height of the Cold War.[14]

The music, as noted above, is loaded with strategic intertextual references to 1967 Beatles songs. Figure 12.2(a) shows a transcription of the repeating vamp that sounds throughout the verses, with Wurlitzer electric piano chords in pulsing quarter notes over a McCartney-like bass pattern of constant eighth notes, moving with the chord changes and punctuated erratically by fifth leaps. The groove and texture here directly evoke that of the verses to "I Am the Walrus," which Smith himself admits to "ripping ... off shamelessly" (*Spotify Landmark* 2014). Yet when Orzabal says "It's just a matter of plugging in the major version of 'I Am the Walrus'" he's not exactly correct, since *all* the chords in "Walrus" are in fact major (a feature unique to rock harmony) while the verses to "Sowing the Seeds of Love" are set in G minor, albeit with a bit of Dorian mixture.[15]

[14] For a close intertextual analysis of "Back in the USSR," see Benitez (2019, 215–17); see also Whitley (2000).
[15] For a detailed analysis of the oddball harmonic design of "I Am the Walrus," see Everett (1999, 136–38).

a) Verse vamp ("I Am the Walrus")

b) Chorus ("Hello, Goodbye")

c) Baroque trumpet in the third chorus ("Penny Lane," "All You Need Is Love")

d) Curt Smith's countermelody in Verse 3 (self-reference to Tears for Fears' own "Shout")

Figure 12.1 Strategic intertextual musical references in "Sowing the Seeds of Love."

Furthermore, the opening verse of the song is prefaced with electronic noise and a tumbling introductory drum fill that echoes Ringo Starr's legendary fills in "A Day in the Life."

Figure 12.2(b) shows the main melodic hook sung by Curt Smith during the chorus. Here the reference to a 1967 Beatles song goes beyond just groove and texture, as Tears for Fears have strategically borrowed the exact chord changes and irregular three-bar phrases from the chorus of the Beatles' 1967 UK Christmas #1 hit "Hello, Goodbye"—complete with the sudden interjection of octave-doubled punches on $\hat{b6}$–$\hat{5}$ (A♭–G)—in the same key of C major, no less.[16] Smith's melody does not match the main chorus melody of "Hello, Goodbye," yet its rhythmic and melodic profile is strikingly similar to that of the guitar countermelody (shown in parentheses) also sung by John Lennon and George Harrison during the song's second chorus.[17]

The first of the song's two extended bridge sections (at 2:15) begins quietly— despite its Janovian lyrics that reference feeling pain and shouting about it— but then quickly builds into a chaos of string and horn flourishes and operatic wordless vocals that sounds eerily reminiscent of the coda to "I Am the Walrus," as well as the famous orchestral crescendo linking John's and Paul's separate parts of "A Day in the Life." This bridge section culminates with a retransition into the third chorus, marked by the triumphant entrance of a Baroque trumpet (at 3:08), thus making another overt reference to a 1967 Beatles song. This trumpet tune, transcribed in Figure 12.2(c), is not a direct quotation from Paul McCartney's "Penny Lane," but the distinctive timbre of the instrument alone is enough to make the connection clear.[18]

For the third and final verse (at 3:54), Curt Smith sings a brand-new countermelody, shown in Figure 12.2(d). He first sings this melody alone, and then Orzabal joins in with a reprise of the first verse. The Beatles reference here

---

[16] The chorus to "When I Was a Boy," the lead single from ELO's stunning 2015 comeback album, *Alone in the Universe*, also strategically borrows the distinctive chord changes and $\hat{b6}$–$\hat{5}$ punches from the "Hello, Goodbye" chorus (Spicer 2018, 123–25). One might say then that Jeff Lynne's reappropriation of "Hello, Goodbye" in "When I Was a Boy" comments on Tears for Fears as well as the Beatles.

[17] With tongue firmly planted in cheek, Orzabal himself plays the "Hello, Goodbye" guitar countermelody during the final chorus of "Sowing the Seeds of Love" in the 2014 *Spotify Landmark* performance of the song.

[18] The Baroque trumpet is also featured prominently during the coda of "All You Need Is Love," where it plays the quotation from J.S. Bach's Two-Part Invention in F major (transposed to fit the G major key of the song) and hence helps to make the strategic intertextual reference sound quintessentially "German" (Spicer 2009, 358). The use of the trumpet in "Sowing the Seeds of Love" serves therefore as a kind of two-pronged reference to both "Penny Lane" and "All You Need Is Love."

is more subtle, but the effect here evokes the final section of the Beatles' 1969 song "I've Got a Feeling," where John and Paul sing their respective different parts of the song together in a cumulative texture that has been deliberately saved for the song's ending.[19] Thinking back to when I first heard "Sowing the Seeds of Love" in 1989, shortly after the single was released, I remember my head being awash with the swirl of Beatles references and yet this moment in the song sounded to me like the "old" Tears for Fears. The reason for this became obvious once I compared the melodic and rhythmic profiles of Smith's new countermelody with the main chorus hook of their 1985 megahit "Shout." (I have aligned the two melodies above one another in Figure 12.2(d) to facilitate comparison.) No transposition is necessary, since both tunes are in the same key and begin with repeated notes on the tonic G followed by a rising fifth leap to D, then four eighth notes with the first two on the pitch D and the fourth tied into the next beat. Furthermore, the lyrics seem to be direct opposites of one another: "Shout! Shout! Let it all out" vs. "Time to eat all your words, swallow your pride." The reference to "Shout" here is somewhat disguised, yet Tears for Fears are essentially deploying the same tactic the Beatles had done two decades earlier by quoting their own "She Loves You" during the fadeaway coda of "All You Need Is Love."

To summarize, strategic intertextual references in "Sowing the Seeds of Love" are made to at least five Beatles songs, all from 1967: "All You Need Is Love," "I Am the Walrus," "Penny Lane," "A Day in the Life," and "Hello, Goodbye." This goes well beyond mere pastiche, as these multiple references combine to create a sort of mega-reference to a particular period from the Beatles' history. John Covach (1991) describes a similar strategy adopted by Neil Innes when composing the songs for his dead-on Beatles parody group, the Rutles (1978). As Covach points out, Rutles songs like "Hold My Hand" are particularly successful as satire because they make pointed references to multiple Beatles songs all at once, both in the lyrics and the music. (in this case, "I Want to Hold Your Hand," "She Loves You," "Please Please Me," and "All My Loving.") The difference with "Sowing the Seeds of Love," of course, is that the song was not necessarily intended as humor.[20]

---

[19] "I've Got a Feeling" is an early example of what I have called "cumulative form" in pop and rock music (Spicer 2004). Tears for Fears had earlier employed a similar technique—waiting to combine two melodies that had previously only been heard separately—for the climactic endings of both "Shout" and "Everybody Wants to Rule the World."

[20] For a useful account of the history and major distinctions between the concepts of pastiche and parody, see Duvall (1999).

Taking more than two years and costing over a million pounds to produce, *The Seeds of Love* was finally released in September 1989 and the duo embarked on another extensive world tour, this time complemented by a full backing band that included African American jazz pianist and singer Oleta Adams. Roland and Curt had discovered her performing in a hotel lounge in Kansas City in August 1985, during their US tour in support of *Songs from the Big Chair,* and were so impressed that they contacted her in 1987 and invited her to perform on three songs for the album—"Badman's Song," "Standing on the Corner of the Third World," and "Woman in Chains"—giving those songs a decidedly soulful flavor that was quite a departure from the synth-driven sound of their first two albums.[21] Ironically, the title track was the only song on *The Seeds of Love* that sounded overtly Beatlesque, and yet this detail is what all the critics seemed to focus on. Stephen Holden, for example, titled his *New York Times* review of Tears for Fears' February 1990 performance at the Meadowlands, "Disciples of the Beatles" (Holden 1990). Never fond of being on the road, Roland and Curt reportedly fought a lot during the tour, and when it was over Smith decided to leave the group and relocated permanently to the United States to concentrate on solo projects. Orzabal continued, however, releasing two albums during the first half of the 1990s under the Tears for Fears moniker, 1993's *Elemental* (which yielded the international top-forty hit "Break It Down Again") and 1995's *Raoul and the Kings of Spain* (which included another duet with Oleta Adams, "Me and My Big Ideas").[22]

Channeling the McCartney Within

We did not hear much from Tears for Fears for almost a decade, but in the early 2000s Roland and Curt decided to settle their differences and secretly began working together again on songs for a new Tears for Fears record. The resultant

---

[21] "Woman in Chains" was released as the second single from *The Seeds of Love,* reaching the top forty on both sides of the Atlantic (UK #26, US #36). During the world tour in support of the album, Adams would perform solo as the opening act and then join the full band for the remainder of the show. Her work with Tears for Fears boosted her solo career and led to international fame. Adams' biggest hit remains her 1991 cover of Brenda Russell's "Get Here," which reached the top five in the United States and United Kingdom and became something of a theme song for families of troops deployed overseas during the Gulf War.

[22] *Elemental* also includes the track "Brian Wilson Said," which serves both as an homage to Wilson and as further evidence of Orzabal's skill at creating pastiches of 1960s pop (in this case, the Beach Boys).

album, *Everybody Loves a Happy Ending*, was released in 2004 and came as quite a surprise to us longtime fans. Since my space is limited, I will not be able to offer a detailed analysis, but suffice it to say that the duo seems to have picked up right where they left off on "Sowing the Seeds of Love" in channeling their inner Beatle. The overt Beatles references on *Happy Ending* did not go unnoticed by the critics. In his review of the album for *Pop Matters,* Michael Pucci (2004) writes,

> The leadoff title track is a cleverly arranged update of "A Day in the Life," which kicks off with an alarm clock, breaks off midway into a separate segment altogether before triumphantly reprising the first part, and ends on a high note— literally—with Orzabal channeling the McCartney within as he sings "oooh." Can it be a coincidence that the first part of "Who Killed Tangerine?" adopts the same stutter-step beat of "Come Together"? And much like the shimmering 1985 hit "Head Over Heels" ended with a "Hey Jude"-like chorale, "Tangerine" ends similarly, with the repeated and apt refrain "And when you think it's all over / It's not over."

We could go further in teasing out the Beatles references on the album: for example, as if the alarm clock on the title track was not enough, the lyric "wake up … " along with the bouncy piano quarter notes make the connection to the "woke up, fell out of bed" middle section of "A Day in the Life" entirely obvious. Yet not all the songs on *Everybody Loves a Happy Ending* are Beatles pastiches. In "Ladybird," for instance, though the title might come across as a conflation of two of Paul McCartney's Beatles songs, the music does not contain any overt Beatles quotations (although I do hear a little nod to Simon and Garfunkel in there).[23] This is Tears for Fears at their best—a huge-sounding record loaded with carefully crafted hooks and a soaring chorus melody.

I must admit that on first hearing *Everybody Loves a Happy Ending*, I could not help but chuckle at the overt Beatles references, wondering why Roland and Curt would have chosen once again to pastiche the Beatles for their reunion

---

[23] The Simon and Garfunkel reference in "Ladybird" comes right after the first chorus at the onset of the second verse, where the line "let us be lovers we'll melt after midnight" bears an uncanny resemblance to the opening line of "America" ("let us be lovers we'll marry our fortunes together"). In a recent YouTube video (2022), Orzabal and Smith were asked to name their top-five favorite albums of all time. Orzabal acknowledges his Beatles influence ("I'm a big Beatles fan, and, of course, McCartney, Lennon, all the Beatles were on another level, and … I wouldn't compare them to any other band") but claims that Paul Simon "is my God" and chooses Simon's 1975 album *Still Crazy After All These Years*. Orzabal has also cited the title track from that album as one of his main inspirations for writing "Mad World" (Csathy 2021).

album, as they had been criticized for doing over a decade earlier. Yet while the songs with overt Beatles references may have conjured a laugh even from longtime Tears for Fears fans like myself, I believe Roland and Curt composed these Beatles quotations into the songs quite deliberately, almost as if to defy their critics. The fact is we cannot exactly be sure if Tears for Fears' allusions to the Beatles are intended as earnest or ironic. The term that comes to mind here is *post-irony*, a label that has been applied to works of visual art or literature in recent decades in which earnest and ironic intents become muddled, and what at first glance appears absurd is meant to be taken seriously.[24] Using the term to describe a wide swath of pop music in the new millennium (groups like the Strokes and the Darkness), music and culture writer Jazz Monroe (2014) claims that "post-irony is pretty much everywhere. Anything overtly cliché[d]—things that should attract ridicule but actually make you warm and tingly—is post-irony."

As if to cement the Beatles' connection, and suggesting to fans that *Everybody Loves a Happy Ending* would indeed be the last Tears for Fears album, the back cover of the CD booklet was emblazoned with two words: "The End." But rock history works in funny ways, and it turns out that we had not heard the last from Tears for Fears. In 2013, as they celebrated the thirtieth anniversary of *The Hurting,* Roland and Curt began touring again and making plans to record and release a new album. Various factors delayed their progress, not the least of which was the global pandemic that shut down much of life for all of us in 2020–21. Most tragically, in 2017 Roland's wife of 35 years, Caroline Orzabal, died following a ten-year battle with depression and substance abuse. The grief from his wife's passing was too much for Roland: "I went kind of mad, which is not uncommon. So trying to get back from that, which I eventually did after two rehabs ... it was the worst time in my life" (Rosen 2022). Thankfully, Roland was able to recover, remarry, and reconnect with his longtime musical partner to resume writing and recording the songs for their new album. Released in February 2022, more than seventeen years after *Happy Ending, The Tipping Point* marks Tears for Fears' triumphant return, and is in my opinion their strongest album since *The Seeds of Love.* In many respects, this album represents the duo coming full circle, returning to the ideas of personal trauma and suffering that

---

[24] The origin of the concept is usually linked to American non-fiction writer David Foster Wallace; see, for example, his seminal 1993 essay, "E Unibus Pluram: Television and U.S. Fiction." For a book-length study on the subject, see Hoffmann (2016), particularly the chapter "Postirony: Conceptualizing an Idea" (37–64).

pervaded their debut album, *The Hurting*.[25] Yet not all the songs on *The Tipping Point* are about grief and madness. In reviewing the album for *Tidal,* Craig Rosen (2022) astutely notes about the opening track, "No Small Thing": "It begins with an acoustic guitar strum and features a wheezy organ before shifting into a bit of sing-song vocalizing reminiscent of the Lumineers. ... The song tags other touchstones before arriving at a Beatlesque climax." Orzabal shrugs off Rosen's comment about sounding like the Lumineers, but is quick to acknowledge the Beatles reference: "It's kind of like 'A Day in the Life' meets Led Zeppelin."[26]

Closing Thoughts

I will conclude this chapter with a few more words on the larger topic of musical influence. Musicologist Dai Griffiths has suggested that artists like Elvis Costello who openly show the influence of others in their songs end up being not especially influential themselves:

> [F]or Costello, there is an additional problem: ... to celebrate him as a great alluder, reference-maker, soaker-up-of-influence, there is the strong possibility that his own work acts only as generous gateway to, and education in, other music. Costello wears the plumes, rather than being among "the fowl who originally grew them."
>
> (Griffiths 2008, 176)[27]

The same I think could be said of Tears for Fears. Much as I admire "Sowing the Seeds of Love" and the post-ironic Beatles pastiches on *Everybody Loves a Happy Ending* and *The Tipping Point,* my favorite Tears for Fears album remains *The Hurting,* when Roland and Curt chose music as psychotherapy and still sounded like no one but themselves.

---

[25] Much of *The Tipping Point* can be interpreted as a kind of musical catharsis for Roland, with lyrics speaking directly to his departed wife—"Please Be Happy," for example, and the chorus to the title track: "So who's that ghost knocking at my door? (You know that I can't love you more.)"

[26] To my ears, the climactic swirl of guitars, huge-sounding drums, and white noise at the end of "No Small Thing" reminds me more of the infinity coda to "I Want You (She's So Heavy)."

[27] Griffiths here is quoting from William Walsh's *Handy-Book of Literary Curiosities* (1909) on the subject of plagiarism: "For although we are pleased to say, in our metaphorical language, that a plagiarist shines in golden plumes, not a plume is really lost by the fowl who originally grew them" (cited in Ricks 2002, 239).

References

Benitez, Vincent P. 2019. "'That Was Me' in 'Vintage Clothes': Intertextuality in the White Album Songs of Paul McCartney." In *The Beatles through a Glass Onion: Reconsidering the White Album*, edited by Mark Osteen, 213–29. Ann Arbor: University of Michigan Press.

Bloom, Harold. 1973. *The Anxiety of Influence: A Theory of Poetry*. New York: Oxford University Press.

Covach, John. 1991. "The Rutles and the Use of Specific Models in Musical Satire." *Indiana Theory Review* 11: 119–44.

Csathy, Peter. 2021. "The Story Behind Tears for Fears' Unexpected Hit 'Mad World.'" *Consequence Podcast*, October 18, 2021. https://consequence.net/2021/10/tears-for-fears-mad-world-story-behind-song/.

Duvall, John N. 1999. "Troping History: Modernist Residue in Fredric Jameson's Pastiche and Linda Hutcheon's Parody." *Style* 33, no. 3: 372–90.

Everett, Walter. 1999. *The Beatles as Musicians: Revolver through the Anthology*. New York: Oxford University Press.

Griffiths, Dai. 2008. *Elvis Costello*. Bloomington: Indiana University Press.

Hoffman, Lucas. 2016. *Postirony: The Nonfictional Literature of David Foster Wallace and Dave Eggers*. New York: Columbia University Press.

Holden, Stephen. 1990. "Disciples of the Beatles." *New York Times*, February 21, 1990.

Janov, Arthur. 1970. *The Primal Scream*. New York: G.P. Putnam's Sons.

Janov, Arthur. 1980. *Prisoners of Pain: Unlocking the Power of the Mind*. New York: Anchor Books.

Monroe, Jazz. 2014. "Post-Irony Is the Only Thing Left in the World That Gets a Reaction." *Vice*, October 22, 2014. https://www.vice.com/da/article/6vm4md/the-past-explains-our-present-wave-of-post-irony.

Moore, Allan F. 1997. *The Beatles: Sgt. Pepper's Lonely Hearts Club Band*. *Cambridge Music Handbooks*. New York: Cambridge University Press.

Pucci, Michael. 2004. "Review of *Everybody Loves a Happy Ending*." *Pop Matters*, November 29, 2004.

Reynolds, Simon. 2011. *Retromania: Pop Culture's Addiction to Its Own Past*. New York: Faber and Faber.

Rickett, Oscar. 2014. "How We Wrote Our First Record: Tears for Fears Revisit *The Hurting*." *Vice*, January 23, 2014. https://www.vice.com/en/article/65jvzr/how-we-wrote-our-first-record-tears-for-fears-revisit-the-hurting.

Ricks, Christopher. 2002. *Allusion to the Poets*. New York: Oxford University Press.

Riley, Tim. 2002. *Tell Me Why—The Beatles: Album by Album, Song by Song, the Sixties and After*. Revised and updated edition. Cambridge, MA: Da Capo Press.

Riley, Tim. 2011. *Lennon: The Man, the Myth, the Music—the Definitive Life*. Croydon, UK: Virgin Books.

Rosen, Craig. 2022. "After Tragedy and Recovery, Tears for Fears Come Back." *Tidal*, February 23, 2022. https://tidal.com/magazine/article/tears-for-fears/1-83471.

Samarotto, Frank. 2012. "The Trope of Expectancy/Infinity in the Music of the Beatles and Others." Paper presented at the annual meeting of the Society for Music Theory, New Orleans, November 2, 2012.

Scenes from the Big Chair. 2006 [1985]. Directed by Nigel Dick. Mercury B000EQ5VEU.

Sharp, Cecil, ed. 1916. *One Hundred English Folksongs*. Boston: Oliver Ditson.

Sheffield, Rob. 2017. *Dreaming the Beatles: The Love Story of One Band and the Whole World*. New York: HarperCollins.

Sinclair, Paul. 2013. Liner notes for the remastered CD boxed set of *The Hurting*. Universal I.S. B01N0CEQ62.

Spicer, Mark. 2004. "(Ac)cumulative Form in Pop-Rock Music." *Twentieth-Century Music* 1, no. 1: 29–64.

Spicer, Mark. 2009. "Strategic Intertextuality in Three of John Lennon's Late Beatles Songs." *Gamut* 2, no. 1: 347–75.

Spicer, Mark. 2017. "Fragile, Emergent, and Absent Tonics in Pop and Rock Songs." *Music Theory Online* 27, no. 2.

Spicer, Mark. 2018. "The Electric Light Orchestra and the Anxiety of the Beatles' Influence." In *The Pop Palimpsest: Intertextuality in Recorded Popular Music*, edited by Lori Burns and Serge Lacasse, 106–36. Ann Arbor: University of Michigan Press.

Spicer, Mark and Stephen Spencer. 2023. "'A Tsunami of Voices': 10cc's 'I'm Not in Love' (1975)." In *Analyzing Record Music: Collected Perspectives on Popular Music Tracks*, edited by William Moylan, Lori Burns, and Mike Alleyne, 144–60. New York: Routledge.

Spotify Landmark: Tears for Fears. 2014. Documentary video to commemorate the thirtieth anniversary of the release of *Songs from the Big Chair*, November 24, 2014. https://www.youtube.com/watch?v=W4_mMl0B5mA.

Tears for Fears. 2022. "My Record Collection." YouTube video. https://www.youtube.com/watch?v=FVjqgI-XqQ8.

Wallace, Wyndham. 2013. "This Is Going to Hurt: The Mad World of Tears for Fears' Debut LP." *The Quietus*, September 20, 2013. https://thequietus.com/articles/13379-tears-for-fears-the-hurting-interview.

Whitley, Ed. 2000. "The Postmodern White Album." In *The Beatles, Popular Music, and Society: A Thousand Voices*, edited by Ian Inglis, 105–25. New York: Macmillan.

Editor and Contributor Bios

Mike Alleyne is Professor Emeritus in the Department of Recording Industry at Middle Tennessee State University (MTSU) and a visiting professor at the Pop Akademie in Germany. His work focuses on aspects of popular music history and music production, with material published in *Popular Music & Society, Rock Music Studies, Ethnomusicology Forum, Billboard* magazine, among other journals and outlets. His books include the co-edited *Analyzing Recorded Music: Collected Perspectives on Popular Music Tracks* (2023), *The Essential Hendrix* (2020), the co-edited Prince and Popular Music (2020), and *The Encyclopedia of Reggae* (2012). He recently contributed liner notes to the groundbreaking *Smithsonian Anthology of Hip-Hop and Rap* (2021).

John Covach is Director of the University of Rochester Institute for Popular Music and Professor of Theory at the Eastman School of Music. He has published dozens of articles on popular music, twelve-tone music, and the philosophy and aesthetics of music. He is the principal author of the textbook *What's That Sound? An Introduction to Rock Music*, now in its sixth edition, and has co-edited *Understanding Rock (1997), American Rock and the Classical Tradition and Traditions, Institutions, and American Popular Music* (2000), *Sounding Out Pop* (2010) and *The Cambridge Companion to the Rolling Stones* (2019). He is editor of the forthcoming *Cambridge Companion to Prog.*

Walter Everett is Professor Emeritus of Music at the University of Michigan. He has authored 35 peer-reviewed articles and book chapters, in addition to presenting to more than 80 audiences for conferences or by invitation on various aspects of both common-practice repertoires and pop and rock music. His books include *The Beatles as Musicians* (two volumes, 1999; 2001), the edited collection *Expression in Pop-Rock Music* (2007), *The Foundations of Rock* (2008), *What Goes On: The Beatles, Their Music, and Their Time* (2019, co-authored with Tim Riley). Walt's most recent book is *Sex and Gender in Pop/Rock Music: The Blues through the Beatles to Beyoncé* (2023).

Stephanie Hernandez is a PhD student of Literature and Music at the University of Liverpool. Using interdisciplinary approaches, she is researching Romantic legacies in popular music of the 1960s and 1970s, from the Doors to Patti Smith. While completing her Bachelor's and Master's degrees in English Literature, she worked at The Beatles Story and Handel & Hendrix in London, which fostered her interest in the cultural legacy of historically musical spaces. Stephanie is also a music journalist who has written for *Rolling Stone UK*, *Ultimate Classic Rock*, and other publications.

Matthias Heyman is Assistant Professor at Vrije Universiteit Brussel and Lecturer at Koninklijk Conservatorium Brussel, where he is Vice-chair of Research and leads the research group on jazz, improvised music, and popular music. He is also active as a freelance double bassist in jazz and classical music. Matthias obtained his PhD at the University of Antwerp in 2018 and his MA in jazz performance at the Royal Conservatoire Antwerp. His research interests include Belgian jazz history and double bass performance. His favorite moment of Beatles comedy is the interview by Torsten Jungstedt for Swedish television filmed in Stockholm on July 28, 1964.

Aviv Kammay is a music educator at Wingra School in Madison, Wisconsin. He has presented on humor in Beatles music, as well as the band's relevance to progressive education. His chapter on tribute shows appears in *Fandom and the Beatles* (2021). A composer and a performing musician, Aviv founded Madison Mystery Tour, an ensemble dedicated to note-for-note live renditions of the complete Beatles catalog.

Katie Kapurch is Associate Professor of English at Texas State University. Her scholarship focuses on icons and the iconic, especially popular phenomena at the intersections of literature, music, and film. In addition to chapters and articles, publications include the monograph *Victorian Melodrama in the Twenty-First Century* (2016) and the co-edited collection *New Critical Perspectives on the Beatles* (2016). Forthcoming books include *Blackbird: How Black Musicians Sang the Beatles into Being—and Sang Back to them Ever After* (2023), supported by the National Endowment for the Humanities, as well as a monograph about the Disneyfication of pop icons.

Richard Mills is Associate Professor in Literature and Popular Culture at St Mary's University, London. He has published extensively on popular music, Irish literature and culture, film, fashion, and British television. Mills is the author of *The Beatles and Fandom: Sex, Death and Progressive Nostalgia* (Bloomsbury). He is co-editor of *Mad Dogs and Englishness* (Bloomsbury), and he is author of the forthcoming *The Beatles and Black Music: Post-colonial Theory, Musicology and Remix Culture*. Richard is a regular contributor to BBC4's Last Word, Sky News, RTE, Portobello Radio, and BBC Live and serves on the editorial board of *The Journal of Beatles Studies*.

Jeffrey Roessner is Dean of the Humanities and professor of English at Mercyhurst University, where he leads classes in contemporary literature, popular music, and creative writing. He is co-editor of *Write in Tune: Contemporary Music in Fiction*. Recent publications include essays on the Beatles, along with articles on Roddy Doyle, Robert Johnson, rock mockumentaries, the post-confessional lyricism of R.E.M., and satellite radio and the re-conception of musical genres. Along with his academic writing, he has authored a book on songwriting, *Creative Guitar: Writing and Playing Rock Songs with Originality*.

Matthew Schneider is Professor of English and Associate Dean of the School of Humanities and Behavioral Sciences at High Point University in North Carolina. His previous writings on the Beatles have appeared in *Things We Said Today: New Critical Perspectives on the Beatles*, and *Fifty Years with the Beatles*. His book *The Long and Winding Road from Blake to the Beatles* explores the band's deep roots in late eighteenth- and early-nineteenth century British literature.

Mark Spicer is Professor and Chair of Music at Hunter College of the City University of New York and Professor of Music Theory at the CUNY Graduate Center. His writings on the reception history and analysis of popular music, especially British pop and rock since the 1960s, have appeared widely in scholarly journals and essay collections. He co-edited *Sounding Out Pop* (2010), edited the volume on *Rock Music* for the *Library of Essays in Popular Music* (2011), and served as Associate Editor of *Music Theory Spectrum* from 2013 to 2015. Spicer's article "Fragile, Emergent, and Absent Tonics in Pop and Rock Songs" (*Music Theory Online*, 2017) won the 2020 Outstanding Publication Award from the Society for Music Theory. He is also a professional keyboardist and vocalist.

David Thurmaier is Associate Professor of Music Theory and Chair of the Music Studies Division at the University of Missouri-Kansas City Conservatory. He has published and presented on topics including Charles Ives, the Beatles, music theory pedagogy, and the history of music theory. His most recent publication about the Beatles examined *White Album* cover songs released in communist Czechoslovakia and appeared in the journal *Interdisciplinary Literary Studies.*

Kenneth Womack is the author of such titles as *Long and Winding Roads: The Evolving Artistry of the Beatles* (2007), the *Cambridge Companion to the Beatles* (2009), *The Beatles Encyclopedia: Everything Fab Four* (2014), and a two-volume biography devoted to the life and work of Beatles producer George Martin, including *Maximum Volume* (2017) and *Sound Pictures* (2018). His recent books include *Solid State: The Story of Abbey Road and the End of the Beatles* (2019) and *John Lennon 1980: The Last Days in the Life* (2020). Womack holds a tenured appointment as Professor of English and Popular Music at Monmouth University.

Ed Zareh is a graduate of the Second City and the Upright Citizen's Brigade. He has worked as a writer/researcher for SNL Studios on *Live! from New York.* He served as writer/producer of *Del Close: The Godfather of American Comedy* for Studio 360, which aired on National Public Radio. He has also worked as Associate Producer of *Thank You, Del Close* for UCB Comedy. His prize-winning play *Long Lost John* was featured at the Broadway Bound Theater Festival in 2018.

Index

The Index alphabetically lists the Beatles' songs, albums, and films by their titles in the main heading. For work by other artists, including solo Beatles, please refer to the artist or band name; subheadings include some titles, but are not comprehensive to all of the artists' output covered herein.

10cc 95, 235, 250

Abbey Road (album) 9, 21n.1, 48, 71, 90, 101, 128, 162, 235n.1
Abbey Road (studio) 117, 182–83; *see also* EMI Studios
ableism 47, 121; *see also* disability
absurd 13, 64, 116, 119, 158, 166, 222, 223, 224, 230, 231, 247
"Act Naturally" 8–9, 67
aggression, aggressive 64, 116, 119–29
Alexander, Arthur 65, 105
Alice (fictional), *see* Carroll
Ali, Muhammad 78
All Caribbean Steel Band 86–87
"All My Loving" 244
"All Together Now" 46
All You Need Is Cash 12 163n.26, 164; *see also* Rutles
"All You Need Is Love" 53, 69
allusion(s) 4n.1, 9, 16, 22, 36, 82, 89, 91, 128, 149, 226n.10, 247–48; *see also* intertext(s); meta-textual
anger, angry 97, 118, 125, 152, 154, 155, 158, 166, 192
Animals, The 31
Anthology (project) 6, 17, 39, 56, 72, 94, 97, 98, 109, 111, 150, 197, 198, 201, 215, 233, 249, 251
Apple Boutique 41
Apple Corps (includes label) 9–10, 41, 42 n.3, 75n.1, 76n.5, 96n.39, 101–2, 126
Aristophanes 3
Around the Beatles 21, 27–30, 48, 169
"Ask Me Why" 66, 92

Astaire, Fred 137, 139–41, 146, 148–49
Atlantic Records 97
authenticity, authentic 9, 28, 87, 95, 96, 116, 127, 128, 130, 141, 146
avant-garde art 15, 70, 124–25, 187, 189–91, 193, 96, 228
    Dadaism 188–89, 192, 195–96
    Fluxus 188–89, 192, 194–96

"Back in the USSR" 142, 241
Bagism 194–96
Bakhtin, Mikhail 3, 193, 218, 220, 225n.9, 228–31; *see also* carnivalesque
"Ballad of John and Yoko, The" 194
Bath (city) 236, 239
Beach Boys, The 227, 235, 241, 245n.22
Beatlemania 44, 45, 68, 161, 201, 202, 204, 205, 206, 214, 235
Beatles for Sale 49, 228
Beatles: Get Back, The (film), *see Get Back*
"Because" 124
Bed-In 41, 194–95
Beethoven, Ludwig van 7, 32, 82
Berry, Chuck 69, 79, 80–83, 85, 102, 105, 241
Beyond the Fringe 15, 217–32
birds (as/in relation to jokes) 3, 7, 9, 64, 93, 164, 195
"Blackbird" 142
Bloom, Harold 39, 249
"Blue Jay Way" 139, 157, 159, 160
blues (as genre) 8, 65, 68 n. 9, 81, 102, 104, 157; *see also* rhythm and blues
Bonzo Dog Doo-Dah Band 12, 164
braggadocio 90
Brambell, Wilfrid, *see* Grandfather

bromance 30; *see also* homoeroticism, lovers
Bruce, Lenny 157–58
Buckingham Palace 4
bug(s) 15, 85, 88, 201, 205–8, 215
Burke, Kenneth 22–25, 30, 38
butcher cover, *see Yesterday and Today*

Cage, John 189–91
calypso 9, 77, 85–92
Candlestick Park 43
Capitol Records 54, 101, 111, 211, 223, 228
carnivalesque, carnival 3, 11, 15, 46, 117,
          157, 163, 218, 220–32; *see also*
          Bakhtin
Carroll, Lewis 14, 21n.1, 22, 33–38, 52, 78,
          181, 187, 218, 229
     Alice (character) 33–37
     Through the Looking-Glass 34–37
"Carry That Weight" 71, 162, 211
casuistic stretching 25, 30
Cavern Club 10, 43, 47, 95n.36, 187
Chaplin, Charlie 47
Charles, Ray 76, 97–98, 101–2, 106
Christianity 53, 76, 103–4
Christmas Shows, The Beatles' 48, 118
Clash, The 235
clown, clowning 3–4, 14, 41–56, 117, 123,
          126, 128, 196, 220, 221, 226,
          233; *see also fool*
clown types
     class clown 44
     evil clown 41, 52
     sad clown 49, 50, 55
clowns, famous
     Harlequin 50, 52
     Pierre the Clown 41
     Pierrot 49, 50, 55
Coasters, The 154–55
collaboration 4, 16, 53, 90, 141, 144, 170,
          173, 180, 189, 192, 194, 196; *see
          also* eyeball-to-eyeball
"Come Together" 51, 246
Comédie-Italienne 49
Commedia dell'Arte 41
competition 78, 90–92, 99, 173, 175, 203,
          207
"Continuing Story of Bungalow Bill, The"
          122, 126–27
Cooke, Sam 76, 106

Costello, Elvis 236, 248
counterculture 44, 60, 117, 192, 202, 226
country and western (C&W) 8–9, 79,
          101–3, 160
Covach, John (as source) 6n.4, 12, 244;
          see also Covach's contribution to
          this volume
Crosby, Bing 148, 164, 206, 207
crossdressing 48; *see also* drag
cry, crying 14, 30n.14, 48–50, 115, 122,
          124, 136, 188; *see also* tears

Daily Howl, The 52
dance -ing, -ability (includes songs with
          entry in title) 15, 94, 105, 133,
          137–38, 141, 144–46, 148, 155,
          158, 171, 173, 190, 207, 222,
          225
Dawkins, Richard 201–3, 207
"Day Tripper" 54, 83
deadpan 5, 44, 84, 116, 117, 126, 133, 183,
          204, 205; *see also* dry; straight
"Dear Prudence" 127
Decca Records 91, 116, 175, 178
Detroit 77, 97
"Dig A Pony" 51
disability 43–44, 47, 116, 119–23, 129
          see also ableism
Disney+ 75–76, 102
Domino, Fats 79, 82
Donegan, Lonnie 83
doo-wop 104, 136
doublespeak 78–79, 85
drag 47–48, 219n.3, 223, 226
"Drive My Car" 54
drugs 122, 125, 222, 227
     marijuana 117, 193
     LSD 125–26, 223, 227
dry (delivery) 1, 6, 28, 83, 117, 126, 137,
          209; *see also* deadpan; straight
Dylan, Bob 42, 49–50, 69, 79n.12, 106,
          115, 125, 127, 159, 164

Ed Sullivan Show, The 119, 205, 208
"Eleanor Rigby" 22n.23, 54, 67, 117, 223
Electric Light Orchestra (ELO) 235,
          243n.16, 250
embarrassment 62–63, 67, 120, 177
Emerick, Geoff 95, 117

EMI Studios 77n.8, 125, 169, 173–178, 180, 182, 221

"End, The" 21n.1, 71, 223, 230, 247

Epstein, Brian 27, 39, 43, 47, 53–54, 91, 118–20, 125, 128–29, 182, 209–210

Esher demos 139

Everett, Walter (as source) 10, 22n.2, 60, 61, 66, 67, 70, 80–83, 97, 128; *see also* Everett's contribution to this volume

Everly Brothers (Phil and Don) 10, 49

exaggeration 1, 8, 64, 68, 79, 136, 143, 145, 146, 156, 164, 208, 224 *see also* hyperbole

eyeball-to-eyeball 90, 93

falsetto 66, 71, 93, 119, 126, 136, 141, 227

"Flying" 102

folk music, folklore 26, 71, 83, 134, 142, 210, 211–13, 230, 239–40

food (includes references to beverages, eating, and drinking) 10, 24–25, 34, 36–38, 93, 154n.7, 156–57, 171, 188, 203, 212, 228–29, 232, 244

fool (comedic type) 3, 9, 16–17, 25, 26, 30, 42, 52, 55, 56, 117, 126, 127, 221, 224; *see also* clown

"Fool on The Hill, The" 55, 153n.5

"For No One" 83, 129

"For You Blue" 82, 107

Friar Park 160–64
    Crisp, Sir Frankie (joke) 160

fun 2, 3, 12, 16, 27, 61, 70, 75, 93, 98, 143, 146, 158, 160, 166, 180

fun, poking or making 121, 154, 162, 203, 206, 220, 221 *see also* mockery

Gates, Jr., Henry Louis 78, 91

gender 3, 11, 13–14, 22–26, 30, 22, 42, 47–48, 54–55, 60n.2, 223, 232

gender fluidity (including gender play and reversals) 22, 25–26, 30–31, 33n.15, 42, 47–48, 54–55

generation(s), generational 3, 27 n. 11, 33–34, 42, 45–46, 55, 59, 70, 174, 180, 191, 206, 213–15, 232, 235

gesture(s), physical 12, 27, 42, 47, 97, 164, 202

"Get Back" 29, 80–81, 90, 100, 101, 103

Get Back (film/sessions) 9, 14, 29, 30, 75–77, 79–108, 111–12, 119–20, 130, 143

"Getting Better" 53, 125, 129

"Girl" 30, 85, 124

"Glass Onion" 37, 70

"Golden Slumbers" 46, 71

"Good Night" 70

Goons, *Goon Show, The* 3, 4, 7, 28, 34, 43, 52, 78, 117, 151, 177–81, 184–85, 218, 221

gospel 76, 101–4

Grandfather, Paul's (fictional character) 16, 17, 26, 45; *see also* A Hard Day's Night

granny music/songs (derogatory) 15, 93, 149

Grapefruit 15, 188–194

grotesque, "grotty" (slang) 46, 119, 124, 193, 223, 228–29

hair (including -cut, -style) 1, 22, 26, 151–52, 161–62, 172, 182, 192–95, 202, 204–5, 208–9, 211–14, 219, 222, 237, 238n.7; *see also* moptop(s)

ham(my) 119, 143

Hamburg 43, 47, 63, 64, 75, 76, 118, 137, 227

"Hard Day's Night, A" 44, 68

Hard Day's Night, A (album) 48

Hard Day's Night, A (film) 1–2, 5, 9, 16, 26–27, 45–47, 55, 61, 66, 96, 98, 115, 116, 154, 160, 207, 211

Harrison, George 1–2, 7, 15, 27, 34, 44–48, 51, 65–70, 75–76, 79, 82–83, 86–87, 89–90, 98, 100, 102, 117, 119, 126, 137, 139, 141, 151–66, 183, 184, 213, 217, 243

All Things Must Pass (album) 99, 157
    "All Things Must Pass" 108
    "Let It Down" 98, 99, 108

Cloud Nine 164–65
    "When We Was Fab" 164–65
    "This Is Love" 165

Dark Horse 159, 161

"Ding Dong, Ding Dong" 47, 159, 160, 163, 165
George Harrison
    "Blow Away" 164–65
    "Faster" 165
    Living in the Material World 158, 159
        "Living in the Material World" 158, 159
        "Sue Me, Sue You Blues" 158, 159, 163, 166
    "Pirate Song, The" 163.26
    Thirty-Three & 1/3, 46n.13, 162–64
        "Crackerbox Palace" 46, 163, 164, 165
        "This Song" 162–63, 165–66
        "True Love" 164–65"
"Hello, Goodbye" 242–44
"Help!" 50, 127
Help! (album) 47, 49, 97
Help! (film) 2, 5, 30, 45n.11, 47, 67n.8, 143n.6, 154n.8, 160, 211
"Helter Skelter" 220
Hendrix, Jimi 80
"Her Majesty" 70-1
"Hey Bulldog" 51, 122
"Hey Jude" 239n.9, 246
high art 32-3, 60-2, 64-5, 67, 69, 71, 192
Hill, Benny 47
Hinduism 153, 213; *see also* India
hip-hop 4, 80, 91
homoeroticism 30; *see also* bromance; lovers
"Honey Pie" 139–42, 144–46, 148
hyperbole 103; *see also* exaggeration

"I Am the Walrus" 5, 21-2, 31-7, 51, 115, 124, 139, 164, 219, 223, 228–29, 232, 240–244
"I Call Your Name" 94
"I Feel Fine" 51, 229
"I Have a Dream" (speech) 79, 101
"I Me Mine" 119, 166
"I Need You" 152, 160
"I Saw Her Standing There" 45
"I Wanna Be Your Man" 67, 72
"I Want to Hold Your Hand" 205, 207, 244
"I Want to Tell You" 152

"I Want You (She's So Heavy)" 101, 108, 239n.9, 248n.26
"If I Fell" 66, 124
"If I Needed Someone" 152
Idle, Eric 12, 46n.15, 163–64, 218, 222, 229–31; *see also* Monty Python
improvisation 5, 11, 101, 103, 117, 147; *see also* unscripted
incongruity 14, 22–38, 65, 68, 70, 93, 152, 157–58; *see also* perspective by incongruity
India, Indian influences 4, 15, 68, 70, 84, 126, 151–66, 213; *see also* Hinduism; Rishikesh
Indra Club 43
"Inner Light, The" 155, 156n.14, 160
Innes, Neil 12, 164, 244; *see also* Rutles
inside joke(s) 9, 29, 84–85, 135–36, 144, 149; *see also* jokes
insult(s)(-ing), 53, 90, 116; *see also* granny music
intertext(s), intertextuality 4n.1, 9, 12, 17, 22–38, 134, 240–44
irony 2, 5, 8, 11–12, 16, 22, 24, 27, 29, 69, 78, 80, 81, 88, 93, 95–97, 100n.56, 136, 143, 156, 241, 245–48; *see also* post-irony
Isley Brothers 238
"It Won't Be Long" 157n.16

Jacaranda Club 86
Jackson, Peter *see Get Back* (film)
Jagger, Mick 120, 162
Jamaica, Jamaican influences 94–96, 236n.3
Janov, Arthur 190, 236–37, 243
jazz (-y) 80, 94, 98, 101, 137, 141, 144–45, 147–48, 173, 207, 245
Jesus comments 53–54; *see also* Christianity; religion
JFK Airport 2, 201
jokes, running/well-known
    Beatles' name, *see* man on a flaming pie; for bug-related jokes *see* bug; pun(s)
    cranberry sauce 70
    "crips" (derogatory) 47; *see also* ableism; disability

clean/dirty/little old man 16, 45, 98
fish-and-finger pie 38, 85; *see also*
    sexual content
granny music/songs (derogatory), see
    entry
I don't like your tie 151, 183
mocker(s); see entry
plastic soul, see entry
rattle your jewelry 44, 119, 220
"spastic" routine (derogatory) see entry
tit(s) (slang) 1, 30
toppermost of the poppermost, see
    entry; *see also* inside jokes
"Julia" 45, 122, 137

"Kansas City" 64n.4, 106, 207
Keaton, Buster 47
King, Jr., Rev. Dr. Martin Luther 79, 101
King Lear, see Shakespeare

"Lady Madonna" 31, 108, 223
laughter 2, 4, 6, 12–14, 16, 23–24, 28–29,
    32, 41, 44, 48–49, 52, 54, 55,
    59–61, 70–71, 76–77, 81,
    83–84, 86, 115–18, 120–24,
    126–28, 130, 159, 166, 174,
    184–85, 196, 220–21, 231, 228,
    232, 247
Laurel and Hardy 6
Lead Belly (Huddie Ledbetter) 83
Lear, Edward 38, 78, 218
Leary, Timothy 68, 155, 157n.16
Led Zeppelin 248
Leiber, Jerry 88, 154
Lennon, Cynthia 89, 120, 125
Lennon, John 1–3, 6, 8–9, 13–15, 21n.1, 22,
    28–38, 41–55, 61, 64–70, 75–95,
    98, 100–2, 104, 115–34, 137,
    140–41, 143, 149, 151, 154n.9,
    155, 157, 160, 170, 179, 180–81,
    184–85, 187–89, 193–96, 198,
    218, 225, 227–30, 236, 243, 246
    "Beautiful Boy" 129
    "Calypso Rock" 86–87
    "Crippled Inside" 123, 128, 129
    "Give Peace a Chance" 53, 96n.39, 194,
        195
    "God" 104, 106

"How Do You Sleep?" 120, 128
In His Own Write 34, 52, 218n.1, 229
Spaniard in the Works, A 52, 218, 229
Lester, Richard 1, 9, 26, 45–47, 61, 66; *see
    also Hard Day's Night* and *Help!*
"Let It Be" 96, 98, 102, 107, 119
Let It Be (album) 70–71, 75–76, 81, 92, 97,
    105, 235n.1
Let It Be (film) 9, 71, 75–77, 102; *see also
    Get Back*
Lewisohn, Mark 34–35, 38, 43, 47, 49,
    52, 60–61, 63–64, 66–67, 86,
    88, 119, 121–23, 126, 175, 179,
    181–84
"Little Child" 45n.12
Little Richard (Richard Penniman) 64n.4,
    76–77, 79, 81, 84, 85, 106, 149
Live at the BBC 2
Liverpool 8 (L8) 9, 86
Liverpool, Liverpudlian 6–11, 14, 17,
    26, 28n.13, 47, 61–63, 59, 67,
    69–71, 82–83, 85–86, 95n.36,
    96, 110, 126, 128, 133n.1, 137,
    156n.12, 171, 181, 183, 204, 208,
    210, 212, 220, 227, 236; *see also*
    Mersey
London 8, 10–11, 21, 60, 69, 94, 98, 125,
    171–72, 174, 176, 181, 183, 204,
    208, 217, 220, 235, 239, 241
"Long and Winding Road, The" 82n.20,
    97, 99, 107
Lord Kitchener (Aldwyn Roberts) 77, 85,
    88, 89, 91
Lord Woodbine (Harold Phillips) 85–87
"Love Me Do" 108
"Love You To" 152, 156n.14
lovers 21, 26–29, 246n.23; *see also*
    bromance; romance
"Lucy in the Sky With Diamonds" 36–37,
    115, 223, 227
lullaby 46, 195; *see also* folk music

Maciunas, George 189, 194
"Maggie Mae" 71, 83
Magical Mystery Tour (album) 55, 69n.10,
    138–39, 157, 160
Magical Mystery Tour (film) 5, 12, 42, 47,
    138, 229

Maharishi Mahesh Yogi 84, 125–26, 153

malapropism 26–27, 68

man on a flaming pie (joke) 38

Martin, George 5, 15, 67, 76, 85, 90, 99, 100, 105, 120, 141, 151–52, 169–85, 221, 222, 225

Marx Brothers 5–7, 117, 180

McCartney, Linda 42n.3, 95n.36, 147

McCartney, Paul 1, 9, 11, 15–16, 21–23, 26–30, 32, 35, 42, 44–47, 54–55, 59, 61, 64, 66–69, 71, 75–76, 79–100, 102, 115, 117–21, 124–26, 128–29, 131, 133–48, 151, 153, 155, 157, 162, 164, 181, 182, 184, 227, 236, 241, 243, 245, 246

Back to the Egg 146, 148

"Baby's Request" 146–48

James Paul McCartney (television special) 144

"Gotta Sing, Gotta Dance" 144–45, 148

Kisses on the Bottom 137, 144, 146

"Bye Bye Blackbird" 9

McCartney 142

"Hot as Sun/glasses" 142

One Hand Clapping 143

"Suicide" 142–45, 148

"Jet" 95

Venus and Mars 145–46

"Letting Go" 146

"Listen to What the Man Said" 146

"Rockshow" 146

"You Gave Me the Answer" 145–46, 148

McCartney, Paul, and Wings 142, 145–49

"Mean Mr. Mustard" 126

melodrama, melodramatic 11, 30n.14, 124

meme(s) 2, 10, 15, 75, 201–5, 207–8, 210, 212–15

Memphis 97

"Memphis" 82

Merseyside, Mersey beat 7, 67, 204, 207, 223, 227

metaphor 22–25, 31–32, 38, 66, 78, 91, 103, 143, 163, 248

meta-textual 10, 21, 27–29, 34–35, 78, 84; *see also* self-awareness; self-conscious(ness)

"Midnight Special" 83, 93

Midsummer Night's Dream, A, see Shakesepeare

Mighty Sparrow (Slinger Fransico) 77, 88, 91–93

Milligan, Spike 3, 177–80, 184, 221

mime, pantomime 9n.7, 28, 48, 50–51

Miracles, The 106; *see also* Robinson, Smokey

"Misery" 66

mocker(s) 1, 5, 116

mockery 4, 9, 14, 28, 43–44, 52–54, 64–66, 68–69, 71, 116–19, 121, 123, 126, 128–29, 131, 143, 156, 169, 178, 192, 194, 215, 218, 220, 225, 230, 232

Mods, mod subculture/style 1–2, 96, 116, 236, 241

Monkees, The 210–11

Monty Python 12–13, 15, 46, 116, 151, 154, 163, 164, 217–223, 229–232

Monty Python's Flying Circus 15, 151, 154, 218, 221–23, 229–31

moptop(s) 21, 202, 213, 237; *see also* hair

"Mother Nature's Son" 65n.6

Motown Records 96–97

music hall, British 2, 7, 29; *see also* vaudeville

New York City (NYC) 2, 71, 176

nonsense 5, 22, 31–32, 34–38, 51, 93, 218, 219, 225, 230, 231

"Norwegian Wood (This Bird Has Flown)" 83, 124

nose (clown, artificial, or humor-related) 26, 42, 47, 54, 71, 161

"Nowhere Man" 50, 67, 129

"Ob-La-Di, Ob-La-Da" 48, 92–95, 155

"Octopus's Garden" 90

"Oh! Darling" 102, 107

"Old Brown Shoe" 99, 107

"On the Road to Marrakesh" 99, 108

"One After 909, The" 80–83, 98, 107

"Only a Northern Song" 155–57, 159, 160, 162
Ono, Yoko 6, 10, 15, 41, 45, 70, 100, 106, 122, 125, 187–96
optimism 129, 142, 160, 164
Orzabal, Roland, *see* Tears for Fears
Owens, Buck, and the Buckaroos 8

pantomime, *see* mime
"Paperback Writer" 218n.1
Parlophone Records 7, 15, 169, 172–83, 221–23, 225
parody (-ic) 3–5, 11–13, 15, 22, 27n.12, 29, 38, 79n.11, 118–21, 134–35, 141–42, 177, 190–191, 193, 211–12, 224, 226–27, 244
partnership 22, 29, 30n.14, 90, 101, 116, 137, 143, 158, 181, 184–85, 247; *see also* collaboration
pastiche 4, 11–13, 15–16, 94, 133–49, 244–46, 248
"Penny Lane" 38, 69, 70, 85, 242, 243, 244
perspective by incongruity 14, 22–23, 30, 34, 36, 38; *see also* incongruity; Burke, Kenneth
pie 24, 38
"Piggies" 5, 44, 155–56, 159
Plastic Ono Band 53, 96, 236n.4
plastic soul (joke) 96
play (theatrical) 21–33; *see also* Shakespeare
play, playfulness 3–7, 10–11, 13–15, 17, 21–31, 42–56, 64–65, 69, 75–77, 79–80, 84, 90, 93, 98–99, 115–17, 127, 130, 141–42, 144, 152–66, 178, 180–91, 206, 209–12, 223, 225, 229, 237
Please Please Me 45n.12, 66, 235n.1
"Please Please Me" 38, 82, 244
Poe, Edgar Allan 37, 219, 229
poetic 42, 79, 88, 89, 91, 92
poetry, poem(s) 7, 34–37, 78–79, 160, 166, 188–89, 197, 213, 225, 235
police 36, 180
Police, The 95, 96n.38, 236n.3
"Polythene Pam" 48
Porter, Cole 135, 140, 154, 164

post-irony 16, 235, 247–48
Presley, Elvis 2, 53, 69, 88n.31, 106, 115, 147, 181
Preston, Billy 14, 75– 77, 79–81, 85, 90, 96–108
primal scream therapy 129, 190, 236, 239
psychedelia (-ic) 31, 68, 139, 155, 157, 160, 213–14, 219, 227
Psychedelic Experience, The, see Leary
pun(s), punning 4, 22, 24, 30, 35, 38, 45n.10, 78, 79, 85, 87, 96, 116, 117, 172, 180, 189, 203, 204, 205, 218, 220, 225, 227, 229–30, 241; *see also wordplay*
punchline 1, 6, 70, 83, 87, 211
punk 119, 147, 195, 211, 235, 241

Quarry Men, The 82
queer (derogatory) 54, 120–121
queer (identity) 121
    for queer readings *see* bromance, homoeroticism, lovers, romance

Rabelais (-ian) 220, 228–29
racism 15, 65, 121, 187–88, 213
"Rain" 6, 51
rap 80, 90–91
RCA Records 87, 91
reggae 94–96
religion 37, 71, 158n.17, 213, 229, 231; *see also* Christianity, Hinduism
repetition 1, 30, 37, 47, 78, 79, 89, 85, 93, 95, 97–8, 101, 115, 117, 119, 122–24, 126, 128–29, 137, 196, 211, 214, 231, 236n.4, 239, 244, 246
reversal(s) 22, 25–26, 51, 89, 208
"Revolution" 51, 70, 74, 142, 193, 241
"Revolution 9" 51, 70, 142
Revolver 44, 66n.7, 67n.8, 68, 235
rhyme(s), rhyming 31, 35, 50, 78, 81–83, 154, 155, 214, 229
rhythm and blues (R&B) 77, 81, 85, 88, 92, 100, 102
Richards, Keith 162
"Rip It Up" 106

Rishikesh 4, 84, 125; *see also* India; Maharishi

Robinson, Smokey 77, 79, 164

rock and roll, rock (genre) 1–3, 8, 22 n. 4, 32, 43, 54, 59–69, 77–87, 91, 103, 116, 118, 136–38, 144, 146–49, 161, 190, 202, 204, 206–7, 210–11, 214, 235, 241, 244, 247; *see also* rhythm and blues

rocksteady 94

"Roll Over Beethoven" 82

Rolling Stones, The 79, 162
  Rock and Roll Circus 79

romance 25–30, 45n.12, 46, 64, 66, 92, 94, 116, 127, 147–48, 152, 164

Romanticism 128, 134

rooftop performance 51, 76n.5, 81, 102, 105

Royal Command Performance 44, 119

Rubber Soul 53, 67n.8, 152n.4

Rutles, The 6n.4, 12, 16, 164, 244
  All You Need is Cash 12, 18, 163, 164

satire 4, 5, 12, 129, 169, 172, 179, 181, 217–31, 233, 244

Savile Row 98

"Savoy Truffle" 155, 159–60

Scouse (accent), Scouser 12, 43, 182

scripted 1, 27–30, 61, 205

self-awareness (textual) 5, 27–28, 64–65, 90, 128, 149, 153, 187

self-conscious(ness) (artistic) 66, 68, 122–23, 172

self-deprecation 8–9, 11, 96, 117, 133, 183

self-directed (humor) 14, 61–64, 66, 70–71

self-referentiality, *see* meta-textual and self-awareness

Sellers, Peter 3, 5, 47, 116, 177–80, 184, 221

Sentimental Journey 9, 137
  "Bye Bye Blackbird" 9

sex work(er) 71, 83, 92

sexism 15, 24, 48, 121, 222, 232

sexual content (including jokes, puns, and innuendo) 8, 24–25, 30, 38, 48, 64, 79, 82–89, 91–92, 126–27, 172, 193–95, 220, 222

sexuality 13, 24, 30, 48, 54, 120, 222; *see also* bromance, homoeroticism, lovers, romance

"Sexy Sadie" 84, 122, 126, 127

Sgt. Pepper's Lonely Hearts Club Band 22, 32, 37, 46, 53, 69–71, 125, 129, 136, 152n4, 155, 158n.17, 161, 232, 239–240

"Shake, Rattle and Roll" 81, 106

Shakespeare, William 7, 14, 21–33, 37–38, 48, 52, 170, 231, 235
  Plays/Adaptations/Performances
    All's Well That Ends Well 22–26
    Around the Beatles, see entry
    Hamlet 26
    King Lear 21, 30–33, 36, 40
    Kiss Me Kate 154
    Midsummer Night's Dream, A 5, 21–22, 26–30, 48

shame 116, 120, 122–24, 170; *see also* embarrassment

Sharp, Cecil 250

"She Loves You" 69, 75, 205, 239, 244

Shea Stadium (concert) 44, 81

Sheffield, Rob 93, 126, 235n.2

Signifyin(g) 4, 78, 79, 80, 91, 97, 103

Simon and Garfunkel 236

Simon, Carly 195

Sinatra, Frank 143–44, 148–49

ska 93, 94, 236

Smith, Curt, *see* Tears for Fears

"Something" 97, 108

soul 76, 95–96, 103–4

"spastic" routine (derogatory) 119, 121, 123, 126; *see also* ableism, disability

spoof (-ing) 5, 15, 21, 38, 136n.3, 159, 163n.26, 241; *see also* parody, mockery

Springsteen, Bruce 238

Star Club 63–66; *see also* Hamburg

Starr, Ringo 1–2, 5, 7, 9, 11, 16, 17, 21n.1, 26–28, 30, 42, 45–46, 62, 66–68, 70, 72, 84–86, 90, 93, 96, 106, 116–17, 120, 133, 137, 141, 151, 158, 164, 201–2, 205, 211–13, 243

Stax Records 97, 102

Steptoe and Son 16, 45

Stoller, Mike 88n.31, 154
straight (delivery) 1, 28, 84, 86, 147, 163,
        164; *see also* deadpan, dry
"Strawberry Fields Forever" 70
Strokes, The 247
Summer of Love 69, 240–41
"Sun King" 51, 128
Supremes, The 77, 97
surreal 3, 5, 15, 23, 31, 33–34, 37, 46, 51–52,
        115–16, 124, 180–81, 187–88, 193,
        196, 218–22, 224, 227–29, 231–32

"Taste of Honey, A" 64, 65, 75
"Taxman" 44, 68, 80, 152, 154, 155, 156,
        159, 241
Taylor, James 195
tea 10, 34, 171, 212; *see also* food
tears 50, 106, 120, 123, 124, 183, 249, 250;
        see also cry, crying; clown: sad
        clown
Tears for Fears 16, 235–48
    Elemental 238, 245
    Everybody Loves a Happy Ending 238,
        246–48
    Hurting, The 236–38, 247–48
    Raoul and the Kings of Spain 238, 245
    Seeds of Love, The 238–8
        "Sowing the Seeds of Love" 240–48
    Songs from the Big Chair 237–39, 245
    Tipping Point, The 238, 247–48
Television shows/programs
    Addams Family, The 201, 206, 210
    Bewitched 201, 209, 214
    Coronation Street 43
    Dick Van Dyke Show, The 201, 209
    Ed Sullivan Show, The, see entry
    F Troop 201, 207–8, 212–13
    Get Smart 201, 213
    Gilligan's Island 201, 207–8, 212
    Gilmore Girls 195, 198
    Monkees, The, see entry
    Monty Python's Flying Circus, see entry
        under Monty Python
    Munsters, The 201, 206–7, 210
    Power Puff Girls, The 191
    Saturday Night Live 181, 224n.7
    Simpsons, The 187, 193
    South Park 192, 198

Steptoe and Son, see entry
    Patty Duke Show 201, 209
"Tell Me Why" 48
Tennyson, Alfred Lord 79, 160
"That Means a Lot" 143n.6
Thatcher, Margaret 16, 240–41
"Three Cool Cats" 116
Through the Looking-Glass, see Carroll
"Till There Was You" 64, 118, 148
"Tomorrow Never Knows" 27, 68, 155, 227
toppermost of the poppermost (joke) 2
Townsend, Ken 182
trauma 129, 170, 226, 237, 247
trickster 16, 26, 78–80, 82
Trinidad, Trinidadian music 85, 87–89,
        91, 92, 96, 110, 111
Twickenham Studios 46, 75n.1, 98, 229
Twiggy 145
"Twist and Shout" 238

ukulele 7, 84, 177
unscripted 5, 47, 61, 217; *see also*
        improvisation

vaudeville 7, 139, 140, 141, 142; *see also*
        music hall

Wenner, Jann 18, 111
"What Goes On" 67n.8
"When I'm Sixty-Four" 46, 137–39, 141,
        143, 148
"While My Guitar Gently Weeps" 95
White Album 65n.6, 68n.9, 70, 84, 95, 98,
        127, 140, 232
Who, The 2
Williams, Hank 8
Williams, Larry 79, 102, 105
With the Beatles 45n.12, 82, 238
"Within You Without You" 34, 70, 152n.4,
        156n.14, 166
Womack, Kenneth (as source) 12, 61,
        67, 221; *see also* Womack's
        contribution to this volume
"Word, The" 53, 128
wordplay 4–5, 13–14, 23, 30–38, 50,
        77–78, 79n.84, 85–87, 89, 91–93,
        100n.56, 103, 116, 154, 230–31;
        see also nonsense; pun

"Yellow Submarine" 46, 66, 90, 117
Yellow Submarine (album) 70, 155
Yellow Submarine (film) 41, 45n.11, 46, 67, 160
"Yer Blues" 68n.9, 127, 129
"Yesterday" 67, 228
Yesterday and Today 53, 223, 228, 232
Yokorolling 191
"You Can't Do That" 123

"You Know My Name (Look Up the Number)" 5, 51, 66
"You Like Me Too Much" 152
"You Never Give Me Your Money" 9–10
"You Really Got a Hold on Me" 106
"You Won't See Me" 83
"Your Mother Should Know" 138–39

Zappa, Frank 135–36

Printed in the USA
CPSIA information can be obtained
at www.ICGtesting.com
LVHW021935021123
762773LV00022B/13